MUSIC IN AMERICAN LIFE

A list of books in the series Music in American Life appears at the end of this volume.

The Erotic Muse

SECOND EDITION

The Erotic Muse

AMERICAN BAWDY SONGS

ED CRAY

University of Illinois Press
Urbana & Chicago

Illini Books edition, 1999
© 1992 by the Board of Trustees of the University of Illinois
Manufactured in the United States of America
1 2 3 4 5 C P 5 4 3 2 1

This book is printed on acid-free paper.

Library of Congress Cataloging-in-Publication Data

The Erotic muse.
    Bawdy American folksongs, principally American; unacc.
    Includes bibliographical references.
    1. Bawdy songs—United States. 2. Folk music—United
States. 3. Folk-songs, English—United States.
I. Cray, Ed.
M1977.B38ET6 1992   90-45334
ISBN 0-252-01781-1 (cloth : alk. paper)
ISBN 0-252-06789-4 (pbk. : alk. paper)

Once more this book is dedicated to
Sara N. Shaffer,
my mother,
and to the memory of
Wayland Debs Hand,
my friend

Teachers both

When I travelled, I took a particular delight in hearing the songs and fables that are come from father to son and are most in vogue among the common people of the countries through which I passed; for it is impossible that anything should be universally tasted and approved by a multitude, tho they are only the rabble of a nation, which hath not in it some peculiar aptness to please and gratify the mind of man. Human nature is the same in all reasonable creatures, and whatever falls in with it will meet with admirers amongst readers of all qualities and conditions.

—Joseph Addison, *The Spectator*

Contents

UNDERGRADUATES COARSE
295

BLESS 'EM ALL
377

Introduction to the Second Edition

WE ARE NOT often afforded the opportunity to correct the
errors of our youth, to revise the ill-considered judgments
and the hasty conclusions, and thus to leave for posterity
a somewhat more judicious record of our times or our wisdom. Such
a reassessment or self-examination is a heady opportunity not to be
missed.

Of course, one launches such a project with some trepidation. After
all, an eighteenth-century epigram reminds:

> C[url]l, let me advise you, whatever betides,
> To let this third volume alone;
> The second's sufficient for all our backsides,
> So pray keep the third for your own.[1]

Still, two decades and more after the first appearance of this book,
there are valid reasons for a new edition.

In the first place, *The Erotic Muse* made no claim to being comprehensive; most of the collecting was done in a single urban setting, the
songs gathered from a well-educated group of informants. They were
a "folk," to be sure, and the songs in this collection were a part of
their folklore. Still there were so many other social and economic
groups not sampled, so many people with *their* bawdy lore untouched.

A number of books, in the intervening years, have followed *Muse's*
lead, publishing unexpurgated folk songs gathered from other areas
and social groups. Together, these various collections make possible
the work of defining the field of bawdy folksong.

Secondly, a number of songs were given relatively short shrift in
the notes of the first edition. Some lacked "clean" relatives, those
analogues out of which endnotes could be spun. Little was known
about others. Generally, still less was known about the melodies. The
serious study of the popular and country music industry, which has
yielded important information about aural tradition, was in its infancy
when the book first went to press.

Finally, the organization of the book, dictated by the publisher, presented problems. Notes were separate from jury texts and tunes, set off where they wouldn't interfere with the reader's prurient pleasures. Further, considerations of space, not inherent relationships, dictated the order of the songs.

For these reasons and more, the editor believed the first edition of *The Erotic Muse* would quickly be supplanted by later scholars. *Muse* would have its moment of note or notoriety, then would be subsumed within later scholarship. But such has not been the case. More than two decades later, the book remains virtually the sole scholarly work devoted to so-called dirty songs. It has been in print, in authorized and in pirated editions, for much of that period.

Meanwhile, the editor continued to collect the odd song that came his way, and to add annotations and marginalia to his last copy of the book. Only when it became clear that no other comprehensive work was in the offing did it seem worthwhile to consider a new edition.

At the same time, another and compelling motive for a second edition emerged. *The Erotic Muse* in expanded form might represent a fair sample of American bawdy song in oral tradition today. Some twenty years of intermittent collecting—plus searches in folklore archives across the country—suggest that, contrary to expectation, the canon of bawdy folksong in urban oral tradition is relatively small. One would have expected to find more songs, especially from differing occupational groups or regions.

Consider: From 1919 to at least 1954, the great folklorist Vance Randolph gathered folk songs throughout the Ozarks, from hill- and townsfolk alike. The State Historical Society of Missouri agreed to publish the collectanea, but only on condition that the ribald material be excised. Randolph reluctantly agreed, excising the still unpublished manuscript of 207 " 'Unprintable' Songs from the Ozarks."

Randolph's manuscript has sixty-two ballads, English and American, plus forty traditional songs. (Another forty-three entries are clusters of quatrains, most to fiddle tunes, and may be mnemonics; fifty-seven are fragments or single-stanza ditties.) While Randolph's collectanea and that included here are largely discrete in both geographical and social senses, and the present editor's collecting begins about the time Randolph leaves off, forty-eight of Randolph's 102 identifiable ballads and songs are represented here. Given the social and generational difference between Randolph's informants and the largely urban, well-educated men and women who contributed to this collection, one might have expected greater variety in repertoire.

Similarly, the "Inferno" holdings of the Robert W. Gordon collection in the Archive of American Folk Song at the Library of Congress contained versions of about half of the songs in this anthology. Three different university archives—at UCLA, Indiana, and Western Kentucky—yielded even greater overlap. An inspection of the titles in the archives of Memorial University, St. Johns, Newfoundland, revealed far greater diversity, but that province stands as a mid-point between British and American traditions.

This is not to suggest that *The Erotic Muse* presents a closed canon. It does not. It *would* appear, however, that this collection contains a large percentage of the bawdy songs still in oral tradition in urban America and that the number of bawdy songs currently in oral tradition is dwindling, compared to what has been recorded by earlier collectors. The surviving corpus may number two hundred or so songs and ballads—fragments and quatrains excepted.

There are three possible reasons for this:

1. The diminished role of self-entertainment given television, phonograph, tape deck and car radio;[2]

2. The urban folk music revival of the 1950s and 1960s, which fostered the preservation of at least some of these songs, has waned;[3] and

3. Though there is no hard evidence to support this conclusion, the impression is that the widely noted sexual revolution, wrought by the introduction of The Pill in June, 1960, has had an impact. As "Roll Your Leg Over," one of the songs in this collection, notes, those who are doing it, don't sing about doing it.

Such conclusions would not have been possible heretofore. There simply was no comparative data.

Thirty years ago, the open publication of this book would have been difficult, if not impossible. The guardians of public morality, self-appointed or legally constituted, would have seen to its suppression. But the United States Supreme Court, in a succession of enlightened decisions, has opened the way to wisdom. Not that bawdry has ever been wholly suppressed by censors, even in parlor-polite circles.

Any number of stories are told of noted people who have known and sung some of the ballads and songs in this collection. In his definitive study of *The Limerick*, Gershon Legman notes that Learned Hand, one of the more influential jurists in the first half of the twentieth century, sang a version of "The Wayward Boy" for Oliver Wendell Holmes and Felix Frankfurter, those equally eminent figures in American law. A United States senator contributed two songs to this collection, and a former California attorney-general another. (Similarly, William O. Douglas, who served on the United States Supreme Court longer than any other justice in history, proudly asserts he had a hand in writing one of the songs here.)

In his widely noted, reluctantly concurring opinion in the case of *Roth* v. *United States*, Judge Jerome Frank of the federal Court of Appeals made discrete reference to other learned bearers of bawdy oral tradition: "Those whose views most judges know best are other lawyers. Judges can and should take judicial notice that, at many gatherings of lawyers at bar association or of alumni of our leading law schools, tales are told fully as 'obscene' as many of those distributed by men, like defendant, convicted for violation of the obscenity statute."[4]

Not only is the bawdy song found in such good company, but frequently it is said to be sired by equally prominent poets. Rudyard Kipling, the team of Gilbert and Sullivan, Robert Service, Gene Fowler, Ogden Nash, James Joyce, even Alfred Lord Tennyson have all been so honored—in some cases, deservedly. Indeed, Eugene Field turned out so many of these underground ballads that friends privately published an anthology of his "secret" poems.

Still, the bawdy song needs no apologetic introduction as the consort of those in high places. It can stand or fall on its own merits—as song. If it is rarely great poetry, in the commonly accepted sense of what may or may not be great poetry, it *is* humorous. If the melodies are only a notch or two above the ditty class, they are, for all that, the borrowed melodies of popular songs or the same oft-praised tunes used for "clean" folk songs.

This borrowing, in fact, rather vexed one scholar who wrote with undisguised distaste: "In general, the rule has been that a good traditional tune is good enough to put to spiritual uses. In fact, folk-music, morally speaking, is virtually incorruptible. Folk-tunes have within them as their inalienable birthright such a gift of purity that they are a standing contradiction of the axiom, 'Evil communications corrupt good manners.' They associate unhesitatingly with the dirtiest companions, and come away unsoiled. In spite of Falstaff's allusion to 'filthy tunes,' there never has been such a phenomenon in folk-music, apart from momentary nonce-associations."[5]

Some of those nonce-associations in the body of ribald songlore, no less than in folk song generally, are happy accidents: an occasional doggerel lyric and pedestrian tune will unite in that particular alchemy of folk song to create a song so appealing that it may persist in popularity literally for centuries.

For more than a hundred years, One-Eyed or One-Balled Reilly (his infirmity varies) has been melodically reamed in the following:

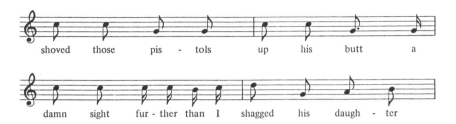

Similarly, "Kathusalem" contains these lines and music well met:

In the even younger "Fuck 'Em All," a merry-go-round tune is coupled with a sprightly internal rhyme to fashion another of those particularly effective amalgams:

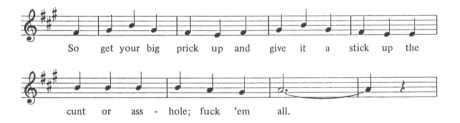

Regardless of the particular merit, or lack of it, of an individual scrap, bawdy songs have survived when other folk songs have died, victims of urbanization and the blight of the mass media. The endurance of the bawdy song, this ability to charm or entertain successive generations of singers, is the single most important point of this collection.

The reason for this staying power is easily found: bawdy songs are funny. They have an elemental appeal; they entertain.

This same humor, it should be added, removes the bawdy song from the plainly prurient. The immodest ballad has only one overt function, that of entertainment. Titillation is incompatible with humor; the person doubled over in belly-aching laughter is not one capable of copulation.

At other times and in other places, many of the songs in this collection would not have been considered to be obscene. Some of the older have, in fact, survived cycles of both public acceptance and public censure. Times change and people's attitudes change with them.

Prior to the sixteenth century, the word "fuck" carried no opprobrium. Sometime after 1571, when it appeared in a poem satirizing the clergy, the word fell into disrepute, to appear only in learned dictionaries and underground literature.

As early as 1300, "shit" appears in print as a verb; "piss" is equally as old. Until perhaps the middle of the eighteenth century, their use was perfectly acceptable. Up to the fifteenth century, "cunt" meant "cunt" and there was no attempt to find new euphemism or dysphemism for this anatomical feature.

Though it was considered to be correct from 1000 A.D. on, the word "breast" fell into disrepute with the Victorians, and was replaced by the more ambiguous "bosom." A hundred years later, "breast" is again in use, and "bosom" relegated to flowery valentines and women's clothing patterns.

According to Peter Fryer's *Mrs. Grundy, Studies in English Prudery,* the word "cock," even when it did not refer to the penis, was banned well before the Age of Queen Victoria. The male chicken was a rooster after 1772. Cockroaches became just roaches in the 1820s. Haycocks were renamed haystacks at the same time.

If such practicing moralists as poets and preachers cannot agree upon a single measure of the obscene, lawyers hardly do any better. Obscenity remains a legal as well as a literary and social variable.

By 1792, each of the fourteen states ratifying the Constitution of the United States had adopted laws providing for the prosecution of either blasphemy or profanity.[6] As early as 1712, Massachusetts made it a crime to publish "any filthy, obscene, or profane song, pamphlet, libel or mock sermon" that mimicked a religious service. Apparently, "filthy," "obscene" and "profane" referred to the anti-clerical; that which is now considered to be "obscene" little troubled the legal profession of the colony, however much it may have agitated the clergy. (It might be added too, that even the anti-clerical could be tolerated, so long as it was not directed at the predominant Protestant faith.)

A similar circumstance prevailed in the Mother Country. Though there were prosecutions under various acts that made it a crime to publish "obscene" works, "obscenity" was defined as that which offended established institutions. Great Britain did not formulate a legal test for sexual expression until 1868.

Not until postal inspector Anthony Comstock mounted his crusade in the 1870s did the United States Congress get around to passing laws against mailing sexually graphic matter. Paradoxically, the United States Constitution now protects those speeches and pronouncements that in defaming a particular religion were once felt to be criminally actionable.

Clearly, the definition of "obscene" or "prurient," the pivotal word in legal circles, depends upon subjective interpretation and shifting cultural norms. The "folk" can hardly be more certain of the meaning of the word.

Folk song collectors have reported, for example, that informants were reluctant to sing "Little Musgrave and Lady Barnard" (Child 81) because it deals in modest terms with the pair's concupiscence.[7] The most explicit stanzas are these:

> "Lie down, lie down, little Matthy Groves,
> And keep my back from the cold;
> It is my father's shepherd boys
> A-blowing up the sheep from the fold."

> From that they fell to hugging and kissing
> And from that they fell to sleep;
> And the next morning when they woke at break of day
> Lord Arnold stood at their feet.

> "And it's how do you like my fine feather-bed,
> And it's how do you like my sheets?
> And it's how do you like my gay ladie
> That lies in your arms and sleeps?"

> "Very well do I like your fine feather-bed.
> Very well do I like your sheets
> But much better do I like your gay ladie
> That lies in my arms and sleeps."

> "Now get you up, little Matthy Groves,
> And all your clothes put on;
> For it never shall be said in Old England
> That I slew a naked man."[8]

As late as the 1960s, the sexual revolution or the new freedom notwithstanding, Louise Manny's older informants in New Brunswick declined to sing "Our Goodman" for her, "though this is so popular

xix

that dozens of songs made up on the Nor'West River have been set to its tune."[9]

Were this not vagary enough, to the temporal and temperamental nature of obscenity must be added what would appear to be levels or gradations of the obscene, reflected in an inordinate number of adjectives that describe all that might be called bawdy: improper, coarse, risque, ribald, blue, basic, dirty, gross, prurient, indelicate, rakish, smutty, roguish, indecent, lewd, loose, racy, randy, crude, and, of course, obscene. Except to the most puritanical, these are not strict synonyms; their meaning varies—from word to word and from individual to individual.

Still, in the last decade of the twentieth century, a folk song is considered subject to censorship in some quarters if it is more or less specific in dealing with matters amorous, if it discusses excretory functions and products, if it uses such tabooed words as "fuck," "shit," "piss," "cunt" or the more indelicate dysphemisms for these.

Even if the song does not concern itself with biological functions, a sprinkling of currently prohibited words (especially when they are involved in hard-to-edit rhymes) is enough to ban a song. In "The Lehigh Valley," for example, the triple rhyme of the last line—"I'll hunt the runt who stole my cunt"—simply cannot be edited in a fashion suitable for presentation to polite company. Into locked files went this hobo classic.

The collector's self-censorship at least leaves the slate clean. Worse is the bowdlerization that might permit publication while distorting the record. The first stanza of "The Lehigh Valley," with chip on shoulder, runs:

> "Don't look at me that way, mister;
> I didn't shit in your seat.
> I just came down from the Lehigh Valley
> With my balls all covered with sleet."

Edited, this has appeared as:

> "Don't look at me that way, mister;
> I didn't sit in your seat.
> I've just come down from the Lehigh Valley
> With my beard all covered with sleet."

The redacted text leaves all the rhymes in the right place and it doesn't hurt the story. But the rewrite lacks the virility of the original—a virility that the mock lament demands. After all, the narrator *is* a former pimp hunting the city slicker who stole away his true love and meal ticket.

Until recently, the collector who gathered a bawdy song or tale had but three alternatives: he could make no mention of the text at all (a hard choice); he could merely insert ellipses for the forbidden words or lines; or he could rewrite the offensive portions.

Whatever the course elected, the result was uncomfortable. One editor who elected to bowdlerize his texts—carefully telling the reader he was doing so — was forced to concede that he could not print *en clair* a rare find in "Put Your Shoulder Next to Mine and Pump Away": "The pumping song we now give is in print for the first time. Owing to its ribald theme, much 'blue-penciling' has been done. It was popular in British ships only. It may have given rise to the popular war-song 'Roll Me Over in the Clover!' "[10] The irony is inescapable. The editor felt constrained to edit a forerunner of an equally ribald ditty that is one of the most popular of bawdy songs in the United States, known and sung by literally thousands.

The losses to history, to scholarship, to our picture of ourselves have been considerable. N. Howard "Jack" Thorp, commenting on cowboy songs in general, noted, "Often the language was rough and for publication had to be heavily expurgated."[11] The result is that not one bawdy cowboy song collected before the turn of the century survives. Bawdy lumberjack songs are also rare. It is impossible to believe that cowhands and shantyboys, living far from women for long periods of time, did not have songs reflecting that fact. Similarly, the late Jim Garland noted on a tape recording made by the collector Lou Curtiss that Kentucky's coal miners spoke or sang "blackguardy" below the surface through the entire shift; not one example seems to survive. The absence of those songs thus distorts our understanding of their lives.

So too, self-censorship skewed appreciation of the sheer popularity of these songs. Arthur Kyle Davis, Jr. surveyed the reports of "Our Goodman," the expurgated version of "Five Nights Drunk," noted its occurrence in fifteen states and added, "If ribald versions were collected and printed, no doubt every state would be represented."[12] The same could be said for a number, if not most, of the songs in this collection.

Censorship inevitably creates more problems than it solves. Students of American culture, whatever their particular specialty, have much to learn from unexpurgated folklore. So obvious a notion is hardly new. Over a century ago, one Pisanus Fraxi, the pseudonymous herald of English erotic studies, argued:

> I hold that for the historian, or the psychologist, these [erotic] books, whether in accordance with, or contrary to the prejudices and tendencies

of the age, must be taken into account as well as, if not in preference to those in many other and better cultivated fields of literature. . . . I maintain that no production of the human brain should be ignored, entirely disregarded, or allowed to become utterly lost; for every writing, however trifling or insignificant it may seem, has a value for the *true* student, in estimating the individual who wrote it, or the period in which it was produced.[13]

Nearing the end of the twentieth century, the shelf of American folk song collections scarcely hints at the number of bawdy songs still in oral tradition. One could well assume that the folk singers of the English-speaking world, with a few notorious exceptions, were innocent romantics.[14]

Yet bawdry is a part of life, and folklore. Early on, children learn a good deal about sex and excretion. A close personal friend of the editor, then just six years old, recited, "A," pointing to her head, "B," pointing to her buttocks, "C," to her eyes, and then progressing from her nose to her pudenda in inch-long steps, "D, E, F, G, H, I, J, K, L, M, N, O," to end triumphantly at "P."

Moments later, she chanted what may fairly be called her first bawdy song, pointing out as she sang, her breasts, genitals, and buttocks:

> Milk, milk, lemonade,
> Around the corner where fudge is made.

Obviously there is a sexual content to children's lore, some of it of respectable age and surprising geographical dispersal. About 1944, the editor was singing to the tune of "My Bonnie Lies Over the Ocean":

> My bonnie lies over the ocean.
> My bonnie lies over the sea.
> My father lies over my mother,
> And that's how I came to be.

That the editor was not unduly precocious is substantiated by the fact that twenty years later, Jacqueline Brunke garnered the same rhyme from her ten-year-old daughter in West Los Angeles.

The twice-told tale of Johnny Fuckerfaster and Mary Holdstill is yet another example of the continuity of this lore:

Once there was a boy named John Fuckerfaster and a girl named Mary Holdstill. One day, Mary was walking past John's house and John came out and said, "Mary, I will give you two bags of candy if you will come in my house, and four more if you will come in my bedroom and take off your dress." She did and she laid down and he began fucking her. Her mother came in and said, "John Fuckerfaster and Mary Holdstill!"[15]

This joke was a favorite twenty years earlier when the editor first heard it in the schoolyard. Roger Abrahams had it from Philadelphia blacks, describing it as one of "the first kind of joke a child learns and remembers. . . ."[16]

To the historicity of such children's lore, one can add a geographical dimension little appreciated. Afanasyev's *Stories from the Folk-lore of Russia* reprints a tale told by Ukrainians sometime about the middle of the nineteenth century:

> A louse met a flea. "Where are you going?"
>
> "I am going to pass the night in a woman's slit."
>
> "And I am going into a woman's backside."
>
> They part. The next day they meet again. "Well, how did you sleep?" asked the louse.
>
> "Oh, don't talk about it. I was so frightened. A kind of bald head came to me and hunted me about. I jumped here and there, but he continued to pursue me. At last he spat on me and went away."
>
> "Well, gossip, there were two persons knocking about outside the hole I was in. I hid myself, and they continued to push about, but at last they went away."[17]

A similar story narrating the adventures of three fleas who spend the night upon and within the body of a famous movie actress — the identity of the hostess changes with the fortunes of film popularity — circulates among school children in Southern California. One flea nestles between her breasts but complains the heaving landscape was unsettling. Another beds down in her navel, but complains of the rumbling beneath him which disturbs his sleep. The third finds "a cave," enjoys the deep warmth, but is routed by "some bald-headed bastard who kept spitting at me."

Material such as this is common among youngsters. That it has so rarely seen print may, in part, be laid to the infirmities of field workers. Kenneth S. Goldstein has warned: "Because children's materials are so in-group oriented, there is a real challenge to the collector to obtain anything more than simply those materials which the children are willing to permit him to hear and observe. But children have a whole world of private beliefs, rhymes, and erotica which only a few sensitive and understanding adults are ever allowed to penetrate."[18]

We live in changing times. Urbanization and the mass media over the course of this century have made self-entertainment less a necessity of life. Television in the living room has replaced the family musicale in the parlor. Motion pictures have preempted the play-party, the square dance, the house-raising, the corn-shucking. The phonograph record has supplanted the homemade music of local, self-taught instrumentalists and singers.

With the passing of the need for local or community musicians, so have passed the songs, ballads, and instrumental tunes these musicians carried. The recovery of a good text of one of the 305 English and Scottish ballads raised to peerhood by Francis James Child is now comparatively rare. Old-timey fiddlers' contests are staged to artificially inseminate tradition; the winners frequently turn out to be professional or semi-professional instrumentalists. Creatures, or victims of this mass culture, younger singers are not learning the songs their grandparents cherished. The old order passeth.

Or almost passeth. Two types of folk song are stubborn exceptions to this general rule: children's rhymes and bawdy songs. These persevere, each for good reason.

Children's lore is the product of a very special social group. For all the imposed activities that teachers, recreation leaders, and parents hope will mold the youth of America, there remains a considerable body of lore that children stubbornly share among themselves. It provides an in-group form of communication, a code, or a password to cross the boundary between the adult world and the child's domain. This material is sometimes disrespectful of authority, frequently fanciful, often antagonistic; it is the jargon of throttled rebellion. How many generations of schoolchildren have laughingly sung, "Mine eyes have seen the glory of the burning of the school / We have torn up all the books and have broken all the rules"?

Such lore flourishes because all of the organized recreational activities in the world cannot supplant the momentary independence offered by a game of stickball or kick-the-can played in a vacant lot or busy street.

The great bearers of children's verbal lore, the five- through ten-year-olds, have only partially learned the art of conformity. They do conform to parental standards; they have early on learned the taboos. They know the ways to adult, that is, social approval. Yet within their games, rituals, and rhymes are the seeds of the rebellion, the outraged protest against cultural discipline, and the means to provide the temporary security of identification with a group of similarly afflicted children.[19]

As they grow older, these five- to ten-year-olds are more and more pressured into adaptive conformity. They discard the songs and folksay of their childhood, replacing this with the lore and rituals deemed appropriate to adult behavior. In the meantime, of course, younger children are there to learn the "right" way to play hopscotch, or jump double dutch, or choose up sides on a playground.

Bawdy songs are remembered and sung by adults because they, too, feel a need to rebel. The prevailing public opinion, that somehow bawdy songs are not appropriate for polite society, permits the bawdy songster to thumb his nose at convention even as he relieves his own fears and guilt with laughter. Further, he must confine his songs to select audiences, like the stag smoker or the fraternity party, far from prying ears. The very locale of the presentation lends a covert, underground sense of group identification—a usually masculine camaraderie so necessary for the emotionally mature male.[20]

Women who learn bawdy songs use them in closed circles also—college sororities and living groups are great trading grounds—but here, too, there is acceptance and shelter. In mixed groups, the songs are sung when the women have been accepted, on the male's terms, as broadminded or modern or sophisticated.

Even in those settings, bawdy songs reflect their strong masculine viewpoint. They can be said to be reinforcing the male view of the woman's sexual role for, at least until the feminist revolution of the 1960s, "women's idea of their own sexuality (at least in a majority of cultures) is historically a response to what men want and demand that sexuality to be, and that in general women are content to accept whatever model of their own sexuality men offer to and demand of them."[21]

Freudian-oriented psychiatrists have probed for the social significance of obscenity, following the lead of the master's *Wit and Its Relation to the Unconscious.* According to Freud and his followers, the function of bawdy lore is to permit people to air or momentarily relieve their fears of matters that are ordinarily taboo in polite society. By laughing at a joke about castration, the listener is coping with the massive fear most American males have of losing their manhood. By laughing at the antic bedding of One-Eyed Reilly's daughter and the subsequent sodomy perpetrated upon that lady's irate father, the listener is responding to his own desires to knock off the pubescent girl living across the street. The deed is done, One-Eyed Reilly violated as well, and the listener has vicariously participated, and escaped punishment—all because the wit of the song makes the unmentionable momentarily acceptable.

Because the story is funny and "O'Reilly's Daughter" an indecorous delight, the listener laughs. The wit, as Freud had it, is the license to thumb one's nose at convention; without wit, as singer and audience define it, the song or the story has no point, no saving grace, and no social function.

This humorous assault on fear is most immediate and most apparent in the songs of the military. A number of songs, bawdy or otherwise, confront the ever-present reality of death. For example, between 1945 and 1948, members of the 504th Parachute Infantry Regiment of the 82d Airborne roared this ballad about "Roman candles"—to the tune of "The Battle Hymn of the Republic."

"Is everybody ready?" cried the sergeant looking up.
Our hero feebly answered, "Yes," and then they stood him up.
He leaped right out into the blast, his static line unhooked,
He ain't gonna jump no more.

Chorus:
Gory, gory, what a helluva way to die. (3)
He ain't gonna jump no more.

* * * * * * * * * *

He hit the ground, the sound was splat, his blood was spurting high.
His comrades were heard to say, "What a helluva way to die."
They picked him up, still in his chute and poured him into his boots,
He ain't gonna jump no more.

The ambulance was on the spot, the jeeps were running wild.
The medics jumped and danced with glee and rolled their sleeves and
    smiled
For it had been at least a week or more since last a chute had failed.
He ain't gonna jump no more.[22]

Similarly, in commenting on what he termed the "smutty" joke, the prose analog to the bawdy songs in this collection, Martin Grotjahn asserted that off-color stories "pretend convincingly to be aimed at sexual satisfaction. Actually they serve, like wit, as the outlet of disguised aggression and for the satisfaction of infantile pleasures. While doing so, they continue to work on residual anxieties and conflicts which began in the time before the Oedipal phase of our development."[23]

Grotjahn sees the "smutty" story as something other than wit, or the "wit" of Freud's essay. Freud makes no such distinction. For him laughter is the result of the sudden unleashing of the forbidden as the result of wit. Suppressed or repressed, this forbidden thought is triggered by the aggression of the witticism. The listeners disguise their own vicarious aggression unconsciously; that aggression emerges in the conscious as harmless play, and in the company of others as laughter.

A few songs here appear to be exceptions to the Freudian argument that the public function of bawdy song is to entertain. One is the work song "Sound Off," which may amuse, but also sets the cadence of the march. Early versions of the sea shanty "Put Your Shoulder/ Belly Close to Mine and Pump Away" certainly served the same purpose, however remote its descendants are from the holystoned deck of a four-master. Another exception is the couplet sung to the opening bars of "The Billboard March," used as a form of social control of those who become too friendly with people in authority:

> There is a brown ring around his nose,
> And every day it grows and grows.

These exceptions notwithstanding, laughter remains crucial to the bawdy song. If the song is not humorous, the listener is left with fear and guilt unassuaged by amusement. The loss of laughter is disastrous not only to the quality of the song, but also to the individual; the humorless fellow who cannot chuckle at the dirty joke or bawdy song is frequently the most sexually guilt-ridden.

Bawdy songs and so-called dirty jokes are analogous forms of folklore. As Gershon Legman pointed out in his article, "The Rationale of the Dirty Joke," that form of humorous folktale falls largely into two classes: those with sexual themes involving castration or pseudocastration, and the scatological. The sexual jokes dealing with castration, says Legman, have one purpose: to reassure the listener with laughter; the scatological joke's function is to shock.[24]

A few bawdy songs seem to exist purely for their shock value: "I Love My Girl" with its coprophagy stands out. Rarely is shock the sole point or focus of the song. The deliberately offensive, or rebellious, is more likely to appear as incidental detail in ballads or as occasional verses inserted into portmanteau songs like "I-Yi-Yi-Yi" (limericks in that case).

Castration — in the form of contracting venereal disease — appears frequently in the songs here, in particular those with a strong occupational currency. "The Chisholm Trail," "The Fire Ship," "Lee's Hoochie," "The Sewing Machine," among others, have an occupational circulation and deal with the problem. Similarly, "The Gay Caballero," lacking a particular occupational association, is also a diseased whoremonger's complaint.

While there are some bawdy songs that may be considered to be homosexual — a psychoanalytic form of castration — none seems to have achieved wide currency in oral tradition. Sodomy, buggery, and related acts usually take place, as in "The Tinker" or "Christopher

Columbo," only after the horny hero has run through the available women. In effect, he is reasserting his super-masculinity by this act.

The most explicit example of this occurs in "Sam MacColl":

> If the girls want no more, want no more,
> Or they say they're very sore, very sore,
> If the girls moan and weep,
> Or they say they want to sleep,
> I try horses, cows and sheep, cows and sheep.

Bawdy songs are emphatically heterosexual. Their viewpoint is masculine, even when sung by women. Sexual intercourse, often in heroic bouts; penises of equally heroic proportions; cunts worthy of such cocks; seduction of the innocent but agreeable maiden—this is the stuff of bawdry.

It is also the stock material of that which, for lack of a better definition, is labeled "hard-core" pornography. There is one major difference: pornography is rarely humorous. Indeed, if it has any distinguishing characteristic, it is this lack of humor. Pornography is grim in its determination, its single-minded insistence upon clinical detail.

Not so the bawdy song, which rushes to climax the scene in laughter; the pornographer meanwhile grinds relentlessly for tumescence.

It is probably no accident that rape rarely figures in bawdy song. Seemingly, the social—and sexual—stigma attached to that act makes such a subject, by its very nature, beyond the bounds of true masculinity. The rapist uses force; the hero of bawdry uses wit. He may be as much a scoundrel as the rapist, but by guile or sexual attractiveness, by deceit or straightforward seduction, he achieves his heterosexual ends.

At the same time, rape is a staple of "hard-core" pornography, a reflection of the medium's abiding interest in sadism. That particular aberration, and its mirror image, masochism, may be rationalized in bawdy song; they do not serve as the basis for erotic episodes, openly dealt with. The brutality—genteel, to be sure—of most flagellational fiction is obvious; one must read into bawdy song such sadistic satisfaction.

The pornographic world is preeminently a sexual *Schlauraffenland,* the erotic pervading the fantasy, fantasy pervading the erotic. The people of Pornographia are capable of unending sexual bouts, only now and again fortified by aphrodisiacs. (Their use by the characters in such fiction is a nod toward the reality of sexual depletion; the fact remains that the potions prescribed are more effective in fiction than in life.) The men ejaculate in super-human streams, again and again, past all limits of known capability. The women are pliant, cardboard receptacles whose response—how different from the real world—is invariable, predictable, oriented to the gratification of their partners, male or female. Sexual intercourse results in no untoward effects. The female is rarely impregnated, despite the interminable coitus. Venereal disease goes unmentioned. Nothing, not even an incidental menstrual period, is permitted to intrude upon paradise.

Above all, pornography is a male-oriented art form. It is loveless, mechanistic, centered upon the act itself, not upon the emotive aspects that women in Western European cultures demand of sex. Its concern apparently is to provoke the reader to potency.[25]

"Hard-core" pornography—there seems to be no better phrase current—is not unlike the songs in this collection in certain ways. Both pornography and bawdy song are all but devoid of character development, of narrative detail, of descriptive setting. Pornography eschews this material as unimportant to its main purpose: sexual titillation. Bawdy song has no time for it; the lack of characterization, of detail, of setting is a trait shared with all of folk balladry. As part of the larger corpus, bawdy songs reflect the characteristics of the whole oral tradition. That folk balladry and pornography have some similar traits is accidental.

To some extent, a handful of the songs in this collection would seem to be closer to "hard-core" pornography than others.[26] Like "Casey Jones," these are the exception, and even these have the requisite leavening of wit lacking in "hard-core" literature.

Most of the songs here, and most bawdy songs in oral tradition, make it clear that even the "loose" sorts who sing bawdy songs retain some form of self-restraint or cultural censorship. "Hard-core" pornography has no such limitations; sexual taboos are openly flouted, their violation explicit and glorified. (The incest taboo is particularly assaulted, perhaps because it is the most deeply held.)

This cultural censorship is reflected in a number of songs, which avoiding the basic Anglo-Saxon, rely instead on the wit of the poetry. They might be fairly, if imprecisely, termed more "clever" or "naughty" than "dirty." Except by implication, they are not obscene.

In some gradation determined by the ratio of humor to the overtly shocking, the bawdy song becomes increasingly pornographic. Thus "My Husband's a Mason" appears to be more waggish than "Five Nights Drunk"; "The Ball of Kirriemuir" is more to the obscene end of the spectrum than the crapulous "Four Old Whores."

To some, all of the songs in this collection are beyond the pale.

Without making that value judgment, the singers themselves class the songs together, for when bawdy songs are sung, the actual obscenity quotient will vary from number to number. Apparently, once beyond the singers' estimate of the contemporary community consensus—whatever that is—a song, however bawdy, is "dirty." It goes underground, to emerge only when that consensus is momentarily waived or ignored.

This is not to suggest that the singers do not recognize that one song is less "offensive" than another, or more suitable for a mixed or unknown audience. They do. The singer's awareness of the bawdry is, though, less important than his appreciation of the humor within the song. After all, the function of bawdy song is to amuse the audience, be that audience only the singer, or a hundred men crowded into a noisy saloon.

The forms of humor within the songs vary from the play-upon-words to the satirical, from the witty to the sly. Generally, one may suspect the hand of better-educated authors in those songs such as "Caviar Comes from Virgin Sturgeon" or "I Used to Work in Chicago" or "Roll Your Leg Over," all of which depend upon special knowledge or plays upon words for their humor.

A significant proportion of the songs in this collection, perhaps as high as one-half, bear these marks of a literate or gifted author(s) at work. While this surprisingly high proportion may be inflated by a biased sample—a very large percentage of the informants who contributed to this collection were themselves college-educated—nonetheless, a good share of bawdy songlore still in oral tradition is the apparent product of literate creators.

There is precedent for this literate as opposed to "folk" origin. G. Malcolm Laws has identified several hundred ballads that began life in the cheap-print shops of 7 Dials and Grub Street. George Pullen Jackson spent a lifetime winnowing the traditional sources of shape-note hymns, incidentally underscoring the role of the singing school masters and hymn writers as stimulators of oral currency. Working in quite a different idiom, Gershon Legman has flatly identified the limerick as almost exclusively the work of educated authors and the property largely of educated narrators or singers. (These same people seem to be responsible for a significant amount of graffiti on the walls of some of the better restrooms.)

This literate authorship and currency of bawdy songlore is reflected most clearly in the great number of parodies gathered here. Parodies of more recent origin are almost invariably set to the borrowed melodies of popular, and familiar, songs. The tune comes first; the words are written to fit the melody. This new text is patterned, to some degree, after the old, and usually there is some attempt to imitate in the first line(s) of the bawdy parody at least the first line(s) of the song vehicle.[27]

This deliberate copying immediately provides a humorous shock, in and of itself. The unexpected lyrics may be so effective as humor that nothing more than the first lines of the new song will ever be written. So it is that a parody of "The Anniversary Waltz" (actually Ivanovichi's "Danube Waves") is set only to the tune's opening musical phrases:

> Oh, how we danced on the night we were wed;
> We danced and we danced 'cause the room had no bed.[28]

On the other hand, when a bawdy song's melody is drawn from the entire stock of Anglo-American folk tunes, it would seem that the words come first and are then set to an appropriate tune, the two fitted together as seems most effective. This would be the only possible explanation for the fact that textual variants of bawdy songs set to traditional tunes may be carried by completely unrelated melodies.

The parody, of course, cannot lose its tune and still retain its identity as a parody. In that extra-musical sense, the parody is far more intimately related to its melody than is the non-parodic folk song.

Published collections of American folk song do not indicate the prevalence of parody, bawdy or otherwise, in oral tradition. Few parodies, at least those recognized as such, have been included in the various regional collections, and only a handful have been published in the academic journals.

But parody is common, both in popular and folk musics. In their introduction to *The Songs of the Gold Rush*, Richard A. Dwyer and Richard E. Lingenfelter noted that the forty-niner

> mended his tunes to suit his life, and, as that life was hard, the songs were rough. Parody was the chief result. . . . It seems not too improbable that prospectors sang the same parodies they heard in the saloons, for the miners' taste for the familiar-with-a-difference may have been more basic than has hitherto been suspected. . . . Apparently, along with their diet of imported Eastern ballads and plays, the forty-niners relished a saltier draught of their own making. The parodic note seems to have been pervasive in their entertainment, and not restricted to song.[29]

Earlier, Duncan Emrich had noted the same prevalence of parody in the songlore of Western miners. Hugh Anderson divined the hand "of itinerant professional ballad-monger(s)" in Australian balladry. John Greenway's survey of *American Folk Songs of Protest*, the Carawan compilation of the recently composed songs from the 1960s Freedom Movement in the South, and Reuss's overview of campus songlore all reflect this same dependence on a second-hand muse.[30] Judging from the available, though scattered, evidence and from this collection, it would appear that the role of parody in folk song must be more seriously considered.

If, as the present editor believes, parody is predominantly the product of the better educated or of the professional entertainer, then it is another example, to use the phrase of Cazden, Haufrecht, and Studer, of "feedback" from urban to rural settings.[31]

Parody, bawdy or otherwise, is not apparently the way of the folk, if "folk" is to be defined conventionally, and wrongly, as a relatively isolated, relatively uneducated, relatively insular group. Instead, parody is a borrowed technique, or, more properly, the products of that technique are borrowed. This borrowing implies contact with, and interest in, a world beyond the local or regional "community."

In another manner, too, the analysis of bawdy song texts reveals a variance from generally accepted definitions of folklore and song.

It is axiomatic in the study of folklore that there is no one, single "correct" version of a song or story as there is of the latest popular tune or even a Beethoven symphony. A folk song has no single melody or set of words; every singer has his or her own version. One may be better than another in an aesthetic sense, but none is the *right* way to sing the song. Further, many folk songs are sung with stanzas interposed, transposed, dropped, or borrowed from entirely different songs because the singer felt like it at the moment.

Bawdy songlore defies that axiom. With such obvious exceptions as "Roll Your Leg Over" and the limerick omnibuses, versions of bawdy folk songs seem to exhibit less variation than their non-bawdy kin. There appear to be standard versions of bawdy songs, or what seem to be closely adhered to measures of what "Ball of Yarn," "The Fucking Machine," or "No Balls at All" should contain. Ribald songs do change over time, but at a rate much slower than do non-bawdy songs.

This anomaly can only be explained by the suggestion that the people who sing bawdy songs take some pains first to learn and then to remember them. They do so because of the wit or humor of the piece; the comic element serves as both the *raison d'être* of the song and the mnemonic device preserving the integrity of the text. In short, the songs have meaning. They are valued. Thus they are important to singer and to scholar alike.

This lack of variation cannot in this case be attributed to that enemy of oral tradition, the printed word. Normally, when a folk song gets into print that particular version acquires a certain sanctity; it becomes the "correct" form of the song in the mind of the singing public, and it is this version that is likely to survive, driving out of oral tradition equally good texts and tunes.[32]

In more recent years, the great enemy of oral tradition has been the phonograph record, not the printed page. The Andrews Sisters' recording of "Down in the Valley" during World War II, and the Weavers' rendition of "On Top of Old Smoky" a few years later, to cite just two examples, gained wide circulation, and these songs, long dormant in oral tradition, were once more widely known. But they were known only in the variants recorded by those groups. Parodies quickly popped up, but these were completely new songs, not rewrites ground piecemeal, as oral tradition refashions a song.

A few bawdy songs, mostly in expurgated versions, have been recorded. (The so-called party records of the 1930s and 1940s sold furtively in comparatively small numbers and did not achieve enough circulation to fix a "standard" version in oral tradition.) In the 1950s, however, versions of "Bell Bottom Trousers" and "The Fire Ship" achieved great popularity, and, for a generation at least, seem to have defined the "correct" tune for even the bawdy versions. Less decisively, the multiple recordings of Oscar Brand during the 1950s and 1960s seem to have influenced oral tradition in that some songs recovered since then reflect Brand's textual and melodic handiwork.[33]

A last conclusion about the nature of bawdy lore in oral tradition has emerged in the two decades since *The Erotic Muse* first saw print: bawdry can travel rapidly.

At one time it appeared to take whole generations for songs and ballads to spread from region to region, or nation to nation. No longer. A British soldiers' song of the First World War, "Bless 'Em All," had become, in little more than twenty years, common property of Brits, Anzacs, Yanks, and Canucks.

Travel, of course, is no longer by horse-drawn wagon, but by airplane. Equally important, it is comparatively inexpensive. It is common during wartime for men bearing songs to be shipped around the globe in great numbers. Thus it might be argued that wartime conditions encourage the broadcasting of folk song.

In the postwar years, students too have moved far and wide, studying abroad in increasing numbers, exchanging songs with their hosts. In one case, students from Britain have introduced not only a game, rugby football, but a large body of songs that travel with the sport. (See "The Rugby Song," below.)

Withal, the study of bawdy song demands that the conventional habits of thought concerning folklore need revision. Good reason, then for the editor of a work such as this to state the ground rules of his collection.

The songs here are all traditional. Some are literally centuries old. Others are rather new.

This editor believes a folk song to be any song—no matter its origin, no matter if the composer is known, no matter how rudimentary or sophisticated text and tune may be—that has passed from a first generation to a second. Generation is defined not in the demographer's twenty-five years, or the biblical thirty-three, but in terms of occupational or sub-group limits.

If a college freshman writes a song lampooning a rival institution, and it is still sung after the author has graduated, that song is a folk song. A college generation lasts but four or five years; at the end of that period, a largely new student body is on campus.

Similarly, a generation of miners is six-, eight-, or ten-years long, depending upon whose estimate of the job longevity in the mines one accepts.

A generation of elementary school children is seven years, and in highly transient communities may well be less. As long as the great majority of the first generation has moved on, consider a generation to have passed.

Should a song persist for only one generation, then it is considered a topical or local song, of great interest in and of itself, since this is the stuff from which folk song comes.

One last, and important, qualification to this definition: the singers must remain unconcerned with changes in the song. Change is not mandatory, only permissible.[34]

All of the songs in this collection are, by that definition, folk songs.

One rule governed the selection. *The Erotic Muse* is conceived as a cross-section, a sampling of bawdy songs sung in urban America, circa 1960-90. The editor required two reports of a song to establish its currency, and thus its claim upon traditional status.

This is not a closed canon. Absent are many bawdy songs known to have been sung in the past, poems really, since tunes often were not recovered or noted by earlier collectors. Unless the editor had a version from contemporary oral tradition, a song was left for another day, another scholar.

Absent too are songs unique to black America. ("Frankie and Johnny" and "Stagolee" have passed from black provenance to general currency; it is the white tradition that is sampled here.) The omission of black material is deliberate; the editor's collection in this area is small, his understanding correspondingly limited. Black bawdy song needs, and merits, its own study, not the incidental attention that black folk song is too often afforded.

This anthology then samples a white, generally urban tradition as it is currently carried by largely middle-class, educated informants. It records but sparingly the bawdy song repertoires of either rural or less well-educated urban dwellers.

Still, the limited collecting done among those groups suggests that class distinctions make little difference in the songs that will be gathered from an informant. "Charlotte the Harlot" and "The Ring-Dang-Doo" are common to all. "Bang Away, Lulu" is seemingly ubiquitous. Soldiers and marines, regardless of rank, who served in Korea during the police action sang at least a bit of "Movin' On."

A second major change differentiates the first and second editions: the use of conflations. The first edition, published in 1968 was, to the best of the editor's knowledge, the first unexpurgated collection of theretofore banned or bowdlerized songs and ballads offered openly for sale. So it seemed useful to present, as exemplars, the fullest possible versions, and to conflate, if necessary.

Other popular collections now provide those model texts. Therefore the conflations have been eliminated in this second edition. In some cases, instead of the single full text of the first edition, two or three more or less partial versions must be fitted together to make a "whole."

The skeletal melodies notated here are reasonable approximations of what the singers actually sang, more or less a mean of the tunes for each stanza. Folk song is a free art, the singers take liberties that would be considered indecent in art song (though not in jazz or opera). In times past, the range of variation, the idiosyncratic and regional performance styles, has been as multifarious as the singers themselves. Apparently, this absolute freedom, within little understood cultural limits, has been narrowed in recent years.

In earlier collections of folk song, the skeletal melodies were suggestions of the framework upon which singers embroidered interpolations, glissandi, grace notes and a dozen other stylistic devices. In this collection, the skeletal tunes seem to be far closer to actual performance. In that sense, these notations are examples of what Charles Seeger has termed prescriptive music writing.[35]

This lessening of variation seemingly flows from a combination of factors, primarily an emphasis upon *pro forma* performance within the limited musical education of the public schools. The inculcated stress upon "excellence" in performance also serves as an inhibiting factor, since one of the aesthetics of art music is accurate recreation of the given melody.

There are other reasons, too, for this shift in traditional performance standards. Above all else, bawdy song is *speech-oriented* music, more so certainly than other forms of traditional singing.[36] In contemporary bawdy song sessions, the performance is geared to delivery of the words; music is secondary. Beyond some gesture in the direction of popular music's performance standards, the vehicle for the text is little considered.

If accompanied—and in recent years more and more singers have considered accompaniment mandatory when singing in company, that is, while *performing*—the arrangements tend to fall into two distinct categories. One includes the simplest of ump-pa-pa, ump-pa-pa harmonic props for the text, usually played on the guitar, sometimes on a piano. The second category is more elaborate, delivered by a performer with sufficient talent or skill to embellish the tune with melodic figures or haphazard counterpoint. Even with this second group of singer-instrumentalists, the performance is likely to be simple and direct, again, one geared to the presentation of the words. (The editor has heard any number of guitar accompaniments to bawdy song, but never one that suggested the performer had consciously prepared an "arrangement." Either bawdy songs are unrehearsed—probably true—by casual singers, or there is some feeling that complex musical arrangements would detract from the text.)

Viewed as a body of music, bawdy song is apparently an audience-oriented music, and there is no question but that the reactions of the listener affect the performance. Bawdy song, again thought of as a body of music, is fundamentally a social experience, one dependent for full appreciation upon this x-factor the audience provides. (Lest the reader think this all very simple, all very obvious, consider the range of permissible audience responses to church music as sung in a High Mass and a Pentecostal Holiness service.)

The editor has seen a singer stop in lame confusion when he realized that a favorite song had somehow alienated his listeners. He has seen other singers erupt in laughter, their song suddenly interrupted. He has seen performers topped by the laughter of the audience, which drowned out the song. Such incidents strongly underscore the immediate social function of the performance.[37]

Wherever possible the editor has sought to include not only citations to textual analogs, but to musical as well. The textual are reasonably easy to agree upon. The musical are something else.

Bawdy songs tend not to borrow the ballad clichés, the stray stanzas of "clean" folk songs; bawdy songs tend to be dirty through and through. It is through the melodies that the relationship of bawdy folk song to "clean" folk song is most clearly shown. The two bodies of material share a common vehicle.

But tune-hunting is an imperfect business. Results are open to question the farther a given melody varies from a clearly acknowledged tune such as "Villikins and His Dinah" or "My Bonnie Lies Over the Ocean." (And while this editor considers these two markedly different tunes, the redoubtable Norman Cazden argues that they are related.) There is no agreement on just what constitutes a tune family, or even how its members are to be identified.[38] The most authoritative statement on the subject is Samuel Bayard's suggestion that there are perhaps thirty-five basic melodies within British folk music.[39]

The present editor tends to rely on the general contour of the tune's melodic phrases and with that their range, coupled with what seem to be particular "trademarks" or characteristic figures. "Sweet Betsy" generally begins with these notes:

That trademark phrase present in the first bar, the rest usually follows.

"My Bonnie" is marked by the unusual initial leap of a sixth and the falling phrase that follows. Given that, identification of a member of the tune-family — if "My Bonnie" deserves to be called an "ur-type" — is simple.

Similarly, "The Wild Colonial Boy" family is set off by the abrupt fall of a fifth or a sixth in the middle of the tune. It is not always present, but when it is there, the likelihood is that other identifying elements are also at hand.

These minimal identification elements ignore a number of other factors that would at one and the same time refine the identification and make for broader classifications. Cadence, mode, phrase recurrence, repeated notes, rhythm are all discounted.

Consequently, the tune identifications made here are comparatively conservative. In general, the identified tune analogs are clearly related and serve no more than as a starting point in identifying clusters of related melodies. As such, they should present little problem for future workers.

This collection of American bawdy songs, or, more properly, bawdy songs sung in America, was gathered by the editor and a number of former students. The collection made by Dean Burson at UCLA during 1960 was especially rich and so systematically collected as to prove a "table of contents" of the most popular songs then circulating on that campus. It has been supplemented in this second edition by an even larger collection made at the University of California, Berkeley, between 1958 and 1963 by guitarist-singer Harry A. Taussig.

A goodly number of people were generous to the point of collaboration in preparing the first edition. Bess Lomax Hawes permitted the use of songs collected by her former students at then San Fernando Valley State College, Northridge, California, between 1961 and 1963. J. Barre Toelken forwarded more than fifty songs and fragments from the holdings of the Robert W. Gordon Collection of American Folk Song at the University of Oregon; he then combed the Utah State University archives for additional material. Roger D. Abrahams, now of the University of Pennsylvania, contributed numerous items gathered by his former students at the University of Texas, frequently with helpful notes.

Equally generous scholars have helped to ready this second edition: Joseph Hickerson guided me through the Library of Congress's Archive of American Folk Song; Sean Galvin worked the Indiana University holdings. Lydia Fish, of Buffalo State College, shared songbooks dating from the Vietnam War era. Guy Logsdon generously forwarded portions of the manuscript of his important cowboy song collection, *The Whorehouse Bells Were Ringing*, and research material, but, more important, extended friendly advice.

Two scholars read this manuscript: Frank Hoffmann of Buffalo State University, a pioneering scholar in erotic folklore; and the late D. K. Wilgus of UCLA. Wilgus not only shared notes, texts, and tunes from his own sturdy repertoire and the Western Kentucky Folklore

Archive at UCLA, but generously gave of his last vital hours to this writer.

With their assistance, this second, expanded edition includes a number of changes from the first. More than forty songs have been added, while a few were stricken on the basis of dubious oral currency. Meanwhile hundreds of additional citations to both the words and the music have been added.

Whenever possible, both collectors and informants are credited. A few not identified in the first edition have elected to throw off the cloak of anonymity, or are beyond caring. The wishes of the balance are respected.

ED CRAY
Los Angeles
1990

NOTES

1. *A Collection of Epigrams* (London: J. Walthoe, 1735), No. 76.

2. See Peter A. Munch's "What Became of 'Little Powder-Monkey Jim,'" *Journal of American Folklore* 84 (1971): 311-20, for a discussion of the impact of electronic entertainments even in the remote fastness of Tristan da Cunha. Paradoxically, urban "feedback" to rural communities can revitalize a folk song in oral tradition, Cazden, Haufrecht, and Studer note in their excellent *Folk Songs of the Catskills*, p. 247. See too Norman Cohen, "Tin Pan Alley's Contribution to Folk Music," *Western Folklore* 29 (1970): 9-20.

3. After the publication of the first edition of this work, Oscar Brand wrote on May 13, 1971, to claim a "proprietary interest" in a number of the songs presented. Noting that he rewrote traditional bawdy songs as early as 1938, and recorded others as early as 1941, Brand stated that he believed himself responsible for the "traditional" versions of many of the best-known bawdy songs. He requested that his authorship be acknowledged with copyright notices for sixteen songs included in this second edition. The sixteen included "Ball of Yarn," "I Don't Want to Join the Army," "Blinded by Turds," "Old Gray Bustle," "I Used to Work in Chicago," "Bang Away, Lulu," "The Jolly Tinker," "The Bastard King of England," "The Ring Dang Do," "O'Reilly's Daughter," "The Cod Fish Song," "We Go to College," "Red Wing," "My God, How the Money Rolls In," "No Balls at All" and "The Wayward Boy." Brand asked for no fee, merely credit. In appropriate cases here, Brand's claim is acknowledged.

4. 237 F. 2d 796. In a footnote, Judge Frank added this observation from an earlier opinion: "One thinks of the lyrics sung at many such gatherings by a certain respected and conservative member of the faculty of a great

law school which considers itself the most distinguished and which is the Alma Mater of many judges sitting on upper courts." *Roth* was eventually appealed to the United States Supreme Court, which used it as a vehicle to formulate a new test of obscenity—one that has lead to a more mature evaluation of sex in the arts.

5. Bronson, 2, p. 15, in the headnote to "The Carnal and the Crane" (Child 55). See also the notes of Norman Cazden, Herbert Haufrecht, and Norman Studer regarding "humorous tunes" in their model study of *Folk Songs of the Catskills*, p. 139.

6. The statutes are collected in *Roth* v. *U.S.*, 354 U.S. 483-84, nn. 12, 13. Most states have considerably expanded the coverage of these laws. California's Penal Code went so far as to proscribe songs such as those in this collection. Section 311.6 at one time read, "Every person who knowingly sings or speaks any obscene song, ballad, or other words in any public place is guilty of a misdemeanor."

7. See Manny and Wilson, p. 205. Similarly, David J. Winslow reports a seven-year-old Pennsylvania girl who thought "there was some impropriety in saying the word 'girdle' in this rhyme: In nineteen-forty-four / My mother went to war; / Her girdle snapped / And killed the Japs, / And that was the end of the war." See "An Annotated Collection of Children's Lore," *Keystone Folklore Quarterly* 11 (1966): 160.

8. Stanzas twelve through sixteen from "Little Mathy Groves" as given by Belden, *Missouri*, p. 58.

9. Manny and Wilson, p. 205.

10. Hugill, *Shanties*, p. 508.

11. *Songs of the Cowboy* (Estancia, N.M., 1908).

12. *More Traditional Ballads of Virginia*, p. 301. Davis added, "Perhaps the indelicacy or obscenity of many versions has reduced the number of texts that reach collectors, certainly the number of published texts. Since some of these more free-spoken texts and their tunes may be among the best ballad versions, there is need of a serious scholarly project which will reduce such squeamishness to a minimum."

13. *Index Librorum Prohibitorum* (London: Privately printed, 1877; New York, 1962), pp. xix-xxv. According to Legman (*Hornbook*, 13), Pisanus Fraxi was the punning pen name of Henry Spencer Ashbee.

14. Donal O'Sullivan notes that "the pitiful theme of girls led astray and betrayed, being unhappily a commonplace of rural life everywhere, is naturally represented in folk song. So far as Ireland is concerned, such songs are found more frequently in manuscripts than in printed books, for reasons that may be readily understood; but it would be wrong to conclude from this (as has sometimes been done) that the subject is avoided by folk singers. . . ." See his *Songs of the Irish*, p. 162.

15. As collected by Nancy Leventhal from a 12-year-old boy in Hawthorne, California, in 1959.

16. *Deep Down in the Jungle*, p. 239. Martha Wolfenstein discusses the story in *Children's Humor*, pp. 63-91.

17. *Ribald Russian Classics*, p. 57. See also Legman, *The Horn Book*, pp. 182-83. Hoffmann has assigned this Tale Type 282D.

18. *A Guide for Field Workers in Folklore*, pp. 150-51.

19. In commenting on the function of children's lore, the editor is co-opting certain observations of Roger D. Abrahams, who took sharp exception to the manuscript of the first edition.

20. William Hugh Jansen has termed this "esoteric" folklore. See "The Esoteric-Exoteric Factor in Folklore," *Fabula* 2 (1959): 205-11.

21. Steven Marcus, *The Other Victorians*, p. 113. Arguing on behalf of women defining their own sexuality, some of the more outspoken feminists, such as Andrea Dworkin, advocate the censorship of all they deem to be pornography. Waving aside distinctions between "obscenity" and "indecency" that the Supreme Court of the United States recognizes, these women would surely demand this book be banned.

22. Written out by former paratrooper Jacques Vidacam of Los Angeles. An Australian version is in Lowenstein, p. 21. Les Cleveland, "Soldiers' Songs: The Folklore of the Powerless," *New York Folklore* 11 (1985): 79-97, makes the point that such songs may function also as a form of social protest.

23. *Beyond Laughter*, p. 110. See also Sigmund Freud, *Wit and Its Relation to the Unconscious*, as translated by A. A. Brill, and printed in *The Basic Writings of Sigmund Freud*, A. A. Brill, ed. (New York, 1938), pp. 728-42.

24. *Neurotica*, No. 9 (1951): 49 ff. In effect, this is a précis of Legman's bulky book of the same name and its second volume, *No Laughing Matter*.

25. Grotjahn, p. 60, sums this: "Where the man discovered love through sex, the woman discovered sex through love."

26. Guy Logsdon's introduction to *The Whorehouse Bells Were Ringing* notes that British erotic songs are less graphic or dysphemistic than are American songs, and that Australian bawdy songs seem to fall somewhere between the two. Research for this book suggests this might hold true for material dating from the nineteenth century and earlier; the newer British rugby song corpus is as raunchy as any American material.

27. See A. S. Limouze, "The Hump Song," *Journal of American Folklore* 63 (1950): 463. In his *Larry Gorman, the Man Who Made the Songs*, Edward Ives notes that Gorman, like Robert Burns before him, carefully fashioned new lyrics to traditional folk tunes, but these melodies were so widely known in their communities that they served the same function as do today's popular songs.

28. Collected by Robert Easton in Los Angeles in 1960.

29. Dwyer and Lingenfelter, *Songs of the Gold Rush*, pp. 2-4.

30. Emrich, "Songs of the Western Miners," *California Folklore Quarterly* 1 (1942): 216 ff.; Anderson, *Colonial Ballads*, p. 147; John Greenway, *American Folksongs of Protest*, passim; Guy and Candie Carawan, *We Shall Overcome*, passim; and Richard A. Reuss, "An Annotated Field Collection of Songs from the American College Student Oral Tradition," unpublished M.A. thesis, Indiana University, 1965.

31. *Folk Songs of the Catskills*, p. 263.

32. This Gresham's Law of oral tradition is demonstrated in the editor's study of the texts of "Barbara Allen in America: Cheap Print and Reprint," in *Folklore International*, D. K. Wilgus, ed. (Hatboro, Pa., 1967), pp. 41-50. Reuss, op. cit., independently has made similar observations, pp. 11 ff.

33. See Note 3 above.

34. This creates an anomalous group of songs, those once traditional that have been "frozen" by the corrective of print and phonograph. It might well be that a singular version is traditional, but no longer of the folk. For whatever reasons, that particular melding of text and tune is no longer theirs to change—even though parodies, entirely new lyrics, set to the familiar tune may flourish. This seems to have occurred in the case of the Carter Family's version of "The Wreck of the Old Ninety-Seven" and the Weavers' "On Top of Old Smoky."

35. See his "Prescriptive and Descriptive Music Writing," *The Musical Quarterly* 44 (1958): 184-95.

36. In traditional ballad-singing, even though the narration is seemingly all-important, singers are, or were, conscious of their vocal performance, and neighbors did judge to some degree a ballad singer's singing style—the ability to project the story—if not the actual vocal quality.

37. These brief notes on the description of bawdy song as a music form were shaped largely by conversations with Charles Seeger and by three of his crucial articles: "On the Moods of a Music-Logic," *Journal of the American Musicological Society* 13 (1960): 224-61; "Systematic Musicology—Viewpoints, Orientations and Methods," ibid., 4 (1951): 240-48; and "Preface to the Description of a Music," a report read to the International Society for Musical Research, Fifth Congress, Utrecht, July, 1952.

38. See Samuel Bayard, "Prolegomena to a Study of the Principal Melodic Families of Folk Song," in MacEdward Leach and Tristram P. Coffin, *The Critics and the Ballad*, pp. 103 ff.; and Norman Cazden et al., Nos. 58, 70, and 101, for discussions of the problem.

39. Bayard, p. 116. This must be read in conjunction with the earlier discussion of Béla Bartók's "styles."

Old, New, Borrowed, Blue

MOST earlier collections of traditional ballads and songs have omitted bawdy material. Consequently, these songs of Anglo-Irish origin, as ancient as those frequently anthologized, as worthy of consideration as those frequently praised, have been denied their just due. This omission has obscured a fundamental point: the bawdy song is simply one form of folk song, subject to the same process of change as every other folk song. Entirely new lines, or even whole stanzas, may be inserted into old songs; snips and fragments may be revised; verses from other songs may be added — all at the singer's discretion.

The constant change and smoothing of rough-hewn lyrics has produced these Anglo-American favorites.

The Sea Crab

"The Sea Crab" is one of those living artifacts of another era, passed down in oral tradition for more than 300 years. As a song, it can be dated to 1620, and in tale form, it was first printed ten years before that. Well known in Elizabethan England, it was apparently recognized as an old song even then.

[A]

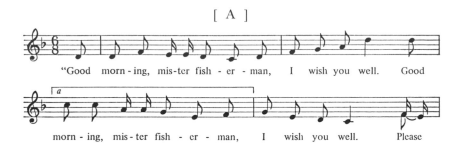

"Good morn-ing, mis-ter fish-er-man, I wish you well. Good

morn-ing, mis-ter fish-er-man, I wish you well. Please

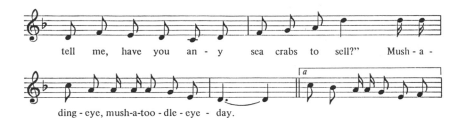

tell me, have you an - y sea crabs to sell?" Mush - a -

ding - eye, mush-a-too - dle - eye - day.

"Good morning, mister fisherman, I wish you well.
Good morning, mister fisherman, I wish you well.
Please tell me have you any sea crabs to sell?"
    Mush a ding eye, mush a toodle eye day.

"Yes, I have got sea crabs, one, two and three.
Yes, I have got sea crabs, one, two and three.
Take any you want; it makes no matter to me."
    Mush a ding eye, etc.

He grabbed one old sea crab by his back bone. (2x)
He hustled and tussled till he got that crab home.
    Mush a ding eye, etc.

When the old man got home, the old wife was asleep, (2x)
So he put him in the pisspot just for to keep.
    Mush a ding eye, etc.

The old wife got up for to take a long shit. (2x)
The God damned old sea crab grabbed her by the slit.
    Mush a ding eye, etc.

"Husband, oh, husband, now what shall I do? (2x)
The devil's in the pisspot and he's got me by the flue."
    Mush a ding eye, etc.

The old man ran over and lifted her clothes, (2x)
And he took his other pincher and he grabbed at his nose.
    Mush a ding eye, etc.

"Now, Johnny, have the doctor hitch his horse and cart, (2x)
Come get your father's nose and your mother's cunt apart."
    Mush a ding eye, etc.

It tickled the children right down to their soul (2x)
To see their pa's nose in their mother's peehole.
    Mush a ding eye, etc.

[B]

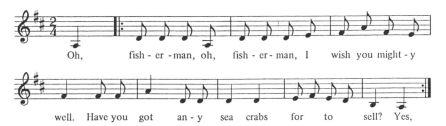

Oh, fish-er-man, oh, fish-er-man, I wish you might-y well. Have you got an-y sea crabs for to sell? Yes,

"Oh, fisherman, oh, fisherman, I wish you mighty well.
Have you got any sea crabs for to sell?"
"Yes, I have. That's one, two, three,
And the best of them I'll sell to thee."

Chorus:
Come a dal-a-daddle-ding, a dal-a-daddle-ding,
A knick knack now.

He picked one up all by the backbone
And he put him on his shoulder and he wagged [?] off home.
When he got home, for the want of a dish,
He put him in the pot where his old woman pished.

The old woman got up to do what she want.
The sea crab grabbed her right by the twat.
"Oh, yes, old man, as sure as you're born,
The devil's in the pisspot and hooked me with his horn!"

The old man rose as you may suppose,
And the sea crab grabbed him right by the nose.
"Oh, son, oh, son, oh, daughter, daughter, daughter,
Get the [poker to pry] your dad's nose and your mammy's ass apart."

"The Sea Crab" is one of the few bawdy songs to have been accorded scholarly attention. In an article in *Midwest Folklore* (8 [1958]: 91-100), Guthrie Meade, Jr., noted, "In America, the song seems to have flourished over a large area," but he had only two versions from oral tradition and a report of a third.

Both Meade and Legman (*The Horn Book,* 190) give tale references to this *conte-en-vers.* Thompson has assigned to it the motif number J 2675, describing it delicately as "Bungling Rescuer Caught by Crab. He tries to rescue woman caught by crab. Is caught himself and found in embarrassing position." Hoffmann reassigns it to X726.3.2.

The earliest song text—from the *Percy Folio Manuscript*—is re-

3

printed in Farmer (4:14 ff.); and Cray (*Anthology*, 42-44). The three oldest versions recovered from American oral tradition are in Randolph's "Unprintable" manuscript (p. 38), dating to the 1890s.

Nettleingham (*More*, 28) has an expurgated variant from first world war British currency. The original edition of *Immortalia*, dated on the title page to 1927, has it on pages 58-59. The 1968 reprint has it on page 76.

The Robert W. Gordon Collection of American Folk Song, at the University of Oregon, has an undated but late 1920s text forwarded by J. Barre Toelken which adds this chip-on-the- shoulder verse:

> Now my story is done, and I don't know anymore.
> There's an apple up my ass-hole and you can have the core.

Morgan 2 (pp. 117-18), and Getz 2 (RR-8, under the title of "Roll-Tiddle-ee-o"), have this tag as well.

The song seemingly continues in oral tradition. Guy Logsdon had it from his excellent cowboy informant, Riley Neal; Logsdon prints it, with notes, at pages 246-48.

Arthur Argo sings a variant from Scotland under the title "The Lobster" on *A Wee Thread o' Blue* (Prestige 13048). Laycock (pp. 37-38) says his text is from Scotland as well. Fowke ("Bawdy Ballads," 57) has a text and tune from Ontario. An American version, with a tune, is in the University of Illinois mimeographed collection, "Songs of Roving and Raking" (p. 2). Babab (p. 101) has a version, different from that here, acknowledging Oscar Brand's copyright of that text and tune.

The "A" version here is from John Terrence O'Neil who learned it as a boy from the singing of his father, circa 1940 in New York City. (See the endnote to "The Foggy, Foggy Dew," below.) The melody O'Neil used, and recognized as such, is the first half of "The Limerick Rake," a copy of which is in O Lochlainn (p. 84). The tune is also used for the unrelated "The Galbally Farmer" in O Lochlainn's second volume (p. 114).

The "B" version is from the singing of Lewis Winfield of Plainfield, Wisconsin, recorded for the Archive of American Folk Song on AFS 4169 by Helene Stratman-Thomas and Robert Draves on August 27, 1940. Tapes of that recording session were forwarded by James P. Leary of Mt. Horeb, Wisconsin. A similar version from Minneapolis with the "Musha De, Musha Die" chorus was contributed to the Indiana Folklore Archives in 1952.

4

Cod Fish Song

The crab of old has become a cod fish, the poor creature is beaten to death with brush and broom, and the song has acquired a moral, of sorts, yet it is still "The Sea Crab." The melody for this version is that of "The Chisholm Trail."

Chorus:
Singing ti yi yipee, yipee ya, yipee ya,
Singing ti yi yipee, yipee ya.

There was a man who had a little horse.
He saddled it, bridled it, and threw his leg across.

He rode and rode until he came to a brook,
And there sat a fisherman baiting his hook.

"Oh, fisherman, fisherman," said he,
"Have you a codfish for my tea?"

"Oh, yes," said he. "There's two:
One for me and one for you."

Well, he took that codfish by [the] leg bone
And mounted on his horse and galloped back home.

But when he got home he couldn't find a dish,
So into the chamberpot he put the little fish.

All night he could hear his woman cry,
"There's a devil down below; I can see his beady eyes."

Well, in the morning, she sat down to squat,
And the codfish jumped up her you-know-what.

She yelled bloody murder; "Well," cried she,
"There's a bloody big something getting up me!"

Well, she hopped and she jumped and she gave a roar.
There went the codfish a-skating 'round the floor.

They chased that codfish all around the room.
They hit him with a brush and banged him with a broom.

First they hit him on the belly and they hit him on the side.
They hit him on his arse until the poor fellow died.

Well, the moral of the song is easy for to define:
None of us has got an eye on our behind.

So better be sure before you squat
There's nothing swimming in the chamberpot.

5

This unusual variant of "The Sea Crab" was given to the editor by D. K. Wilgus, curator of the Western Kentucky Folklore Archives at UCLA. It was collected, from an anonymous informant at Campbellsville College, Campbellsville, Kentucky, by two of Wilgus's former students in the fall of 1964. The text was not accompanied with a melody as it was submitted to the archive; scanson and chorus, however, suggest the proper tune. In the interest of making the narrative a bit more coherent, the tenth and eleventh stanzas have been transposed here.

This is one of sixteen songs upon which Oscar Brand claimed a copyright after the appearance of the first edition of this book.

Four Old Whores

One of the most persistent notions in folklore is the belief that the greater the size of the sexual organ, the greater the sexual pleasure or capacity. The idea appears again and again in folk song, sometimes as an incidental line, and sometimes, as in this sea song, as a series of outlandish lies.

The number of women who match wits and physical endowments varies from version to version; there are sometimes three, sometimes four, and, in the "B" version here, five. They generally call Baltimore home; just why is impossible to say, except that "Baltimore" neatly fits the meter.

[A]

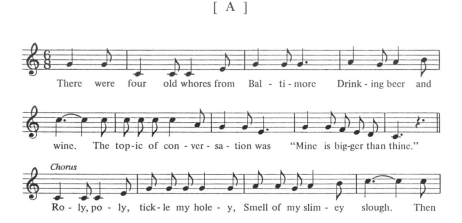

drag your nuts a - cross my guts, I'm one of the whore - y crew.

There were four old whores from Baltimore
Drinking beer and wine.
The topic of conversation was
"Mine is bigger than thine."

Chorus:
Roly, poly, tickle my hole-y,
Smell of my slimy slough.
Then drag your nuts across my guts,
I'm one of the whorey crew.

The first old whore from Baltimore said,
"Mine's as big as the air.
The birds fly in, the birds fly out,
And never touch a hair."

The second old whore from Baltimore said,
"Mine's as big as the moon.
The men jump in, the men jump out,
And never touch the womb."

The third old whore from Baltimore said,
"Mine's as big as the sea.
The ships sail in, the ships sail out,
And leave their rigging free."

The fourth old whore from Baltimore said,
"Mine's the biggest of all.
A man went up in the springtime,
And didn't come out till fall."

[B]

There were five women in Canada
Sipping their cherry wine.
The topic of conversation was:
"Is yours as big as mine?"

Chorus:
Oh, rub my tits and belly,
And slip in my slimy slough,
And rattle your nuts against my guts,
I'm one of the whorey crew.

7

"Mine is the biggest," said the first one,
"For mine's as big as the sea.
A full-rigged ship can sail right in
With all her riggin' free."

"You're a liar," said the second,
"For mine's as big as a well,
And all the pricks in Canada
Can't make my belly swell."

"You're a liar," said the third one,
"For mine's as big as the moon.
A man went up in October
And never came out until June."

"You're a liar," said the fourth one,
"For mine's as big as the air.
The sun and moon can kiss in my ass
And never singe a hair."

"You're a liar," said the fifth one,
"For mine's the biggest of all.
The average flow of my monthly
Is as big as Niagara Falls."

The theme of unusually large sexual organs is probably as old as any in folklore. Thompson's motif index lists only two entries, both from the oral tales of India, under F 547.3.1, long penis; and F 547.5.2, enormous vagina. Hoffmann adds three more at that number, two from the Ozarks, one from France; and a number at X712. This song, as "women boast of size of vaginas," is specifically cited at X749.4.2.

These citations would hardly seem to reflect the international distribution of the theme in oral tradition; most collectors and editors have felt constrained in the presentation of this sort of folklore. Two collections or collectors are exceptions, Aleksandr Afanasyev's *Stories from the Folk-lore of Russia* and Vance Randolph's *Pissing in the Snow*, and both have a number of stories dealing with unusual sexual organs.

A close parallel to the version here is recorded by Arthur Argo on his collection of Scots bawdy songs, *A Wee Thread o' Blue* (Prestige International 13048). John Greenway's album notes assert this is probably the oldest indecent song in the English language, descended from "A Talk of Ten Wives on Their Husbands," which dates from about 1460. That ballad deals with the size of the husband's equipment.

Legman's *Hornbook* (pp. 414-15) is even more assured, describing "Four Old Whores" as "a version of the oldest surviving erotic folksong in English." Legman judges the Scots song, "Our John's Brak Yestreen," in Burns, *The Merry Muses of Caledonia* (p. 84), to be a midpoint between the older form of the ballad and the newer. Burns's text begins:

> Twa neebor wives sat i' the sun,
> A twynin' at their rocks, [spinning thread]
> An' they an argument began
> An' a' the plea was c--ks.
>
> 'Twas whether they were sinens [sinews] strang,
> Or whether they were bane? [bone]
> An' how they row'd about your thumb,
> And how they stan't themlane? [themselves]

It seems strained to insist that a Scots song about the nature of the penis would give rise to another about the size of the vaginas of four draggletails from Baltimore.

"Four Old Whores" has seen print a handful of times. Logsdon (pp. 167-68) has a cowboy version as "Three Old Whores in Mexico." Another American variant, the boasts of "Three Whores of Winnipeg," is in "Songs of Roving and Raking," (p. 117), and reprinted in Babab (p. 133); the tune there is related to "Ninety-Nine Bottles of Beer" and "Our Goodman." Vicarion's text, No. XXXII, is to be sung to the tune of the otherwise unidentified "My Love Lies Dying." Getz 2 (pp. TT 8-9) and Laycock (pp. 223-24) have texts. Morgan 1 (p. 16) is close to Argo, sharing the nautical chorus:

> So take up the sheets, me hearties,
> Water the decks with brine,
> Bend to the oars, you lousy whores,
> None is bigger than mine.

Under the title of "Dark and Dreamy Eyes," Getz 2 (pp. DE 2-3) prints two versions of an unusual air force song of obvious English origin that is related to, or inspired by "Four Old Whores." The first, dating from World War II, begins:

> A few old whores of Portsmith town
> Were drinking Spanish wine.
> The gist of conversation was,
> "Is your cunt bigger than mine?"
>
> Then up there spake the airman's wife,
> And she was dressed in beige;
> And in one corner of her funny little thing,
> She had a Handley-Page. [a WW II bomber]

9

> She had a Handley-Page, my boys,
> With a joy stick and its knob,
> And in the other corner
> Were two airmen on the job.
>
> Chorus:
> She had those dark and dreamy eyes,
> And a whizz-bang up her jacksey. [*sic*]
> She was one of the flash-eyed 'hores
> One of the old brigade.

The second is from a songbook dating from the Vietnam War era. Its chorus runs:

> She had those dark and dreamy eyes,
> With a whiz bang up her nighty.
> Singing, "Hi, Jack, come and have a skin back;
> Come and have a bang at Liza, singing,
> 'Old Soldiers never die, they just smell that way.' "

Partridge's *Slang Dictionary* has "jacksy-pardy," the posteriors, dating from 1850. *The Supplement* defines it as "jacksie, posteriors, Army and Navy late 19th-20th C. slang." The tune for the Getz song is likely to be "She Had a Dark and Roving Eye," a folk melody given wide currency by a popular recording in the 1950s.

The Archive of American Folk Song contains two recorded versions: "Four Old Whores of Mexico" on AFS 3323 and "The Three Old Whores from Canada" on AFS 2291.

The "A" version of "Four Old Whores" used here was collected by Dean Burson from an anonymous informant who learned the song at Carnegie Tech, Pittsburgh, prior to 1959.

Burson's last stanza is probably influenced by, or influences "The Darby Ram." At any rate, they share the motif of the extraordinarily long absence. The melody for this version is a set of "The Lincolnshire Poacher," which frequently carries the words of other bawdy songs. See, for example, "The Chandler's Wife" in Brand (pp. 24-25), Babab (p. 57), or Morgan 2 (pp. 69-70); and "The Dog's Meeting" in Meredith and Anderson (pp. 160-61). The melody is also used for numerous non-bawdy ballads.

The "B" version is from the Robert W. Gordon "Inferno" collection in the Library of Congress's Archive of American Folk Song. While no source nor date are given on the slip, it can be dated to the mid-1920s. It is similar to the earliest text the editor has handled — reportedly sung by members of the 5th Infantry Regiment near New Bedford, Massachusetts, in 1914. It is No. 2432 in Gordon's Oregon collection in the AAFS. Gordon's versions are similar to the fragments reported in Randolph, "Unprintable" (pp. 78-81). Randolph's first version is sung to a worn down set of "The Lincolnshire Poacher."

Two unpublished texts, from Indiana University rugby players, are in the Indiana University folklore archives.

Five Nights Drunk

Folklore usually has the cuckolded husband remain ignorant of his wife's gambols outside the marriage bed. This British ballad, seemingly one of the two or three most popular of the bawdy songs imported from the Old World, is the exception to the rule. Most of the printed versions of this "merry" or ribald song suggest the lady's dalliance delicately; this one is very straightforward.

When I came home last Sat-ur-day night, As drunk as a skunk could
be, I saw a hat up-on the rack Where my hat ought to
be. *spoken* I said, "Come here, hon-ey. *sung* Explain this thing to me. How come this hat up-on the rack Where
my hat ought to be?" *spoken* "Oh, you damn fool, you
sung sil-ly fool, You're drunk as a skunk could be. That's

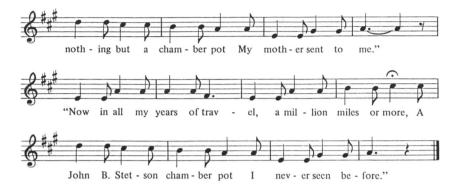

noth - ing but a cham - ber pot My moth - er sent to me."

"Now in all my years of trav - el, a mil - lion miles or more, A

John B. Stet - son cham - ber pot I nev - er seen be - fore."

When I came home last Saturday night,
As drunk as a skunk could be,
I saw a hat upon the rack
Where my hat ought to be.
I said, "Come here, honey.
Explain this thing to me.
How come this hat upon the rack
Where my hat ought to be?"
 "Oh, you damn fool, you silly fool,
 You're drunk as a skunk could be.
 That's nothing but a chamber pot
 My mother sent to me."
 "Now in all my years of travel,
 A million miles or more,
 A John B. Stetson chamber pot
 I never seen before."

When I came home last Saturday night,
As drunk as a skunk could be,
I saw some pants upon the chair
Where my pants ought to be.
I said, "Come here, honey.
Explain this thing to me.
How come these pants upon the chair
Where my pants ought to be?"
 "Oh, you damn fool, you silly fool,
 You're drunk as a skunk could be.
 That's nothing but a bed quilt
 My mother sent to me."
 "Now in all my years of travel,
 A million miles or more,
 A fly hole on a bed quilt
 I never seen before."

12

Now, when I came home last Saturday night,
As drunk as a skunk could be,
I saw a head upon the bed
Where my head ought to be.
I said, "Come here, honey.
Explain this thing to me.
How come this head upon the bed
Where my head ought to be?"
        "Oh, you damn fool, you silly fool,
        You're drunk as a skunk could be.
        That's nothing but a cabbage
        My mother sent to me."
        "Now in all my years of travel,
        A million miles or more,
        A mustache on a cabbage
        I never seen before."

Now when I came home last Saturday night,
As drunk as a skunk could be.
I saw an ass upon the bed
Where my ass ought to be.
I said, "Come here, honey.
Explain this thing to me.
How come this ass upon the bed
Where my ass ought to be?"
        "Oh, you damn fool, you silly fool,
        You're drunk as a skunk could be.
        That's nothing but a pumpkin
        My mother sent to me."
        "Now in all my years of travel,
        A million miles or more,
        An asshole on a pumpkin
        I never seen before."

When I came home last Saturday night,
As drunk as a skunk could be.
I saw a cock in the hole
Where my cock ought to be.
I said, "Come here, honey.
Explain this thing to me.
How come this cock in the hole
Where my cock ought to be?"
        "Oh, you damn fool, you silly fool,
        You're drunk as a skunk could be.
        That's nothing but a candle
        My mother sent to me."

13

"Now in all my years of travel,
A million miles or more,
Bollocks on a candle
I never seen before."

[B]

Well, it was Sat - ur - day night when I came home As
drunk as I could be. There in the sta - ble I
saw a horse where no horse ought to be. So I
turned to my wife And I said un - to she,
What's that horse a - do - ing there Where my horse ought to
be? "Well, you blind fool, you stu - pid fool, You
fool, Why can't you see? *(spoken)* That ain't noth - ing but a milk cow Your *(sung)*
moth - er gave to me." "Now man - y miles have I trav -
eled, A thou - sand miles or more, But a

milk cow with a sad-dle on I nev-er saw be-fore."

Well, it was Saturday night when I came home
  As drunk as I could be.
There in the stable I saw a horse
  Where no horse ought to be.
So I turned to my wife
  And I said unto she,
"What's that horse a-doing there
  Where my horse ought to be?"
"Well, you blind fool, you stupid fool,
  You fool, why can't you see?
That ain't nothing but a milk cow
  Your mother gave to me."
Now many miles have I traveled,
  A thousand miles or more,
But a milk cow with a saddle on
  I never saw before.

Well, it was Saturday night when I came home
  As drunk as I could be.
There on the hatrack was a hat
  Where my hat ought to be.
So I turned to my wife
  And I said unto she,
"What's that hat a-doing there
  Where my hat ought to be?"
"Well, you blind fool, you stupid fool,
  You fool, why can't you see?
That ain't nothing but a chamber pot
  Your mother gave to me."
Now many miles have I traveled,
  A thousand miles or more,
But a chamber pot size six seven-eighths
  I never saw before.

Well, it was Saturday night when I came home
  A-buzzing like a bee,
There in the parlor was a coat
  Where no coat ought to be.
So I turned to my wife
  And I said unto she,
"What's that coat a-doing there
  Where my coat ought to be?"

15

"Well, you blind fool, you stupid fool,
    You fool, why can't you see?
That ain't nothing but a blanket
    Your mother gave to me."
Now many miles have I traveled,
    A thousand miles or more,
But a blanket with buttons on it
    I never saw before.

Well, it was Saturday night when I came home
    A-buzzing like a bee.
There on the pillow was a head
    Where no head ought to be.
So I turned to my wife,
    And I said unto she,
"What's that head a-doing there
    Where my head ought to be?"
"Well, you blind fool, you stupid fool,
    You fool, why can't you see?
That ain't nothing but a cabbage
    Your mother sent to me."
Now many miles have I traveled
    A thousand miles or more,
But a cabbage with a mustache
    I never saw before.

[C]

"Last night when I came home, love, and hung my hat on the tree,
I found another man's hat, love, where my hat ought to be."

"Why, you old fool, you blind fool, say, can't you see?
It's nothing but a flower pot my mother sent to me."

"Oh, it's many a mile I've traveled, a thousand miles or more,
But I never saw a flower pot look like a hat before."

"Last night when I came home, love, and hung my coat on the tree,
I found another man's coat, love, where my coat ought to be."

"Why, you old fool, you blind fool, say, can't you see?
It's nothing but a blanket my mother sent to me."

"Oh, it's many a mile I've traveled, a thousand miles or more,
But I never saw a blanket with buttons on before."

"Last night when I came home, love, and hung my coat on the tree,
I found another man's gun, love, where my gun ought to be."

"Why, you old fool, you blind fool, say, can't you see?
It's nothing but a beanpole my mother sent to me."

"Oh, it's many a mile I've traveled, a thousand miles or more,
But I never saw a beanpole have a trigger before."

"Last night when I came home, love, and hung my coat on the tree,
I found another man's boots, love, where my boots ought to be."

"Why, you old fool, you blind fool, say, can't you see?
It's nothing but a bootjack my mother sent to me."

"Oh, it's many a mile I've traveled, a thousand miles or more,
But a bootjack with spurs on I never saw before."

"Last night when I came home, love, to the barn the horse and me,
And there in the stable a strange horse I did see."

"Why you old fool, you blind fool, say, can't you see?
It's nothing but a milking cow my gramma sent to me."

"Oh, it's many a mile I've traveled, a thousand miles or more,
But I never saw a cow with a saddle on before."

"Last night when I came home, love, and hung my hat on the tree,
I looked into the bedroom, love, and a strange face I did see."

"Why you old fool, you blind fool, say, can't you see?
It's nothing but a baby my mother sent to me."

"Oh, it's many a mile I've traveled, a thousand miles or more,
I never saw a baby with whiskers on before."

"Last night when I came home, love, and hung my hat on the tree,
I saw a pair of feet, love, in bed where mine should be."

"Why you old fool, you blind fool, say, can't you see?
It's nothing but a warming pan my mother sent to me."

"Oh, it's many a mile I've traveled, a thousand miles or more,
I never saw a warming pan with toes on before."

"Last night when I came home, love, and hung my hat on the tree,
I saw another ass, love, in bed where mine should be."

"Why, you old fool, you blind fool, say, can't you see?
It's nothing but a pumpkin shell my mother sent to me."

"Oh, it's many a mile I've traveled, a thousand miles or more,
I never saw a pumpkin shell with asshole on before."

"Last night when I came home, love, and hung my hat on the tree,
I saw a pair of bollocks, love, where my bollocks ought to be."

"Why, you old fool, you blind fool, say, can't you see?
It's nothing but some lemons my mother sent to me."

17

"Oh, it's many a mile I've traveled, a thousand miles or more,
I never saw two lemons with hair on them before."

"Last night when I came home, love, and hung my hat on the tree,
I saw another man's cock, my love, in the hole where mine should be."

"Why, you old fool, you blind fool, say, can't you see?
It's nothing but a candle which in play I stuck in me."

"Oh, it's many a mile I've traveled, a thousand miles or more,
But I never saw a candle with a red head on before."

[D]

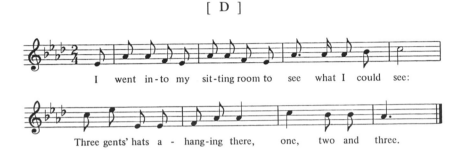

I went into my setting room to see what I could see,
Three gents' hats a-hanging there, one, two by three.
I called to my dear loving wife, "Kind sir," she answered me.
"What's these three gentlemen's hats a-doing here, unless they belong
      to me?"
"You old fool, you blind fool, can't you very well see?
Here's three soup bowls my mammy sent to me."
"Hey, oh, soup bowls with hat bands on, such things I never have seen.
They're always here when I am gone, here they must be."

I went into my dressing room to see what I could see,
Three gentlemen's coats a-hanging there, one, two and three.
I called to my dear loving wife, "Kind sir," she answered me.
"What's these three coats a-doing here, unless they belong to me?"
"You old fool, you blind fool, can't you very well see?
Here's three coverlids my mammy sent to me."
"Hey, oh, coverlids with buttons on, and soup bowls with hat bands on,
      such things I never did see.
There're always here when I am gone, and here they must be."

I went into my drawing room, to see what I could see,
Three gentlemen's boots a-setting there, one, two and three.
I called to my dear loving wife, "Kind sir," she answered me.

"What's these three gentlemen's boots a-doing here unless they
  belong to me?"
"You old fool, you blind fool, can't you very well see?
Here's three pudding bags my mammy sent to me."
"Hey, oh, pudding bags with spurs on, and coverlids with buttons on,
  and soup bowls with hat bands on, such things I never did see.
They're always here when I am gone, and here they must be."

I went into my bedroom to see what I could see.
Three gentlemen a-lying there, one, two and three.
I called to my dear loving wife, "Kind sir," she answered me.
"What's these three gentlemen a-doing here, unless they live with me?"
"You old fool, you blind fool, can't you very well see,
Here's three milkmaids my mammy sent to me."
"Hey, oh, milk maids with whiskers on, and pudding bags with spurs on
  and coverlids with buttons on and soup bowls with hat bands on,
  such things I never did see.
They're always here when I am gone, and here they must be."

I went into my backyard to see what I could see.
Three gentlemen's dogs a-lying there, one, two and three.
I called to my dear loving wife, "Kind sir," she answered me.
"What's these three gentlemen's dogs a-doing here, unless they belong
  to me?"
"You old fool, you blind fool, can't you very well see?
Here's three sucking calves my mammy sent to me."
"Hey, oh, sucking calves with flopping ears, and milkmaids with
  whiskers on and pudding bags with spurs on and coverlids with
  buttons on and soup bowls with buttons on, such things I never
  did see.
They're always here when I am gone, and here they must be."

I went into my horse lot to see what I could see.
Three gentlemen's horses a-standing there, one, two and three.
I called to my dear loving wife, "Kind sir," she answered me.
"What's these three horses a-doing here, unless they belong to me?"
"You old fool, you blind fool, can't you very well see?
Here's three milch cows my mammy sent to me."
"Hey, oh, milch cows with saddles on and sucking calves with flopping ears,
  and milk maids with whiskers on and pudding bags with
  spurs on and coverlids with buttons on and soup bowls with hat
  bands on, such things I never did see.
They're always here when I am gone, and here they must be."

Joseph Hickerson of the Library of Congress's Archive of American
Folk Song has suggested that "Our Goodman" (Child 274) may well
be the most popular of the English and Scottish popular ballads in

oral tradition. In one or another form, he notes, it has appeared as a college and camp song, on race and country-western records, even as a popular hit under the title of "Seven Drunken Nights." According to Hickerson, were not informants and collectors handicapped by modesty, printed texts and tunes would surpass in number the acknowledged leader, "Barbara Allen" (Child 84). Child himself had only five texts of "Our Goodman," none bawdy, though he cited scores of continental analogues.

Collectors and editors have found themselves in an awkward position in dealing with bawdy versions of the much-prized Child ballad. Discretion sufficed for some. H. M. Belden, for example, noted a two-stanza version sent to him by a student, appending the comment that "there are some twenty verses to it, each one 'rottener' than the one before. It is often sung by the older generation of miners." In Belden's version (p. 90), the wife responds, "You old fool, you damn fool, you son of a b-----, says she."

Eloise Hubbard Linscott (pp. 259-62) was a bit more bold:

When he thought no one could overhear him, a certain young man of North Irish extraction sang this naughty song to his little sister. Since this little sister is today too much of a gentlewoman, she could not sing the last verse; but she finally consented to write it.

> Oh, the old man he came home one night,
> As drunk as he could be,
> He saw a face between the sheets,
> Where no face ought to be.
>
> * * * * * * * *
>
> It's nothing but a little kid
> My uncle sent to me."

Significantly, that gentle woman remembered the three-stanza version from puberty to adulthood before modestly writing it down for Mrs. Linscott.

The ballad is widely reported, if not always printed in full. Cox (p. 154) noted that "by variation or extension several vulgar stanzas are current in West Virginia and elsewhere" though he included none. Hudson elected to print only "a fragment of a ribald version of the old English and Scottish ballad, said to be well known among students of the University of Mississippi" (p. 122). In 1929, Arthur Kyle Davis reported the Virginia archives contained "none of the more or less ribald stanzas superimposed upon this ballad . . ." (p. 485). In 1960, Davis concluded, "If ribald versions were collected and printed, no doubt every state would be represented!"

More bawdy versions might have been reported but for similar reasons of modesty. Hubbard (pp. 34-37) noted that one of his versions had unprintable stanzas, and gave a tune used for the teasing song "Two Irishmen, Two Irishmen." Flanders, *Ancient Ballads* (4:63-71), prefaced her texts with this comment on the gap between informant and collector: "Many informants refuse to sing this ballad on moral grounds. . . ." Quite obviously though, her informants learned the "usually bawdy" (Mrs. Flanders's phrase) verses. Manny and Wilson had a similar problem, and never could collect "Our Goodman"; they print a tune (pp. 158-59) for the unrelated "Peelhead," that is also used for "Goodman." (Interesting enough, that melody borrows a musical phrase from "The Ball of Kirriemuir." Apparently a tune used for one bawdy song suggests itself for other bawdy songs.)

For references to reported versions, expurgated or otherwise, see Belden (p. 90); and Brown (2:181). Additional versions from the British Isles are in Morgan 1 (pp. 18-21); Hamer (p. 24); Bold (pp. 174-75), in which a parson is cuckolded; Karpeles, *Sharp's* (1:193-94); and Purslow (*Wanton Seed*, 37), where the lady entertains three men in her bed. Arthur Argo sings "Hame Drunk Came I" on *A Wee Thread o' Blue* (Prestige International 13048). Jack Elliott sings it on *The Elliots* [*sic*] *of Birtley* (Folkways FG 3565). McCarthy (pp. 102-5) has it as "Seven Nights Drunk," sung to the melody of "The Wearing of the Green," changed from 6/8 to 4/4 time.

Songs of Roving and Raking (p. 80) credits its version—likely from English tradition--to Logue's underground Parisian publication, *Count Vicarion's Book of Bawdy Ballads*, where it is No. 52. That text has a hat upon the rack, chamber pot with head band; a head upon the bed, baby bum with whiskers; a nob betwixt her legs, rolling pin with balls attached; a mess on her nightdress, clotted cream that smelt of fish. Babab (p. 97), reprints it with a melody close to that used here for the "A" text.

Australian versions are in MacGregor (pp. 29 ff.); Laycock (pp. 16-18); Hogbotel and Ffuckes (p. 48); and Wannan (pp. 56-57), where the unique Yiddishism, "shickered," is substituted for "drunk." Cleveland (p. 95) notes that New Zealand troops sang "One Evening I Came Home My Darling Wife to See" during World War II.

Additional versions from North American sources are in Brand (pp. 76-77); Shay (*More*, 31); Lynn (*Housemothers*, 128); Davis (*More*, 300 ff.); Rosenbaum (pp. 98-99); Roberts and Agey (pp. 78-80); McNeil, *Southern Folk Ballads* (2:35-40); and Getz 1 (p. L-2), from an air force songbook. McCulloh ("Some Child Ballads," 123-28), prints transcriptions of three versions from country music records.

The oldest reported American ribald texts are in Randolph's "Unprintable" manuscript (pp. 22-28), as "The Old Man Came Home One Night." Fowke, "Bawdy Ballads," offers another of the more raunchy variants. The mimeographed "The One, the Only Baker House . . . Song Book" (p. 12) has it from M.I.T. circa 1950.

There are two recordings of American versions. John Greenway sings it on *The Cat Came Back* (Prestige 13011). "The Merry Cuckold" on the recording *The Unexpurgated Folk Songs of Men* has pants on the chair, blanket with fly hole; head upon the bed, turnip with whiskers; ass upon the bed, an asshole on a pumpkin; a thing within the thing, a foreskin on a carrot.

Hoffmann (p. 170) has assigned this the tale type number of 1355B, "unfaithful wife always manages to have excuse when husband catches her with lover." See too the motif numbers K1513.1 and J1251.2.

The editor learned the "A" version here in 1958 from the late United States Senator Clair Engle in one of those legendary smoke-filled rooms at a political convention.

The "B" version was forwarded by Roger D. Abrahams as learned by a student in Amarillo, Texas, about 1964. The editor adjusted apparent errors in the notation by Abrahams's former student at bars 12, 15, and 26 to relieve two unnatural stresses placed on unaccented syllables.

The lengthy "C" text is No. 3851 in the Gordon collection in the Archive of American Folk Song. It was forwarded to Gordon by Jean Bordeaux of Los Angeles, on February 6, 1932. Bordeaux added, "The song continues almost interminably, telling the story of how the poor blind husband, supposedly unaware, but with malice afore-thought, proceeded to 'shag' the alleged pumpkin shell, much to the distress and pain of the adulterous wretch who was cuckolding the husband. Having thoroughly cowed the intruder by judicious sod-omies, the husband threw wife and her Don Juan out. [The] song ends with this verse:

> "Oh, it's many a mile we've traveled, a thousand miles or more,
> But never heard such goings-on in all our lives before."

Bordeaux learned the song about 1898 from a Nova Scotian farm-hand who claimed to have gotten it from an English sailor. That sailor, in turn, is said to have learned the song as a boy in or near London. Thus Bordeaux dated his version "back to the middle seventeen hundreds."

As "The Jealous Hearted Husband," the "D" version of "Our Goodman" was sung by Mrs. Emma Dusenberry of Mena, Arkansas,

for Sidney Robertson Cowell about 1940. A gifted singer, Mrs. Dusenberry often had unusual variants of songs, including this cumulative
version. (Hickerson noted that a copyist's oversight caused Child to
miss one other cumulative text.) This transcription of text and tune,
probably by Ruth Crawford Seeger, was contained in a manuscript
of ninety songs collected by Charles Seeger from Mrs. Dusenberry
on behalf of the federal Farm Security Administration. A copy is on
deposit in the Library of Congress's Archive of American Folk Song.

The Darby Ram

This song of marvels apparently was to be sung by masked or
costumed visitors who stopped at various homes in English villages
bringing luck upon the house during the year to come. Early versions
may well have had verses later generations would deem obscene. Over
time, Gresham's law of folk balladry — bawdy verses drive out clean —
has transformed some versions of "The Darby Ram" into salacious
celebrations of the monster ram.

In the United States, the changes have been even more extreme.
First, a military marching band during the Civil War used the tune
on parade; later Negro jazzmen refashioned the song into the New
Orleans jazz standard, "Didn't He Ramble?"

[A]

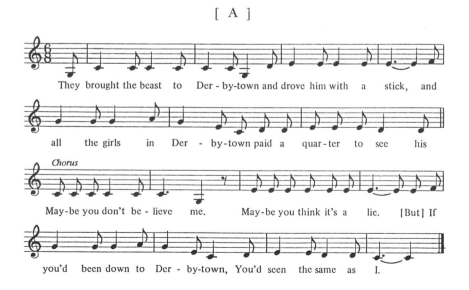

They brought the beast to Der - by-town and drove him with a stick, and

all the girls in Der - by-town paid a quar-ter to see his

Chorus

May-be you don't be - lieve me. May-be you think it's a lie. [But] If

you'd been down to Der - by-town, You'd seen the same as I.

They brought a beast to Derbytown,
And drove him with a stick,
And all the girls in Derbytown
Paid a quarter to see his

Chorus:
Maybe you don't believe me,
Maybe you think it's a lie,
But if you'd been down to Derbytown
You'd seen the same as I.

The legs upon this monster,
They grew so far apart,
That all of the girls in Derbytown
Could hear him when he

The hair upon this monster,
It grew so very thick,
That none of the girls in Derbytown
Could see the head of his

The horns upon this monster,
They grew up solid brass.
One grew out of his forehead
And the other grew out of his

And when this beast got hungry,
They mostly fed him grass.
They did not put it in his mouth;
But shoved it up his

He did not care for grass so much;
He always wanted duck.
But every time he ate a bird,
He had to take a

The garbage bill was awful,
And it cost us quite a bit,
But we had to keep a special truck
To haul away the

There's something else I'd like to say.
Now what do you think of this?
The folks would come from miles around
Just to watch him take a

The girls that live in Derbytown
Will all sit in your lap.
One night a girlie sat on mine
And now I've got the

24

[B]

As I went down to Der-by-town all on a mar-ket day [and]
there I saw the fat-test sheep that ev-er was fed on hay.
Chorus Did-n't he ram - ble! Did-n't he ram - ble! Yes, he
ram-bled till the butch-er cut him down.

As I went down to Derby town
All on the market day,
There I saw the fattest sheep
That ever was fed on hay.

Chorus:
Didn't he ramble, didn't he ramble?
He rambled till the butchers cut him down.

Oh, the sheep that had two eyes, sir,
And four feet to stand, sir,
And every foot he had, sir,
Covered an acre of land.

Oh, the sheep that had two horns, sir,
Reached up to the moon.
A man went up in April
And never got down till June.

Oh, the wool that's on his back
Reached to the sky.
The eagles built their nest
For I heard the young ones cry.

Oh, the wool that's on his sides, sir,
Reached to the ground,
And the wool that's on his tail, sir,
Weighed four thousand pound.

25

> Oh, the man who killed the sheep, sir,
> Got drowned in the blood
> And the boy that held the basin
> Got washed away in the flood.
>
> Oh, the blood run ten miles, sir,
> I'm sure it run no more
> And there it turned a water-mill
> That it never turned before.
>
> Oh, the man that owned the sheep, sir,
> Was called very rich,
> But the boy that made this song, sir,
> Was a lying son of a bitch.

Child's unspoken rule that the heroes and heroines of popular balladry had to be of the genus *homo sapiens* was enough to exclude "The Darby Ram" and the equally likely candidate, "The Frog and the Mouse," from his multi-volume canon. The ballad is an old one, despite the reference to a garbage truck in the "A" text of "The Darby Ram," collected by Sidney Robertson Cowell in 1940 from Charles Fulton of Oakland, California. Its roots lie somewhere in English pre-history, and the ballad is commonly thought to be a remnant of the winter luck-visits of masked and costumed dancers once common in England.

Exaggerations involving tremendous animals are widely known, and figure extensively in folktales. (Thompson has assigned the song motif number X1243.1; Hoffmann has reassigned it to X749.4.4.) The Old Testament, borrowing from an even older tale, tells the story of David's climb up the side of a monstrous animal, the reem (ram?). When the animal stands up, the young David finds himself in stratospheric peril. Praying for aid, he offers to build a temple as high as the animal's horns if he is saved. That mythical reem sounds much like the Darby monster. Variants of the ballad sometimes note:

> The horns upon this ram, sir,
> They reached up to the sky,
> And eagles built their nests up there
> For I heard the young ones cry.

While sanitized or nursery versions of "The Darby Ram" or "The Old Tup" have seen print often enough, few bawdy texts have. A. L. Lloyd has a modestly robust version on *English Drinking Songs* (Riverside 12-618). The fullest version of the bawdy ballad seems to have appeared in Logue-Vicarion, No. XXIII. The same appears in Morgan 1 (p. 152). McCarthy (pp. 30-31) has a six-stanza text and tune, presumably from Australia. Another Australian version in Wannan (p. 66) contains this unusual verse:

> The pizzle on that ram, sir—believe me, I'm no
>   liar—
> It was so large it could have stretched from Cairns to Nevertire.

The earliest of American bawdy versions is apparently in Randolph's "Unprintable" manuscript (pp. 49-51), dated to the 1930s. A tune there is a worn-down set of the melody used for "Our Goodman." Legman (*Horn Book*, 424), prints two undated stanzas garnered from the first American scholar to collect and study bawdry, Josiah Combs:

> It took all the boys in Darby Town
>   To haul away his bones.
> It took all the girls in Darby Town
>   To roll away his stones. *(Chorus.)*
>
> The man that owned this mighty ram
>   Was 'counted very rich,
> But the one that made this silly song
>   Was a dirty son-of-a-bitch.

The "teasing" form of the ballad, like "A" here, is intermediate between the frankly ribald and the nursery versions. It is this teasing form that Roger Abrahams, who has devoted considerable study to the song, considers the most common. Reuss (p. 58) has a single stanza from a Pine Bluff, Arkansas, informant, circa 1957:

> There was a cow in barber town
> Who had two horns of brass.
> One grew out of her upper lip,
> The other grew out her
>   Hinky dinky, tiddly winky,
>   You may think I lie,
>   But if you go down to barber town,
>   You'll see the same as I.

Brand sings a variant of this verse on volume two of his record series (Audio Fidelity 1806). The editor heard another sung by country and western musician Buddy Wright at a noontime concert at Alpine Meadows, a ski resort near Truckee, California, on April 12, 1987. Wright said he learned it from his father, an Arkansawyer. Meredith and Anderson (p. 153) have a four-stanza teasing version from Australia; Tate (pp. 45-46) presents another of eight verses under the title of "The Wattle Flat Ram."

For references to inoffensive versions and variants, See Dean-Smith

(p. 63); Randolph 1 (pp. 398-400); Brown 2 (p. 439); Hudson (p. 273); and Belden (p. 224). Add to those Grieg (*Northeast*, No. 14); Williams (pp. 43-44); Broadwood and Maitland (pp. 44-47); Cazden (*Nonsense*, 87); Hubbard (p. 390); Karpeles, *Sharp's*, 2 (pp. 375-78); and Hamer (*Garner's Gay*, 21). Hamer's *Green Groves* (pp. 50-52 and 70-71) has two versions of "The Darby Tup." The second has its chorus sung to the melody of the chorus for "The Ball of Kirriemuir"—a faint hint it may have been expurgated. Hugill (pp. 437-38) says of his version: "I have had to camouflage quite a lot as the sailors' version was markedly obscene." Gardner and Chickering (p. 462) do some judicious editing in the last stanza.

Peter Kennedy has it as "The Ram Song" (pp. 660-61, with notes on 679). See too "The Wonderful Sucking Pig" in Purslow, *Marrow Bones* (p. 100).

Music analogues cited by Norman Cazden are included in Fowke's *Lumbering Songs* (p. 43) and expanded in Cazden, Haufrecht, and Studer (*Catskills*, 566-69), and the indispensable companion *Notes* (pp. 109-11).

For the ram in mummers' plays see, Alan Brody, *The English Mummers and Their Plays* (Philadelphia, 1970). Abrahams noted the song in S. O. Addy, *Household Tales and Traditional Remains* (1895), p. xxi; S. O. Addy, "Local Pamphlets" (Sheffield Public Library, Vol. 90 n.d. [circa 1900]); Ivor Gatty, "The Old Tup and Its Ritual," JEFDSS, 5 (1946): 23-30; *Folk* 1 (October, 1962): 9-10; and Reginald Nettel, *Sing a Song of England* (London, 1954): 32-34.

The "A" version, forwarded by Joe Hickerson, is on record 4216B1 and 2 as "Beast of Derbytown" in the Library of Congress's Archive of American Folk Song. The melody is the familiar nursery tune "The Farmer in the Dell."

The "B" version, collected by Charles Seeger from the legendary Emma Dusenberry in the late 1930s, stands midway between the common British form and the jazz band version, "Didn't He Ramble." It is one of ninety Dusenberry songs contained in a manuscript compiled by Charles Seeger while a member of the staff of the federal Farm Security Administration, circa 1940. The manuscript of the transcriptions is deposited in the Library of Congress's Archive of American Folk Song.

A country music version of "Didn't He Ramble," based on the singing of Charlie Poole on Columbia 15407, is in *New Lost City Ramblers Song Book* (pp. 190-91).

The Tinker

Popular belief in the British Isles once had it that gypsies possessed, among other supernatural assets, the power of *glamour,* or an irresistible sex appeal. The venerable "Gypsy Laddie" (Child 200) recounts the story of the legendary Davey Faa's abduction-seduction of an impressionable young lady. But where "The Gypsy Laddie" is discreet and gentle, "The Tinker" is coarse. Indeed, contemporary versions of the ballad explicitly assign the tinker's attraction to the size of his kidney-wiper, and not upon some supernatural charm.

[A]

There was a jolly tinker And he came from Dun-gar-ee, With a yard and a half of fore-skin Hang-ing down be-low his knee.

Chorus

With his long dong did-dly whack-er, Ov-er-gro-own kid-ney-crack-er, Moth-er-fuck-ing ba-by-fetch-er hang-ing to his knees.

There was a jolly tinker
And he came from Dungaree,
With a yard and a half of foreskin
Hanging down below his knee.

Chorus:
With his long dong-diddly-whacker,
Overgrown kidney-cracker,

29

Mother-fucking baby-fetcher
Hanging to his knees.

My lady she was dressing,
Dressing for the ball,
When she saw the jolly tinker
Lashing piss against the wall.

"Oh, tinker, oh, tinker,
I'm in love with you.
Oh, tinker, oh, tinker,
Will half a dollar do?"

Oh, he screwed her in the parlor;
He fucked her in the hall,
And the servant said, "By Jesus,
He'll be cramming on us all."

There were fifty naked women
Running up and down the hall,
Shouting, "Jesus Christ, Almighty,
Is he gonna fuck us all?"

"Oh, daughter, oh, daughter,
You were a silly fool,
To get busy with a man
With a tool like a mule."

"Oh, mother, oh, mother,
I thought I was able,
But he split me up the belly
From the cunt up to the navel."

Said the daughter to the mother,
"Why you God damned whore!
If he gave you twenty inches,
You would ask for twenty more."

[B]

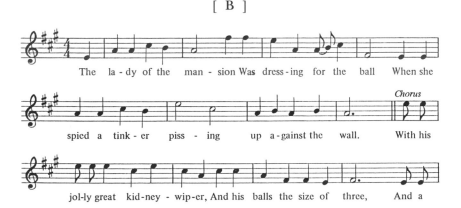

The la-dy of the man-sion Was dress-ing for the ball When she
spied a tink-er piss-ing up a-gainst the wall. With his
jol-ly great kid-ney-wip-er, And his balls the size of three, And a

yard of dirt-y fore - skin Hang-ing down be-low his knee.

The lady of the mansion
Was dressing for the ball
When she spied a tinker
Pissing up against the wall.

Chorus:
With his jolly great kidney-wiper,
And his balls the size of three,
And a yard of dirty foreskin
Hanging down below his knee.

The lady wrote a letter
And in it she did say,
["I'd rather be fucked by a tinker
Than my husband any day."]

When the tinker got the letter
And in it he did read,
His balls began to fester
And his prick began to bleed.

So he mounted on his charger
And on it he did ride
With his balls slung o'er his shoulder
And his penis by his side.

Oh, he rode up to the mansion
And he gave a loud call,
"Jesus!" yelled the lady,
"He has come to fuck us all!"

[He fucked them in the kitchen.
He fucked them in the hall.]
But when he fucked the butler,
'Twas the dirtiest trick of all

He rode off from the mansion.
He rode into the street,
Little drops of semen
Pitter-pattering at his feet.

Oh, the tinker's dead and buried.
I'll bet he's gone to Hell.
He said he'd fuck the Devil,
And I'll bet he's done it well.

31

[C]

Oh, there was a little tinker,
And he came from France;
He came to America
To fiddle, fuck and dance
With his long, lean liver, kidney-wash and baby-maker
Hanging to his knees!

The ship that he came over on,
The women were but few.
So first he fucked the captain,
And then he fucked the crew
With his long, lean liver, kidney-wash and baby-maker
Hanging to his knees!

The little tinker died,
And he went to hell.
He swore he'd fuck the Devil
If he didn't treat him well.
With his long, lean liver, kidney-wash and baby-maker
Hanging to his knees!

"How do you do, Mr. Devil.
God bless your soul
Let me exercise my pecker
In your hairy ass hole."
With his long, lean liver, kidney-wash and baby-maker
Hanging to his knees!

Then all the little devils
Went shouting through the hall:
"We'd better get him out of here
Before he fucks us all!"
With his long, lean liver, kidney-wash and baby-maker
Hanging to his knees!

This ballad, also known as "The Highland [Jolly] Tinker," has had a long and involved history in oral tradition. It is a descendant of a bawdy parody of "The Jolly Beggar" (Child 276) crossed with an older broadside, "Room for a Jovial Tinker: Old Brass to Mend." Legman (*The Horn Book*, 226-27), sketches this history, adding that Robert Burns collected another version of the bawdy parody, calling it "The Jolly Gauger." Burns's gathering is in *The Merry Muses*, p. 78. (A mosaic of marginalia in Dick, and especially in the "Appendix," p. 119, of the added *Notes on Scottish Songs*, points out that both bawdy and non-obscene versions of "The Jolly Tinker" coexisted in Scots oral tradition.) Contrary to Legman, the present editor suspects that Burns's bawdy song, "The Jolly Gauger," is an earlier offshoot of the ribald versions of the Child ballad, but otherwise unrelated to the modern-day song.

Child handled two distinct version of "The Jolly Beggar" collected by the indefatigable William Macmath from his aunt in Kirkcudbrightshire in 1893. As printed in Child, 5 (p. 113) the first verse and chorus of the first of Macmath's pieces run:

> There was a jolly beggar, as mony a ane has been,
> And he's tae up his lodging in a house near Aberdeen.
> Wi his yi yi yanti, his eerie eerie an
> Wi his fine tan taraira, the jolly beggarman.

Macmath's second version, which Child felt constrained to bespatter with asterisks to indicate the expurgation of offensive lines, has a chorus rhythmically similar to that of "The Tinker" and one which shares the same rhyme:

> Wi his long staff, and ragged coat, and breeches to his knee,
> And he was the bauldest beggar-man that eer my eyes did see.

The second Macmath text is still clearly a version of the Child ballad, but within it are obviously the seeds of the modern bawdy song, "The Tinker." Ten similar texts are in the Shuldham-Shaw/Lyle edition of the Grieg-Duncan collection (pp. 296-301).

More likely, the contemporary bawdy song is the result of a coupling of Macmath's or some more bawdy variant of the Child ballad, with an equally old broadside, "Room for a Jovial Tinker." Dated to 1616 in *The Roxburghe Ballads*, 3 (pp. 230 ff.; a more accessible text is in Kronhausen, 33 ff.), "Room" has these stanzas analogous to those in the present day ballad:

1. It was a lady of the North she loved a Gentleman,
   And knew not well what course to take, to use him now and then.
   Wherefore she writ a Letter, and sealed it with her hand,
   And bid him be a Tinker, to mend both pot and pan,
   With a hey ho, hey, derry derry down; with hey trey, down down,
      derry.

2. And when the merry Gentleman the Letter he did read,
   He got a budget on his back, and Apron with all speed,
   His pretty shears and pincers, so well they did agree,
   With a long pike staff upon his back, came tripping o'er the
      Lee,
   With a hey ho, hey, derry derry down; with hey trey, down down,
      derry.

7. But when the Lady knew his face, she then began to wink,
   "Haste, lusty Butler!" then quoth she, "To fetch the man some
       drink.
   Give him such meat as we do eat, and drink as we do use,
   It is not for a Tinker's Trade good liquor to refuse."
   With a hey ho, hey, derry derry down; with hey trey, down down,
       derry.

10. At last being come into the Room, where he the work should do,
    The Lady lay down on the bed, so did the Tinker too:
    Although the Tinker knocked amain, the Lady was not offended,
    But before that she rose from the bed, her Coldron was well
        mended,
    With a hey ho, hey, derry derry down; with hey trey, down down,
        derry.

An example of the intermediate form between Roxburghe broad-side and contemporary bawdy song is in Kennedy (p. 405) as "The Jolly Tinker." The analogous stanzas to the Roxburghe text include:

2. She wrote to him a letter
   And she sent it with a friend
   She said: My jolly tinker
   I've some kettles for you to mend.

3. She wrote to him another
   And she sealed it with a stone
   She said: My jolly tinker
   I can never lay alone.

6. She brought him up the stairs
   For to show him what to do
   She fell on the feather-bed
   And he fell on it too.

7. She took up a frying pan
   And he began to knock
   Just to let the servants know
   That he was hard at work.

Another of these intermediate forms is reconstructed in Palmer's edition of the Vaughan Williams folk song collection. "The Barley Straw" there (pp. 135-36) has a rich young squire disguise himself as a tinker, and adopt the name of the legendary David Faw to seduce the maiden. Palmer notes that as "The Pollitick Begger-Man" this appears in Samuel Pepys's ballad collection.

The matter of the gypsy's *glamour*, mentioned by Brand (p. 69) is also of some interest. The gypsy appears not infrequently in balladry

34

in a stereotyped role, that of the super-sexed wanderer alternately mending pots and rupturing hymens. The supernatural *glamour* of the oldest ballads involving gypsies, Child 200 A-F and Gb, for example, has been rationalized into something more comprehensible to the more or less sophisticated singers of recent years. In Child it is transformed into romantic love; in "The Tinker," it is sheer good-natured lust. Both are more understandable than the business of spells and charms to singers who no longer pay credence to the lore of the witches.

In any event, the rowdy version of "The Tinker" does not seem to be old. Peter Fryer's *Mrs. Grundy* (p. 41) and Partridge identify "kidney wiper" as a twentieth century dysphemism for the male organ. Partridge cryptically adds: "Ex a ribald song." (The phrase "kidney-wiper" appears in the very rare ribald anthology apparently cobbled together by Chicago newspapermen about 1885, "The Stag Party" [n.p., n.d.] in "Special Notice/Secretary's Office/Whore's Union/New York/April 1 '85." A copy of that work was forwarded by Frank Hoffmann.)

A number of versions of the modern bawdy song have been reported. Hoffmann has assigned it motif number X749.4.1.1. *Immortalia* (1927): 91-92 Brand (pp. 68-69); Babab (p. 68) credited to Brand, but textually quite different though the tunes are similar; *Songs of Raunch and Ill-Repute* (p. 29); *Songs of Roving and Raking* (p. 57); and Getz 2 (p. DE-7) from air force currency, all have American versions. Randolph's "Unprintable" collation (pp. 71-76) has three versions, two of which are apparent meldings of the bawdy ballad, Child 278, and the sea shanty "Whup Jamboree."

British texts are in McCarthy (pp. 52-53); Morgan 2 (pp. 54-55); Sedley (p. 29); and Pinto and Rodway (p. 438). The text in Logue (No. 54) has been retouched—to no great advantage. The tune there is a pastiche of borrowed melodic phrases, partially reminiscent of "Solomon Levi." Hopkins (pp. 182-83) has a Canadian servicemen's variant from World War II. McGregor's text (pp. 63-64); Hogbotel and Ffuckes (p. 29); and Laycock's conflation (pp. 231-33), are from Australia.

Kennedy's version of "The Knife in the Window" (p. 406) borrows the refrain "With his long fol-the-riddle-do right down to his knee."

A distinctly separate song, from British broadside tradition, involves a tinker who visits a home, eats and drinks, kisses a maid behind the door, then (in some versions) tap, tap, taps or mends the pot behind the door. This song may well have been inspired by the bawdy song. A text and tune are in Baring-Gould (*Folk Song*, 60-61).

Lowenstein (p. 42) has a vaguely related song/rhyme beginning:

There was a priest, a dirty beast,
Whose name was Michelanjo.
He had a prick two inches thick
And balls as big as a banjo.

The editor's files contain eight variants of "The Tinker" gathered from Pennsylvania, Indiana, Texas, and California. At least one of the California texts comes directly from the singing of British troops during World War II, when the song was wide-famed. That version, as do many of the British texts, adds this tag to the chorus:

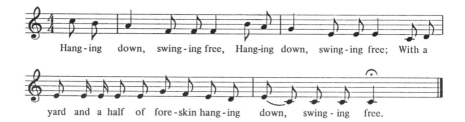

Hang-ing down, swing-ing free, Hang-ing down, swing-ing free; With a
yard and a half of fore-skin hang-ing down, swing-ing free.

Hanging down, swinging free,
Hanging down, swinging free,
With a yard and a half of foreskin
Hanging down below his knee.

The first version of the ballad printed here was collected by the editor in Los Angeles in 1964 from a psychiatric social worker who said he learned it from a patient.

The second came from a Los Angeles housewife and retired school teacher in 1963 who learned it from an older brother about 1945. The material in brackets filling in lacunae is from a text forwarded by Abrahams from Texas.

For references to the tune of the second version, "Rosin the Beau," see Dean-Smith; Belden (pp. 255 ff.); Brown, 3 (p. 61), and 5 (pp. 32-35); Spaeth (pp. 40-44) and see Samuel Bayard's note to "Heavenly Welcome" in Jackson, *Another Sheaf* (p. 164).

The "C" text under the title "The Little Tinker," was contained in Larson's "Barnyard" anthology, learned from Idaho school children prior to 1952.

The Monk of Great Renown

Bawdy lore intends to shock. The greater the shock, the greater the catharsis. Which explains the popularity of this song with its story of clerical indiscretion, seduction, necrophilia, and anal intercourse, all with a happy ending.

[A]

There was a monk of great renown.
There was a monk of great renown.
There was a monk of great renown.
He fucked the girls around the town.

Spoken:
The dirty old man. The dirty old man.
The bastard deserves to die. Fuck him.

Chorus:
Brothers, let us pray.
Glory, glory, hallelujah.

37

He met a girl with lily-white thighs,
He met a girl with lily-white thighs,
He met a girl with lily-white thighs,
And teats that grew to enormous size.

He laid her down on a downy bed,
He laid her down on a downy bed,
He laid her down on a downy bed,
And busted in her maidenhead.

He shoved it in until she died,
He shoved it in until she died,
He shoved it in until she died,
And then he tried the other side.

He carried her to the burial ground.
He carried her to the burial ground.
He carried her to the burial ground.
He thought he'd go another round.

The monk lamented his grief and shame,
The monk lamented his grief and shame,
The monk lamented his grief and shame,
So he fucked her back to life again.

[B]

There was an old monk of London town.
There was an old monk of London town.
There was an old monk of London town.
He fucked all the women of great renown.

Chanted:
The old sod. The old sod.
The bastard deserves to die. Fuck him.

Chorus:
Let us pray.
Glory, glory, hallelujah.

His brother monks cried out in shame.
His brother monks cried out in shame.
His brother monks cried out in shame.
So he rolled the women over and did it again.

His brother monks said, "We'll stop his frolics."
His brother monks said, "We'll stop his frolics."
His brother monks said, "We'll stop his frolics."
So they rolled him over and cut off his bollocks.

[C]

The Friar of Great Renown

There was a friar of great renown, (3)
And then he fucked the girl from out of town,
Fucked the girl from out of town.
Ha, ha, ha,
Ho, ho, ho.
Horse shit.
That dirty ol' sonovabitch,
That rotten ol' cocksucker.
Fuck him.

Tales of ecclesiastics who stray from the path of righteousness to diddle local girls are frequent in folklore and classic erotica. These fancies were a staple of such early tale collections as Boccaccio's *Decameron* (first day, second story; seventh day, fifth story; eighth day, second story; ninth day, second story) or the earliest of the deliberate erotica like Pietro Aretino's *Ragionamenti* (1534 [?], reprinted North Hollywood, California, 1966). Baskervill (p. 245) notes more generally that the "intrigues of churchmen" were a common motive in Renaissance jest and farce. "Early in the seventeenth century [George] Chapman in *May Day* (2, 4) says of 'a friar's weed' that the 'disguise is worn threadbare upon every stage and so much villany committed under that habit that 'tis grown as suspicious as the vilest.' "

The reputation of the various monkish orders was fearsome. Rabelais, himself a vicar, has Friar John warn the pilgrim Dogweary: "Were your wife uglier than Proserine, by God, she'd find herself jerkthumped as long as there was a monk within a thousand miles. Good carpenters use every kind of timber. The pox riddle me if you don't all find your wives pregnant on your return. The very shadow of an abbey spire is fecund!"

For some indication of the currency of such stories in oral tradition—as distinguished from literary redactions—see Arne-Thompson MT 1726, 1730, 1775A, 1776, 1781, and 1825A. Add to those full tale references the motifs J 1211.1; K 1814.1; V 465 and the references there; T 401.1 and X457.1. Hoffmann's typing of the erotic folktale adds MT 1358, 1725, 1726C, and 1770.

Pisanus Fraxi [Henry Spencer Ashbee], *Centuria Librorum Absconditorum* (London, 1879; New York, 1962), surveys the appearance of anti-clerical erotica.

Perhaps in reaction to the very prevalence of the material, it is noteworthy that English obscenity law evolved from court actions against anti-clerical erotica. In 1739, Edmund Curll was receipted for the first fine for publishing an "obscene" book because fifteen years before he had issued *Venus in the Cloister or the Nun in Her Smock*. The first suppression of a book as an obscene work by English courts occurred in 1868 when "The Confessional Unmasked, Shewing the Depravity of the Romish Priesthood; the Inequity of the Confessional, and the Questions Put to Females in Confession" was banned.

In spite of the prevalence of the theme of clerical incontinence in folktales and classic literature alike, there are few published folk songs dealing with the topic. In addition to "The Monk of Great Renown," there are two others: "The Priest and the Nuns," in Harlow (pp. 166ff.); and "The Friar in the Well," Child 276. For possibly linked tunes, see Simpson (pp. 239, 242); Chappell, *Popular Music* (p. 146); Chappell, *Old English*, 2 (p. 296).

Of less certain oral currency are "The Tyrannical Wife," Farmer, 2 (p. 47) and "A Beggar Got a Beadle," Farmer, 3 (p. 141), both with an anti-clerical bent. The latter is sung to "The Friar and the Nun," according to Simpson (p. 239). Baskervill (pp. 26-27) gives a handful of notes on other songs of questionable oral circulation.

Limericks, deliberately piling shock upon shock, often center on

the priapic inclinations of the priesthood. Legman's *The Limerick* gives
over a chapter to "Abuses of the Clergy" (pp. 109-17), containing
forty-four limericks on that subject. The clergy and the fallen sisterhood are the only professions to which Legman felt called upon to
devote an entire chapter.

"The Monk" has not often been reported, but its geographic dispersal is impressive. Brand (pp. 84-85) masks his as a "Squire of Great
Renown." Morgan 1 (p. 91) is from British rugby tradition. Hopkins
(p. 184) has a Canadian military version, Getz 2 (p. MM-7), two from
American airmen.

There are six versions of "The Monk of Great Renown" in the
editor's files. The first here was sung by an insurance salesman to the
editor in Los Angeles in 1963. A variant of "A" collected on the
Michigan State University campus in 1949 is in the Indiana University
Folklore Archive.

The "B" text was collected by a former student of Bess Lomax
Hawes, the informant a former member of Her Majesty's armed
forces. This "English" text is close to a version of the song printed
in Pinto and Rodway's *Common Muse* (p. 439):

> There was an old monk of great renown. (3)
> Who f-----d all the women of London town.
>
> > The old s-d, the dirty old s-d.
> > The b----r deserves to die.
> > Glory, glory, hallelujah.
>
> The other monks cried out in shame,
> But he turned them over and did them again.
> The other monks to stop his frolics
> They took a great knife and cut off his b-----ks.
>
> And now deprived of all desire
> He sings soprano in the choir.

Morgan 1 (p. 91) has a version with an explicit crucifixion:

> His brother monks to stop his frolics,
> Put a nail through his **** [cock] and cut off his ********
> [bollocks].

Getz 2 (pp. MM7-8) has a version unusual for its last stanzas:

> The other monks all cried "For shame." (3)
> They took up a knife and cut off his fame.
>
> But on that Resurrection morn, (3)
> The dirty old bugger still got a horn.

And so that monk has gone to Hell, (3)
And we've heard that he's fucking the devil as well.

The one-stanza "C" text and tune are of college and air force currency. The song, transcribed from a tape of music exampla forwarded by Bill Getz, is from the singing of Wally Fey, an air force veteran of the Vietnam era. It is an intermediate version between the older "Monk" and the next song.

Horse Shit

The dramatic title notwithstanding, this is still another version of "The Monk of Great Renown." The monk has become a pilot and the narrative has been lost, yet the derivation is clear.

There was a pilot of great renown.
There was a pilot of great renown.
There was a pilot of great renown,
Until he fucked a girl from our town,
    Fucked a girl from our town.
    Ha, ha, ha. Ho, ho, ho.
    Horse shit.

He laid her down beside a stump.
He laid her down beside a stump.
He laid her down beside a stump.
And then he missed her cunt and split the stump,
    Missed her cunt and split the stump.
    Ha, ha, ha. Ho, ho, ho.
    Horse shit.

Successive verses follow the same pattern, substituting:

He laid her in a feather bed,
And then he twisted in her maidenhead.

He laid her on a winding stair,
And then he shoved it in clear up to there.

He laid her down beside a pond,
And then he fucked her with his magic wand.

This offspring of "The Monk of Great Renown" was included in a collection of bawdy songs sung by air force officers on Guam between 1956 and 1959. The collection, owned by Colonel G. W. P., was transcribed by James W. Kellogg in 1963 as a project for a folklore class at the University of Texas where the colonel was then serving.

No tune was indicated. It is included here through the courtesy of
Roger D. Abrahams. A longer version in Getz 2 (pp. MM 7-8) adds
three stanzas that even more clearly tie this to the "English" versions
of "Monk":

> He laid her on the dewy grass, (3)
> And then he shoved the old boy up her ass,
>   Shoved the old boy up her ass.
>   Ha, ha, ha. Ho, ho, ho, horseshit!
>
> He took her to the countryside, (3)
> And then he fucked the girl until she died,
>   Fucked the girl until she died.
>   Ha, ha, ha. Ho, ho, ho, horseshit!
>
> He took her to the burial ground, (3)
> And then he thought he'd have another round,
>   Thought he'd have another round.
>   Ha, ha, ha. Ho, ho, ho, HORSESHIT, HORSESHIT.

Samuel Hall

In 1701, an otherwise undistinguished chimney sweep by the name
of Jack Hall was hanged at Tyburn Hill in London for the crime of
burglary. As was the custom of the time, a hack writer dashed off
some bathetic poetry purporting to be the last sentiments of the dead
man, and these lines were hawked about the streets even as Jack was
being stretched.

This "last goodnight," as folklorists morbidly refer to the usually
repentant ballads, passed into oral tradition. There, sometime after
Jack had been elevated to office (to borrow Francis Grose's phrase),
a curious thing happened. Jack became Samuel—or, more familiarly,
Sam—and no longer remorseful. He was instead contemptuous, profane, and disdainful of hangman, preacher, spectators and all.

43

name is Sam-uel Hall   And I've on-ly got one ball,   But it's

bet-ter than none at   all.   Fuck 'em   all.

Oh, my name is Samuel Hall, Samuel Hall.
My name is Samuel Hall, Samuel Hall.
My name is Samuel Hall
And I've only got one ball,
But it's better than none at all. Fuck 'em all.

Oh, I killed a man they said, so they said.
I killed a man they said, so they said.
I killed a man they said.
Christ, I bashed his bloody head
And I left him there for dead. Fuck 'em all.

Oh, they say that I must die, I must die.
They say that I must die, I must die.
They say that I must die,
And they'll hang me up so high.
Then I'll piss right in their eye. Fuck 'em all.

Oh, the parson, he will come, he will come.
The parson, he will come, he will come.
The parson, he will come
With his tales of Kingdom come.
He can shove them up his bum. Fuck 'em all.

Oh, the sheriff will come too, will come too.
The sheriff will come too, will come too.
The sheriff will come too
With his motherfucking crew.
They've got fuck all else to do. Fuck 'em all.

I see Molly in the crowd, in the crowd.
I see Molly in the crowd, in the crowd.
I see Molly in the crowd,
And I feel so God damned proud
That I want to shout out loud, "Fuck 'em all!"

It would be hard to find a more fertile source of traditional balladry
than "Samuel Hall," or, more properly, "Jack Hall"—to which Hoffmann has assigned the motif number Q 413.4.1. Both the tune and

the stanzaic form of the ballad have had great influence in oral tradition. For some hint of this—and these articles barely begin to itemize all the descendants of "Jack Hall"—see Bertrand Bronson, "Samuel Hall's Family Tree" (*California Folklore Quarterly* 1 [1942]: 47 ff., reprinted in Bronson, *The Ballad as Song* [Berkeley: University of California Press, 1969]: 18 ff.) and G. P. Jackson, "The 400-Year Odyssey of the 'Captain Kidd' Song Family" (*Southern Folklore Quarterly* 15 [1951]: 239 ff.).

Bronson concludes from the available record that the contemporary bawdy song "took its rise ultimately in the bosom of the Church, in England, at some time in the later Middle Ages." (The assertion that Hall and Kidd are not related—made by Eckstorm and Smyth [pp. 246-49]—may be discounted.)

To the references Bronson and Jackson supply, add "Remember O Thou Man" in Thomas Ravenscroft, *Melismata* (London, 1611; reprinted by the American Folklore Society, 1961): 144; "God Save Great King George" in Chappell, *Popular Music*, 2 (p. 45); "Ye Jacobites by Name" on Ewan MacColl, *Songs of Two Rebellions* (Folkways FW 8756); "Aikendrum" on Ewan MacColl, *Classic Scots Ballads* (Tradition 1013); "The Shan Van Vocht" in Galvin (p. 27); "The Famine Song" also in Galvin (p. 44); "Admiral Benbow" in Cecil Sharp, *Folk Songs from Somerset*, 3d Series (London, 1906): 5, and Karples, *Sharp's*, 2 (pp. 273-74); "Benjamin Bowmaneer" in Vaughan Williams and Lloyd (pp. 20-21), and *Sing Out* Vol. 32, No. 2; and "The Bold Benjamin," ibid. (p. 23). O Lochlainn notes in *More Irish Street Songs* (p. 215) that "The Shan Van Vogt" [*sic*] has "ribald" verses about "the tight old Hag," but gives none; he does have two more songs using the "Sam Hall" stanzaic formula. For further references to "The Shan Van Vocht," see D. K. Wilgus, "The Aisling and the Cowboy," *Western Folklore* 54 (1985): 255-300; and Wilgus and Eleanor R. Long, "The Banks of Mulroy Bay," in *Ballades et Chansons Folklorique* (Quebec, 1989): 267-68.

"Hurrah Lie" in Lomax (*North America*, 260), and the references there introduce the nursery branch of the family. Silber (p. 189) has "Drink It Down," a Civil War drinking song.

G. P. Jackson has extensively documented the God-fearing members of the family. In addition to his article cited above, see *Spiritual* (pp. 90, 114, 159, and 162); *Down-East* (pp. 196, 241, 259-61 [text only], 267-68, and 271 [text only]); and *Another* (pp. 27-28, 196).

Jackson credits the great popularity of the tune and stanzaic form to William Walker's *Southern Harmony* (Philadelphia, 1836, 1854; reprinted Los Angeles, 1966) which borrowed the text from *Mercer's Cluster*. The melodic grafting was Walker's.

Further references to the tune family are in Brown, 5 (p. 495); and Buchanan (pp. xv, 12-13). See too "The Freemason's Song," in Simpson (p. 234), which seems as if it were at any moment to break into "God Save the King"; and "Sound a Charge" (p. 673).

Textual references for the "Jack Hall" ballad and its congener, "Captain Kidd," are in Laws, *American Balladry* (pp. 158-59, 167-68). Mackenzie (pp. 278-79) has excellent notes on the ballad of the throttled pirate captain, as well as a parody dated to 1797. Add Peacock, *Songs* 3 (p. 837-39); Karpeles, *Sharp's*, 2 (pp. 149-51); and Cazden, *Nonsense* (p. 84). An English music hall version is reconstructed in Davison (pp. 13-15).

Art songs set to traditional tunes have used the same stanzaic form. See "A Young Man and a Maid," in D'Urfey's *Pills*, 6 (p. 251). The tune there was borrowed by Burns for "Ye Jacobites by Name," according to Dick (pp. 264, 464). Burns also used a variant of the Kidd tune to bear the words for his poem "The Tailor." See J. Johnson, 1 (p. 505); and Stenhouse's notes, 2 (p. 431).

The bawdy version of the original broadside is definitely dated to the middle of the nineteenth century. Defending the inclusion of Commonwealth and Elizabethan indelicacies in his edition of *Choyce Drollery*, J. W. Ebsworth gamely rationalized in 1876:

> There are tokens of a debased taste that would be inconceivable, did we not remember that, not more than twenty years ago, crowds of M.P.s, Lawyers, and Baronets listened with applause and encored tumultuously, songs far more objectionable than these (if possible) in London Music Halls, and Supper Rooms. Those who recollect what R..s sang (such as "The Lock of Hair," "My Name It Is Sam Hall, Chimbley Sweep," etc.) and what "Judge N-----" [G. Renton Nicholson] said to his Jury Court, need not be astonished at anything which was sung or written in the days of the Commonwealth and at the Restoration.

In a footnote to the version in his *Garland*, Kidson (p. 39) identifies "R . . s" as G. W. Ross, who "in the fifties of the last century . . . sang a version of the above named 'Sam Hall,' but with a very blasphemous chorus. This drew a big audience of a certain kind."

In the end papers of the copy of John S. Farmer's *Musa Pedestris*, now held by the UCLA Research Library's Department of Special Collections (PR 1195 V2F2), former owner Edgar Syers of London wrote in pencil, apparently about 1904:

"The Ballad of Sam Hall which used to be sung at Evans' Supper Rooms Covent Garden circa 1845 is not mentioned here.
    "I only remember fragments of it.

"First Verse
    "My name it is Sam Hall, chimney sweep, (2)
    My name it is Sam Hall, and I tell you one and all
    That you're buggers great and small.
    Damn your eyes.

    "Part of Penultimate Verse
    And now the parson's come, damn his eyes, (2)
    And now the parson's come, telling me of Kingdom Come, etc.

"Last Verse
    "And now I hear the bell, damn your eyes, (2)
    And now I hear the bell, calling me to bloody hell
    Where all poor buggers dwell, damn their eyes."

This may be the oldest folk redaction of the ballad recovered.

Kennedy (pp. 706-7), Davison (p. 13), and Morgan 1 (pp. 80-81) have contemporary British versions. The last verse of the Kennedy ballad has the contemptuous narrator, true to the very end, even mock himself:

> Up the ladder I did grope, that's no joke, that's no joke.
> Up the ladder I did grope, that's no joke.
> Up the ladder I did grope and the hangman pulled the rope
> But the devil a word I spoke coming down, coming down.
> But the devil a word I spoke coming down.

The song has traveled widely. Laycock (pp. 81-82) and Hogbotel and Ffuckes (p. 59) have Australian versions. Lowenstein (p. 43) has a teasing form of the song from Australian schoolchildren. Cleveland (pp. 18-19) reports it as sung by New Zealand troops during World War II.

Wallrich (p. 171) carries an American air force version of "Sam Hall." Another is in Getz (p. B-7) as "Beer Hall Chant" and three more versions are at pages S-4 ff. Getz 2 (pp. SS-2,3) has two more versions, one of which is dated to 1977 as sung in Korea by air force types. He notes he has seen variations of the following text, "Sammy Small," in no less than thirteen air force songbooks:

O, come 'round us fighter pilots, fuck 'em all, (2)
O, we fly the goddamn plane through the flak and through the rain,
And tomorrow we'll do it again, fuck 'em all.

*   *   *   *   *   *   *   *   *   *   *

O, my bird got all shot up, fuck 'em all, (2)
O, my bird got all shot up, and I'll probably cry a lot,
But I still think that it's shit-hot, so fuck 'em all.

While I'm swinging in my chute, fuck 'em all, (2)
While I'm tangled in my chute, comes this silly, fucking toot,
Hangs a medal on my root, so FUCK 'EM ALL!

The text and tune of "Samuel Hall" used here were sung to the
editor in Los Angeles in 1955 by Donald Weiner, who had learned
it while serving in the military in Japan during the Korean conflict.

Sam MacColl's Song

Jack Hall's last goodnight is remarkable not only for its unrepentant
nature, but also for his unparalleled progeny. Dozens of songs have
either been modeled on the stanzaic pattern and rhyme scheme of
Jack's ballad or have borrowed the melody which, in turn, led to a
remolding of the host-text.

"Sam MacColl's Song" is one of those that deliberately followed
the indelicate versification of "Jack Hall," using a tune that ultimately
can also be traced to the gallows cry of the chimney sweep.

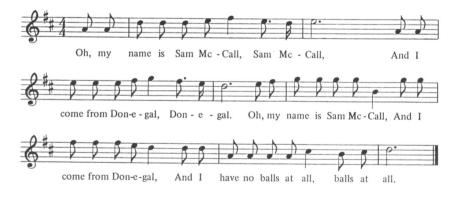

Oh, my name is Sam MacColl, Sam MacColl,
And I come from Donegal, Donegal.
Oh, my name is Sam MacColl,
And I come from Donegal,
And I have no balls at all, balls at all.

There can be no room for balls, room for balls,
When your pecker fills the halls, fills the halls,

So I kicked the walls all out,
And I chased the girls about,
And I skewered them with a shout, with a shout.

When it stands erect with pride, erect with pride,
And the girls want to hide, want to hide,
But they aren't so very meek;
At least once or twice a week,
They take a curious peek, curious peek.

Oh, the girls laugh and sing, laugh and sing,
At the length and breadth of my enormous thing, enormous thing.
For it fills them with delight
Through the day and through the night,
'Cause it fits secure and tight, secure and tight.

If the girls want no more, want no more,
Or they say they're very sore, very sore,
If the girls moan and weep,
Or they say they want to sleep,
I try horses, cows and sheep, cows and sheep.

This is more closely related to the head of the clan than most of the derivative songs and ballads. There are two versions of this in the author's collection; the variant here comes from the singing of a woman in her mid-forties who learned it from her husband about 1940. It was collected in San Francisco by the editor in 1963.

Immortalia ([1927]: 77-78) and its 1968 reprint (pp. 92-93) have a somewhat cobbled version, attributed to Jim Tully.

The melody is a set of the tune usually associated with "I Was Born Almost Ten Thousand Years Ago," a version of which is in Sandburg (pp. 330-31). That same tune is used for an air force version of "Sammy Small."

In Kansas

Still another of the "Jack Hall" cycle or family, "In Kansas" is actually a mocking parody of a haunting lament that commemorates the Irish famines of the 1840s. The beauty of that dirge is only suggested by this stanza:

How I wish that we were geese, night and morn, night and morn.
How I wish that we were geese, night and morn.
How I wish that we were geese,
And could live and die in peace
'Til the hour of our release, eating corn, eating corn.

49

The stanza of the lament which probably inspired the American
parody—often included though not in this version—is:

> Oh, the praties, they grow small over here, over here.
> Oh, the praties, they grow small over here.
> Oh, the praties they grow small,
> And we eat them in the fall.
> Yes, we eat them skins and all over here, over here.

From that lament comes this screed.

Oh, the ea-gles, they fly high in Kan-sas. Oh, the
ea-gles, they fly high in Kan-sas. Oh, the
ea-gles, they fly high, And they shit right in your eye. Thank the
Lord that cows don't fly in Kan-sas.

> Oh, the eagles, they fly high in Kansas.
> Oh, the eagles, they fly high in Kansas.
> Oh, the eagles, they fly high,
> And they shit right in your eye.
> Thank the Lord that cows don't fly in Kansas.
>
> There's a shortage of good whores in Kansas.
> There's a shortage of good whores in Kansas.
> There's a shortage of good whores,
> But there's keyholes in the doors,
> And there's knotholes in the floors in Kansas.
>
> Oh, they say to drink's a sin in Kansas.
> Oh, they say to drink's a sin in Kansas.
> Oh, they say to drink's a sin,
> But they guzzle all they kin,
> And the drys are voted in in Kansas.

They drink their whiskey neat in Kansas.
They drink their whiskey neat in Kansas.
They drink their whiskey neat
'Til it knocks them off their feet
And it petrifies their meat in Kansas.

Oh, I chased a parson's daughter in Kansas.
Oh, I chased a parson's daughter in Kansas.
Oh, I chased a parson's daughter,
And I banged her when I caught her.
Now I cannot pass my water in Kansas.

There's no paper in the bogs in Kansas.
There's no paper in the bogs in Kansas.
There's no paper in the bogs.
They just sit there 'til it clogs,
Then they saw it off in logs in Kansas.

If you ever go to jail in Kansas,
If you ever go to jail in Kansas,
If you ever go to jail,
And you need a piece of tail,
The sheriff's wife is for sale in Kansas.

Directly parodied upon "The Famine Song," a variant of which is in Galvin (p. 44), "In Kansas" itself has spawned a number of offspring. The closest is "In Mobile," texts of which are in Legman, *The Limerick* (pp. 321-22); deWitt (p. 54); Logue-Vicarion, No. 10 (with the editor's handiwork visible); both the 1927 *Immortalia* (p. 81) and the 1968 edition (p. 88), as "In Mobile"; and Getz 2 (pp. II-5).

Randolph's "Unprintable" (pp. 233-35) seemingly has the oldest version of "The Taters They Grow Small" in oral tradition, dating to about 1910; it is sung to the common Irish tune, shifted from the minor to the major. The 1927 *Immortalia* (p. 151) and the reprint (p. 119) have a second version as "Over There," beginning:

Oh, the peters they grow small, over there,
Oh, the peters they grow small, over there,
Oh, the peters they grow small,
Because they work 'em for a fall,
And then eats them, tops and all, over there.

The Robert W. Gordon "Inferno" of bawdy songs at the Library of Congress contains an uncredited text, number 3801, dated to 1931, and apparently stemming from American soldiers stationed in the Philippines between the wars. Its last two stanzas run:

> Oh, the women get no tail in Zamboanga. (2)
> Oh, the women get no tail
> For their husbands are in jail.
> Oh, the women get no tail in Zamboanga.
>
> There's a virgin in Cebu, so they say. (2)
> There's a virgin in Cebu
> And today she is just two.
> There's a virgin in Cebu, so they say.

There are many others, especially those with college currency. See, for example, Randolph, "Unprintable" (p. 633); Ford's *Traditional Music* (p. 356) as "'Way Out West in Kansas"; Cazden, *Nonsense* (p. 106); Dolph (pp. 64-65); Hudson (pp. 216-17); and Lynn (p. 104). Spaeth (p. 33) has a popular redaction dated to 1844, placing it hard on the heels of the famines during which the undated song in Galvin was seemingly written.

This traditional song apparently received a boost from the popular music industry. Sheet music for "The Wonderful Song of 'Over There,'" arranged for voice and piano, and published in New York by Atwill, 1844, was listed in the Cantabrigia Book Store Catalog, Vol. 1, No. 1 (Cambridge, Mass., May, 1957). It is reprinted in Levy, *Flashes* (pp. 334-35). A humorous version is included in *100 Comic Songs* (Boston: Oliver Ditson, 1858): 11. A number of citations to ephemeral prints are included by Reuss (pp. 190-91).

The editor collected a one-stanza complaint from Lee Bluestone in Los Angeles in 1964, a fragment of a longer song ultimately traceable to "In Kansas."

> It's a helluva situation up at Yale.
> It's a helluva situation up at Yale.
> As a means of recreation,
> They rely on masturbation.
> It's a helluva situation up at Yale.

Legman's *Limerick* (p. 320) has a two-stanza version of "Yale." Hart's *Immortalia* (pp. 78-80) has a variant with a tune, and adds, to be sung to the same music:

> Oh, the eagles they fly high in Mobile,
> Oh, the eagles they fly high in Mobile,
> Oh, the eagles they fly high;
> And they shit right in your eye—
> Oh, it's good the cows don't fly in Mobile!

This song is seemingly popular on college campuses. Bess Hawes forwarded from then San Fernando Valley State College, now California State University Northridge:

> Oh, we have some Chi Omegas at IU,
> Oh, we have some Chi Omegas at IU,
> But the Beta Theta Pi's,
> They still sleep with Sigma Chi's,
> Even though we have some Chi O's at IU.

Roger Abrahams has forwarded a seven-stanza slander from the University of Texas related to this college-centered sub-group. Two stanzas of that, sung to the tune of "There's No Hiding Place Down There," are:

> Oh, the Thetas they are a bunch of wrecks, a bunch of wrecks. (2)
> Oh, the Thetas are a bunch of wrecks,
> Turn out the lights, turn on the sex.
> There's no hiding place down there.

> Oh, the Chi O's they wear the low cut dress, the low cut dress (2)
> Oh, the Chi O's wear the low cut dress.
> It's so low, I must confess,
> There's no hiding place down there.

Finally, it is worth noting that the song is known throughout the English-speaking world. Laycock has a staggering 39 verses with two different choruses for the Australian song he calls "In Mobile" (pp. 87-93). Hogbotel and Ffuckes (p. 52) have another. Cleveland (p. 94) notes it was sung by New Zealand troops in World War II.

The first phrases of the melody of "In Kansas" printed here—collected by the editor from an informant who had learned it in his boyhood in Philadelphia in the 1930s—are a variant of "I Was Born Almost Ten Thousand Years Ago." (A version is in Sandburg, pp. 330-31.) The use of that tune strongly suggests a link beyond the textual form with both "Sam Hall" and "Sam MacColl's Song," printed above. The balance of the tune used here is otherwise a derivative of the "Aikendrum" branch of "Sam Hall's" family tree.

I Am Growing Old and Gray

This minor lament for a lost youth is another of the songs modeled upon the tune and stanzaic pattern of Jack Hall's last goodnight.

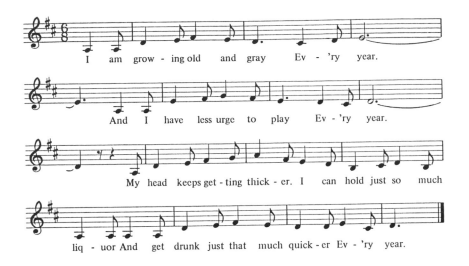

I am growing old and gray every year.
And I have less urge to play every year.
My head keeps getting thicker.
I can hold [just that] [a lot] less liquor
And get drunk just that much quicker every year.

The women all are sweeter every year.
And they ask for much more peter every year.
But mine can get no bigger
And it's slower on the trigger
And cuts less and less a figure every year.

One of two versions in the editor's collection, this was sung by Carl Fertig, a fifty-year-old carpenter in Los Angeles in 1964. He had learned it, perhaps in 1945, while working in a shipyard in Seattle, Washington. The melody is an adaptation of the familiar "She'll Be Comin' 'Round the Mountain When She Comes." He varied the fourth line of the first stanza.

The only other reported texts, with no tune, are in the once-scarce underground anthology, *Immortalia*, on page 126 of the 1927 original and page 137 of the 1968 reprint. Hart's unrelated *Immortalia* 2 (p. 25) also has it.

The sentiment of the song is echoed in "When I Was in My Prime," in Randolph's "Unprintable" anthology (pp. 131-33); "Old Man's Lament" in Logsdon (pp. 238-40); and Getz 1 (p. O5).

My Husband's a Mason

The pun, considered the lowest form of humor, is put to good use in service of the lowest form of songlore. Despite its modern allusions, "My Husband's a Mason" can be traced to a song printed first in the early eighteenth century—one that was probably old then.

[A]

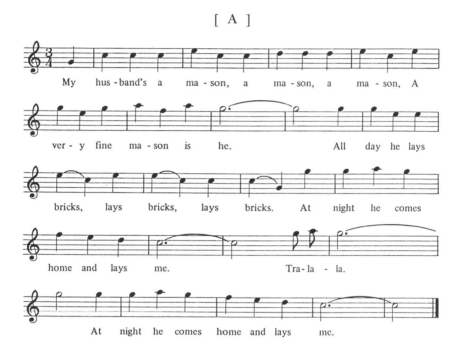

My husband's a mason, a mason, a mason,
A very fine mason is he.
All day he lays bricks, lays bricks, lays bricks.
At night he comes home and lays me.
    Tra la la,
    At night he comes home and lays me.

My husband's a butcher, a butcher, a butcher,
A very fine butcher is he.
All day he stuffs sausage, stuffs sausage, stuffs sausage.
At night he comes home and stuffs me.
    Tra la la,
    At night he comes home and stuffs me.

55

My husband's a miner, a miner, a miner,
A very fine miner is he.
All day he bores holes, bores holes, bores holes.
At night he comes home and bores me.
    Tra la la,
    At night he comes home and bores me.

My husband's a pilot, a pilot, a pilot,
A very fine pilot is he.
All day he flies planes, flies planes, flies planes.
At night he comes home and flies me.
    Tra la la,
    At night he comes home and flies me.

My husband's a jockey, a jockey, a jockey,
A very fine jockey is he.
All day he rides horses, rides horses, rides horses.
At night he comes home and rides me.
    Tra la la,
    At night he comes home and rides me.

My husband's a carpenter, carpenter, carpenter,
A very fine carpenter's he.
All day he pounds nails, pounds nails, pounds nails.
At night he comes home and pounds me.
    Tra la la,
    At night he comes home and pounds me.

[B]

My fa-ther's a driv-er, bus driv-er, bus driv-er, A
might-y fine driv-er is he. All day he drives bus-es, drives
bus-es, drives bus-es, And then he comes home and drives me. So
dance a lit-tle bit, fuck a lit-tle bit, Fol-low the band With your

balls in your hnad. Sing-ing, Dance a lit-tle bit, fuck a lit-tle bit,

Fol-low the band, Fol-low them all the way home.

Chorus:
Dance a little bit, fuck a little bit.
Follow the band, follow the band
With your balls in your hand, singing,
Dance a little bit, fuck a little bit.
Follow the band. Follow them all the way home.

My father's a postman,
A postman, a postman,
A mighty fine postman is he!
All day he licks stamps,
He licks stamps, he licks stamps,
And when he comes home, he licks me.

My father's a baker,
A baker, a baker,
A mighty fine baker is he!
All day he creams puffs,
He creams puffs, he creams puffs,
And when he comes home, he creams me.

[C]

My father's a mason, a mason, a mason,
A very fine mason is he.
All day he lays bricks, he lays bricks, he lays bricks.
At night he comes home and lays me.

Chorus:
Hi, jig-jig a jig, kiss a little pig.
Follow the band, follow the band, follow the band.
Hi, jig-jig a jig, kiss a little pig.
Follow the band, follow the band, follow the band.

My father's a baker, a baker, a baker,
A very fine baker is he.
All day he makes bread, he makes bread, he makes bread.
At night he comes home and makes me.

My father's a sailor, a sailor, a sailor,
A very fine sailor is he.
All day he climbs ropes, he climbs ropes, he climbs ropes.
At night he comes home and climbs me.

My father's a drummer, a drummer, a drummer,
A very fine drummer is he.
All day he beats drums, he beats drums, he beats drums.
At night he comes home and beats me.

[D]

My old man was a miner,
Worked all day in the pit.
Sometimes he'd shovel up coal dust,
Sometimes he'd shovel up shit.

Chorus:
Singing, hey, jig-a-jig, fucken little pig,
Follow the band, follow the band,
With your cock in your hand.

My old man was a carpenter,
And a fine carpenter is he.
All day long he screws in,
And then he comes home and screws me.

My old man is a taxidermist,
And a fine taxidermist is he.
All day long he stuffs animals,
And then he comes home and stuffs me.

My old man is a trumpeter,
And a very fine trumpeter is he.
All day long he blows trumpets,
And then he comes home and blows me.
    Drink a little, little, chug a little, little,
    Follow the man, follow the man, follow the man.

[E]

My husband's a pilot, a pilot, a pilot.
A very fine pilot is he.

All day he flies planes, flies planes,
At night he comes home and drinks tea.

My boy friend's a carpenter, a carpenter, a carpenter.
A very fine carpenter is he.
All day he pounds nails, pounds nails.
At night he comes home and drinks tea.

My boy friend's a mason, a mason, a mason,
A very fine mason is he.
All day he lays bricks, lays bricks.
At night he comes home and drinks tea.

[F]

My husband's a baker, a baker, a baker,
My husband's a baker is he.
All day he makes bread, he makes bread, he makes bread,
And at night he comes home and drinks tea.

Chorus:
Hey-rig-a-dig, kiss a little pig,
Follow the band, follow the band,
Fall in and follow the band.

Similarly:
A bricklayer . . . All day he lays bricks
A farmer . . . All day he forks hay
A glazier . . . All day he blows glass
A cabby . . . All day he strips gears

According to MacColl and Seeger, *Travelers' Songs,* "The English and Scots traditional repertoires are rich in euphemistic songs and scores of trades and occupations have contributed their terminologies and their tools to the vocabularies of sexual symbolism." Though McCarthy (p. 41) has one such in "A German Clockmaker," relatively few of these seem to have retained any great currency today.

Still, it is an old tradition. The same punning device appears in "A Ballad for All the Trades" reprinted from the 1707 edition of *Pills to Purge Melancholy* in Farmer, 3 (p. 101):

V.   O the weaver, the wicked, wicked weaver,
     That followeth a weary trade;
     He never shoots his shuttle right,
     But he shoots, but he shoots, but he shoots first at his maid.

VIII. O, the blacksmith, the lusty, lusty blacksmith,
    The best of all good fellows;
    He never heats his iron hot
    But his maid, but his maid, but his maid must blow the bellows.

A similar stanzaic form appears in a sea shanty forwarded by J. N. West in 1924 to Robert W. Gordon. That one-stanza song, now Number 365 in the Gordon "Inferno" in the Library of Congress's Archive of American Folk Song, runs:

> Every ship has a capstan, has a capstan, has a capstan.
> Every ship has a capstan and a capstan has pawls,
> And every young girl likes a young man
> With a big pair of balls.
>
> Sheet out your main t'gan't'sail,
> Your main t'gan't'sail,
> Your main t'gan't'sail,
> Sheet out your main t'gan't'sail,
> And let the good ship go free.

Other versions of "My Boy Friend's" are in Pinto and Rodway, *The Common Muse* (pp. 438-39); MacGregor (pp. 65-66); Morgan 2 (p. 115); and in Babab (p. 85), as "The Professions Song." Popular on college campuses, this song has been collected at Indiana University no less than thirteen times; no doubt students at other institutions of higher learning can match that.

The "A" version was recited in parlando style by Max Cray of Burlingame, California, in 1964. He had learned it as a youth in Sherbrooke, Quebec, about 1925.

Christian Gunning wrote out the "B" text and tune as they were sung by members of the University of Southern California marching band in 1989.

The "C" text was collected by Betty Golom from Rusty Ward at then Michigan State College in 1949. It is in the Indiana University folklore archives.

The "D" text was one of a group of songs sung by rugby players at Indiana University and deposited in the Indiana University Folklore Archive in 1970 by Drake Francescone.

Jon W. Krainock gathered the "E" text, a "teasing" form of the song, at then San Fernando Valley State College in 1964; he told Bess Hawes, "This song is also improvised upon by the participants."

The "F" versions is one of seven "teasing" versions in the Indiana University Folklore Archives. It was collected from Gene Cope of Ft. Knox, Kentucky, in 1954, by Janice Elkins of Pontiac, Michigan, while attending Michigan State University. Six other versions were collected between 1950 and 1955 at that school. A similar version is included in the mimeographed "Scientific and Professional Personnel Song-book," produced by a classified unit associated with the Army Chemical Corps, circa 1959, and forwarded by Lydia Fish of Buffalo State University.

The Foggy, Foggy Dew

This is one of the most beautiful of British love songs, delicately suggestive of the sexual, perhaps the least bawdy of the songs in this anthology. The third stanza has sometimes suffered excision when the song has been printed.

Now I am a bach-el-or; I live by my-self And I
work at the weav - er's trade. And the
on - ly, on-ly thing I ev - er did wrong Was to
woo a fair young maid. I
wooed her in the sum - mer time, And
part of the win-ter time too. But the
on - ly thing I ev-er did wrong Was to
[on - ly, on-ly]

keep her from the fog - gy, fog - gy dew.

Now, I am a bachelor, I live by myself
And I work at the weaver's trade.
The only thing I ever did wrong
Was to woo a fair, young maid.
    I wooed her in the summer time,
    And part of the winter time too;
    But the only thing that I ever did wrong
    Was to keep her from the foggy, foggy dew.

One night this maid came to my bed
Where I lay fast asleep.
She laid her head upon my chest
And then began to weep.
    She sighed, she cried, she damn near died.
    She said, "What shall I do?"
    So I took her into bed and I covered up her head
    Just to keep her from the foggy, foggy dew.

All through the first part of the night,
We did laugh and play.
And through the latter part of the night,
She slept in my arms 'til day.
    Then when the sun shone down on our bed,
    She cried, "I am undone."
    "Hold your tongue, you silly girl.
    The foggy dew is gone."

Now I am a bachelor; I live with my son.
I work at the weaver's trade,
And every time I look into his face
He reminds me of the fair young maid.
    He reminds me of the summer time
    And part of the winter time too,
    And the many, many times I took her in my arms
    Just to keep her from the foggy, foggy dew.

As "The Foggy Dew," this English ballad was included in the first edition of *The Erotic Muse*. It has been retitled to differentiate it from the Irish lyric that travels under the title of "The Foggy Dew." See Cazden, Haufrecht, and Studer (pp. 284-89) for a discussion of the confusion that has ensued because two songs are known by the same title.

Under either title, this is representative of a group of gently erotic folk songs once much more common in New World oral tradition than now appears to be the case. (Edith Fowke's remarkable informant, O. J. Abbott, sang three of these "last leaves" for her: "A Young Man Lived in Belfast Town," "Nellie Coming Home from the Wake," and "The Weaver" in her *Traditional Songs*, 34-39.) Recent British publications such as the Kennedy, Sedley, Palmer, and Purslow anthologies listed in the bibliography, contain a number of these euphemistic and symbolic ballads, largely from rural or suburban informants. Characteristically, they are celebrations of the erotic, avoiding profanity, treating sex and seduction with elliptical delicacy. The frankest of these rarely surpasses this stanza from "She Was a Rum One" in Kennedy (p. 421):

> My trouble lies between my thighs
> And e'er it is abidin'
> It tickles me baith night and day
> And it keeps me from my stridin'.

This version of "The Foggy, Foggy Dew," as is the case with most, only hints gently at the bawdy. It was learned by the editor in 1956 from John Terrence O'Neil, an advertising artist who remembered it from the singing of his father, a New York City construction worker. O'Neil's melody, in the mixolydian, with the sixth of the scale added, is one of the handful of clearly modal tunes in this collection. The addition of the sixth in this melody suggests that it too will eventually shift from the modal to the major, conforming as it were to more modern tastes.

Hoffmann has assigned the song the motif number X724.10.1.1.

The oldest version of this ballad in the United States, said to have been learned about 1900, is in Randolph, "Unprintable" (pp. 227-29). Josiah Combs's text, as "The Bugaboo," is probably of similar vintage; it was the first printed, in his *Folk Songs du Midi des Etats-Unis* (pp. 214-15). John Dos Passos's *Nineteen Nineteen* notes the ballad was sung by Americans on the Italian front during the First World War.

Other North American texts of this widely known ballad are cited in Laws, as O3 (pp. 227-28), to which may be added Hubbard (p. 115); Brand (p. 55); *Immortalia* ([1927]: 124); and *Immortalia* ([1968]: 136). Fowke, *Traditional* (pp. 108-9) gives additional references at page 186. (The melody in Fowke, known usually as "The Rambling Rake of Poverty," is unrelated to the usual tunes for the ballad.) Logsdon too gives extensive references (p. 206). The mimeographed M.I.T. song collection entitled "The One, the Only Baker

House . . . Song Book" (p. 13), prints a text, perhaps from the version recorded by Burl Ives in the late 1940s. The Indiana University Folklore Archives contain an unpublished text from that school's rugby team, circa 1970. There are two recorded versions in the Library of Congress's Archive of American Folk Song, on AFS 2261 and 2280.

Getz 1 (p. F-15) has a variant with an unusual third stanza:

> Now a year has gone by,
> Still a bachelor am I,
> And I work at the weaver's trade.
> Comes a-knocking at my door,
> It's a voice I've heard before,
> It's the voice of the fair young maid.
> She handed me a little one.
> She said, "What can I do?"
> So I took him into bed
> Just to cover up his head,
> Just to shield him from
> The foggy, foggy dew.

English versions of the song are in Kennedy (p. 400); Sedley, *Seeds* (p. 179); Purslow, *The Foggy Dew* (p. 31), McCarthy (pp. 34-35); and McGregor (pp. 21-22), each with a stanza in which the two wed. *English Dance and Song* 36, No. 2 (Summer, 1974): 59, has a five-stanza variant from Somerset, collected in 1905; it is set to a "Villikins" tune variant. Five other Somerset variants — to other melodies — are in Karpeles, *Sharp's Collection*, 1 (pp. 410-18).

The tune for "The Foggy, Foggy Dew" is used for "The Nutting Girl" in McCarthy (p. 79); and "Banks of Panama," in Leach, *Folk Ballads* (p. 242). It has also influenced "Old Garden Gate," in Palmer, *Vaughan Williams* (p. 34).

A-Rovin'

Perhaps because of its fine tune, perhaps because of the sailor's intent which bowdlerizing has not obscured, this is one of a handful of former sea songs with currency ashore. It cannot be claimed that "A-Rovin' " is as frequently sung as it was in the days of sail when it reportedly served as a chantey accompanying work aboard ship. Still versions do turn up, far from the tradition which spawned them.

In Amsterdam there lived a maid.
Mark well what I do say.
In Amsterdam there lived a maid
And she was a mistress of her trade.
I'll go no more a-rovin' with you, fair maid.

Chorus:
A-rovin', a-rovin', since rovin's been my ruin.
I'll go no more a-rovin' with you, fair maid.

I put my hand upon her knee.
Mark well what I do say.
I put my hand upon her knee.
She said, "Young man, you're rather free."
I'll go no more a-rovin' with you, fair maid.

I put my hand upon her thigh.
Mark well what I do say.
I put my hand upon her thigh.
She said, "Young man, you're rather high."
I'll go no more a-rovin' with you, fair maid.

I put my hand upon her snatch.
Mark well what I do say.

I put my hand upon her snatch.
She said, "Young man, that's my main hatch."
I'll go no more a-rovin' with you, fair maid.

She rolled me over on my back.
Mark well what I do say.
She rolled me over on my back
And fucked so hard my balls did crack.
I'll go no more a-rovin' with you, fair maid.

And then I slipped her on the blocks.
Mark well what I do say.
And then I slipped her on the blocks.
She said, "Young man, I've got the pox."
I'll go no more a-rovin' with you, fair maid.

And when she spent my whole year's pay,
Mark well what I do say,
And when she spent my whole year's pay,
She slipped her anchor and sailed away.
I'll go no more a-rovin' with you, fair maid.

This sea song has seemingly survived largely on college campuses. The earliest reported versions, expurgated, to be sure, are frequent in turn-of-the-century collections of campus favorites.

In the late 1920s, Robert W. Gordon collected a seven-stanza version entitled "The Maid of Amsterdam." The last three stanzas of that text (No. 221 in Gordon's Oregon collection at the University of Oregon and the Library of Congress) either influenced or borrowed from "The Monk of Great Renown":

I laid my hand right on her quin [*sic*].
Mark well what I do tell!
When I laid my hand upon her quin,
Said she, "For Christ's sake! shove it in!"
I'll go no more a-rovin' with you, fair maid.
A-rovin', a-rovin', since rovin's been my ru-in,
I'll go no more a-rovin' with you, fair maid!

I took her to her snow-white bed.
Mark well what I do tell!
I took her to her snow-white bed
And I fucked her there till she was dead.
I'll go no more a-rovin' with you, fair maid.
A-rovin', a-rovin', since rovin's been my ru-in,
I'll go no more a-rovin' with you, fair maid!

And when the bell tolled out "Amen."
Mark well what I do tell!

66

And when the bell tolled out "Amen,"
I fucked her back to life again.
   I'll go no more a-rovin' with you, fair maid.
   A-rovin', a-rovin', since rovin's been my ru-in,
   I'll go no more a-rovin' with you, fair maid!

Other texts and tunes for "A-Rovin' " are to be found in Cecil Sharp et al., *A Selection* (2:1); Cazden, *Abelard*, Part 2 (pp. 26-27); Hugill (pp. 48-52); Colcord (pp. 87-88); Shay (pp. 80-81); and Harlow (pp. 49-51). The collegians' song is in *The Remick Favorite Collection of College Songs* (p. 87), among others.

A bawdy version is recorded on *Barely Alive* (Sault Antlers Recordings). An early unexpurgated printing is in *Immortalia* ([1927], 113), and the reprint (p. 127).

Randolph's "Unprintable" (pp. 87-88) has a song that has borrowed (?) the formula. It is possible too that "A-Rovin' " has thrown off another formulaic song; see "Yo Ho, Yo Ho," below.

In *The Wanton Seed*, Purslow includes a curiosity that seemingly textually borrows from "A-Roving." "All Under the New Mown Hay" (p. 8) has this stanzaic pattern:

As I was going over the fields,
Mark you well what I do say.
As I was going over the fields,
A fair pretty lass came close to my heels
Which caused me to go a-screwing,
And brought me to my ruin,
Which caused me to go a-screwing
All under the new mown hay.

Purslow's tune is not clearly related to the familiar one here. Nonetheless, he argues his song is the original, since "ruin" and "roving" don't rhyme.

A portion of the conventional tune for "A-Rovin' " intrudes into "Jolly Waggoner" in Baring-Gould (pp. 68-69); and in "Bonnie Susie Clelland" and "Horn Fair," both in Palmer, *Vaughan Williams* (pp. 9-10, 134).

The version included here — to which Hoffmann has assigned motif number X724.8.1 — is from a student at the University of California, Berkeley. It was collected by the editor in 1967. That young man said he learned the song on campus from friends; it may well be a product of the urban folk song revival, since "A-Rovin' " was recorded both as a folk and a popular song. The unusual melody, which fuses both stanza and chorus into a single entity, is shaped ABCBC.

The Fire Ship

In a sanitary version, this sailors' ballad was revived in the 1950s
as a popular song. Needless to say, the popular recording lacked the
realism of seventeenth century versions which contained verses like:

> She gave to me a syrup sweet
> [That] was in her placket box,
> But e'er three minutes went about
> It proved the French-pox.

> The fire ship she did blow me up
> As my effigy shows,
> And all may read upon my face
> The loss of teeth and nose.

Modern-day bawdy texts also avoid this graphic detail, the singers
apparently preferring to treat venereal disease humorously — if at all.

As I stepped out one ev-en-ing up on a night's career, I spied a loft-y clip-per ship and aft-er her I
steered. I hoist-ed up my sig-in-als which she so quick-ly
knew, And when she seen my sig-in-als, she im-
med-i-ate-ly hove to. She had a dark and a rov-in'

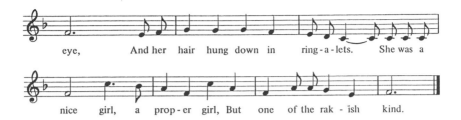

eye,   And her   hair   hung down in   ring-a-lets.   She was a

nice   girl,   a prop-er girl, But   one   of the rak-ish   kind.

[A]

As I stepped out one evening upon a night's career,
I spied a lofty clipper ship and after her I steered.
I hoisted up my sig-in-als which she so quickly knew,
And when she seen my sig-in-als fly, she immediately hove to.

Chorus:
She had a dark and a rovin' eye,
And her hair hung down in ring-a-lets.
She was a nice girl, a proper girl,
But one of the rakish kind.

Oh, sailor, please excuse me for being out so late,
But if my parents knew of it, oh, sad would be my fate.
My father is a minister, a good and honest man.
My mother is a Methodist; I do the best I can.

I eyed that girl both up and down for I'd heard such talk before,
And when she moored herself to me, I knew she was a whore.
But still she was a pretty girl; she shyly hung her head.
"I'll go along with you, my lad," this to me she said.

I took her to a nice hotel; I knew she wouldn't mind.
But little did I ever think she was one of the rakish kind.
I played with her for quite some time, and learned to my surprise,
She was nothing but a fire ship rigged up in a disguise.

So up the stairs and into bed I took that maiden fair.
I fired off my cannon into her thatch of hair.
I fired off a broadside until my shot was spent,
Then rammed that fire ship's waterline until my ram was bent.

Then in the morning she was gone; my money was gone too.
My clothes she'd hocked; my watch she stole; my sea bag was gone too.
But she'd left behind a souvenir, I'd have you all to know,
And in nine days, to my surprise, there was fire down below.

Now all you jolly sailormen who sail upon the sea
From England to Amerikay take warning now from me.

Beware of lofty fire ships, they'll be the ruin of you.
They'll empty out your shot locker and pick your pocket too.

[B]

As I went down to the city hotel to get my night's career.
T'was there I spied a pretty little miss, straightway to her I did steer.
Said she, "Kind sir, I think you're bold to stop me on my way,
But just come down to the green front door if you've got anything for
    to say."

Chorus:
She had a dark and a rolling eye,
Cold black cock and lily-white thighs.
She had a dark and lolling eye.
She had a tapering thigh.

Oh, I went down to the green front door and I treated her to wine,
And I drank a healthy round for her and I wished that girl was mine.
I begged and teased her 'til at length I gained consent,
And I slipped five dollars in her hand and away to bed we went.
    We rolled and we toppled 'til I got my heart's desire,
    And less than ten days afterward, I thought my ass was on fire.

Chorus
As you go down in New York town, inquire for number nine,
And shag them whores all around and among them you'll fuck mine.

Chorus
As you go down in Brooklyn town, they call her the Rising Sun,
And many a chap she's given the clap, and among them, me for one.

Chorus
The clothing that this damned bitch wore was fine enough for any queen.
Two coal black eyes, two tapering thighs, and a red-hot magazine.

Chorus
She gave me the shankers, likewise the runners too.
And in about ten days the blue balls was in view.

Chorus
Oh, but now my song is ended and to you I'll sing no more.
That apple's in the maiden's ass and you can suck the core.

While remembered as the inoffensive popular song of the 1950s,
"[She Had a] Dark and a Roving Eye," bawdy versions are scarce.
McCarthy (pp. 32-33) has it, with the same tune as here. Randolph's
"Unprintable" (pp. 639-40) offers a seven-stanza version. Hugill (pp.
171-72) had one, but chose to omit the two indelicate stanzas in his

text. Other versions are in Shay (p. 205); and Niles, Moore, and Wallgren (pp. 152-55).

The two broadside stanzas quoted in the headnote are from "As I Cam up to Arpendeen," in Loth (pp. 77-78) credited there to "Elizabethan yeomanry." Simpson (p. 461) puts "Arpendeen" in print very early in the seventeenth century, sung to a tune he calls "London Is a Fine Town." It is difficult to perceive any direct relationship between Simpson's melody and that used for modern versions of "The Fire Ship" or its variants such as "The Brisk Young Butcher," in Purslow, *Marrow Bones* (p. 13).

An analogous text, possibly a forbear of "The Fire Ship," appears in the *Pepys Ballads*, 6 (pp. 153-55). Legman (*Horn Book*, 190) marks it an antecedent of the "Cruising Round Yarmouth" songs.

The "A" version of "The Fire Ship" here was forwarded to the editor in 1960 after he broadcast a radio appeal in Los Angeles and San Francisco for "bawdy or dirty" songs. The letter was postmarked in San Francisco and contained this note: "I learned this from my father who worked on the docks here when he was a boy about 1900. I suppose he learned it there. I am not sure if the melody is the way my father sang the song. I picked it out on the piano the way I sing it." The editor has corrected what appear to be two errors in the barring of the musical transcription forwarded with the text. That melody is essentially that of the popular song.

The "B" text was forwarded by Barre Toelken from the Utah State University archives. Under the title of "The Dark and Rolling Eye, Cold [*sic*] Black Cock and Lily-White Thighs," the text was set down by M. Stubblefield at the behest of his son, singer-collector Blaine Stubblefield. The elder Stubblefield had learned it sometime prior to the 1930s from W. P. Warnock of Enterprise, Oregon. No tune was given and Toelken has followed the stanzaic division of the typescript.

The Stubblefield text is notable in that it identifies the Rising Sun as the name of a bawdy house in Brooklyn. An establishment by that name also appears in the otherwise unrelated blues, "House of the Rising Sun." As printed in John A. and Alan Lomax, *Our Singing Country* (New York: Macmillan [1949]: 368), it is the lament of a prostitute long gone in drink, drugs, and/or debauchery. The Lomaxes note the name "occurs in a number of unprintable songs of English origin."

Bell Bottom Trousers

Sailors, tinkers, lawyers, millers, and tailors have fearful reputations in British folklore. Tailors are inevitably cowards; millers and lawyers are just as inevitably dishonest. Tinkers are oversexed, and sailors are seducers of innocent maidens. Many of the once numerous songs about lawyers, millers, and tailors have not survived the wear and tear of oral transmission, but those about tinkers and sailors persist.

[A]

When I was just a serv-ing girl I lived in Dru-ry Lane, My mas-ter he was kind to me; my mis-tress was the same. When a-long came a sail-or boy with laugh so bright and gay, And he was the source of all my mis-er-y.

Chorus

With his bell bot-tom trou-sers, coat of na-vy blue, He would climb the rig-gin' like his dad-dy used to do.

When I was just a serving maid who lived in Drury Lane,
My master he was kind to me; my mistress was the same.
When along came a sailor boy with laugh so bright and gay,
And he was the source of all my misery.

72

Chorus:
With his bell bottom trousers, coat of navy blue,
He would climb the riggin' like his daddy used to do.

He asked me for a candle to light him to his bed.
He asked me for a nightcap to put upon his head.
Now I was just a simple lass and didn't mean no harm,
So I hopped into the sailor's bed to keep the sailor warm.

In the morning he was gone and he left a five pound note,
With a bit of writin', and this is what he wrote:
"Now you may have a daughter, lass. You may have a son,
And this should help to pay for the trouble I have done.
       Now if you have a daughter, you can bounce her on your knee,
       But if you have a son, you can send him off to sea."

[B]

Now once there was a waitress in the Prince George Hotel,
Her mistress was a lady, and her master was a swell.
They knew she was a simple girl, and lately from the farm,
So they watched her carefully, to keep her from all harm.

Chorus:
Singing a bell bottom trousers, coats of navy blue,
Let him climb the rigging like his daddy used to do.

The Forty-second fuselears [Fusiliers] came marching into town,
And with 'em came a complement of rapists of renown.
They busted every maidenhead that come within their spell,
But they never made the waitress from the Prince George Hotel.

Next came a company of the Prince of Wales' Hussars.
They piled into the whore houses and they packed along the bars.
Many a maiden, mistress, and a wife before them fell,
But they never made the waitress from the Prince George Hotel.

One day there came a sailor, an ordinary bloke,
A-bulging at the trousers with a heart of solid oak.
At sea without a woman for seven years or more,
There wasn't any need to ask what he was looking for.

He asked her for a candlestick to light his way to bed,
He asked her for a pillow to rest his weary head,
And speaking very gently, just as if he meant no harm,
He asked her if she'd come to bed, just so's to keep him warm.

She lifted up the blanket, and a moment there did lie,
He was on her, he was in her, in the twinkling of an eye.

He was out again, and in again, and plowing up a storm.
But the only word she spoke to him: "I hope you're keeping warm."

Then early in the morning, the sailor he arose,
Saying, "Here's a two-pound note, my dear, for the damage I have caused.
If you have a daughter, bounce her on your knee,
And if you have a son, send the bastard out to sea."

And now she sits aside the dock, a baby on her knee,
Awaiting for the sailing ships, a-comin' home from sea.
Waiting for the jolly tars in Navy uniforms.
And all she wants to do, my boys, is keep the Navy warm.

[C]

When I was a servant girl, down in Tennessee
Along came a sailor, a sailor from the sea.
I, like a foolish girl, thinking it no harm,
Jumped into bed that night to keep the sailor warm.

Early the next morning, the sailor he awoke
And reaching in his pocketbook, he handed me a note.
"Take this, my gentle maiden, for the damage I have done.
In nine months' time, just drop a line, a girlie or a son.

"And if it be a little girl, just bounce her on your knee,
And if it be a little boy, just send him out to sea
With belly button jacket, and trousers navy blue,
So he can charm the ladies as his daddy used to do."

Now all you gentle maidens, just take a tip from me
And never let a sailor boy an inch above your knee.
They'll hug you, they'll kiss you, they'll swear there's none like you,
Until they've copped your cherry, then they'll say to hell with you.

In both its presumably older form, "Home, Dearie, Home," and the frequently bowdlerized form here, "Bell Bottom Trousers" is well known. Hoffmann has assigned it motif number X724.8.3.

Despite its presumed age and derivation, the earliest recovered printing of "Bell Bottom Trousers" is in an American song collection, Leach's *Bottoms Up!* (p. 113) according to Fuld (p. 139).

There is some indication that the bawdy song is much older. Hopkins (p. 138) speaks of "First War versions," but gives only one from Canadian servicemen during World War II. Similarly, Winnans (p. 31) reprints a variant of the "B" version here, stating it was current in the Royal Australian Navy in the early 1940s. Such geographical dispersion would suggest the age of the song, even in the well-traveled twentieth century.

In addition to the references in Laws (p. 163), add the following appearances of the song: MacColl and Seeger (pp. 166-67), under the title "Rosemary Lane"; Karpeles, *Sharp's*, 1 (pp. 671-79, nine versions); Hugill (p. 498); Brand (pp. 41 ff., two versions); McCarthy (pp. 46-47); and Stubbs (p. 54), as "The Oak and the Ash." "Rosemary Lane" in Purslow's *Wanton Seed* (p. 99), and Baring-Gould, *Folk Songs* (pp. 90-91) are variants of "Bell Bottom Trousers." The distinctive melody of "Bell Bottom Trousers" seems to have influenced the tune for "The Whip and the Spurs," in Meredith and Anderson (p. 93). There are unexpurgated versions of both "Bell Bottom" and "Home Dearie Home" in Randolph's "Unprintable" (pp. 623-25). One or the other is in Shaw (pp. 116-17); *Immortalia* ([1927]: 136) and the 1968 reprint (p. 150); Morgan 1 (pp. 41-43); *Songs of Raunch and Ill-Repute* (p. 26); *Songs of Roving and Raking* (p. 103); and Logue-Vicarion, No. 22. Babab (p. 115) credits Brand for his version. There seems to be considerable air force currency—likely traceable to college tradition—judging from Wallrich (pp. 60, 63) with two songs set to the familiar tune, but textually unrelated. See also Getz 1 (p. G-12), for an air force version, "'G'-Suits and Parachutes."

There are five versions of "Bell Bottom Trousers" in the editor's files. The "A" version was collected in 1957 by Charles Marshall from Thorsten Gunther who learned the song in Pomona, California, while attending college there in 1936.

The "B" version is from Massachusetts Institute of Technology where the anonymous editors of the mimeographed "The One, the Only Baker House Super-Duper Extra Crude Song Book" chose it to lead the collection.

The "C" text is No. 3144 in the Archive of American Folk Song's Gordon Inferno. It was mailed to Gordon by Frank A. Partridge of Auburn, California, about 1927.

In a sanitized version, the song was recorded in the early 1950s for Columbia Records by Guy Mitchell. That record seems to have refurbished memory of the tune in oral tradition.

When I Was Young

Change is the hallmark of oral tradition. In some cases, the changes are for the better; other times, the changes corrupt the song and lead eventually to its demise. In some instances, one song is so changed that it becomes a new effort, and both old and new songs continue side by side in oral currency. Such is the case with this American redaction of "Bell Bottom Trousers."

When I was young and fool - ish, I used to take de - light At-tend - ing balls and danc - es And stay - ing out at night.

When I was young and foolish,
I used to take delight
Attending balls and dances
And staying out at night.

'Twas at a ball I met him.
He asked me for a dance.
I knew he was a sailor
By the buttons on his pants.

His shoes were neatly polished.
His hair was neatly combed.
And when the dance was over,
He asked to take me home.

As we walked home together,
I heard the people say,
"There goes another girlie
That's being led astray."

'Twas on my father's doorstep
That I was led astray.
'Twas in my mother's bedroom
That I was forced to lay.

He laid me down so gently.
He raised my dresses high.
He said, "Now, Maggie, darling,
Take it now or die."

"Here is half a dollar
For the damage I have done,

For soon you will have children,
A daughter or a son.

"If it is a daughter,
Take her on your knee.
But if it is a son, then
Send him out to sea.

"I hope next time I see you
That you'll remember me,
And thank God for the blessing
That I have brought to thee."

Collected in Northern California, this was furnished by Dale Koby. It is sung to the tune usually associated with the American folk song known variously as "Johnson's Old Gray Mule" or "Simon Slick."

D. K. Wilgus, a graduate of Ohio State University, noted the sea song had come ashore in a version of "When I Was Young" at his alma mater in the late 1930s:

'Twas at a dance I met him.
He asked me for a dance.
I knew was a Lambda Chi
By the way he wore his pants.

His shoes were brightly polished,
His hair was neatly combed,
And when the dance was over,
He asked to see me home.

As we were strolling homeward
I heard somebody say,
"There goes another Alpha Phi
Being led astray."

'Twas in my father's hallway
That I was led astray.
'Twas in my mother's bedroom,
That I was made to lay.

Now listen all my children,
Listen to my plea,
Don't ever let a Lambda Chi
Get an inch above your knee.

For if you do he'll hold you
And promise to be true,
And when he's got your cherry,
He'll say, "To hell with you."

Wilgus' college variant is close to a seven-stanza version from naval currency collected in 1926 and numbered 482 in the Robert W. Gordon Collection of American Folk Songs at the University of Oregon. The Gordon text, forwarded by J. Barre Toelken, probably dates from the First World War; how much older this redaction of "Bell Bottom Trousers" may be is debatable. A World War II rewrite is in Getz 2 (p. WW-2) as "The WASP National Anthem."

The Wilgus text is also similar to "The Buttons on His Pants" in Logsdon (pp. 256-58).

Other texts are in *Immortalia* ([1927]: 88-89); and the 1968 reprint (p. 103). The "inch-above-the-knee" warning floats as a two-stanza fragment (p. 93 of the original, and p. 107 of the reprint). Sandburg (p. 219) has a three-stanza fragment to be sung to a set of the "Goodnight Irene" tune family. His melody is probably more familiar now as the vehicle for James Stevens's "The Frozen Logger." It turns up too in a version from Idaho, set down in Larson's "Barnyard" collection. The sailor-narrator of "An Inch Above the Knee" there makes some unique offers:

> I offered her a silver necklace;
> I offered her a pin;
> I offered her a wooden cradle
> To rock her baby in.
>
> She wouldn't accept the necklace;
> She wouldn't accept the pin;
> But she did accept the cradle
> To rock her baby in.

Reuss (pp. 46 ff.) provides an extended discussion of the appearance of the fateful warning in ribald songlore. For other occurrences, see Randolph ("Unprintable," 541-42); Fowke (*Lumbering,* 194); Purslow (*Wanton Seed,* 33, 37, 50); and O Lochlainn (*More,* 147). This bit of wandering folk poetry is echoed in "Navvy Boots," collected in London and printed in *Sing* 2 (1955), p. 2, and Sedley (*Seeds of Love,* 79-80):

> Come all you pretty fair maids, take heed what I have said.
> Don't ever let a navvy come into your bed
> For their hearts do run light and their minds do run young
> Sure they'll jump on your bones with their navvy boots on.

The Gatesville Cannonball

At first impression "The Gatesville Cannonball" would have little but its theme in common with "Bell Bottom Trousers." However, interpose the connecting link in the evolutionary scheme, "When I Was Young," and the relationship becomes clear.

As sung at Gatesville State School for Boys in Texas, this was apparently fashioned by someone who knew the older "When I Was Young" or another song quite like it. Adapting older songs to new environments, setting them to familiar tunes—in this case, the perennial favorite "The Wabash Cannonball"—continually renews oral tradition.

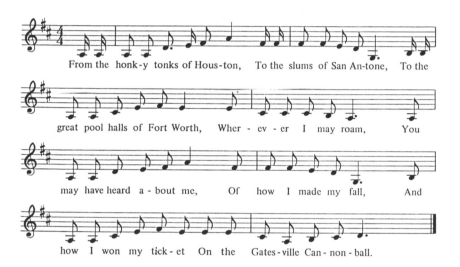

From the honk-y tonks of Hous-ton, To the slums of San An-tone, To the great pool halls of Fort Worth, Wher - ev - er I may roam, You may have heard a - bout me, Of how I made my fall, And how I won my tick - et On the Gates - ville Can - non - ball.

Gather 'round me all you maidens,
And I will tell my tale,
Of how I got my ticket
On the Gatesville Cannonball.

From the honky tonks of Houston,
To the slums of San Antone,
To the great pool halls of Fort Worth,
Wherever I may roam,
You may have heard about me,
Of how I made my fall
And how I won my ticket
On the Gatesville Cannonball.

When I was young and handsome,
It was to my heart's delight
To go to balls and parties,
To stay out late at night.
It was at a ball I met her.
I asked her for a dance.
She could tell I was a Gatesville boy
By the way I wore my pants.

My stomps were neatly polished.
My ducks were neatly combed.
Before the dance was over,
I asked to walk her home.
Walking down the sidewalk,
You could hear the couples say,
"There goes the fair young maiden,
Just throwing her life away."

It was at her father's doorstep,
I asked if I may try.
It was at her mother's bedside,
I forced her down to lie.
I pulled her pants so gently.
I raised her dress so high.
I said, "I'll be a son of a bitch.
I'll go the rest or die."

It was the very next morning.
The sheets were spotted red.
Her mother said, "You son of a bitch,
You've got her maiden's head.
Gather 'round me all you fair maidens,
Listen to my pleas.
Never trust a Gatesville boy
An inch above the knee."

A singular text, sung to the frequently used tune of "The Wabash Cannonball" made popular during the 1920s by hillbilly singers, this was given to the editor by Marilyn Eisenberg Herzog. Herzog had it from a girl friend who learned it at Newport Beach, California, in 1961 from unidentified youths who had spent time at Gatesville. This version of the song can be dated to the 1950s, when "ducks" and "ducktail" hair styles were common among teenage boys.

Cohen (pp. 373-81) details the history of the song, providing an exhaustive discography of country music records. "Cannonball" is a traditional quatrain ballad despite the copyright D. K. Wilgus notes was issued to one William Kindt in 1904, or the later copyrights by A. P. Carter (1939) and Roy Acuff (1940).

Something approaching the original "Cannonball" is in Milburn (pp. 188-91) without a melody. Randolph's "Unprintable" anthology has a variant, said to date from 1894, sung to the melody of the unrelated "Jealous Lover," better known lately as the setting for Woody Guthrie's "Philadelphia Lawyer." This is the same tune Kindt used, according to Cohen.

Much recorded, "The Wabash Cannonball" has been used as a model for other songs. Wallrich (pp. 80 ff.) has an air force adaptation. Greenway (pp. 291 ff.) has Guthrie's "Grand Coulee Dam," modeled in part upon, and using the melody of the hillbilly song. A set of the melody carries "The Bootlegger's Song" on Oscar Brand, *American Drinking Songs* (Riverside 12-630).

The tune has also been used to carry two otherwise unrelated north woods songs. See Peacock (p. 746) and Fowke (*Lumbering*, 91).

Bollochy Bill the Sailor

This song, unlike so many folk songs, has little to recommend it. Its melody is monotonous; its lyrics are repetitious to the point of idiocy. But weak tune and foolish lyrics notwithstanding, the song has an appeal all its own. Singers can add new lyrics as they go, unburdened by the necessity of observing rhyme schemes; the repetitive tune is easily learned and seems to gather momentum as the song goes on. So, for a hundred or more years, Bollochy Bill has been paying his respects to the fair young maiden.

Stanza I only

"Who's that knock - in' at my door? Who's that knock - ing at my door. Who's that knock - ing at my door?" Cried the fair, young maid - en.

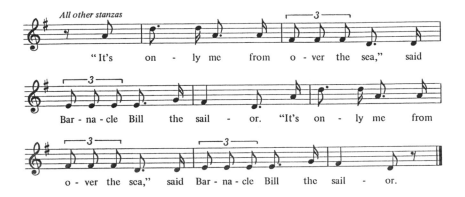

All other stanzas

"It's on - ly me from o - ver the sea," said Bar - na - cle Bill the sail - or. "It's on - ly me from o - ver the sea," said Bar - na - cle Bill the sail - or.

"Who's that knocking at my door?
Who's that knocking at my door?
Who's that knocking at my door?"
Cried the fair young maiden.

"It's only me from over the sea,"
Said Bollochy Bill the sailor.
"It's only me from over the sea,"
Said Bollochy Bill the sailor.

"I'll come down and let you in,"
Cried the fair young maiden.
"I'll come down and let you in,"
Cried the fair young maiden.

"Just open the door and lay on the floor,"
Said Bollochy Bill the sailor.
"Just open the door and lay on the floor,"
Said Bollochy Bill the sailor.

"What if Ma and Pa should see?"
Cried the fair young maiden.
"What if Ma and Pa should see?"
Cried the fair young maiden.

"We'll fuck your ma and shoot your pa,"
Said Bollochy Bill the sailor.
"We'll fuck your ma and shoot your pa,"
Said Bollochy Bill the sailor.

"Stop shouting at the door,"
Cried the fair young maiden.
"Stop shouting at the door,"
Cried the fair young maiden.

82

"I just got paid and want to get laid,"
Said Bollochy Bill the sailor.
"I just got paid and want to get laid,"
Said Bollochy Bill the sailor.

"What's that thing between your legs?"
Cried the fair young maiden.
"What's that thing between your legs?"
Cried the fair young maiden.

"It's only a pole to shove up your hole,"
Said Bollochy Bill the sailor.
"It's only a pole to shove up your hole,"
Said Bollochy Bill the sailor.

"What's that fur around the pole?"
Cried the fair young maiden.
"What's that fur around the pole?"
Cried the fair young maiden.

"It's only some grass to tickle your ass,"
Said Bollochy Bill the sailor.
"It's only some grass to tickle your ass,"
Said Bollochy Bill the sailor.

"What if we should have a child?"
Cried the fair young maiden.
"What if we should have a child?"
Cried the fair young maiden.

"We'll dig a ditch and bury the bitch,"
Said Bollochy Bill the sailor.
"We'll dig a ditch and bury the bitch,"
Said Bollochy Bill the sailor.

A sea song come ashore, "Bollochy Bill the Sailor" now appears to survive on college campuses in the United States, where it is known also under the euphemistic title of "Barnacle Bill the Sailor." Its progenitor, "Abel [Abram] Brown the Sailor," is much less well known, and may well be extinct.

Sightings of "Abel Brown" ashore are scarce. It is described as a diddling or mouth-music melody in Tongue (pp. 33, 91). J. Barre Toelken forwarded this undated text (No. 1109) from the Robert W. Gordon collection at the University of Oregon:

"Who's that knocking at my door?"
Said the fair young maiden.
"Who's that knocking at my door?"
Said the fair young maiden.

"It's me and' I wanna get in,"
Said Abram Brown the sailor.
"It's me and I wanna get in,"
Said Abram Brown the sailor.

Successive stanzas follow the same pattern, each question and answer repeated.

"Open the door and walk in,"
Said the fair young maiden.

"There's only room in the bed for one,"
Said Abram Brown the sailor.

"You can sleep between my thighs,"
Said the fair young maiden.

"What is that hairy thing I see?"
Said Abram Brown the sailor.

"That is my pin cushion,"
Said the fair young maiden.

"I have a pin and it must go in,"
Said Abram Brown the sailor.

"What if we should have a child?"
Said the fair young maiden.

"I'd kill the dirty son of a bitch,"
Said Abram Brown the sailor.

Non-offensive, possibly expurgated versions of "Bollochy Bill"—all from a sea tradition—are in Hugill (pp. 440-42); Colcord (pp. 112-13); Harlow (pp. 164-65); Shay (*American*, 204), and Greenleaf and Mansfield (p. 105). Lynn (pp. 54-55) carries an edited version without a source. Hugill also prints a variant of "Oh Aye Rio," which has bawdy stanzas of its own, that begins with the first verses of "Bollochy Bill" (p. 96).

The fullest version of "Bollochy Bill" the editor has handled is in the Robert W. Gordon Collection of American Folk Song at the University of Oregon. That text (No. 480), forwarded by J. Barre Toelken, borrows much from "Bell Bottom Trousers."

"Oh, who's that knocking at my door?"
Says the fair young maiden.
"Oh, who's that knocking at my door?"
Says the fair young maiden.

"Oh, this is me and no one else,"
Says Bolakee Bill the sailor.

"I'll open the door and let you in,"
Says the fair young maiden.

"Now I am here; I'll stay to dawn,"
Says Bolakee Bill the sailor.

At that point the typewritten copy in the Gordon collection has a broken rule, suggesting that the informant has omitted verses. The song continues after the obvious lapse:

"But a babe now I shall have,"
Says the fair young maiden.

"But it will never see its daddy,"
Says Bolakee Bill the sailor.

"And if it be a lass?"
Says the fair young maiden.

"Strangle it as soon as it's born,"
Says Bolachee Bill the sailor.

"But if it be a laddie?"
Says the fair young maiden.

"Send him out to sea,"
Says Bolachee Bill the sailor.

"I'll make him bell bottom trousers,"
Says the fair young maiden.

"Get him a suit of navy blue,"
Says Bolachee Bill the sailor.

"And he will climb the riggin's,"
Says the fair young maiden.

"Like his daddy used to do,"
Says Bolachee Bill the sailor.

Other ribald versions of "Bollochy Bill" are in *Immortalia* ([1927]: 109), and the 1968 reprint (p. 123); this is apparently the earliest recovered text. Linton (pp. 115-17) has the song.

Shay's version in *More Pious Friends* (p. 102) follows hard on the heels of *Immortalia;* Shay says of his unoffending text that there are "many versions, all of them far better" than his, obviously alluding to the bawdry he excised.

The wide currency of the melody may be attributed to the Frank Luther and Carson Robison version copyrighted in 1929; Luther recorded it commercially (RCA Victor V40043) that same year. *Songs of Roving and Raking* (p. 100) gives credit to Oscar Brand for its variant.

Babab has an Illinois text (p. 112) with the nursery tune used here. Reuss (pp. 240-43) has two texts from Indiana University as well as references to the appearance of the song in ephemeral collections of bawdy songs.

Unpublished American texts are in Larson's "Barnyard" anthology from Idaho; and the USC Marching Band's mimeographed "Hymeneal" (1988).

Morgan 1 (p. 46) has a British version. Laycock (pp. 218-23) contains an unusually full Australian text.

The song is well known in the military. Getz 2 (pp. BB-10) prints two from American air force currency. Another air force adaptation is in Wallrich (p. 15). Hopkins (p. 151) has it from Canadian servicemen during World War II. Cleveland (p. 94) lists it as sung by New Zealand troops at the same time.

Roger Abrahams has noted in a letter to the editor that "Bollochy Bill" is usually sung with alternating tempi — "Bill" rapidly, the girl slowly. This alternation was not indicated by the two former students who collected similar texts at UCLA in 1960.

The Wayward Boy

This ballad is widely known, and probably owes some of its popularity to the catchy melody, the familiar "The Girl I Left Behind Me," and some to the sprightly internal rhymes.

I walked the street with my prick to my feet, I heard a voice come to me. A love-ly maid looked out and said, "I need some-one to screw me." Said I, "My dear, you need-n't fear, For I have heard your plead-ing. It's

ver - y plain   I can   ease your pain. I've   got just what you're need - ing."

She stood right there in the midnight air,
With nothin' on but her nightie.
Her tits swung loose like the balls on a goose,
Jesus Christ Almighty!

She jumped in bed and covered up her head
And said I couldn't find her.
But I knew damn well she lied like hell,
So I jumped right in behind her.

Quick as a wink she grabbed my dink
And shoved it up her grinder.
The white of an egg ran down her leg
And shit flew out behind her.

I screwed her once, I screwed her twice,
I screwed her once too often.
I broke the mainspring in her box
And now she's in her coffin.

Nine days went by, I heaved a sigh,
A groan of pain and sorrow.
The pimples thick ran up dick,
And there'll be more tomorrow.

Nine months went by, she heaved a sigh,
A sigh of pain and sorrow.
For two little mutts were in her guts
But they'll be out tomorrow.

Quatrains set to the familiar "The Girl I Left Behind Me" abound. Two are included in the "Ditties" section below. James Barke, in his essay "Pornography and Bawdry in Literature and Society" in *The Merry Muses of Caledonia* (p. 20), also gives this Scots children's song:

O Mary Ann had a leg like a man
And a great big hole in her stockin';
A chest like a drum and a big fat bum
And a hole to shove your cock in.

As popular as the tune may be, "The Wayward Boy" has been infrequently collected. Legman (*The Limerick*, 454) quotes one stanza from a full text from Michigan dated to 1935. Gainer (pp. 173-74) has a fuller text to the standard melody from a West Virginian woman.

A recorded version is on *Unexpurgated Folk Songs of Men*. Brand sings another on *Bawdy Songs and Backroom Ballads*, 4 (Audio Fidelity 1847), with his own stanzas added. *Songs of Raunch and Ill-Repute* (p. 21) is somewhat close to that here, which was sung by Thomas Thompson in Los Angeles in 1978. Thompson learned it as a youth in Texas in the 1940s.

Unpublished texts include a fragment of "The Wayward Boy" in the Robert W. Gordon Collection of American Folk Song, University of Oregon (No. 3900). It can be dated to the late 1920s, and is the earliest text the editor has seen. That fragment, too, contains the venereal intrusion. Harry A. Taussig learned a variant of the song at the University of California, Berkeley, between 1958 and 1963. Both the Indiana University and the Western Kentucky Archives at UCLA contain short forms of the ballad.

Abrahams has garnered a brisk variant from a Philadelphia informant, "Kid" Mike, including it in the unpublished portion of his doctoral thesis, "Negro Folklore from South Philadelphia, A Collection and Analysis" (University of Pennsylvania [1962]: 252):

> Last night I slept in a sycamore tree
> The wind blowing all around me.
> Tonight I'll sleep in a nice warm bed,
> All the girls beside me.
>
> Well, she jumped in bed and covered her head
> And swore I couldn't find her.
> She knew damn well she was lying like hell,
> So I jumped on in behind her.
>
> She rolled her gut against my nut
> And told me not to mind her,
> And like a damn fool, I took my tool,
> And in her sausage grinder [*sic*].
>
> Nine months rolled by and I heard a cry.
> She rolled with pain and horror.
> Three little grunts jumped out of her cunt,
> I'm booting ass tomorrow.

The first stanza, Abrahams adds in a letter to the editor, indicates some relation to "The Gypsy Laddie" tradition. That ballad and this at least share the notion of the wandering hero and the charmed, sexually-hungry girl.

Texts and tunes for the British ballad "The Girl I Left Behind Me" may be found in Shay (pp. 202 ff.); and in Dolph (pp. 507 ff.); the latter also includes other (inoffensive) parodies (pp. 194 ff., and p.

392). The brisk tune has served for other texts, too. Silber has a mock military song from the Civil War, "I Goes to Fight mit Siegel" (pp. 325 ff.); and credits the original words to Samuel Lover (p. 327).

Chappell's *Old English Popular Music,* 2 (pp. 187-89), or his *Popular Music* (p. 708), have a history of the song, dating it to 1758. Fuld (p. 243) asserts the melody was first published under this title in 1810, and that Thomas Moore revised it in 1818.

Another song with the same title and using the familiar tune is in O Lochlainn (pp. 3-7). There, too, is "The Real Old Mountain Dew" (p. 128) using a set of the melody. O'Neill's *Music of Ireland* has it as a dance tune under the title of "The Rambling Laborer" (p. 52); and as "The Spalpeen March" in his *Dance Music.*

In the United States, the melody has also been put to good service. Hudson (pp. 229-30) has a localized version of the song. Jackson has sniffed out the tune's influence on two hymns in *Another Sheaf* (p. 85), and *Spiritual Folk-Songs of Early America* (p. 111). Finally, worn-down versions of the ballad, fragments really, double as play-parties. See Wolford (p. 277); Botkin (pp. 188-92); and Wyatt (pp. 16-17) for examples. As a singing call for a dance, it appears in David S. McIntosh, *Folk Songs and Singing Games of the Illinois Ozarks* (Carbondale: Southern Illinois University Press [1974]: 76). Ford's *Traditional Music* presents the melody as a square [?] dance tune (p. 116, with floating verses at pp. 211, 417). Bayard has it from Pennsylvania fiddlers (p. 325).

Ball of Yarn

There are any number of disingenuous, even obscure euphemisms for sexual intercourse in folk balladry. In some songs, a soldier plays his fiddle; in others, the girl's thyme is stolen away. Rest assured whatever the poetic device chosen, it will sound wondrously innocent to the uninitiated. Were it not for the rather frank story of this song, the true meaning of "winding up that little ball of yarn" might be similarly vague.

In the merry month of May when the lambs did sport and play,
I went to take a walk around the town.
I met a pretty miss and politely asked her this:
"Will you let me wind your little ball of yarn?"

Chorus:
Ball of yarn, ball of yarn,
It was then I wound her little ball of yarn.
Ball of yarn, ball of yarn,
It was then I wound her little ball of yarn.

With my arm about her waist, we went to a quiet place,
And I gently laid her down upon the grass.
While the birdies and the bees did the same among the trees,
She let me wind her little ball of yarn.

It was shortly after this I went out to take a piss
And to see if she had done me any harm.

With her crack beneath her lap, she had given me the clap
When she let me wind her little ball of yarn.

It was nine months after that in a bar room where I sat,
A policeman put his hand upon my arm.
Said the officer in blue, "Now, young man, we're after you
Just for winding up that little ball of yarn."

To the judge straightway we went, and I offered to repent,
But the judge said, "I do not give a darn.
Guilty in the first degree! To the penitentiary!
Just for winding up that little ball of yarn."

In the jailhouse I sit with my fingers dipped in shit,
And the bedbugs play billiards with my balls.
And the women as they pass stick their hatpins up my ass
Just for winding up that little ball of yarn.

[B]

It was in the month of June and the roses were in bloom
Where the grass grew the thickest on the farm.
There I met a little miss, and to her I whispered this:
"Let me ravel up that little ball of yarn."

It was with her consent, so behind the fence we went,
Where the grass grew the thickest on the farm.
There I gently laid her down, and I ruffled up her gown,
And I raveled up that little ball of yarn.

It was nine months after that and in my club I sat,
Thinking that I'd done her no harm,
Came a policeman dressed in blue, said, "Young man, I'm after you.
You're the father of a nine-pound ball of yarn."

In my prison cell I set with my shirttail full of shit,
And my pecker a-dripping through the bars.
And the women as they pass throw hot peanuts up my ass
For raveling up that little ball of yarn.

[C]

It was early in the month of June when the roses are in bloom
And the little folks are playing on the lawn,
When I met a pretty miss and I simply asked her this:
"Can I wind up your little ball of yarn?"

Oh, she gave me her consent, to the living room we went,
And I asked her where she kept her ball of yarn.

She says, "Underneath my gown," and I gently lyed [*sic*] her down,
And wound up her little ball of yarn.

It was nine days after this when I tried to take a piss,
That my balls did burn and ache and scratch like hell,
When I found to my mishap that I had caught the clap
For winding up her little ball of yarn.

It was nine months after this, I was sitting all in bliss,
When the doctor came a-knocking at my door.
He said, "Son, have no more fear, for your baby boy is here.
You're the father of a nine-pound ball of yarn."

Here in the jailhouse I sit, my shirttail soaked with shit.
The rats play ping-pong with my balls.
The day will come to pass, they'll throw baseballs at my ass
For rolling up that little ball of yarn.

In its present version, "Ball of Yarn" is apparently a music hall or
buskers' rifacimento of an older Scots folk song. Legman (p. 225)
follows the lead of Vance Randolph in according parentage of "Ball
of Yarn" to "The Yellow, Yellow Yorlin," a traditional Scots song
collected by Robert Burns and printed in *The Merry Muses* (1959
edition, 138).

Wayland Hand and D. K. Wilgus have suggested that the song
involves the widespread popular belief that a young woman might
summon up the *doppelganger* of the man she will marry by throwing
a ball of yarn through a window. The spirit or image will throw the
ball back, or rewind the ball for her. See Hand's notes to No. 4340
in *The Frank C. Brown Collection of North Carolina Folklore* (Durham:
Duke University Press [1961] 6: 584); and *JAF* (7 [1894]: 108).

Hugill (pp. 533-34) has a sailors' version of "Ball of Yarn" sung to
a melodic variant of "Blackbirds and Thrushes," borrowing for its
chorus a stanza of that English country song. D. K. Wilgus has suggested there is a close relationship between the two songs.

Other British versions are in McCarthy (pp. 13-14); and in Kennedy
(p. 408). An Irish text in Healy's pub collection (pp. 94-95) carries
this cautionary last stanza:

> Now come all ye young and old
> Take warning when you're told
> Never rise too early in the morn
> Be like the blackbird and the thrush,
> Keep one hand upon your bush
> And the other on your little ball of yarn.

Morgan 1 (p. 47) under the odd title of "I'm a Gentleman of Leisure, of Nobility and Pleasure," begins his version:

> I'm a gentleman of leisure, of nobility and pleasure,
> With manners of the manor and the morals of the barn,
> And when I met a lady in the forest green and shady,
> I asked if I could spin her ball of yarn.

Gilbert (*Lost Chords*, 74-75) dates "Ball of Yarn" to about 1870 in the United States, but gives no melody. Joseph Hickerson, archivist of the Library of Congress's Archive of American Folk Song, furnished sheet music to "Winding Up Her Little Ball of Yarn" with new words by Earl Marble and the familiar tune credited to "Miss Polly Holmes"; it was copyrighted in 1884 by Boston and Chicago music publisher White Smith & Co. Miss Holmes's text has a young narrator take a job teaching school, meeting the daughter of "Mister School Committee . . . knitting by her side as she wound up her little ball of yarn." They marry and live happily ever after in three stanzas.

By about 1887, according to Gates Thomas, the ballad was "widely distributed over Texas" in what Mack McCormick calls "Negro versions" in *American Folk Music Occasional* (No. 1 [1964]: 10). One of Randolph's nine "Unprintable" reports dates from 1890. Significantly, all three of the tunes he gives are variants of that here, collected 70 years later. (The song has maintained a robust vitality.)

Neither Hugill nor Gilbert print the last three verses of their texts, claiming them to be too bawdy. However, Gilbert's two stanzas correspond closely to Hugill's first and third, suggesting that Hugill's sea song is much the same as Gilbert's buskers' song. This would seemingly explain how the song came to the United States.

Other American variants of this well known ballad are in Babab (p. 69); and Peters (p. 266). Brand claims a copyright on his variant (pp. 56-57). The anonymous editors on the Illinois campus of *Songs of Roving and Raking* (p. 58) and at Caltech of *Songs of Raunch and Ill-Repute* (p. 4) print the song in full. A text dated to the 1930s by an internal reference to the "CCC" or Civilian Conservation Corps is in Linton (p. 98). Abrahams gathered another version from "Kid" Mike in Philadelphia, inserting it in his doctoral dissertation, "Negro Folklore from South Philadelphia, A Collection and Analysis" (University of Pennsylvania [1962]: 251).

At least two other uncensored American texts have appeared in print. Getz 2 (pp. BB 8-9) has an air force variant of the text used here. Hart's *Immortalia* 3 (pp. 55 ff.) begins its six-stanza variant with an uncommon introductory verse:

It was in the month of May,
When the jacks begin to bray,
And the jennies come prancing around the barn;
Said the jennie to the jack,
"Will you climb upon my back,
    And wind up my little ball of yarn?"

J. Barre Toelken has culled a text from the Robert W. Gordon
Collection of American Folk Song at the University of Oregon (No.
135) which, though fragmentary, contains this bucolic metaphor:

I took her by the waist, and I led her to the place.
    Gently, gently I laid her down,
And a jaybird and a thrush raised hell in the brush
    While I wound up her little ball of yarn.

Other unpublished texts are in Larson's "Barnyard" collection made
in Idaho (p. 28); and the Gordon Library of Congress "Inferno," No.
738, from California. It is commonly found in folklore archives, often
in fragmentary form with just the "prison-cell-I-sit" stanza; that quatrain is often sung to the Civil War song "Tramp, Tramp, Tramp"
written by George F. Root and published by Root & Cady, Chicago,
in 1864. (The melody also turns up as a fiddle tune in Bayard, 501.)

The tune presently in use is as new as are the words. It is typical
of English music-hall material and the products of the American
popular music industry, circa 1870-1900. It has a relatively wide ambit
(a ninth) and there is the trademark stress upon the sub-mediant
throughout.

The music for the verse and the words of the last stanza here owe
something to Root's Civil War dirge, "Tramp, Tramp, Tramp," wildly
popular just before "Ball of Yarn" ostensibly came across the sea.
Professional singers, such as buskers—audience-wise and ready to
please—would happily borrow the Root song, expecting an added
laugh from the deliberate parody of the last stanza.

The melody of the chorus is related to the post-Civil War cavalry
song, "She Wore a Yellow Ribbon," the verse of which is also rhythmically similar to "Ball of Yarn." Though extant records do not support
the hypothesis, it is possible that the troopers' song is a remnant of
some earlier form of "Ball of Yarn."

The "A" version of the song printed here is from the editor's
collection, gathered in Los Angeles from a draftsman who learned it
in college in the mid-1950s.

D. K. Wilgus learned the "B" text in Columbus, Ohio, circa 1940.

The "C" version was sung by a student from Cleveland, Ohio, at Western Kentucky State College in 1955 for D. K. Wilgus.

The Ball of Kirriemuir

"The Ball of Kirriemuir" was reportedly written in the 1880s to celebrate an actual social event in the Kirriemuir district of Scotland.

According to James Barke's introduction to the 1959 edition of *The Merry Muses of Caledonia*, the male guests took advantage of the fact that few women of the day wore "panties," and the few styles on the market had open crotches. The men sprinkled the earthen floor with the burred seeds of ripened roses. Once the music started, the seeds and dust swirled. The seeds lodged in the nether bush of the ladies present, setting up a fierce itch. Not content with this external irritation, the men spiked the punch with Spanish fly. Finally, they rigged the hanging paraffin lamp to burn out about the same time that the rose seeds and cantharides took effect.

The result was the most sung-about orgy in the history of the Western world.

[A]

'Twas the gath'ring of the clans, And all the Scots were there, A-
blow-in' on their bag-pipes And strok-in' pus-sy hair.
Sing-ing, "Who hae ye, las - sie, Who hae ye noo? The
ane that hae ye last time He can - na hae ye noo.

'Twas the gath'ring o' the clans,
And all the Scots were there,

A-skirlin' on their bagpipes,
And strokin' pussy hair.

Chorus:
Singing, "Who hae ye, lassie,
Who hae ye noo?
The ane that hae ye last time
He canna hae ye noo."

Maggie McGuire, she was there
A-showin' the boys some tricks,
And ye canna hear the bagpipes
For the swishin' o' the pricks.

Sandy MacPherson, he was there
And on the floor he sat,
Amusin' himself by abusin' himself
And catchin' it in his hat.

The factor's wife, she was there,
Ass against the wall,
Shoutin' to the laddie boys,
"Come ye one an' all."

The factor's daughter, she was there,
Sittin' down in front,
A wreath of roses in her hair,
A carrot up her cunt.

The mayor's daughter, she was there,
And kept the crowd in fits
By jumpin' off the mantle piece
And landin' on her tits.

The village idiot, he was there;
He was a perfect fool.
He sat beneath the oak tree
And whittled off his tool.

The chimney sweep, he was there,
But soon he got the boot,
For every time he farted,
He filled the room with soot.

Johnny McGregor, he was there,
A lad so brave and bold.
He pulled the foreskin over the end
And whistled through the hole.

Down in the square,
The village dunce he stands,

Amusin' himself by abusin' himself
And usin' both his hands.

There was fuckin' in the parlor.
There was fuckin' in the ricks.
Ye canna hear the music
For the swishin' o' the pricks.

The elders of the church,
They were too old to firk,
So they sat around the table
And had a circle jerk.

The bride was in the corner
Explainin' to the groom
The vagina, not the rectum,
Is the entrance to the womb.

The king was in the countin' house
A-countin' out his wealth.
The queen was in the parlor,
A-playin' wi' herself.

The queen was in the kitchen,
Eatin' bread and honey.
The king was in the kitchen maid
And she was in the money.

John Brown, the parson,
Was quite annoyed to see
Four and twenty maidenheads
A-hanging from a tree.

And when the ball was over,
The opinion was expressed:
Although they liked the music,
The fuckin' was the best.

[B]

Chorus:
Balls to your partner,
Ass against the wall.
If you can't get fucked on Saturday night,
You can't get fucked at all.

The ball, the ball,
The ball of Kerrymuir [pronounced: Kerry-more],
Your wife and my wife
Were doing it on the floor.

97

The village parson, he was there
And on the couch he sat,
Thinking of pussy to get it hard
Then ramming it into the cat.

Mrs. Murphy, she was there.
She had the crowd in fits,
Jumping off the mantlepiece
And landing on her tits.

There was fucking in the bedroom,
Fucking on the stairs.
You could not see the carpet
For the come and curly hairs.

The bride was in the bedroom
Explaining to the groom
The vagina, not the asshole,
Was the entrance to the womb.

The groom, he got excited
And raced around the halls
Pulling on his pecker
And showing off his balls.

The king was in the counting house
Counting out his wealth.
The queen was in the parlor,
Playing with herself.

The queen was in the kitchen,
Eatin' bread and honey.
The king was in the kitchen maid
And she was in the money.

There was fucking in the parlor
And fucking in the halls.
You could not hear the music
For the banging of the balls.

------ -------, he was there
Looking for a fuck,
But every cunt was occupied
And he was out of luck.

And when the ball was over
The opinion was expressed:
They all enjoyed the dancing
But the fucking was the best.

"The Ball of Kirriemuir"—assigned motif X745.1 by Hoffmann—

is one of the more commonly encountered bawdy songs in oral tradition. Tongue in cheek, Gershon Legman notes hyperbolically, "It is very much to be doubted whether any male Scot alive today, above the age of twelve, has not at least once heard 'The Ball o' Kirriemuir' sung, and joined in *at least* on the chorus." Furthermore, he suggests that the addition of "at least one outrageously obscene stanza" is obligatory for numerous cultivated persons in Scotland (*The Horn Book*, 228).

"The Ball of Kirriemuir" is a modern song, composed on the occasion of a particularly riotous wedding celebration. Legman (p. 227) suggests that the epic epithalamium may owe something to "Blyth Will and Bessie's Wedding," as gathered by Robert Burns and printed in *The Merry Muses* (p. 131):

> There was a weddin' o'er in Fife,
>> An' mony ane frae Lothian at it;
> Jean Vernor there maist lost hir life.
>> For love o' Jamie Howden at it.
>
>> Blyth Will an' Bessie's weddin',
>> Blyth Will an' Bessie's weddin',
>> Had I been Will, Bess had been mine,
>> An' Bess an' I had made the weddin'.
>
> Right sair she grat, an' wet her cheeks,
>> An' naithing pleas'd that we cou'd gie her;
> She tint her heart in Jeamie's breaks,
>> It came nae back to Lothian wi' her.
>
> [Tam]mie Tamson too was there,
>> Maggie Birnie was his dearie,
> He pat it in amang the hair,
>> An puddled there till he was weary.
>
> When e'enin' cam the town was thrang,
>> An' beds were no to get for siller;
> When e'er they fand a want o' room,
>> They lay in pairs like bread and butter.
>
> Twa an' twa they made the bed,
>> An' twa and twa they layd the gither;
> When they had na room enough,
>> Ilk ane lap on aboon the tither.

Although the Burns song is a sketchy ballad and "The Ball" only a series of interconnected fornications in four lines, the first lines, the third stanza, and the very meter of "Blyth Will" and company would award it paternity for "The Ball."

Withal, the tradition is seemingly older. As printed in Farmer, 4 (pp. 48 ff.), or in *Pills to Purge Melancholy*, 1 (p. 276), the sixth stanza of "The Winchester Wedding" runs:

> Pert Stephen was kind to Betty,
> And blith as a Bird in the Spring;
> And Tommy was so to Katy,
> And wedded her with a Rush Ring:
> Sukey that Danc'd with the Cushion,
> An hour from the Room had been gone;
> And Barnaby knew by her Blushing,
> That some other Dance had been done:
> And thus of Fifty fair Maids,
> That came to the Wedding with Men;
> Scarce Five of the Fifty was left ye,
> That so did return again.

Simpson (pp. 638-39) enters a number of these songs that call out the roster of the wedding guests. Though he terms them "genuine Scotch piece[s]," the present editor is dubious.

"The Ball of Kirriemuir" has reached print or record no less than eleven times. Brand has an antiseptic version (pp. 88-89) which he also sings on Volume 3 of his recorded anthology. It appears as "Scotch Ballad" in *Songs of Raunch and Ill-Repute* (p. 28). *Unexpurgated Folk Songs of Men* has a version. Arthur Argo sings it on *A Wee Thread o' Blue* (Prestige International 13048).

Printed versions/variants from British tradition include those in Morgan 1 (pp. 34-40), a 43-stanza endurance test, without sources but possibly conflated. An expurgated version from Scots oral tradition is printed in *Kerr's "Cornkisters" as Sung and Recorded by Willie Kemp* (Glasgow: James E. Kerr [c. 1950]: 40-41). *Vicarion's Book* (No. 21) has the usual tune, but inexplicably omits the last four bars required by the words of the chorus. The text is a 19-stanza conflation of traditional verses and Logue's penmanship. *The Merry Muses of Caledonia* (pp. 23-25) offers a history of the song.

Hopkins (pp. 168-70) has no less than thirty-eight stanzas, sung by Canadian servicemen during World War II.

Antipodal variants are in Hogbotel and Ffuckes (p. 40); and Cleveland (p. 94), noting the song was sung by New Zealand troops during World War II. Laycock (pp. 33-41) prints a record fifty-seven verses from "half a dozen" Australian informants, and has this alternative chorus:

Sing balls to your partner,
Arse against the wall,
If you can't get fucked on Saturday night,
You can't get fucked at all.

Printed versions from American currency include Hart's *Immortalia* (pp. 60 ff.), a 26-stanza offering with a version of the tune that appears here. Getz 2 (pp. BB 6-8) has a 20-stanza version as well as a 12-stanza supplement from USAF sources. *Songs of Roving and Raking* (p. 114) gives a 20-stanza text to the usual tune, presumably from college tradition. Babab (p. 128) credits Brand, who prints it on pages 88-89; Babab's text is longer than Brand's, however.

The editor has collected four variants, the shortest of which is nine stanzas long. No doubt those figures can be matched easily by other collectors. The "A" version printed here was provided by an anonymous male informant to Dean Burson in Los Angeles in 1960. The "B" text was collected by the editor from a male singer in that same city in 1963. The "king/queen/kitchen maid" verses circulate by themselves as a separate song or rhyme.

The melody is apprently wedded to the text; the editor has heard no other tune used for "The Ball." However, the melody bears the unrelated "Lewiston Falls" sung by Frank Warner on *Our Singing Heritage* (Elektra 153); and "The Derby Ram" in Meredith and Anderson (p. 120); the chorus of "The Derby Tup" [Ram] in Hamer (*Green Beds*, 70); a phrase of "Peelhead" in Manny and Wilson (p. 158); and "The Barley Grain for Me" in Fowke (*Traditional*, 14).

O'Reilly's Daughter

Beyond a doubt, this is one of the most popular of bawdy songs, especially among college students. A British import, "O'Reilly's Daughter" or "One-Eyed Riley" has survived in oral tradition relatively unchanged for at least a hundred years.

[A]

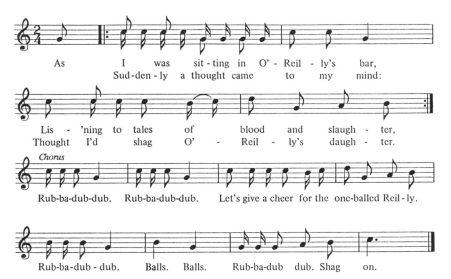

As I was sitting in O'Reilly's bar,
Lis'ning to tales of blood and slaughter,
Suddenly a thought came to my mind,
Thought I'd shag O'Reilly's daughter.

Chorus:
Rubba-dub-dub. Rubba-dub-dub.
Let's give a cheer for the one-balled Reilly.
Rubba-dub-dub. Balls. Balls.
Rubba-dub-dub. Shag on.

Grabbed that bitch by the tits,
Then I threw my left leg over.
Shag, shag, shag some more,
Shagged all night till the fun was over.

Came a knock at the door.
Who could it be but her God-damned father?
Two horse pistols in his hands,
Coming to see who was shagging his daughter.

I grabbed that bastard by the neck,
Stuck his head in a pail of water,
Shoved those pistols up his butt
A damn sight further than I stuffed his daughter.

As I go walking down the street,
People shout from every corner,
"There goes that God damned son-of-a-bitch
Who did shag O'Reilly's daughter."

[B]

As I was walking down the street,
I met the parson's daughter;
The very first thought came into my mind,
That I could finger her hind quarter!

Chorus:
Ho-re-rigga, rigga, ho-re-Riley;
Ho-re-rigga, rigga, one-eyed Riley!

As soon as we had gone to bed,
Who should come in but her damned old mother;
I was shagging away with all my might
When she spatted my ass and drove it in farther!

Then with two pistols in his hand,
Who should come in but her damned old father!
I shoved both pistols up his ass,
And slapped his wife, and shagged his daughter!

Two textual elements provide an approximate dating of "O'Reilly's/Riley's Daughter": "shag" as a euphemism for sexual intercourse dates from the late eighteenth century; and the reference to the necessary in the bedroom places this song to an era prior to the invention or rise of indoor plumbing.

Despite its age and popularity among American college students, the song has appeared relatively infrequently in print. Three Australian versions are in MacGregor (p. 71); Hogbotel and Ffuckes (p. 44); and Laycock (pp. 185-86), which has this unusual stanza:

Her hair was black, her eyes were blue,
The colonel, major and captain sought her,
The company goat and the drummer too,
But they never got into O'Reilly's daughter.

Cleveland (pp. 13-14) is from the singing of New Zealand troops in World War II. Hopkins (p. 158) reports it from Canadians at the same time. Patrick Galvin sings a variant on *Irish Drinking Songs* (Riverside 12-604). Healy's second book (pp. 98-99) has an expurgated military version. Another Irish version is recorded on *Barely Alive* (Sault Antlers

103

Recordings). Morgan's text from Great Britain, 1 (pp. 104-5) adds this last stanza:

> Come you virgins, maidens fair,
> Answer me quick and true no [sic] slyly,
> Do you want it fair and straight and square,
> Or the way I give it to the one-eyed Reilly?

The oldest American report of the song is in Randolph's "Unprintable" manuscript (p. 642), a partial text said to have been learned about 1890. Leach (p. 126), with one harmless verse and a melody, dates to 1933. Larson's "Barnyard" collection (p. 15) has an unpublished version from Idaho schoolboys that dates from the 1930s or 1940s. Brand (pp. 22-23) says his version of the song is at least 100 years old, adding that the song is probably much older. The Brand song is reprinted in *Songs of Roving and Raking* (p. 115).

Suggestive of the interrelationship of bawdy song and folklore in general is the fact that Brand's version begins with an unusual first stanza, apparently a later accretion:

> Oscar Brand is my name, America is my nation,
> Drinking gin my claim to fame, shagging girls my occupation.

This is a portion of a well-known Scots book inscription. *Miscellanea of the Rymour Club*, Edinburgh, 1 (Part 4 [February, 1909]: 129) quotes a version written appropriately enough in a copy of *The Merry Muses of Caledonia* housed in the British Museum:

> William Findlay is my name,
>   And Scotland is my nation,
> Crawford is my dwelling-place,
>   A pleasant habitation.
> When I am dead and in my grave,
>   And a' my bones are rotten,
> Tak' up this book and think of me
>   When I am quite forgotten.

Other printed versions of the song may be found in *Songs of Raunch and Ill-Repute* (p. 27); and Getz 2 (p. OO-16). Logsdon (pp. 249-52) has an extended version; and references.

The song also figures, however fleetingly, in the first act of T. S. Eliot's *The Cocktail Party*. See the appendix (p. 190) of the New York edition of the play for a tune and two stanzas Eliot himself knew.

The "A" version printed here, one of five full texts and four fragments in the editor's collection, was sung by Lee Bluestone, a legislative lobbyist, in Los Angeles in 1964.

The "B" text is from the unpublished Larson "Barnyard" manuscript in the Library of Congress (p. 15).

I Went Down to New Orleans

This is a version of "One-Eyed Riley" notable for its length. The additional stanzas that open the song are borrowed from another, unidentified song.

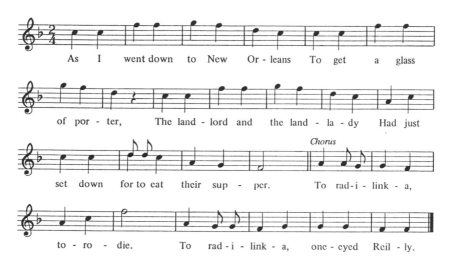

As I went down to New Orleans
To get a glass of porter,
The landlord and the landlady
Had just sat down for to eat their supper.

Chorus:
Too rad-di-link a-too-ro-die
Too rad-di-link a one-eyed Reilly.

Oh, the girls, the girls came flocking 'round
Like the bees a-swarming.
Oh, there I saw one among the crowd
Oh, my Lord, but wasn't she charming.

This pretty fair maid, she went to bed.
She left her doors unbuttoned.
Well, I knew that I might shut
The bolted door that I found open.

I carefully pulling [pulled?] off my shoes.
I went unto her chamber,
Said, "Pretty fair maid, do now you wait
Or would you leave me for a stranger?"

"Away! be gone," replied this maiden.
"I fear you are some rover."
I loved so sweet and I kissed so neat
Till I got her to turn over.

Then I pissed and punched around the hole
Until I got it open.
I run my duty into her
Never touched the bottom.

Then I heard a rumbling up the stairs,
Who should come but her old mother,
Saw me laying between her daughter's thighs,
Clapped her hand and cried out, "Murder!"

I quickly made a sudden spring.
I seized her by the shoulders,
Rammed her ass ag'in the wall,
Played the same tune over and over.

Then I heard another rumbling up the stairs,
Who should come but her old father,
A brace of pistols in each hand
[To] shoot the man who fucked his wife and shagged his daughter.

I quickly made a sudden spring.
I seized him by the collar,
Rammed his pistols up his ass,
Fucked his wife and I shagged his daughter.

And I went out into the county,
There the boys they called me a rouser,
Fucked his wife and I shagged his daughter,
Shook my prick at his old dog [spoken] Towser.

Sung on July 21, 1941, by Lewis Winfield Moody, 75, of Plainfield, Wisconsin, for recording engineer Robert Draves while the credited collector, Helene Stratman-Thomas, waited in the car at Moody's insistence. It is deposited in the Archive of American Folk Song as AFS 4973, No. 3. A dub was furnished by James P. Leary of Mt. Horeb, Wisconsin, who collected with Stratman-Thomas and Draves.

My God, How the Money Rolls In

One of a handful of the most popular bawdy songs, this urban ditty can ultimately be traced to an Irish and Scots tinkers' song, the first stanza of which brags:

> My father was hung for sheep-stealing.
> My mother was burnt for a witch.
> My sister's a bawdy-house keeper,
> And I am a son-of-a-bitch.

The bawdy parent has not flourished. Its offspring meanwhile pops up everywhere, caroled to the innocent melody of "My Bonnie Lies Over the Ocean."

My father makes illegal whiskey.
My mother makes illegal gin.
My sister sells sin in the corner.
My God, how the money rolls in.

Chorus:
Rolls in. Rolls in.
My God, how the money rolls in, rolls in.

107

Rolls in. Rolls in.
My God, how the money rolls in.

We've started an old-fashioned gin shop,
A regular palace of sin.
The principal girl is my grandmother.
My God, how the money rolls in.

My brother's a curate in Sydney.
He's saving poor girlies from sin.
He'll save you a blonde for a dollar.
My God, how the money rolls in.

Grandmother makes cheap prophylactics;
She punctures the end with a pin.
Grandfather performs the abortions.
My God, how the money rolls in.

My bonnie has tuberculosis;
My bonnie has only one lung.
My bonnie spits blood in her pocket
And uses it for chewing gum.

My uncle whittles out candles
With wax especially soft.
He says it will come in handy,
If ever his business drops off.

My sister was once a virgin;
She didn't know how to begin.
I showed her the tricks of the trade.
My God, how the money rolls in.

This is a descendent twice, thrice removed from an English Commonwealth song, "Old Hewson the Cobbler," sung about John Hewson, a former shoemaker who rose through the ranks of the Roundheads to eventually sit in judgment at the trial of Charles I. According to Dick's *The Songs of Robert Burns* (p. 415), "Hewson" is older than its first appearance in the *Vocal Miscellany* 1 (Dublin [1738]: 338), and many "scurrilous and indecent verses" appeared in various Restoration song collections. The popularity of the song is indicated by the fact that a number of other songs and ballads are to be sung to the tune of "Old Hewson." It is not, however, included in Simpson's encyclopedic *The British Broadside Ballad and Its Music*. The tune of "Old Hewson," is printed in Chappell, 2 (p. 163), and *Popular Music of the Olden Time* (p. 451).

The Commonwealth song "Old Hewson" passed into oral tradition in the British Isles, notably with the tinkers and other wandering folk.

That song may have been something close to this from Farmer's *Musa Pedestris* (p. 26):

> A craven my father, a maunder my mother
> A filer my sister, a filcher my brother,
> A canter my uncle that car'd not for pelf,
> A lifter my aunt, and a beggar myself.

No early version of this traditional text seems to have been recovered. However, two descendants, a tinkers' redaction — Legman styles it "The Finest Fucking Family in the Land" — and a busker's/broadside offspring, continue to flourish.

"The Finest Fucking Family" seems to have been reduced to a scatological joke, a tortured remnant of the music halls, if the version in *Songs of Roving and Raking* (pp. 42, 45) is representative.

> I've got a sister Lily, she's a whore in Picadilly,
> And my brother runs a brothel in the Strand.
> My father cocks his asshole at the guards of Windsor Castle,
> We're the finest fucking family in the land.
>
> Oh, please don't burn our shit-house down.
> Mother has promised to pay.
> Dad's laid up with the old D.T.'s
> And the cat's in the family way.
> Brother's been caught selling morphine,
> Sister's been hustling so hard,
> So if you burn our shit-house down,
> We'll have to make do with the yard.

This has been widely reported, in one or another form. The text here is from UCLA, circa 1960, given to the editor by a former student, Alice O'Brien. Babab (p. 52) has it from the University of Illinois. Hopkins (p. 157) presents a Canadian version dated to World War II. Morgan 2 (p. 12); Laycock (pp. 202-3); and Getz 2 (p. DE-5), all have the second verse traveling alone. As sung by Wally Fey on a tape provided by Bill Getz, an air force version for that second verse dating to the Korean conflict runs:

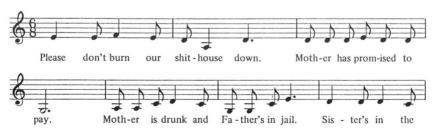

Please don't burn our shit-house down. Moth-er has prom-ised to

pay. Moth-er is drunk and Fa-ther's in jail. Sis-ter's in the

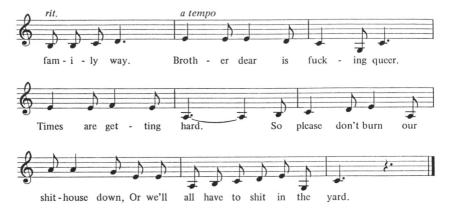

rit.   *a tempo*

fam - i - ly way.   Broth - er dear   is   fuck - ing queer.

Times   are   get - ting   hard.   So   please   don't burn   our

shit - house down, Or we'll   all   have to   shit   in   the   yard.

> Please don't burn the shithouse down.
> Mother has promised to pay.
> Mother is drunk and father's in jail.
> Sister's in the family way.
> Brother dear is fucking queer.
> Times are fucking hard.
> So please don't burn the shithouse down
> Or we'll all have to shit in the yard.

Contrary to Legman's assertion, there is a variety of what appear to be alternative second verses. Legman (*The Horn Book*, 422), seems to insist *his* is the correct second stanza:

> Oh my little sister, Heather,
> Has a maidenhead of leather,
> And she's married to the leader of the band.
> On their wedding-night, the sod,
> (*Spoken:*) Didn't know what to DO, by god!
> So he just reached up and broke it with his hand.

McGregor (pp. 122-23) offers these two rather contemporary stanzas:

> If ye're ever doon in London and ye hae na place to gae,
> An ye canna find a spot to sit ye doon,
> For a penny on deposit
> Ye can hire a water-closet
> And a season ticket costs but half-a-crown.
> There's a gentleman's convenience on the corner of Waterloo,
> And a ladies' one a little further doon,
> If ye've got an aching in your heart
> We need a penny for a fart,
> We own every public lavatory in town.

D'ye ken me sister Tilly, she's a whore in Piccadilly,
And me mither runs a brothel in the Strand,
And me father hawks his asshole
Roond the walls of Windsor Castle,
We're the finest fookin' family in the land!
At the slightest provocation we indulge in masturbation.
We all are ardent followers of Freud!
For the price of copulation
Is the risk of population
And dependents are a thing we must avoid.

These two stanzas are also in Laycock (pp. 230-31). Hogbotel and
Ffuckes (p. 66) give another version. Getz 2 (p. DE-6) has two variants,
said to be fitted to "John Peel." The second of these offers:

Have you met my Uncle Hector?
He's a cock and ball inspector,
At a celebrated English public school.
And my brother sells French letters,
And a patent cure for wetters.
We're not the best of families, ain't it cruel!

Other versions are in Logue-Vicarion, No. 50; Morgan 1 (p. 49); and
Morgan 2 (p. 32).

The buskers' song, meanwhile, has had a lively currency, in print
and in tradition as "Dick Darby [or some such] the Cobbler." Tommy
Makem sings a version on *The Lark in the Morning* (Tradition 1004).
The melody for the Makem song, a set of the music hall mock "Botany
Bay," is printed in *Sing Out!* 11, No. 2 (April-May, 1961). (In the first
edition of this work the editor stated that Makem's tune "is clearly
related to the rudimentary strains of 'Old Hewson' as given by Chappell." Norman Cazden properly corrects that statement in *Folk Songs
of the Catskills,* 269.) Makem's tune runs:

The first stanza of "Dick Darling" printed in Gilbert (pp. 78-79) is:

> Och! my name is Dick Darlin' the cobbler,
> My time I served down there in Kent.
> Some say I'm an old fornicator,
> But now I'm resolved to repent.

Makem's second verse even more clearly shows the paternity of the buskers' song to "My God":

> Now my father was hung for sheep-stealing,
> Me mother was burned for a witch,
> My sister's a dandy housekeeper,
> And I'm a mechanical switch.
> > With me ing-twing of an ing-thing of an i-day,
> > With me ing-twing of an ing-thing of an i-day,
> > With me roo-boo-boo, roo-boo-boo randy,
> > And me lab stone keeps beating away.

Gilbert also cites a DeMarsan broadside, and it may be that the printing houses can take some credit for the song's wide currency in the United States. Gardner and Chickering (pp. 435-38) have two versions from Southern Michigan, and the related "Rusty Old Rover" (p. 434). Flanders and Olney (pp. 176-77) comment on the probable paternity of their version. *The New Green Mountain Songster* (p. 223; the tune there is from Chappell; the informant's has been accidentally omitted); and Randolph, *Ozark Folk Songs,* 1 (pp. 385-86), are also from this broadside/buskers' strain. Louis Pound's Nebraska syllabus reports "They Call Me Dick Turpin the Cobbler" (p. 68). Randolph's "Unprintable" text is at pages 543-44, with a fragment at page 576 under "The Gypsy Maid." Harlow (p. 211) has one stanza from sailors. The Gordon "Inferno" in the Library of Congress, No. 380, from Sullivan County, Missouri, circa 1911, proclaims:

> My father was hung as a horse thief.
> My mother was burned as a witch.

I have seventeen sisters in the whorehouse
And I'm a cocksucking son of a bitch.

Gavin Grieg (*Folk-Song of the Northeast,* No. 18), prints another song—
a maiden's lament about her uncourted state—that borrows its first
stanza from the tinkers' tradition. An analogue is in Williams (p. 226).
A similar text, from Thomson's *Orpheus Caledonius* (p. 69), begins:

My daddy's a delver of dykes,
My minny can card and spin,
And I'm a bonny young lass,
And the siller comes linkin in.
The siller comes linkin in,
And it is fou [*sic*], fair to see,
And it's woe, wow, wow,
What ails the lads at me?

"My God, How the Money Rolls In" is certainly one of the most
frequently encountered bawdy songs in the United States. The earliest
report of the song dates to 1921-22, when, historian Ernest May
wrote,

At a dwelling on K Street, celebrated later as the "little green house,"
there was continuous celebration: card games were always in progress,
the bar never closed, girls came in and out on call, and underworld
figures met with politicians to discuss such matters as pardons, paroles
and withdrawal certificates permitting the purchase of alcohol for in-
dustrial or pharmaceutical use. The host here was Howard Mannington,
who held no office but who was an old friend of [President] Harding's
and an inner member of what was called the "Ohio Gang." Surgeon-
General Sawyer and many others who sat in on White House poker
games were frequent visitors at K Street. The Attorney General came
seldom if at all, but his close friend Jesse Smith was a regular and was
often heard humming in his husky voice, "Good God! How the money
rolls in!" (*War Boom and Bust,* Life History of the United States, 10 [New
York, 1964]: 67)

Reuss reports eighteen archived texts from Michigan State, Indiana
University, and Western Kentucky State College (p. 186). He adds a
text he collected (p. 189), then gives ephemeral references, the earliest
of which he dates to 1928. Other versions are printed in the mimeographed "The One, The Only Baker House . . . Songbook" (p.
4); Brand (pp. 52-53); *Songs of Roving and Raking* (p. 64); and *Songs
of Raunch and Ill-Repute* (p. 9). Versions with air force currency are
in Getz 1 (p. M-11), with the note that he has seen it in no less than
fifteen unit songbooks; and Wallrich (p. 189).

113

Sandburg (p. 381) and Leach (p. 89) each have one stanza of "My God" set to different — and well-worn — sets of the tune that Flanders and Olney, Gardner and Chickering, and Makem offer. This would suggest the strongest possible relationship between "My God" and the inoffensive derivatives of the older tinkers' song. "My God" is now generally sung to the nursery tune of "My Bonnie Lies Over the Ocean." For a short history of that tune, see Fuld (p. 381), who notes it was first printed in an 1881 student song collection in Cambridge, Massachusetts.

British versions survive. MacColl and Seeger (pp. 162-65) have it with excellent notes. A variant from Edinburgh is in Reeves (pp. 103-4). Morgan 1 (pp. 116-17) has a ten-stanza version. Laycock's Australian text (pp. 83-85), with 17 stanzas, smacks of a literate rewrite. Hopkins (p. 161) reports it from Canadian servicemen during World War II.

The editor has handled half a dozen variants of "My God," all sung to "My Bonnie Lies Over the Ocean."

Life Presents a Dismal Picture

This cry of Job, probably of English origin, circulates at times embedded in other, completely separate songs, and sometimes as a full-fledged song in its own right. It is generally sung to the tune of "Hark, the Herald Angels Sing."

[A]

Life presents a dismal picture.
Life is full of tears and gloom.
Father has a penile stricture.
Mother has a fallen womb.
In the corner sits my sister,
Never laughs and never smiles.
What a dismal occupation:
Cracking ice for father's piles.

Brother Bill has been deported
For a homosexual crime.
Sister Sue has been aborted
For the sixth or seventh time.
Little Luke is slowly dying
For he's always having fits.

114

Everytime he laughs, he vomits;
Every time he farts, he shits.

[B]

Life presents a dismal picture,
Dark and dreary as the tomb.
Father's got an anal stricture.
Mother's got a fallen womb.

Sister Sue has been aborted
For the forty-second time.
Brother Bill has been deported
For a homosexual crime.

Nurse has chronic menstruation,
Never laughs and never smiles.
Mine's a dismal occupation,
Cracking ice for grandpa's piles.

In a small brown paper parcel,
Wrapped in a mysterious way,
Is an imitation rectum,
Granddad uses twice a day.

Joe, the postman, called this morning,
Stuck his cock through the door.
We could not, despite endearment,
Get it out till half-past four.

Even now the baby's started
Having epileptic fits.
Every time it coughs it spews.
Every time it farts it shits.

Yet we are not broken-hearted,
Neither are we up the spout.
Aunty Mabel has just farted,
Blown her cunt hole inside out.

Legman terms this a recitation in his *Horn Book* (p. 422). It has, however, acquired various melodies to which it may be sung, and portions of it turn up in other bawdy, quatrain ballads. Hoffmann has assigned to it motif number X726.0.1.

In fact, melodies abound for this, suggesting it has traveled in print, and singers have merely adapted it to whatever melody works best. Randolph's "Unprintable" (pp. 83-85) has the oldest versions turned up: one from 1920; the other, sung to the popular tune of "The

Letter Edged in Black," dating to 1937. Getz 2 (p. LL-3) reprints a four-stanza variant to be sung to the melody of "What a Friend We Have in Jesus." That version is from Royal Canadian air force currency. Hopkins (p. 155) contributes a text sung to the melody of "It's the Same the Whole World Over."

Hogbotel and Ffuckes (p. 20) have the song as well. Laycock (pp. 157-59) has an Australian text of eight stanzas; two of which Laycock wrote. It is to be sung to "Deutschland Uber Alles." Logue-Vicarion, No. 16, is also set to that melody. Morgan 1 (pp. 100-101) shares those quatrains from British tradition without indicating a tune.

The "A" text here was collected by the editor in 1965 while staying at the Detroit YMCA. Roger D. Abrahams forwarded a close variant as sung by college students in Austin, Texas, in 1963; they used the melody of the then popular song "Scarlet Ribbons," a 1949 composition copyrighted by Jack Segal and Evelyn Danzig.

The "B" text is from a collection of rugby songs made at Indiana University in 1970 by Drake Francescone and contributed to that school's folklore archive.

F. M. Rivinus of Philadelphia has forwarded, to the same carol, another song learned in London in 1942:

> If it's warmth that you desire,
> Poke your wife and not the fire.
> If in single state of life,
> Poke some other fellow's wife.
> Poke his wife, or poke your own
> But leave the bloody fire alone.

The Keyhole in the Door

A puzzlement, this may not have been a song originally, but a recitation to which somebody attached a tune. Further, it may not be British in origin, but American. Its assignment here is thus both cautious and arbitrary.

[A]

We left the parlor early, I think it scarcely nine,
And by a lucky fortune, her room was next to mine.
Resolved like old Columbus new regions to explore,

I took a snug position by the keyhole in the door.
    The keyhole in the door, the keyhole in the door.
    I took a snug position by the keyhole in the door.

And while kneeling there in silence upon my bended knee,
Most patiently I waited to see what I could see.
She first took off her collar, and it fell upon the floor,
And I seen her stoop to get it through the keyhole in the door.
    The keyhole in the door, the keyhole in the door.
    I seen her stoop to get it through the keyhole in the door.

This maiden next proceeded to take off her pretty dress,
And then her underclothing, some hundred more or less.
To speak the truth sincerely, I think there was a score,
But I could not count correctly through the keyhole in the door.

She sat down on the carpet, in pretty graceful ease,
And lifted her snowy linen above her lily white knees.
A dainty sky blue garter on either leg she wore
And they looked like Parian marble through the keyhole in the door.

As she arose from her position, looking so nice and warm,
And nothing but a chemise concealed her pretty form,
Thinks I, take off your chemise, and I'll ask for nothing more,
And, by Jove, I seen her do it, through the keyhole in the door.

Then up before the mirror this pretty creature stood,
Revealing her rich beauty and feverishing my blood.
My hair upraised like bristles upon an angry boar,
By Jove, I felt like jumping through the keyhole in the door.

And as she stood reviewing her voluptuous charms,
I wished like an octopus I had a hundred arms,
But as I did not have them, the fact I did [not] deplore
For you can't embrace a maiden through a keyhole in the door.

She next unloosed her tresses of flowing, golden hair;
They fell in a golden torment [torrent?] about her shoulders fair.
And as she quickly rebound them, more firmly than before,
I viewed the pretty process through the keyhole in the door.

She next approached the bed and laid the covers down,
And on the bed Miss Jennie prepared to lay her body down.
The light it was extinguished and I knew the show was o'er
So I abandoned my position by the keyhole in the door.

[B]

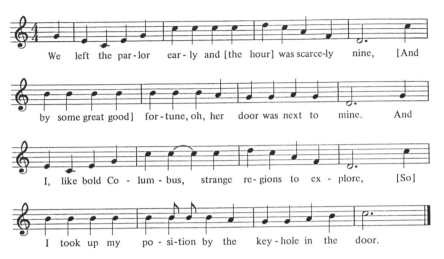

We left the par-lor ear-ly and [the hour] was scarce-ly nine, [And by some great good] for-tune, oh, her door was next to mine. And I, like bold Co-lum-bus, strange re-gions to ex-plore, [So] I took up my po-si-tion by the key-hole in the door.

We left the parlor early and, of course, was scarcely nine [the
　　hour was scarcely nine?]
By some great misfortune, [good fortune?] oh, her door was next to
　　mine.
And I, like bold Columbus, strange regions to explore,
I took up my position by the keyhole in the door.

Well, I waited there in silence upon my bended knee.
I waited there in silence and I waited most patiently.
She first took off her collar and she dropped it on the floor,
And it is a fact I saw her stoop and pick it up through the keyhole in
　　the door.

Then up before the fire, her pretty feet to warm
With nothing but her shimmy on to hide her graceful form.
Says I, "Take off that shimmy and I'll ask for nothing more."
It's a fact I saw her do it through the keyhole in the door.

Then down upon the pillow she laid her little head.
The angels they watched over her till darkness round her spread.
I knew the show was over for I could see nothing more.
A telescope is nothing, boys, to a keyhole in the door.

The editor first heard a portion of this as a recitation while in high
school about 1948 in North Hollywood, California. That it was a
song slipped his ken until he began work on this second edition and
turned up various archived versions.

118

Logsdon suggests in his *Whorehouse Bells* (pp. 253 ff.) that this relatively modern song—to the story of which Hoffmann has affixed motif number X742.1—is probably related to the much older Child 27, "The Whummil Bore." A servant of the king secretly spies upon the princess undressing through a hole made by a gimlet or wimble. It ends, rather inconclusively, like "Keyhole":

> Her neck and breast was like the snow,
> Then from the bore I was forced to go.

The Archive of American Folk Song, in addition to the two here has a Gordon "Inferno" text, No. 3914; and a recording (AFS 1636) by Blaine Stubblefield. A printed text from British sources is in Morgan 1 (p. 82).

A single variant of four stanzas was collected in Michigan in 1954 and deposited in the Indiana University Folklore Archives under the title "I Left the Parlor Early."

The extended "A" text is from the Gordon Inferno, No. 35, from R. M. Davids, 1924, and was forwarded by Guy Logsdon.

The shorter "B" version and tune are from the singing of Lewis Winfield Moody of Plainfield, Wisconsin, recorded on July 21, 1941, by Helene Stratman-Thomas and Robert Draves. James P. Leary contributed a copy of the recording, No. 4971B, made for the Library of Congress.

Seven Old Ladies

Inspired by, and sung to the tune of "Oh, Dear, What Can the Matter Be," this is another of the more discreet "bawdy" songs. Aside from the subject matter, one would be hard put to find anything offensive about the seven old ladies; nonetheless, it is as effectively proscribed as the more indecorous songs in this collection.

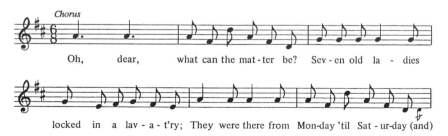

Oh, dear, what can the matter be? Seven old ladies
locked in a lavatory; They were there from Monday 'til Saturday (and)

no-bod-y knew they were there. The first old la-dy was

'Liz-a-beth Por - ter. She was the dea-con of Dor-ches-ter's daugh-ter,

Went to re-lieve a slight pres-sure of wa-a-ter (and) no-bod-y knew they were there.

Chorus:
Oh, dear, what can the matter be?
Seven old ladies were locked in the lavat'ry;
They were there from Monday till Saturday,
And nobody knew they were there.

The first old lady was 'Lizabeth Porter;
She was the deacon of Dorchester's daughter.
Went to relieve a slight pressure of water,
And nobody knew she was there.

The second old lady was Abigail Splatter.
She went there 'cause something was definitely the matter,
But when she got there, it was only her bladder,
And nobody knew she was there.

The third old lady was Amelia Garpickle;
Her urge was sincere, her reaction was fickle.
She hurdled the door; she'd forgotten her nickel,
And nobody knew she was there.

The fourth old maiden was Hildegard Foyle;
She hadn't been living according to Hoyle,
[She was relieved it was only a boil,]
And nobody knew she was there.

The fifth old lady was Emily Clancy;
She went there [when it] tickled her fancy,
But when she got there it was ants in her pantsy,
And nobody knew she was there.

The sixth old lady was Elizabeth Bender;
She went there to repair a broken suspender.
It snapped up and ruined her feminine gender,
And nobody knew she was there.

> The janitor came in the early morning.
> He opened the door without any warning,
> The seven old ladies their seats were adorning,
> And nobody knew they were there.

In the *Oxford Dictionary of Nursery Rhymes* (pp. 248-50), Iona and Peter Opie give a history of the original popular song, which was parodied for political and patriotic purposes long before the "Seven Old Ladies" went into the lavatory. They date it from a manuscript compiled between 1770 and 1780. Chappell (*Popular Music*, 732) fixes the song's date to 1792, when it first appeared in sheet music. Stenhouse's notes in the second volume of Johnson's *Scots Musical Museum* (p. 434) add a concurrent Anglo-Scottish publication. Fuld (p. 398) has a concise survey of the earliest appearances of "Oh, Dear" in print.

A text and tune for the popular song fashioned from the older nursery rhyme is in the *Abelard Folksong Book*, "Songs for Saturday Night" (pp. 6-7).

Williams' *Upper Thames* collection (p. 201) has a stanza from an "old morris fragment" that suggests a folk precursor between the inoffensive "Oh, Dear" and the bawdy song:

> Oh dear, what can the matter be?
> Three old women tied to an apple tree!
> One ran away, the others stopped till Saturday.
> Oh dear, what can the matter be?

Apparently it did not take long for a bawdy parody or paraphrase to appear. Hoffmann has assigned it motif number X726.4.1. The Opies in *Lore and Language of Schoolchildren* (p. 364) deem "Seven Old Ladies" to be a "hoary scatological song concerning the Bishop of Winchester's daughter." Sadly, they do not elaborate.

"The One, The *Only* Baker House Super-Duper Extra Crude Song Book," probably compiled at the Massachusetts Institute of Technology about 1955 (pp. 1-2), presents the oldest recovered American text.

Oscar Brand sings a variant of the bawdy song on Vol. 3 of his record series (Audio Fidelity 1824); that version is reprinted in "Songs of Roving and Raking"(p. 62). Lynn (*Songs for Singing,* 37); Babab (p. 76); and Getz 2 (p. TT-8) have other American versions.

British variants are in Morgan 1 (pp. 118-19); and the Baring Goulds' *Mother Goose* (p. 118), citing "Three Old Ladies" as a "raucous college song," but giving only two inoffensive lines. Two texts from Australia are in print: Laycock (pp. 207-11) has no fewer than twenty-one women in various predicaments, Hogbotel and Ffuckes (p. 45), but five.

The melody, known from the nursery rhyme "Oh, Dear, What Can the Matter Be," was fitted to the shape-note hymn "Send Us a Blessing," according to Jackson (*Spiritual*, 209). It has served too as a contra (?) dance tune; Ford's *Traditional Music* (pp. 351-52) has it under the title "Johnny's So Long at the Fair." Always serviceable, it popped up again in a 1967 popular song, "Round, Round," as recorded by Jonathan King.

Four variants of this have been gathered in Southern California. The one used here was noted by the editor from the singing of a secretary who had volunteered her services as a political campaign worker in Los Angeles in 1964. Two partially missing lines in the fourth and fifth stanzas were patched with the text collected at UCLA by Dean Burson four years earlier.

The Bastard King of England

It's really a very good story; backstairs gossip about palace intrigue is always interesting. As the story goes, Rudyard Kipling wrote "The Bastard King of England" (pronounced "En-ga-land") and that authorship cost him the poet laureate's knighthood. It is too bad that the attribution is apparently spurious; "The Bastard King" would undoubtedly be Kipling's most popular work.

Oh, the min - strels sing of an Eng - lish king Who lived long years a - go, And he ruled his land with an i - ron hand, But his mind was weak and low. He used to hunt the roy - al stag With - in the roy - al

wood, But bet-ter than this he loved the bliss Of

Chorus

pull-ing his roy - al pud. He was dirt-y and lous-y and

full of fleas. His ter-ri-ble tool hung to his knees.

God save the bas-tard king of En - ga - land.

Oh, the minstrels sing of an English king
Who lived long years ago,
And he ruled his land with an iron hand,
But his mind was weak and low.
He used to hunt the royal stag
Within the royal wood,
But better than this he loved the bliss,
Of pulling his royal pud.

Chorus:
He was dirty and lousy and full of fleas.
His terrible tool hung to his knees.
God save the bastard king of England.

Now the Queen of Spain was an amorous dame
A sprightly dame was she,
And she longed to fool with his majesty's tool
So far across the sea.
So she sent a royal message
With a royal messenger
Inviting the king to bring his ding
And spend the week with her.

When news of this reached Philip of France,
He swore before his court,
"The queen prefers my rival
Just because my dork is short."
So he sent the Duke of Zippity-Zap
To slip the queen a dose of clap

123

To pass it on to the bastard
King of England.

When news of this foul, dastardly deed
Reached fair Windsor Hall,
The king swore by the royal whore
He'd have the Frenchman's balls.
So he offered half his kingdom
And the hole of Queen Hortense
To any loyal Briton
Who would nut the King of France.

So the loyal Duke of Essexshire
Betook himself to France.
When he swore he was a fruitier,
The king took down his royal pants.
Then around his prong he tied a thong,
Leaped on his horse and galloped along,
Dragging the Frenchman
Back to England.

Now the king threw up his breakfast
And he shit all over the floor,
For during the ride, the Frenchman's pride
Had stretched a yard or more.
And all the maids of England
Came down to London town,
And shouted 'round the battlements,
"To hell with the British crown."

Last Chorus:
So the King of France usurped the throne.
His sceptre was his royal bone.
Hail to the bastard
King of England.

Like so many of the other bawdy songs in this collection, "The Bastard King of England" clearly shows the marks of a literate creator at work: the story is involved, the meter is correct, the whole well-fitted to the tune.

This is not to suggest that "Bastard King" is not a folk song; it is. Singers have made changes in the text, despite a remarkable faithfulness to an unrecovered "orginal." The tune, a rather difficult one in some versions, changes as well.

A number of versions of this song—to which Hoffmann has assigned motif number X712.2.1.6—have seen print. The oldest recovered dates to 1927 and the privately printed *Immortalia* (pp. 45-46). It is also in the 1967 reprint (pp. 63-64). Hart's unrelated *Immortalia* 3 (pp. 10-15) also has it.

John I. White (p. 35) notes that the novelist Owen Wister, seeking to impart authenticity to *The Virginian,* quoted various cowboy songs, including a frontier boast that seems to be an echo or precursor of "The Bastard King":

> I'm wild and wooly and full of fleas;
> I'm hard to curry above the knees;
> I'm a she-wolf from Bitter Creek, and
> It's my night to howl.

Versions from British or Empire currency are in Morgan 1 (pp. 43-45); Laycock (pp. 216-18); Vicarion, No. 11, which has been harshly served by the anonymous editor.

American texts, some with tunes, are in "Songs of Roving and Raking" (pp. 58-59); Getz 2 (pp. BB-12); and Babab (pp. 74-75), reprinting the Brand variant.

As a testament to the popularity of the ballad, which dates to at least World War I, edited versions appeared at least four times prior to World War II. Leach (p. 79), and Dolph (pp. 140-42), print melodies and censored first stanzas only. Milburn's text (pp. 128-30) has been carefully edited also. So too the Niles-Moore-Wallgren essay (pp. 51-54).

The melody used here, from a version collected by the editor in Los Angeles in 1964, is a variant of the familiar "Irish Washerwoman," transforming a pure mixolydian tune to the major. For a history of the melody, see Fuld (p. 306), who dates it to 1792.

Four other versions of the bawdy ballad are in the editor's collection.

The "Washerwoman" carries not only bawdy quatrains (see the section on ditties below) but versions of "The Ring Dang Doo" in Randolph's "Unprintable" manuscript (p. 119); "There's Fun in the Country" (p. 194); and "Sweet Evalina" (pp. 210-12).

Blinded by Shit

Sexual subjects dominate in bawdy songlore, but there are some ballads concerning the equally natural and equally tabooed functions of excretion. The melody for this sally into the outhouse is "Sweet Betsy from Pike."

[A]

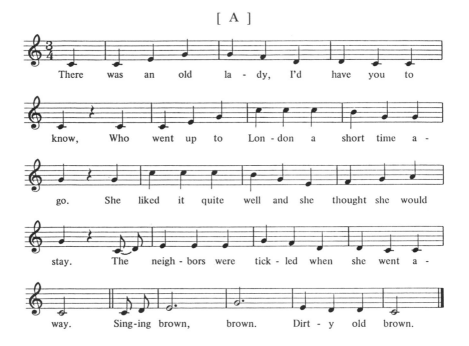

There was an old lady
I'd have you to know
Who went up to London
A short time ago.
She liked it quite well
And she thought she would stay.
The neighbors were tickled
When she went away.
    Singing Brown, Brown,
    Dirty Old Brown.

Now when this old lady
Retired for the night,
She said, "Oh, gor blime,
I believe I must shit."
There's no use in talking
About things that have past.
So up went the window
And out went her ass.

There was an old watchman
Who chanced to pass by,

126

Looked up, got a chunk of shit
Right square in the eye.
He put up his hand
To see where he was hit.
He says, "Oh, gor blime,
I'm blinded with shit."

Now this poor watchman
Was blinded for life.
He had five healthy children
And a fine fucking wife.
On a London street corner
You may now see him sit
With a sign on his chest
Reading, "Blinded with shit."

[B]

There once was a maiden called Adeline Schmidt,
Who went to the doctor 'cause she couldn't shit.
He gave her some medicine all wrapped up in glass.
And up went the window and out went her ass.

Chorus:
It was brown, brown shit falling down.
It was brown, brown shit all around.
It was brown, brown shit falling down.
The whole world was covered with shit, shit, shit, shit.

A handsome young copper was walking his beat.
He happened to be on that side of the street.
He looked up so bashful, he looked up so shy,
When a big piece of shit hit him right in the eye.

That handsome young copper, he cursed and he swore.
He called that young maiden a dirty old whore,
And on London Bridge you can still see him sit,
With a sign 'round his neck saying, "Blinded by Shit."

This was printed as "Blinded by Turds" in the first edition; "Blinded by Shit" is the more common title. Seemingly of British stage origin, it has not often seen print, though Brand recorded a euphemistic rewrite in his *Bawdy Songs and Backroom Ballads* series for Audio Fidelity. Laycock (pp. 228-30); and Hogbotel and Ffuckes (p. 50) have it combined with "Charlotte the Harlot," which shares the "Villikins/ Sweet Betsy from Pike" tune. Laycock (p. 228) and Tate (p. 37) do the same. Morgan 2 (pp. 43-44) has a presumably English text under the title of "There Was an Old Lady" that begins:

> Now there was an old lady who lived on our street,
> She got constipation through too much to eat.
> She took several pills on a Saturday night
> And soon she discovered she wanted to **** [shit].
>> Chorus:
>> Too-ra-la, too-ra-lay,
>> Oh, a rolling stone gathers no moss, so they say.
>> Too-ra-la, too-ra-lay,
>> It's a ******* [fucking] fine song but it's all about **** [shit].

For a discussion of the use of the "Villikins/Betsy" tune in other songs, see the notes to "Charlotte the Harlot I."

J. Barre Toelken forwarded the "A" text from Robert W. Gordon's collection (Oregon No. 385). It was sent to Gordon on May 1, 1925, by H. W. McCormick on stationery of Michigan State Normal College, Ypsilanti. It is also in the Library of Congress's AAFS.

The "Adeline Schmidt" "B" text, from United States air force currency, was sung by Wally Fey on a tape recording provided to the editor by Bill Getz. Getz 2 (pp. AA 2-3) prints two versions under the title of "Adeline Schmidt" and "Brown Brown."

She Was Poor but She Was Honest I

Originally, this was a bathetic lament, sung with tongue in cheek by English music hall singers. The mock lament of "It's the Same the Whole World Over," popularized by British troops, quickly became a bawdy lampoon. In that form it captures the sentiment of the original, but it makes its point in more forthright fashion.

[A]

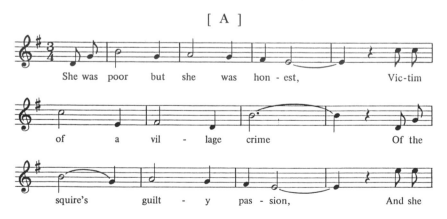

She was poor but she was hon - est, Vic-tim
of a vil - lage crime Of the
squire's guilt - y pas - sion, And she

lost   her   own   good   nyme.

She was poor but she was honest,
Victim of a village crime,
Of the squire's guilty passion
And she lost her own good nyme.

Then she went right up to Lunnon
For to hide her ghastly shyme,
And she met another squire,
And she lost her nyme agayne.

She was poor but she was foolish,
Victim of a rich man's whim,
He seduced her, then he left her,
She'd a little child by him.

You'll find her in the theayter.
See her sitting in the stalls,
And at home an hour lyter
Plying with some strynger's balls.

You'll see her in her limoosin
In the park, and people say
All the squires and nobby people
Stop to pass the time of day.

In a quiet country cottage,
There her aged parents live,
Drinking the champagne that she sends them
But they never can forgive.

You will find her in the gutter
Selling matches by the box.
For a tanner you can up her.
Ten to one you get the pox.

See him passing in his carriage
With his fyce all wreathed in smiles.
See her sitting on the pyvement
Which is bloody bad for pyles.

See him passing to the Commons,
Making laws for rich and pore.
See her walking of [sic] the pyvements,
Nothing but a bloody whore.

129

It's the syme the whole world over.
It's the poor they always blyme,
And the rich, they takes their pleasures.
Isn't it a bloody shyme?

[B]

She was poor but she was honest,
A victim of a rich man's whim.
First he fucked her, then betrayed her,
And she had a child by him.

Chorus:
It's the same the whole world over.
It's the poor what gets the blame.
It's the rich what gets the pleasure,
Ain't it all a bleeding shame.

See him with his handsome horses,
See him strutting at his club,
While the victim of his whoring
Drinks a gin inside a pub.

See him in the House of Commons,
Passing laws to combat crime,
While the victim of his passion
Walks the streets at night in shame.

See him riding in a carriage
Past the gutter where she stands.
He has made a stylish marriage
While she wrings her ringless hands.

See him sitting at the theater,
In the front row with the best.
While the girl that he has ruined
Entertains assorted guests.

Then she came to London city,
Just to hide her bleeding shame.
There a labor leader had her,
Put her on the streets again.

In a little country cottage,
There her grieving parents live.
While they drink the gin she sends them
Still they never can forgive.

130

In a house near Picadilly,
With her hands clasped in her lap,
She awaits her frequent callers.
Ten to one you get the clap.

[C]

She was poor but she was honest,
Victim of a rich man's whim.
He was rich and he seduced her,
And she had a child by him.

See him riding in his carriage,
See him going to the hunt,
Thinking nothing of a marriage,
Only of a piece of cunt.

Now she stands in Picadilly,
Selling matches by the box.
Anyone who buys those matches
Gets a hellfire dose of pox.

This song seemingly began life in English music halls, probably during the latter half of the nineteenth century, and must have acquired bawdy verses early in life. At one time, extended versions were common, probably because it was widely sung by British troops during the First World War.

Logue-Vicarion has a ten-stanza text from British tradition, possibly doctored, and an imperfectly notated tune, No. 3. Morgan 1 (pp. 88-89) contains fourteen verses; a number are different, suggesting this song is undergoing continual recreation. Laycock's Australian text (pp. 94-98) conflates twenty-five stanzas of a "composite" text. Hopkins (p. 162) has a Canadian member of the family.

A version probably closer to the original song is in Sandburg (pp. 200-201). Getz 2 (p. SS-5) has seven stanzas close to some in Morgan. Wallrich (p. 114) carries another song to the same tune.

The "A" text is seemingly the earliest recovered, given in 1923 to Robert W. Gordon, and numbered 246 in the Gordon Collection of American Folk Song at the University of Oregon and the Library of Congress.

The "B" version was from the singing of Walter Burbridge, in 1980 in Los Angeles. Burbridge learned it from an English roommate while attending California State University, San Francisco a decade earlier. The Indiana University Folklore Archives contain a collection of rugby songs made by Drake Francescone at IU in 1970 with a close variant.

The last version was from the singing of an anonymous veteran of the British armed forces, collected by a former student of Bess Lomax Hawes at then California State College Northridge circa 1960.

She Was Poor but She Was Honest II

This English import was adapted in the United States sometime around 1948 to serve as a lampoon of a former governor of Alabama, James Folsom, who was charged with fathering a child on the wrong side of the blanket. The melody for the adaptation is similarly a cross between British and American strains, a fusion of the original tune and "Red River Valley."

She was poor   but she was hon-est,   The vic-tim of   a rich man's whim,   With that south - ern Christ-ian gen-tle-man Big Jim Fol-som, and she had   a child by   him.

> She was poor but she was honest,
> The victim of a rich man's whim,
> With that southern, Christian gentleman, Big Jim Folsom,
> And she had a child by him.
>
> Now he sits in the legislature
> Making laws for all mankind,
> While she walks the streets of Cullman, Alabama,
> Selling grapes from her grapevine.
>
> Now the moral of this story
> Is to never take a ride
> With that southern, Christian gentleman, Jim Folsom,
> And you'll be a virgin bride.
>
> It's the rich what gets the glory.
> It's the poor what gets the blame.

132

It's the same the whole world over, over, over.
It's a lowdown, dirty shame.

Folsom, who died in 1987, deserves recognition for more than fathering a child out of wedlock—a charge he apparently never denied. A genuine populist, six-foot, eight-inch "Kissing Jim" Folsom ran as "the little man's big friend." He was one of the South's first racial moderates, explaining that at age eighteen, "I spent a lot of time below decks on freighters crossing the Atlantic. I slept and ate with men of different colors from all over the world. . . . There are a lot more important things about a man than the color of his skin."

One of four variants of the song in the editor's files, this was forwarded by Roger D. Abrahams from Austin, Texas, where it was apparently current among college students. A second text was learned at UCLA by the editor, circa 1957. Another Texas variant lays the child on the doorstep of a former governor of Texas, suggesting that the song might persist in oral tradition by the expedient of attaching itself to local politicians.

The Western Kentucky Folklore Archives at UCLA contain six texts of the song collected at Murray State College between 1955 and 1958. Curator D. K. Wilgus added that it was sometimes tagged to local basketball players. He also noted that a variant of the song was contributed to the UCLA Folklore Archives by Folsom's daughter.

Getz 1 (p. P-8) prints a text of "Big Jim" in which the "southern bastard gentleman" sits in the legislature while the girl sells "chunks of her behind" in Dothan, Alabama. Getz also mentions another with air force currency in which the woman meets a "rich old gentleman" and ultimately "walks the streets of Austin." In sum, this seems to have a vital and continuing oral tradition.

The uncredited version recorded on *The Unexpurgated Folk Songs of Men* is sung to the melody of the nineteenth-century gospel song "Life's Railway to Heaven"—a melody also used for such southern mountain folk lyrics as "I Don't Want Your Millions, Mister" and "East Virginia." For the original song, copyrighted in 1890 and credited to M. E. Alley and Charles D. Tillman, see Cohen (pp. 611-18).

The tune here is something of a cross between the original melody of "She Was Poor" and the country song "The True and Trembling Brakeman." A melody for that song, recorded at least six times between 1927 and 1939, is in Cohen (p. 257).

133

The Hairs on Her Dicky Di Do

Folk songs are still being made. Though the melody for this celebration, "The Ash Grove," is old and long familiar, the words are seemingly of more recent vintage.

The maid of the mountain, she pees like a bloody fountain
And the hairs of her dicky di do hang down to her knees.

Chorus:
Oh, the hairs, oh, the hairs,
Oh, the hairs on her dicky di do hang down to her knees.
One black one, one white one, and one with a bit of shite on
And the hairs of her dicky di do hang down to her knees.

If she were my daughter, I'd have them cut shorter,
And the hairs of her dicky di do hang down to her knees.

I smelt it. I felt it. By God it's like velvet!
And the hairs of her dicky di do hang down to her knees.

I've seen it. I've preened it. I've been in between it.
And the hairs on her dicky di do hang down to her knees.

She married an Italian with balls like a stallion.
And the hairs on her dicky di do hang down to her knees.

It took a coal miner to find her vagina.
And the hairs on her dicky di do hang down to her knees.

The earliest report of this song that the editor has found is from F. M. Rivinus of Philadelphia, who learned it circa 1942 in Great Britain.

It does not seem to be widely reported. *The Unexpurgated Folksongs of Men* (Berkeley: International Blues Record Club, 1964) and Indiana University's Folklore Archives have it, the latter in a 1967 collection of rugby songs compiled by David Zimmerman.

Two more recent variants, the one perhaps Irish, the other Australian are on *Barely Alive* (Sault Antlers Recordings) and in Hogbotel and Ffuckes (p. 63).

The single version in the editor's collection is from the singing of Walter Burbridge of Los Angeles in 1980. Burbridge learned it from the singing of an English roommate in San Francisco about 1970.

As American
As Mom's Apple Pie

Here's to America, land of the push,
Where a bird in the hand is worth two in the bush,
But if in that bush a fair maiden should stand,
Then a push in the bush is worth two in the hand.
—Collected by Robert Griffis, in Los Angeles, 1958
(Courtesy of Wayland D. Hand)

A MERICAN folk tradition, bawdy or otherwise, has produced far fewer ballads narrating a story than has the British, but it has fashioned numbers of parodies, loosely grouped jokes in rhymed form, and items of social commentary and description.

The reason for this is at least partly a result of the increased tempo of contemporary life. People are less inclined, and perhaps even have less time, to patiently listen to a song which may take five or ten minutes to sing. The pattern of entertainment, especially of the all-pervasive popular music, is for short songs, one following hard upon the other. This entertainment-oriented imperative establishes a model that even the underground of bawdry follows. The older, longer ballads are truncated. Songs of more recent vintage tend to "get on and get off" quickly. The joke, the laugh, become all the more important. Still, American songs and ballads on earthy themes manage not only to entertain, but even to provide a cautionary tale and a moral in some cases.

Frankie and Johnny

Apparently, there was a Frankie—general consensus would have her a hustler in St. Louis—and apparently she supported a natural-born easeman named Albert or Johnny. But Albert or Johnny ran out of luck and died unexpectedly, as they said, along the river before the turn of the century, from a sudden attack of lead poisoning.

137

Sometime after the fact, the habitués of various fancy houses in St. Louis were singing this song. Eventually an expurgated version made the hit parade and the tragedy of Frankie became a national treasure.

[A]

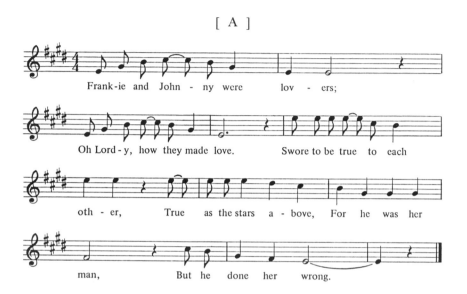

Frank-ie and John - ny were lov - ers;
Oh Lord - y, how they made love. Swore to be true to each
oth - er, True as the stars a - bove, For he was her
man, But he done her wrong.

Frankie and Johnny were lovers;
Oh, Lordy, how they made love.
Swore to be true to each other,
True as the stars above,
    For he was her man,
    But he done her wrong.

Frankie was a good girl,
Most everybody knows.
She gave a hundred dollars
To Johnny for a suit of clothes.
    'Cause he was her man,
    But he done her wrong.

Frankie worked in a crib-joint
Behind a grocery store.
She gave all her money to Johnny;
He spent it on high-tone whores.
    God damn his soul.
    He done her wrong.

138

Frankie was a fucky hussy,
That's what all the pimps said,
And they kept her so damn busy,
She never got out of bed
But he done her wrong.
God damn his soul.

Frankie, she knowed her business,
She hung out a sign on the door:
"Fresh fish cost you a dollar here,
Fancy fucking cost ten cents more."
He was her man.
He done her wrong.

Frankie went down to Fourth Street.
She ordered a glass of beer,
Said to the big bartender man,
"Has my ever-lovin' man been here?"
God damn his soul.
He done her wrong.

"I couldn't tell you no story.
I couldn't tell you no lie.
I saw your Johnny an hour ago
With a whore called Alice Bly.
God damn his soul,
He was doin' you wrong."

Frankie ran back to her crib-joint,
Fixin' to do him some harm.
She took out a bindle of horse
And shot it right up her arm.
God damn his soul.
He was doing her wrong.

Frankie put on her kimono;
This time it wasn't for fun
'Cause right underneath it
Was a great big forty-four gun.
God damn his soul.
He done her wrong.

She ran along Fish Alley,
Looked in a window so high,
Saw her lovin' Johnny
Finger-fucking Alice Bly.
He was doing her wrong.
God damn his soul.

139

Frankie went to the front door.
She rang the whorehouse bell.
"Stand back you pimps and whores
Or I'll blow you straight to hell.
    I'm hunting my man.
    Who's doin' me wrong."

Frankie drew back her kimono,
Pulled out her big forty-four.
Tooty-toot-toot, three times she shoot,
Left him lyin' on that whorehouse floor.
    She shot her man
    'Cause he done her wrong.

"Roll me over, Frankie,
Roll me over slow.
A bullet got me in my right side,
Oh God, it hurts me so.
    You killed your man
    'Cause I done you wrong."

Frankie ran back to her crib-joint,
She fell across the bed,
Saying, "Lord, oh Lord, I've shot my man.
I've shot my Johnny dead.
    He was my man.
    God damn his soul."

Three little pieces of crepe
Hanging on the crib-joint door
Signifies that Johnny
Will never be a pimp no more.
    God damn his soul.
    He done her wrong.

"Bring out your rubber-tired buggy.
Bring out your rubber-tired hack.
I'm taking my man to the graveyard;
I ain't gonna bring him back.
    He was my man
    But he done me wrong."

They brought a rubber-tired buggy,
And brought out a rubber-tired hack.
Thirteen pimps went to the cemetery
But only twelve of them came back.
    He's dead and gone,
    He was doing her wrong.

Frankie went out to the graveyard,
Sorry as she could be,
Ridin' behind a whorehouse band
Playin' "Nearer My God to Thee."
    He was her man.
    He was doing her wrong.

Frankie stood up in the courtroom.
"I'm not talkin' no sass.
I didn't shoot Johnny in the first degree.
I shot him in his big black ass.
    He was my man.
    He was doin' me wrong."

The judge said, "Stand up, Frankie,
Stand up and dry your tears.
You know murder's a hangin' crime
But I'll give you ninety-nine years.
    He was your man.
    But he was doin' you wrong."

The last time I seen Frankie
She was ridin' on that train
Takin' her to the jail house,
Never bring her back again.
    He was her man.
    God damn his soul.

[B]

Frankie and Johnnie were lovers.
Oh my God, how they could love.
They swore to be true to each other
As true as the stars above,
    He was her man
    And he done her wrong.

Frankie she lived in a crip house,
A crip house with only one door.
She gave all her money to Johnnie
Who spent it on a parlor house whore.
    And he was her man
    What done her wrong.

Frankie, she was a good girl,
As all the neighborhood knows.
She gave her Johnnie a hundred dollar bill
Just to buy himself some clothes.

141

And he was her man
What done her wrong.

One night when Frankie was lonely
And nobody came to call,
She put on her dirty kimona [*sic*]
And went down to the nickel crawl.
    She was looking for her man
    What was doin't [*sic*] her wrong.

Oh, Frankie went down to the corner
Just to buy herself a beer.
She said to the big bartender
"Has my lovin' man been here?
    I'm looking for the man
    What's a-doing me wrong."

"Well, I ain't gonna tell you no stories,
And I ain't gonna tell you no lies,
But Johnnie was here 'bout an hour ago
With that high yaller Nelly Bly.
    God damn his soul.
    He's cheating the game."

Oh, Frankie went down to the hop-joint.
This time it wasn't for fun.
Underneath her dirty kimona,
She had a big forty-four gun
    To shoot the man
    What was doing her wrong.

And when she reached the hop-joint
And she looked in the window so high,
There she saw Johnnie a-sittin',
Finger-fuckin' Nelly Bly.
    The son of a bitch,
    He was dealin' it cold.

Frankie, she knocked at the hop-joint
And she rang the hop-joint bell.
She yelled, "Clear out, all you whores and pimps
I'm going to blow my lover to hell.
    God damn his balls,
    He's a-doing me wrong."

Johnnie heard Frankie a-comin'
And yelled, "My God, don't shoot!"
But Frankie pulled her forty-four Gatling gun,
Five times she shoot, tooty-toot-toot,

Right into the man
What had done her wrong.

"Oh, roll me over gently.
Roll me over slow.
Roll me over on my right side
So the bullets won't hurt me so,
    For I was your man
      Though I done you wrong."

"Oh, roll up your rubber-tired hearses,
Hearses all lined with black.
Take me out to the cemetery
And I'll never, never, never come back.
    Oh, I was your man
      And I done you wrong."

"Oh, lock me up in the dungeon
And throw the fuckin' key away.
I've gone and killed my lover, Johnnie,
And I never want to live another day.
    Oh, I've killed my man
      What done me wrong."

But the sheriff said, "Frankie, don't worry.
I guess it was all for the best.
He was always pimping and whoring around.
My God! he was an awful pest
    And he was your man,
      And he done you wrong."

And the judge, he said, "Looka here, Frankie,
This case is as plain as can be.
You went and shot your lover, Johnnie,
And it's murder in the first degree.
    You killed your man,
      What's been doing you wrong."

Frankie said, "Judge, I'm sorry
For all that's come to pass,
But I never shot him in the first degree.
I shot him in his big fat ass
    For he was my man
      And he done me wrong."

Frankie now sits in the parlor,
Underneath the 'lectric fan,
Warning her little granddaughters,
"Beware the God-damn man.

Yes, he'll do you wrong
Just as sure as you're born."

[C]

Frankie and Johnny were lovers,
Lawdy, oh God, how they loved,
Swore to be true to each other,
As true as the blue sky above.
    He was her man,
      But he was doin' her wrong.

Frankie she worked in a hump-house,
A hump-house with only two doors,
Gave all her money to Johnny
Who spent it on the parlor-house whores.
    Damn his soul,
      For he was doin' her wrong.

One night when Frankie was lonely,
Nobody came out to call.
Frankie put on her kimonie
And went out to the nickel crawl
    Lookin' for the man
      That was doin' her wrong.

Frankie blew down to the corner,
Ordered herself up some beer,
Said to the gentle bartender,
"Have you seen my lovin' Johnny here?
    For he's my man,
      But he's doin' me wrong."

"I don't want to tell you no story.
I don't want to tell you no lie,
But Johnny was here about an hour ago
With that fat bitch Nellie Bly.
    He's your man,
      But he's doin' you wrong."

Frankie blew back to the hump-house.
This time 'twasn't for fun.
Under her dirty kimona,
She packed a big .44 gun,
    Lookin' for the man
      That was doin' her wrong.

Frankie blew into the hump-house,
Didn't even ring the bell,

144

Said, "Look out, all you pimps and whores
Or I'll blow you all straight to hell.
    I'm lookin' for the man,
    That's doin' me wrong."

She went on back through the hallway,
Looked over a transom so high.
There she saw her lovin' boy
Finger-fucking Nellie Bly,
    God damn her soul.
    But he was doin' her wrong.

Johnny saw Frankie a-comin',
Said, "My God, Frankie, don't shoot!"
But Frankie pulled out her big .44 gun
And the gun went root-i-toot-toot.
    She shot the man
    That was doin' her wrong.

"Bring on your rubber-tired hearses,
Fill 'em up plumb full of maques [sic]
For they're taking my Johnny to the cemetery,
And they'll never bring his penis back,
    Best part of the man
    That was doin' me wrong."

[D]

Frankie was a good woman,
As everybody knows.
She hocked her rings and all her things
To buy her man some clothes.
    He was her man,
    But he done her wrong.

Frankie and Albert were sweethearts.
They had a quarrel one day.
Said Albert to Frankie, "I'm done with you
And I'm goin' away."
    He was her man,
    But he done her wrong.

Frankie broke down crying.
She bowed her head with woe.
When she looked up she was all alone,
And said, "Where did my Albert go?
    He was my man
    And he's doing me wrong."

Frankie went down to the barroom.
She ordered a bottle of beer.
Said Frankie to the bartender,
"Has my lovin' Albert been here?
    He was my man
    But he's done me wrong."

Said the bartender to Frankie,
"I'll tell you no stories, no lies.
Your lovin' man left an hour ago
With a woman that you despise.
    He was your man
    But he's doing you wrong."

Then Frankie went into the hock shop.
She didn't go there for fun.
She hocked her rings and all her clothes
To buy a great big Forty-one.
    She's going to find her man
    Because he done her wrong.

Frankie started for home then.
She had blood in her eye.
"If I find that dark-skinned man of mine.
He sure is goin' to die.
    He was my man,
    But he's done me wrong."

Frankie climbed the back door stairs.
Looked in the transom high.
There she saw her lovin' man
Bankin' old Nancy Bly.
    He was her man,
    But he's doing her wrong.

Albert rolled over and saw her,
Said "Frankie don't you shoot."
But Frankie pulled that old Forty-one.
It went root-a-toot-a-toot-toot!
    She shot her man
    'Cause he done her wrong.

Frankie shot him the first time.
Then Frankie shot him twice.
Frankie shot him the third time
And he hollared, "Ah, Jesus Christ!"
    He was her man
    But he done her wrong.

146

"Turn me over gently.
Raise my head up high.
I want to see that gal of mine
Once more before I die.
    I was her man
    But I done her wrong."

Then Frankie went down to Misses Jones'.
She fell down on her knees.
She said, "Misses Jones, I done shot your son
But won't you forgive me please?
    He was my man
    But he done me wrong."

"Now go call a policeman
And have him take me away,
Lock me down in a dungeon dark
And throw the old keys away.
    My heart's like lead
    'Cause my Albert's dead."

"Bring on your rubber-tired carriages.
Bring on your rubber-tired hack.
They're goin' to take Albert to the graveyard
And they ain't a-goin' to bring him back.
    He was my man
    But he done me wrong."

The jailer gave her coffee.
The jailer gave her tea.
He gave her everything she wanted
Except the good old jailhouse key.
    She shot her man
    Because he done her wrong.

Frankie stole out one morning.
She didn't make a sound.
She left a note on the jailer's desk
Sayin' she was Alabama bound.
    She shot her man
    Because he done her wrong.

The angels up in heaven
Said, "Here's something we don't get.
Frankie shot Albert a month ago
And the fool ain't got her yet!
    He was her man
    But he done her wrong."

This is one of the handful of American-made ballads most frequently collected prior to 1960. For some estimate of the song's popularity, see Belden (pp. 330 ff.). To the references there, add those in Brown, 2 (pp. 589 ff.); and Fuld, *American* (pp. 20-21). See also Spaeth (pp. 34 ff.); and Henry (p. 338). It is also accorded extensive discussion in John R. David's St. Louis University thesis, "Tragedy in Ragtime," according to D. K. Wilgus. Hoffmann has assigned to it motif number Q411.0.3.

For all the prior reports of the song, "Frankie and Johnny" has been openly printed in all its flaming glory only in the underground *Immortalia* ([1927]: 49-52); and the 1968 reprint (pp. 67-70); and the first edition of this book in 1969.

The song does not appear to be as old as some sources would have it. Fuld (pp. 233-35) puts it at about the turn of the century, when it was copyrighted as "He Done Me Wrong" by Hughie Cannon in 1904. (While Fuld does not say so, it may well be that Cannon got the song from oral tradition, indeed, that he cleaned for publication a bawdy ballad about Frankie and her lovin' Albert.) Bruce Buckley's 1962 doctoral dissertation at Indiana concludes that Johnny does not appear as a hero until 1912. It was about this time that Donald C. Foster of Binghamton, New York, heard the song sung as early as 1912 or 1913 at a gathering of students in the back room of a saloon in Ithaca, New York; it was sung by a "Southerner" to piano accompaniment, according to a letter Foster wrote Robert W. Gordon in 1925.

Other versions or variants of the song are in MacGregor (pp 17-20). Randolph's "Unprintable" manuscript has two fragments (pp. 506-8). Getz (pp. DE-2 and F-17) has two air force parodies, one dating from the First World War. Neither is bawdy.

The "A" version of the song was sent to the editor by an anonymous Los Angeles radio listener who wrote only that the song was learned in Cleveland, Ohio, prior to 1940. The editor has "corrected" what appeared to be errors in the barring of the melody included by the radio listener.

Contributed by Hubert Canfield of Pittsford, New York, the "B" text is number 2087 in Gordon's "Inferno" in the Library of Congress's Archive of American Folk Song. In sending the song on to Gordon on November 5, 1926, Canfield added what he called an "unhappy variant" stanza:

> Frankie climbed up the scaffold
> As calm as a girl can be,

And turning her eyes to heaven, she said,
"Good Lord, I'm a-coming to thee."

Mr. Canfield added the comment that this is "the version that Carl Sandburg says is the best he's ever seen."

The "C" text too is from Gordon, obtained from a California student in 1921. J. Barre Toelken forwarded it from the Gordon Collection of American Folk Song, University of Oregon. The correspondent spelled the pimp's name "Johnie."

At the end of the song, either Gordon or his informant (who was probably white) noted: "This song is pure Negro. I got it from a man that has played in cafes, and he said that it is universal among the Negroes. I have heard it before myself. There are probably more verses to it than are here."

The "D" text too is from the Gordon "Inferno," mailed to him by C. Becker of Chicago, Illinois, who said he learned it at Camp Mills, Long Island, in 1917.

The "nickel crawl" in versions "B" and "C" refers to a taxi-dance charging a nickel admission.

Stackolee

Stackolee, or Stagolee, or Stackerlee, or Stagger Lee, or Stack-o'-Dollars — he's known by all these names — is one of the legendary giants of Negro folklore. Not only is he celebrated in this ballad, but Stack' can boast of dozens of tales and legends that circulate about him. His prodigious feats far surpass those of his Bunyunesque rivals, for who among them can claim to have caused the San Francisco earthquake merely by pulling out the water pipes in a local saloon?

Stackolee's strength was that of ten, not because his heart was pure, but because the Devil made a bargain with him. In exchange for Stack's soul, Old Scratch gave the badman a magic John B. Stetson hat. When a rival tough stole or won the hat in a card game, Stack' killed him.

[A]

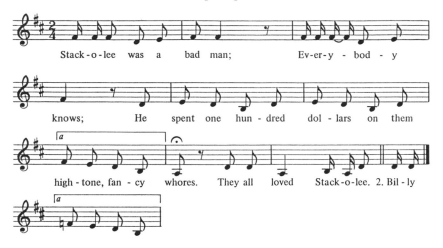

Stack-o-lee was a bad man; Ev-er-y - bod - y
knows; He spent one hun - dred dol - lars on them
high-tone, fan - cy whores. They all loved Stack-o-lee. 2. Bil-ly

Stackolee was a bad man;
Everybody knows
Spent one hundred dollars
On them high-tone, fancy whores.
   They all loved Stackolee.

Billy Lyons said, "Stackolee,
Please don't take my life.
You make an orphan of my son,
And a widow of my wife."
   Mean old bad man, Stackolee.

"I don't give a damn for your son.
I don't give a damn for your wife.
You done stole my Stetson hat.
I'm going to take your life."
   Mean old bad man, Stackolee.

What do you know about this?
What the hell you know about that?
Stackolee killed Billy Lyons
Over a damned old Stetson hat.
   Poor old Stackolee.

They took him to the jailhouse
And they threw his ass in a cell.
All the pimps and whores went on down

To bid poor Stack farewell.
   Poor old Stackolee.

Policeman said to Stackolee—
His eyes all filled with tears—
"The judge sure won't be hard on you;
He'll just give you ninety-nine years."
   Poor old Stackolee.

Stack's girl was a good girl,
None of that low-down trash.
"I'll make the bail for Stackolee,
Give that sheriff a piece of ass."
   Poor old Stackolee.

She hustled in the morning.
She hustled in the night.
She got so thin from hustling
She was an awful sight.
   She'd get the dough for Stackolee.

One night it rained like hell
And she had an awful time.
She said, "I won't break Stackolee's luck."
She shook her fanny for a dime,
   Making bail for Stackolee.

Then she got a dirty old crib
Right behind the jail.
She hung a sign on the front door:
"Fresh fish here for sale."
   She'd get the bail for Stackolee.

One night she had more bad luck.
An old nigger give her a buck.
She said, "You know I got no change,
So give yourself another fuck.
   For poor old Stackolee."

One night there came a telephone call
And everybody cried.
It said that at nine o'clock
Poor old Stack had fried.
   Means a funeral for Stackolee.

When Stackolee's girl friend
Heard this awful news,
She was lyin' on the torn bedspread
Havin' the electric chair blues,
   Havin' the blues for Stackolee.

151

When they got to the graveyard
And saw that awful hole,
Those pimps and whores fell on their knees
And asked the Lord to save their souls.
   Poor old Stackolee.

A high yeller pimp stepped out,
Said, "I ain't got much to say,"
Pulled a bindle and took a shot,
Said, "Like Stack, I'm on my way."
   Poor old Stackolee.

They laid out poor old Stackolee
And laid him in his last hole.
All the whores and pimps gathered 'round and said
"Lord have mercy on his soul.
   Poor old Stackolee."

[B]

One cold an' frosty Christmas night
Stackerlee and Billy Lyons had an awful fight.
   Everybody talk about Stackerlee.

Said Billy Lyons to Stackerlee, "Don't you take my life.
Remember my two children and my loving wife!"
   Everybody talk about Stackerlee.

"Care nothing 'bout your children, care nothin' 'bout your wife.
You spit in my new Stetson hat, an' I'm going' to take your life."
   Everybody talk about Stackerlee.

Billy Lyons, Billy Lyons staggered through the door
'Cause Stackerlee had got him with his forty-four.
   Everybody talk about Stackerlee.

Dogs did howl, dogs did bark,
When Stackerlee the murderer came creepin' through the dark!
   Everybody talk about Stackerlee.

Sergeant and the policeman—Stackerlee behind a tree.
Sergeant say to Stackerlee, "Better come along with me!"
   Everybody talk about Stackerlee.

Up in the jail cell, Stackerlee in despair
Hears them repairin' that ole electric chair.
   Everybody talk about Stackerlee.

Little Lily Sheldon, when she first hear the news,
Sitting on her bedside, lacin' up her shoes.
   Everybody talk about Stackerlee.

She wired to Stackerlee, "Don't you weep an' moan.
Your honey babe'll get you out o' jail, if she have to sell her home!"
   Everybody talk about Stackerlee.

Rubber tires on the carriages, rubber tires on the hack,
Took poor old Stackerlee to the cemetery, never to bring him back.
   Everybody talk about Stackerlee.

Rounders, rounders, you take my advice,
Stop your drinkin' whiskey, stop your shakin' dice.
   Everybody talk about Stackerlee.

Stackerlee, Stackerlee, what do you think o' that?
Killed old Billy Lyons over a damned ole Stetson hat.
   Everybody talk about Stackerlee.

What a bad man he must be, with his forty-four an' his knife,
Never hesitate a minute for to take your life.
   Everybody talk about Stackerlee.

This Negro ballad is widespread throughout the South, the core of the story retold in tale, legend and toast. Strangely enough, it has appeared in comparatively few collections.

Abrahams (pp. 78-83 and 123-36) offers a perceptive analysis in socio-psychological terms to accompany three texts collected from Philadelphia blacks. His notes include a comprehensive bibliography and discography of the song, to which may be added the versions sung by Dave Van Ronk (Prestige 13056); Tom Paley on *The New Lost City Ramblers*, 4 (Folkways FA 2399); and Clarence Edwards, *Country Music Jam Sessions* (Folk-Lyric 111). The Edwards version is only faintly related to the ballad. So too the text in Rosenbaum (pp. 104-5). One Archibald—identified as Speckled Red by Neil Rosenberg—recorded the song commercially in the early 1950s on Imperial X5358. *Immortalia* ([1927]: 33-35, and the 1968 reprint, 52-54) have a seventeen-stanza version. Bruce Jackson prints a version of the Stagolee tale in toast form in "Circus and Street: Psychosocial Aspects of the Black Toast," in *Journal of American Folklore* (85 [1972]: 123-39); Wepman, Newman, and Binderman (pp. 147-50) have another.

Stackolee apparently was a real person, the local bully who ran things circa 1870 in the black section of Memphis, Tennessee. His flouting of the white man's law—no doubt tacitly assisted by a police force traditionally little interested in black intra-racial crime—coupled with his high-handed manner gave to him a reputation far beyond his just deserts. His seeming ability to avoid the clutches of the law and the vengeance of rivals became encrusted with a superstitious aura: he had, some legends say, sold his soul to the Devil in exchange for very mortal powers, sexual and physical. The Devil's end of the bargain lay in a magic John B. Stetson hat, which Stackolee's rival, Billy Lyon, tries to steal. This occasions Billy's death, and the ballad. J. R. David, in his St. Louis University thesis "Tragedy in Ragtime," makes an extended effort to identify the original Stack-o-Lee.

Bruce Jackson, "Stagolee Stories: A Badman Goes Gentle" (*Southern Folklore Quarterly* 29 [1965]: 228-33), recounts tales of Stack's considerable talents aside from devil-dealings.

Though the shorter, more lyric forms of the ballad can be collected, there is some question whether extended *ballad* versions of this song persist in oral tradition. The editor has collected only one version of the longer ballad—the "A" text and tune here. It comes from John Hibbert of Los Angeles, circa 1962. Hibbert, a knowledgeable folk song aficionado, used a melodic variant of the tune Paley sings; the phonograph record may have "contaminated" or reinformed Hibbert's version. According to Roger D. Abrahams, Paley's melody comes ultimately from a recording made by Mississippi John Hurt (Okeh 8654) in 1928 under the title "Stack O'Lee Blues." Hibbert pasted the text together from print and oral sources, at least one of the latter a black semi-professional guitarist who performed on weekends in Los Angeles under the name of "Travelin' Man." The editor has been told that "Travelin' Man" disappeared from his haunts about 1960; rumor had it that he died from an overdose of heroin.

The theme of the faithful girlfriend earning bail and her boyfriend's freedom on her back appears also in "I'll Fuck You for a Nickel" in Randolph's "Unprintable" manuscript (pp. 308-10).

The "B" text was sent by C. E. Roe in June, 1929, to Robert W. Gordon. It is No. 3756 in the Gordon "Inferno" collection in the Library of Congress Archive of American Folk Song. Roe noted his text was written down by Kenneth Olesen of Duluth, Minnesota, in 1903.

Casey Jones

This native American ballad exists in two very distinct versions. One is the story of the fatal train wreck of Engine 382 on the Illinois Central near Vaughan, Mississippi, on April 30, 1900; the other is a mélange of verses concerning Casey's sexual adventures. It would be a toss-up as to which is the more popular.

[A]

Casey Jones was a son-of-a-bitch,
Drove a hot steam engine through a forty-foot ditch,
Pissed on the whistle and he shit on the bell
And he went through Chicago like a bat out of hell.

Chorus:
Casey Jones mounted to his cabin.
Casey Jones had his pecker in his hand.
Casey Jones mounted to his cabin,
Said, "Look out, ladies, I'm a railroad man."

It happened one morning about a quarter to four,
Pulled up in front of a whorehouse door,

155

Climbed through the window with his cock in his hand
And said, "I'll prove I'm a railroad man."

He lined a hundred whores up against the wall,
And he bet ten dollars he could fuck them all.
He fucked ninety-eight and his balls turned blue.
He took a shot of whiskey and he fucked the other two.

Casey Jones said before he died
There were two more drinks he'd like to try.
"Tell me, Casey, what can they be?"
"A glass of water and a cup of tea."

[B]

Casey Jones was a son-of-a-bitch.
His balls were covered with the whorehouse itch.
He went to the door with his pecker in his hand,
Says to the lady, "I'm a railroad man."

Casey Jones said before he died
There were five more things he'd like to ride:
Bicycle, tricycle, automobile,
Bow-legged woman and a ferris wheel.

Casey said before he died
There were two more drinks he'd like to try.
"Well, tell me, Casey, what can they be?"
"A cup of coffee and a cup of tea."

They were rolling down the line 'bout half past two.
Casey pissed in the fire and the boiler blew.
The fireman drowned in a yellow stream
And for miles around you could see yellow steam.

Unlike "Frankie and Johnny" and "Stackolee," whose bawdy verses serve to elaborate upon a story essentially non-ribald, this version of "Casey Jones" has nothing to do with the native American ballad that usually chronicles the fatal last run of John Luther "Cayce" Jones on the Illinois Central's Chicago and New Orleans Limited. It is rather one of a group of satires or parodies of familiar folk songs.

Commenting on the relationship of the tragic "Lord Randall" (Child 12) to the sprightly "Billy Boy," Bertrand Bronson has bemoaned this process of transformation in oral tradition:

Such, incidentally appears to be the destined end of too many fine old tragic ballads: they are not to be permitted a dignified demise, but we must madly play with our forefathers' relics and make a mock of their calamities. The high seriousness of the parents is the children's favorite joke. So it has been with "Earl Brand," "Young Beichan," "Lord Lovel," "Lady Alice," "The Mermaid," "Bessie Bell and Mary Gray," "Queen Jane," and "The Three Ravens." (Bronson, 1, 191.)

To that list might be added "The Golden Vanity," now collected most often as a children's street rhyme.

One traditional ballad about the fatal train wreck was written shortly after the accident by Wallace or Wallis "Wash" Saunders, most authorities agree. A black roundhouse worker in Canton, Mississippi, Saunders used an older, yet unidentified train wreck song as a model. Cohen (p. 147) posits a second or vaudeville song, copyrighted by Eddie Newton and T. Lawrence Seibert in 1909, that existed concurrently in oral tradition. Cohen also delineates a third song about Casey, this essentially the Newton-Siebert text with added verses. Sandburg has a version (pp. 366-69) distinguishable for the added stanzas.

It is those added stanzas that apparently mutated into the bawdy song, but sung to the very popular tune of the vaudeville version. Mack McCormick, "The Damn Tinkers" (*American Folk Music Occasional* 1 [1964]: 12), mentions an early version of the familiar train-wreck ballad, complaining that whites added an off-color stanza to the song:

> Casey said before he died,
> "There's two more women I'd like to try."
> "Tell me what can they bed?"
> "A cross-eyed nigger and a Japanee."

In truth, black singers too added bawdy material to the train wreck ballad before Seibert and Newton heard a traditional song or songs about the high-balling engineer, and published their now "standard" version in 1909. Odum and Johnson (p. 207) include this stanza:

> Went on down to de depot track,
> Beggin' my honey to take me back,
> She turn 'round some two or three times:
> "Take you back when you learn to grind."

See also, Abrahams, *Positively Black* (pp. 93-94) for a toast from Louisville that elaborates on the third stanza here.

The only bawdy version collected prior to this seems to be in the Randolph, "Unprintable" manuscript (pp. 508-11), where two of four texts are dated to 1912 and 1920.

See Cohen (pp. 132-57); and Cazden, Haufrecht, and Studer (p.

598); and Robert Y. Deake, Jr., "Casey Jones: The Man and the Song," in *Tennessee Folklore Society Bulletin* (19 [1953]: 95-101) for discussions of the early history of the song. Cazden's separate *Notes* (p. 114) gives additional citations. References to the classic American ballad may be found in Laws, *Native American Balladry* (p. 204); Brown 2 (p. 510); and Lomax, *Folk Songs of North America* (p. 564); to which may be added the version in Hubbard (p. 364). Wallrich (pp. 31-33, 35, 71, 155); and Getz 1 (pp. C-1,2), have air force parodies to the same tune. Dolph prints an army parody from World War I (p. 180). Randolph's "Unprintable" anthology (pp. 503-4) has a song modeled in part upon "Casey" entitled "Peggy Howatt."

The two variants of "Casey Jones" printed here were notated by the editor from the singing of insurance salesman Stuart Grayboyse and bookseller Ray Fisher as they swapped verses at a party in Los Angeles in 1964. Both men, then approximately 30, had learned the song while in college, ten years earlier. Their stanzas are descended from the vaudeville tradition.

No Balls at All

The theme of the young girl forced to marry the much older man — often for financial reasons — occurs often in folklore and song. The girl usually manages to find solace for her lifeless marriage bed in the arms of a more virile companion. "No Balls at All" is unusual only in that the cuckoldry extends to the second generation.

[A]

Oh, lis-ten, my chil-dren, a stor-y you'll hear. A song I will sing you; 'twill fill you with cheer. A charm-ing young maid-en was wed in the fall. She mar-ried a man who had

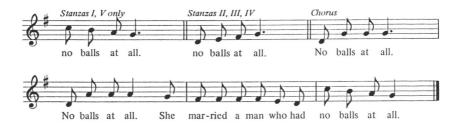

no balls at all.   no balls at all.   No balls at all.

No balls at all.   She mar-ried a man who had no balls at all.

Oh, listen, my children, a story you'll hear.
A song I will sing you; 'twill fill you with cheer.
A charming young maiden was wed in the fall.
She married a man who had no balls at all.

Chorus:
No balls at all. No balls at all.
She married a man who had no balls at all.

The night of the wedding she leaped into bed.
Her breasts were a-heaving; her legs were well spread;
She reached for his penis; his penis was small.
She reached for his balls; he had no balls at all.

"Oh mother, oh mother, oh, what shall I do?
I've married a man who's unable to screw.
For many long years, I've avoided the call,
Now I've married a man who has no balls at all."

"Oh daughter, oh daughter, now don't feel so sad;
I had the same trouble with your dear old dad.
There are lots of young men who will answer the call
Of the wife of a man who has no balls at all."

Now the daughter she followed her mother's advice,
And she found the proceedings exceedingly nice,
And a bouncing young baby was born in the fall
To the wife of the man who had no balls at all.

Spoken: No testicles whatsoever!

[B]

Listen my people and to you I'll tell
The tale of a couple I once knew real well.
The maid she was skinny and not very tall.
The man he was large but had no balls at all.

Chorus:
    No balls at all, no balls at all.
    For she married a man who had no balls at all.

The very first night when they crawled into bed,
Her cheeks they were rosy, her lips they were red.
She reached for his penis and found it quite small
For she married a man who had no balls at all.

"Oh mother, oh mother, I wish I were dead
And buried along with my poor maiden head.
My sorrows are many, my pleasures are small
For I've married a man who has no balls at all."

"Oh daughter, oh daughter, why are you so sad?
Just do to your man like I did to your dad.
There's many a man who will answer the call
Of a wife whose husband has no balls at all."

Some women are pure and free from sin,
But nine out of ten have their bung holes pushed in.

Last chorus:
    Bungholes pushed in, bungholes pushed in.
    But nine out of ten have their bungholes pushed in.

This is a ribald member of a group of folk songs dealing with the mismatch in years of marriage partners. The theme and sentiment of "No Balls at All" are shared by the Scots-English-Irish songs "An Old Man He Courted Me," "My Husband's Got No Courage in Him," "The Old Man from Over the Sea," and others.

For references to "An Old Man," see Fowke, *Traditional Singers and Songs from Ontario* (pp. 32-33, 167); and her article "Bawdy Ballads in Print, Record and Tradition" (*Sing and String*, 2 No. 2 [Summer, 1963]: 3-9). Other texts are in Purslow, *Marrow Bones* (p. 66); Sedley, *Seeds of Love* (p. 230-31); Karpeles, *Sharp's* 2 (pp. 27-29); Palmer, *Vaughan Williams* (pp. 183-84), as "I Courted an Old Man;" McCarthy (pp. 72-73), as "Maids When You're Young"; and Morgan 2 (pp. 126-27), as "Never Wed an Old Man." See too Karpeles, *Sharp's* 2 (p. 30), "Never Marry an Old Man."

"My Husband's Got No Courage" is in Sedley (p. 232); and Purslow, *Wanton Seed* (p. 82). Purslow also has the similar "Seven Months I've Been Married" (p. 103). Frankie Armstrong sings "The Old Man from Over the Sea" on *The Bird in the Bush* (Topic 12T135).

Robert Burns had similar sentiments in mind when he fashioned this stanza in "What Can a Young Lassie?":

He's always compleenin' frae morin to e'ein;
He hoasts [coughs] and he hirples [limps] the weary day lang:
He's doylt [crazed] and he's dozin [shriveled]; his blude it is frozen,
O, dreary's the night wi' a crazy auld man.

Burns's last stanza is much like that in "No Balls":

My auld auntie Katie upon me taks [sic] pity,
I'll do my endeavor to follow her plan;
I'll cross him and wrack [vex] him until I heartbreak him,
And then his auld brass will buy me a new pan.

Dick (p. 417) credits the words to Burns, but it may be that the song, like so many others of the poet, was modeled upon, or suggested by, or an extension of, a song in oral tradition. See also the original version of "John Anderson, My Jo," in *The Merry Muses* (pp. 114-15).

Two Irish members of the group, with the sexual longing delicately put, "Seanduine Chill Chocain" ("The Old Man of Kilcockan") and "An Seanduine" ("The Old Man"), are in O'Sullivan (pp. 73-76). The subject is treated too in Brian Merriman's story *Cuirt an Mheadhon Oidhche (The Midnight Court)*.

Songs such as these are perhaps the inevitable by-product of that land's traditional patterns of family structure and farm ownership. As detailed in Conrad Arensberg's *The Irish Countryman* (New York, 1937), these social institutions tended to create "May-December" matches. The oldest son in a culture that followed the rule of primogeniture could marry only after his father retired and the land passed to the son. Until then he was the "boy," no matter his age, unable to bring a wife home to his own farm, and not ready for marriage until he could support a family with the produce of his own land.

In the United States, the theme of the May-December marriage is in "Get Away, Old Man, Get Away." Shay's version, in *More Pious Friends* (pp. 132-33) has this verse:

Be sure to marry a young man, no matter what the cost,
For an old man's like an apple when bitten by the frost.
For an old man he is old, an old man he is gray,
But a young man knows just how to love—
Get away, old man, get away!

Similar in content and tone is the fragmentary "I'd Wouldn't Marry an Old Man," in Randolph's "Unprintable" (p. 332); and his version of "The Old Man from Over the Sea," "With the Old Thing A-Shaking" (pp. 333-36), sung to the melody of "Barbara Allen."

According to Legman (*Horn Book*, 377), "No Balls at All" dates from the American Civil War, and was modeled upon a then-topical song, "Nothing to Wear." Laycock (pp. 200-201) dates his version to World War I.

Other texts attributable to British Empire singers include Logue-Vicarion, No. 56; Morgan 1 (pp. 111-12); Hogbotel and Ffuckes (p. 13); and MacGregor (pp. 69-71).

Variants from American sources of "No Balls at All" are in Brand (pp. 30-31), with "hips" substituted for the codlings. *Songs of Roving and Raking* (p. 60) borrows a version from a mimeographed song collection, circa 1960, "published" by students at Caltech in Pasadena, under the title of *Songs of Raunch and Ill-Repute*. A recorded version is on *Unexpurgated Songs of Men*. Hart's *Immortalia*, 3 (pp. 30 ff.), with a tune; and Getz 2 (pp. NN-2, 3) have versions.

Logsdon (pp. 38-41) judges his song, "The Mormon Cowboy," to be a member of the song family, if only for the shared theme of the husband's impotence.

There are seven full versions, four with virtually identical tunes, in the editor's files. Harry Taussig's, from Berkeley, circa 1958-63, has an unusual last stanza:

> The doctor examined the baby that night,
> And swore up and down he'd examined him right.
> The thing that was found was most astounding of all:
> The babe had a penis but no balls at all.

The "A" text and tune here are from a recording made by a former student in Los Angeles in 1960. A variant of the melody carries the cowboy song "The Strawberry Roan."

The "B" text is from the Library of Congress's Gordon "Inferno," No. 3913, dated March 3, 1918, and probably from Cleveland, Ohio. No informant is credited.

Charlotte the Harlot I

Sung to one of the most frequently used tunes in the Anglo-American stock, "Sweet Betsy from Pike" or "Villikins and His Dinah," this song celebrates one of the more famous whores in American literature. Her untimely demise is still lamented in college dormitories and neighborhood bars.

Down in cunt valley where gizzum does flow,
The cocksuckers work for a nickel a blow;
There lived pretty Charlotte, the girl I adore,
My free-fucking, cock-sucking cowpunchers' whore.

Chorus:
Charlotte the harlot, the girl I adore,
The pride of the prairie, the cowpunchers' whore.

She's easy, she's greasy, she works on the street,
And whenever you see her, she's always in heat.
She'll do it for a dollar, take less or take more,
She's Charlotte the harlot, the cowpuncher's whore.

163

One day on the prairie, while riding along,
My seat in the saddle, the reins on my dong,
Who should I meet but the girl I adore,
Charlotte the harlot, the cowpunchers' whore.

One day on the prairie, no pants on her quim,
A rattlesnake saw her and slipped right on in.
She wiggled, she giggled; it tickled down there.
She had a vagina with rattles and hair.

I got off my pony, I reached for her crack.
The damn thing was rattling and biting me back.
I took out my pistol; I aimed for its head.
I missed the damn rattler; I shot her instead.

Her funeral procession was forty miles long,
With a chorus of cowpunchers singing this song:
"Here lies a young maiden who'll screw us no more,
Young Charlotte the harlot, the cowpunchers' whore."

There are as many as seven different songs traveling under the name of "Charlotte the Harlot" in oral tradition. One is a full-dress ballad, similar to this, built on the motif of the woman with a serpent in her cunny. This variation on the *vagina dentata*-castration theme appears also in the story "The Half-Wit and the Eel," in Randolph, *Pissing in the Snow* (pp. 77 ff). Hoffmann has assigned to it the number X712.1.2.1. Related to it is a black "toast" from the Brownsville section of Brooklyn, "Mexicana Rose," printed by Wepman, Newman, and Binderman (pp. 40-48). It begins:

Way down in old Sonora where the pot grows tall,
Vultures fly the skies, and the rattlesnakes crawl.

Scorpions creep over dead men's bones,
And coyotes yelp in blood-curdling tones.

It was in this hot, dry desert waste
That I first came face to face

With the queen of all the whores,
Senorita Bonita, the Mexicana Rose.

The second and third forms of "Charlotte" are celebrations of the lady's particular qualities (see "Charlotte the Harlot II and III," below). "Charlotte IV" is a drinking song, known to rugby players both in the United States and Great Britain.

The fifth form of the song, one not collected by the editor, has "Carolina, the cowpuncher's whore . . . using a stick instead of the end of a cowpuncher's dick," then engaging in sexual intercourse with the narrator's pony. The pony "backfires," dooming Charlotte. Morgan 1 (pp. 157-58) has a four-stanza text. Getz 2 (pp. C-2, 3) is close. His last verse runs:

> I found Carolina all covered with muck;
> She said, "Oh, my dear, what a glorious fuck!"
> Then her sexual organ fell out on the floor,
> And that was the end of the cow-puncher's whore.

Two other forms of the song do not seem to have come to great currency in the United States. Morgan 1 (p. 185) has one, a faint echo of "The Unfortunate Rake," that begins:

> Charlotte the Harlot lay dying,
> A piss-pot supported her head,
> The blow-flies were buzzing around her,
> She lay on her left *** [tit] and said:
>
> Chorus:
> "I've been had by the army, the navy,
> By a bullfighting toreador,
> By dagos and drongos and dingos,
> But never by maggots before.
> So roll back your dirty old ****holes [arseholes?]
> And give me the cream of your ****." [nuts]
> So they rolled back their dirty old ****holes, [arseholes]
> And played "Home Sweet Home" on her guts.

Tate (p. 39) has it as "So roll back your greasy white foreskins. . . ." Laycock (pp. 179-80) offers an Australian version that makes "The Unfortunate Rake" connection clearer:

> "So wrap me in foreskins and frenchies,
> And bury me deep down below,
> Where all those old bludgers can't catch me,
> The place where all good harlots go."

Wendy Lowenstein's "Shocking! Shocking! Shocking!" has a variant from Australian schoolchildren dated to the 1950s:

> Charlotte the harlot lay dying,
> Two pisspots supporting her head,
> Two bastards around her were crying,
> As she rose on her left tit and said,
> "I've been fucked by the men of all nations,
> The Germans, the Japs and the Jews,
> And now I have come to Australia
> To be fucked by bastards like youse."

165

Hogbotel and Ffuckes (p. 23) contains two variants of this song of apparent Australian currency.

The last of the "Charlotte" songs is also of limited oral currency in the United States. The ballad entitled "Lupee" in Getz 2 (pp. LL-6, 7) tells of a three-hour sexual bout between Lupee and a "Texan." It ends with the two of them run over by a truck in a Laredo street. That song contains this memorable stanza:

> The bar was of marble and it was well-built,
> But it shuddered and groaned as he drove to the hilt.
> "Viva la Mexico!" Lupee she cried.
> "Remember the Alamo!" the Texan replied.

The texts of these songs are not only different; so are the tunes associated with each. "Charlotte the Harlot I," of which the editor has collected four versions, and "Charlotte II" are sung to the tune of "Villikins and His Dinah," or, as it is known in the United States, "Sweet Betsy from Pike." In these texts she is identified as a "cowpunchers' whore." "Charlotte III" runs to the melody of "Down in the Valley" and styles her a "Mexican whore." "Charlotte IV" is not likely to be confused.

The Villikins melody that carries "Charlotte I" is the most used "come-all-ye" in Anglo-American balladry. A numbing profusion of songs travels on the tune and its variants, perhaps too many to encourage a full study of the tune family. Barry's short essay, "Notes on the Ways of Folk-Singers with Folk-Tunes" (*Bulletin of the Folk-Song Society of the Northeast* 12 [1937]: 2 ff.) is a firm beginning. Dean-Smith's index to the *Journal of the English Folk Dance and Song Society* considers the ballad of "Villikins and His Dinah" to be a "vulgarized" form of the broadside "William and Dinah." As Dean-Smith perceives it:

> This tune, popular amongst folk singers, and to be seen in the Journal associated with The Blackberry Fold, George Keary, The Keepers and the Poachers, Peggy and the Soldier, etc., is found in the famous Skene Manuscript of airs for the lute, c. 1615, and can be seen in the transcription thereof, Dauney's Ancient Scottish Music, 1838, associated with the words "Peggie is over the sie wi' ye soldier."

Dean-Smith stands alone in citing the Skene tune. Fuld (*World Famous*) dates "Villikins'" first printing, in London, to 1853, but suggests it may be a bit older. He also questions the relationship between that tune and the melody in the Skene manuscript. Simpson (p. 572) resorts to silent disagreement; he reprints "Peggie," but makes no reference to the later "Villikins." Cazden, Haufrecht, and Studer, *Folk*

Songs of the Catskills (pp. 155-58) discount the Skene link as well. Fuld (p. 605) presents a number of citations of early British imprints, noting too that Stephen Foster used it in 1856 as the vehicle for a satirical campaign song, "The Great Baby Show." Levy, (*Flashes*, 321) states the British stage song was published in the United States in "the middle 1850's." He reprints the undated cover of a Boston imprint by Oliver Ditson credited to John Parry (p. 340). Even with the date lacking, it is clear that the tune quickly spread through the popular music press, and was popular in its day.

The most comprehensive survey of the history of this melody is to be found in Cazden's Catskills collection and its indispensable *Notes and Sources* (pp. 28-31). Laws, *American Balladry from British Broadsides*, catalogues it as M 31B. Further textual references are also in Moore and Moore (pp. 319-21), to which may be added Shuldham-Shaw/ Lyle (p. 70). For some flavor of the song as performed on stage, add Colyn Davies's singing on *Cockney Music Hall Songs and Recitations* (Tradition 1017).

To the extensive melodic references in the first edition of this work, add the following: Ireland — "Von Shilly, Von Shilly" in Daiken (p. 18). England — "Still I Love Him" in Sedley, *Seeds of Love* (p. 242); "The Bold Princess Royal" in Purslow, *Marrow Bones* (p. 5); "The Cruel Ship's Carpenter" in Purslow, *Wanton Seed* (p. 30); "A German Clockwinder" in McCarthy (p. 41); "Keepers and Poachers" in Palmer, *Vaughan Williams* (p. 39); and "The Foggy Dew," *English Dance and Song* (36, No. 2 [Summer, 1974]: 59). It is said to carry "The Jolly Ploughboys" in Berkshire and Surrey, according to Broadwood and Maitland (p. 65).

Australia — "Botany Bay," in Anderson (pp. 8-9), but lacking the signature first bars, though still "Villikins"; "Caledonia" in Meredith and Anderson (p. 85); and the first melodic phrase of "The Little Fish," ibid., (p. 133).

Canada and the United States — "Lakes of Col Fin," in Flanders et al., *New Green Mountain* (p. 32); and the last two phrases of "Johnny Doyle" (p. 248) which is close to the textually unrelated "William Taylor" in Hamer, *Garner's Gay* (p. 34). Other Canadian sources are "H'Emmer Jane" in Fowke-Johnston, *More* (pp. 156-57); Peacock, 1, has "Hard Times," (p. 57), "Squarin'-Up Time" (p. 98); "A Crowd of Bold Sharemen" (p. 113); and "Fish and Brewis" (p. 123), all to sets of "Villikins." The second half of "Villikins" turns up there as "Leather Britches" (p. 71). Hopkins has two songs, "The Battle of Halifax" and "A-25" to the melody. "The Wild Cart Back on the Pipe Line," in Manny and Wilson (p. 185) is "Villikins" in the first and last phrases, and "Brennan on the Moor," in the middle two. Norman Cazden cites four songs using sets of "Villikins" in Fowke, *Lumbering* (pp. 64, 84, 168, 187); there is another on page 203.

The extent of the tune family, and the relationship of "Villikins" to the melody for some versions of "Lord Randall," is explored in Barry, Eckstorm and Smyth (pp. 67-69). See too Bronson, 1 (p. 378) and Schinhan's references in Brown, 4 (pp. 263-64).

Bronson 1 (pp. 204-12) identifies 26 versions of "Lord Randall" (Child 12) said to be sung to "Villikins" sets. No doubt there is some "Villikins" influence on these tunes, in particular on the second and third phrases, but they do not appear to be central to the tune family. First, the signature phrase is absent. Second, the variants after number 39 are clearly sung to sets of "The Wagoner's Lad," as Bronson himself notes. As great as the "Villikins' " tune family is, it does not stretch to include "The Wagoner's Lad." (For that song, see Brown 4, 157-62, and Sharp-Karpeles 2, 3, 123; Larkin, *Singing Cowboy,* 11; "Farewell to Tarwathie," in MacColl and Seeger; and "Navvy Boots," in Palmer, 6.)

Members of the "Villikins" tune family are most easily spotted by the introductory tonic, then the outline of the major triad in the first bar(s) and the repeated fifth that follows immediately. For an example of the use of that trademark motif, and little else, in a "Villikins"-derived melody, see "Sally Monroe" in Leach, *Folk Ballads* (p. 108); "The Sheepwasher's Lament" in Long and Jenkin (p. 103); or "The Bold Princess Royal" in Kidson, *Garland* (pp. 334-35). "High Germany," ibid. (pp. 82-83) embroiders that formula in the first and last phrases. The signature phrase seems intrusive in "Colin's Ghost" as given in Purslow, *Marrow Bones* (p. 16); and in "Paddy Sheehan" in Matthews and Anderson (p. 88). "The Red Light Saloon" in Brand (p. 50), on the other hand, is sung to "Villikins" with a slight modification of that trademark first phrase.

"Sweet Betsy" carries more than its share of other bawdy texts. Randolph's "Unprintable" (pp. 282-84) has rowdy stanzas added to the familiar Gold Rush text. The melody is also borrowed for "An Inch Above Her Knee" (pp. 541-42). Fowke, "Bawdy Ballads from Ontario" (pp. 53-54), reports the rare "Boring for Oil" to our tune.

"Charlotte the Harlot," in this version, has not seen print often. It appears on Brand's *Bawdy Western Songs* (Audio Fidelity 1920). Tate (p. 38) presents it from Australia. Logue-Vicarion, No. 44, has an incomplete text. Laycock (pp. 228-29) fuses lyric verses from "Charlotte I" to "Blinded by Turds."

The text and tune used here were sung by the late United States

Senator Clair Engle, who also contributed "Five Nights Drunk," in Sacramento in 1961.

Charlotte the Harlot II

Charlotte's story is lost in this version of the song, and in its place is a paean to the prostitute's promiscuity. It also is sung to the familiar "Sweet Betsy" tune.

> She's easy, she's greasy, she lives in the street.
> Whenever you see her, she's always in heat.
> She goes for a dollar, give less or give more,
> She's Charlotte the harlot, the Phi Sig Delt whore.
>
> She's got a cannon tucked down in her lap.
> You know without asking she's always got clap.
> Just ask her to show you her favorite sore,
> She's Charlotte the harlot, the Phi Sig Delt whore.
>
> She sleeps with the stallions each Saturday night.
> Now she gives the stable a terrible fright.
> She works them all night and then asks them for more,
> She's Charlotte the harlot, the Phi Sig Delt whore.
>
> Charlotte's not choosy, no, Charlotte don't care.
> Charlotte once made it with Smokey the bear.
> She's satisfied with 12 inches or more.
> She's Charlotte the harlot, the Phi Sig Delt whore.

This fraternity song was collected by Robert Gyemant at UCLA in 1964, and deposited in the UCLA Folklore Archive.

Charlotte the Harlot III

Still recognizably "Charlotte," this strays even farther from the original song. It is now sung to the tune of "Down in the Valley."

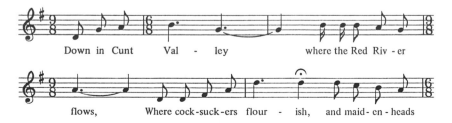

Down in Cunt   Val - ley   where the Red Riv - er

flows,   Where cock-suck-ers flour - ish,   and maid-en-heads

grow, That's where I met Lu - pe, the girl I a -
dore. She's my hot - fuck - ing, cock - suck - ing Mex - i - can
whore. *Chorus* She'll fuck you; she'll suck you; she'll gnaw at your
nuts; She'll wrap her legs 'round you, and squeeze out your
guts. She'll hug you and kiss you 'til you wish you could
die. I'd rath - er eat Lu - pe than sweet cher - ry pie.

Down in Cunt Valley where the Red River flows,
Where cocksuckers flourish and maidenheads grow,
That's where I met Lupe, the girl I adore,
She's my hot-fucking, cocksucking, Mexican whore.

Chorus:
She'll fuck you; she'll suck you; she'll gnaw at your nuts;
She'll wrap her legs 'round you, and squeeze out your guts.
She'll hug you and kiss you till you wish you could die.
I'd rather eat Lupe than sweet cherry pie.

She got her first piece as a girlie of eight,
While swinging like hell on the old Golden Gate.
The cross-member broke and the upright went in,
And ever since then, she's lived a life of sin. [Or: And Lupe embarked
    on her long life of sin.]

Now Lupe is dead and she lies in her tomb.
The maggots crawl out of her decomposed womb,
But the smile on her face seems to say, "Give me more."
She's my hot-fucking, cocksucking, Mexican whore.

The lady's name may change, her qualities do not. *Songs of Roving and Raking* (p. 123) borrowed from *Raunch and Ill-Repute* (p. 31), calls the lady "Lulu" and begins with the first verse here. Its second, and last, runs:

> She's dirty, she's filthy, she'll fuck in the street,
> Whenever you meet her, she's always in heat.
> She'll fuck for a quarter, take less, take more,
> She's a hard-fucking, cocksucking Mexican whore.

The text printed here is from a collection submitted by a former student of Bess Lomax Hawes at then San Fernando Valley State College in 1964. The tune identification comes from a fragment heard in Los Angeles in 1968.

For references to the familiar melody, see Brown, 5 (p. 200). Textual references to "Down in the Valley" are cited in Brown, 3 (p. 330); and Lomax (p. 289). The words to "Down in the Valley" have had some influence on this third form of "Charlotte," especially in the chorus.

Other versions of this song are in Getz 2 (p. LL-6) under the title of "Lupee"; in the Indiana University Folklore Archive as "Down in Cunt Valley"; as "Gallazy" in the Western Kentucky Folklore Archive at UCLA; and in the photocopied, most unofficial songbook of the University of Southern California marching band, "Hymenal" [*sic*], a copy of which was given to the editor by Christian Gunning in 1988. There she is called "Esther, the Trojan Band whore." Gunning confirmed the tune as "Down in the Valley."

Charlotte the Harlot IV

Originally from Great Britain, this version of "Charlotte the Harlot" forgets all about the lady's misadventures with the poisonous serpent. The abrupt ending is deliberate.

'Twas the first time I saw her. She was all dressed in blue.

All in blue, all in blue, I said, "How do you do?" Down in the

171

val - ley where she fol - lowed me. She's eas - y; she's greas - y; she

works in the street. And each time I see her she's al - ways in

heat. She'll do it for a dol - lar, take less or take

more. She's Char - lotte the har - lot, the cow - punch - ers' whore.

'Twas the first time I saw her.
She was all dressed in blue,
All in blue, all in blue,
I said, "How do you do?"
 Down in the valley where she followed me.
 She's easy; she's greasy; she works in the street.
 And each time I see her she's always in heat.
 She'll do it for a dollar, take less or take more.
 She's Charlotte the Harlot, the cowpuncher's whore.

The next time I saw her
She was all dressed in black,
All in black, all in black,
I laid her down on her back.
 Down in the valley where she followed me. (Etc.)

Successive verses follow the same pattern, substituting:

 Pink . . . oh, how my finger did stink
 Green . . . I slipped it in between
 Red . . . oh, how her hymen bled
 White . . . oh, how her pussy was tight

The last stanza, in full, is:

 'Twas the next time I saw her
 She was all dressed in mauve,
 All in mauve, all in mauve. . .

The earliest report of this song, under to title of "Down in the

Valley," is in Nettleingham, *Tommy's Tunes* (pp. 82-83) to a melody analogous to that used here. (The first bar of the imperfectly noted tune is "Villikins.")

Laycock (pp. 20-22) has sixteen stanzas to the tune of "Villikins," and Tate (p. 40) four, also from Australia. Getz 2 (pp. DE-5, 6) has a version from air force currency. Morgan 2 (pp. 108-9) prints another, under the title of "Down in the Valley," with seven stanzas and this philosophical chorus:

> Fol di rol, fol di rol,
> Fol di rol, fol di rol,
> A rolling stone gathers no moss, so they say,
> But a standing stone gets pissed on.

This unusual version of the ballad was contributed by Michael Higer at UCLA in 1959 as learned from an Australian. According to Higer's informant, "Charlotte" is sung Down Under as a drinking song by rugby players. Higer's melody is a thoroughly confused set of "Villikins/Betsy."

Bang Away, Lulu I

Lulu is one of the legendary ladies of American folk song, rivaled in her sexual capacities only by the aforementioned Charlotte. There is no standard version of "Lulu"; like so many other songs from the Southern Appalachians, "Lulu" has hundreds of floating verses. Each singer knows only a handful, to which he will add new stanzas as he thinks of them or as his neighbors sing them.

[A]

I wish I was a dia - mond up - on my Lu-lu's hand, And ev-'ry time she wiped her ass I'd see the prom-ised land, Oh, Lord-y.

Chorus

Bang a - way, my Lu - lu; bang a-way good and strong. Oh,

what-'ll we do for a damn good screw when our Lu-lu's dead and gone?

I wish I was a diamond upon my Lulu's hand,
And every time she wiped her ass, I'd see the promised land,
Oh, Lordy.

Chorus:
Bang away, my Lulu; bang away good and strong.
Oh, what'll we do for a damn good screw when our Lulu's dead and gone?

I wish I was the pee-pot, beneath my Lulu's bed,
For every time she took a piss, I'd see her maidenhead,
Oh, Lordy.

My Lulu had a baby. She named it Sunny Jim.
She dropped it in the pee-pot to see if he could swim,
Oh, Lordy.

First it went to the bottom, and then it came to the top,
Then my Lulu got excited and grabbed it by the cock,
Oh, Lordy.

I wish I was a candle, within my Lulu's room,
And every night at nine o'clock, I'd penetrate her womb.
Oh, Lordy.

My Lulu's tall and sprightly. My Lulu's tall and thin.
I caught her by the railroad track jacking off with a coupling-pin,
Oh, Lordy.

I took her to the Poodle Dog, upon the seventh floor,
And there I gave her seventeen raps and still she called for more,
Oh, Lordy.

My Lulu was arrested; ten dollars was the fine.
She said to the judge, "Take it out of this ass of mine."
Oh, Lordy.

[B]

Lulu had a baby. She named it Tiny Tim.
She put him in the bathtub to see if he could swim,
Oh, Lordy.

Chorus:
Bang, bang, Lulu.
Bang it good and strong.

174

What'll we do for banging
When Lulu's dead and gone?

He swam right to the bottom. He swam right to the top.
My Lulu got excited and grabbed him by the cock,
Oh, Lordy.

Sometimes I got a nickel and sometimes I got a dime,
But when I got a quarter, Lulu lays it on the line,
Oh, Lordy.

I wish I was a pisspot beneath my Lulu's bed,
And every time she'd take a piss I'd see her maidenhead.
Oh, Lordy.

I wish I was a diamond on pretty Lulu's hand
And every time she'd take a crap I'd see the promised land.
Oh, Lordy.

Pappy loved my mammy; mammy loved the men.
Now Mammy's full of buckshot and pappy's in the pen,
Oh, Lordy.

Lulu got religion; she had it once before.
She prayed to Christ with the minister while they did it on the floor,
Oh, Lordy.

My Lulu went to Boston, and there she met a trucker,
She high-balled to the bedroom cryin', "Double-clutch me,
    motherfucker."
Oh, Lordy.

My Lulu had a sister who lived upon a hill.
If she hadn't died of syphilis, we'd be banging still,
Oh, Lordy.

[C]

I took my Lulu to a circus,
To a circus good to see.
She got a hammerlock on an elephant's cock
And wouldn't come home with me.

Chorus:
Oh, bang away at Lulu,
Bang away good and strong.
For what are you going to do for your banging
When your Lulu's dead and gone?

I wish I were a picture
Up in Lulu's room,

175

And every time she let a fart,
I'd smell the sweet perfume.

I wish I were a shithouse
Upon my Lulu's place,
And everytime she took a shit,
She'd shit right in my face.

I wish I were a diamond
Upon my Lulu's hand.
And every time she wiped her ass,
I'd see the promised land.

Some girls wear lace on their pants.
Some girls wear them plain.
My Lulu she wears none at all,
But we get there just the same.

I wish I were a pisspot
Under Lulu's bed,
And every time she took a piss,
I'd see the promised land.

Some girls they use Vaseline.
Some girls they use lard.
My Lulu simply spits on it,
But she gets it just as hard.

[D]

My Lulu, she went fishing.
She caught a string of bass.
She hung them over her shoulder
And they still stink in her ass.

Chorus:
Bang away at Lulu.
Bang her good and strong
What ya gonna do for a midnight screw
When Lulu's dead and gone?

I wish I was a piss pot
Beneath my Lulu's bed,
And every time she took a crap,
I'd see her maidenhead.

I wish I was a diamond ring
Upon my Lulu's hand,
And every time she scratched her ass,
I'd see the promised land.

176

I wish I was a diamond pin
Upon my Lulu's breast.
I'd get between my Lulu's teats
And sink right down to rest.

The rich girl's pants are made of lace.
The poor girl's are chambray.
My Lulu wears no pants at all;
She claims they're in the way.

The rich girl's watch is made of gold.
The poor girl's is of brass.
My Lulu needs no watch at all;
There's movement in her ass.

The rich girl uses Vaseline.
The poor girl uses lard.
My Lulu uses neither
But she gets there [it?] just as hard.

I took her to the circus,
The circus for to see,
But she got stuck on the elephant's cock
And had no use for me.

[E]

Rich girls drive Cadillacs.
Poor girls drive Fords.
Lulu drives a Model-T
And gets it all the more.

Chorus:
Bangin' away on Lulu,
Bangin' away all day.
Who we gonna bang on
When Lulu goes away?

Rich girls wear diamonds.
Poor girls wear glass.
The only ring that Lulu's got
Is the ring around her ass.

Lulu had two boy friends
And both were very rich.
One was a son of a banker.
The other was a son of a bitch.

Lulu had a boy friend
By the name of Diamond Dick.

177

He never gave her diamonds
But he gave her lots of Dick.

The rich man uses Vaseline.
The poor man uses lard.
The nigger uses axle grease
Because he gets it twice as hard.

[F]

Some girls work in offices; some girls work in stores,
But Lulu works in a hotel with forty other whores,
Oh, Lordy.

Bang, bang Lulu.
Bang her good and long.
What'll we do for banging
When Lulu's dead and gone?

Published reports would hardly substantiate the claim, but this may well be one of the most frequently sung quatrain ballads in the repertoire of Southern Mountain singers. Randolph's "Unprintable" (pp. 348-51) has five versions, one of which is said to date to the 1890s, and another to 1912. Brown, 3 (pp. 22-23) has a text with only the barest hint of bawdry in the last stanza. Some mildly suggestive texts are in Henry (pp. 436-37); and see John A. Lomax, *Cowboy Songs* (pp. 263-64). The Archive of American Folk Song's "Supplementary Listing" of 1940 lists versions of "Lulu" in that collection on discs 1768, 3946, and 4225. Guy Logsdon (pp. 154-59) prints the most recent report of it, with extensive notes and sources.

Owen Wister apparently heard a version of this song or yet another song about Lulu. Wister borrowed a stanza to lend authenticity to his 1902 novel *The Virginian,* according to White (*Git Along Little Dogies,* 35). Wister's stanza runs:

If you go to monkey with my Looloo girl,
I'll tell you what I'll do.
I'll carve your heart with my razor, AND
I'll shoot you with my pistol, too.

Sandburg (pp. 378-79) offers "nine of the nine hundred verses," some ribald. Dolph (pp. 93-94) has the tune and one expurgated stanza from a military source. Getz 2 (pp. BB 9-10) has two uncensored versions from air force currency. Another is in *Immortalia* ([1927]: 103-4, and the reprint [1968]: 116).

An English text is in Morgan 1 (p. 14). The Vicarion anthology, probably from British sources, has a text and an idiosyncratic tune notation (the negative of the music was also stripped in upside down), numbered 64. Hopkins (p. 159) presents Canadian compliments to the lady.

There are two recorded versions. Brand sings one on *Bawdy Sea Chanties* (Audio Fidelity 1884), though the song has no special connection with the sea or with sailors. The New Lost City Bang Boys (New Lost City Ramblers) render a Southern Mountain version on *Earth is Earth* (Folkways 869 [that number is no accident]) which they credit to an older recording called "When Lulu's Gone," as sung by "The Bang Boys" (Roy Acuff and his band).

In truth, "Lulu" shares stanzas with a number of songs. D. K. Wilgus points out that the rich girl/poor girl verses are borrowed from or loaned to the familiar childrens' and camp song "She Gets There Just the Same." Similarly, *Songs of Raunch and Ill-Repute's* "The Gruen Watch Song" (p. 7) and Reuss's "Phi Delta Theta" (pp. 88 ff.) borrow the second stanza of the "A" text here. (Reuss also includes three college versions [pp. 264-68] sung to the tune "Goodnight Ladies.") That second stanza printed here has a curious historical antecedent or parallel scratched in a toilet at Hampton Court by "R. M." and dated 1703. It appeared in the pioneering collection of folk epigraphy, *The Merry Thought*, subtitled *The Glass Window and Bog House Miscellany*, published in 1731 in England, and reprinted by the Augustean Reprint Society, Publication No. 216 (Los Angeles: William Andrews Clark Memorial Library, 1982):

> Oh! that I were a t[ur]d, a t[ur]d,
> Hid in this secret place,
> That I might see my Betsy's a[rse]
> Though she sh[i]t in my face.

The "A" version here was sung in 1964 by the late Robert W. Kenny, former attorney general of the State of California and Superior Court judge; he learned it in law school some forty years before. The verses are identical to those in *Immortalia*. The third and fourth stanzas circulate by themselves as an urban, children's street song and jump-rope rhyme.

The "B" text came from a professional musician in Los Angeles in 1963; he had learned it from another musician while performing in a dance band.

The undated, unattributed "C" text is No. 3912 in the Library of Congress's Gordon "Inferno," forwarded by Guy Logsdon. Like the other Gordon material, it can be dated safely to the 1920s. The chorus

179

served as a marching song for the 2d Division in the summer of 1918 in Bellau Wood; "the verses were very vulgar and no doubt are only made up on the moment," wrote another Gordon correspondent on March 16, 1927 (No. 2734). Thomason, *Fix Bayonets!* (p. 67) states it was sung by marines at the same time, but gives no text.

The undated, circa 1925 "D" variant is from the Robert W. Gordon Oregon collection housed at the University of Oregon (No. 3144). It was forwarded by J. Barre Toelken. The Gordon Library of Congress collection has a conflation (?) under that number apparently fashioned by the correspondent, Frank A. Partridge, of Auburn, California.

The "E" is from the collection of bawdy songs and recitations gathered by Harry A. Taussig between 1958 and 1963 at the University of California, Berkeley.

The "F" text is from the singing of insurance agent Stuart Grayboyse in Los Angeles in 1964.

The melody of "Bang Away, Lulu" used here is a set of the "Goodnight, Ladies"-"Bell Bottom Trousers" tune family.

Bang Away, Lulu II

A slightly different version, this one depends on the deliberately unfinished last line of each verse for its humor.

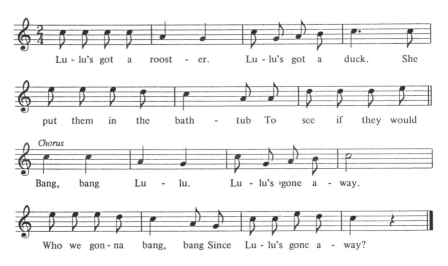

Lu-lu's got a roost-er. Lu-lu's got a duck. She put them in the bath-tub To see if they would

Chorus

Bang, bang Lu-lu. Lu-lu's gone a-way. Who we gon-na bang, bang Since Lu-lu's gone a-way?

Lulu's got a rooster.
Lulu's got a duck.
She put them in the bathtub
To see if they would

Chorus:
Bang, bang Lulu.
Lulu's gone away.
Who we gonna bang, bang
Since Lulu's gone away?

Lulu's got two boy friends.
They are very rich.
One's the son of a banker,
The other's a son-of-a

Cows wear bridles.
Horses wear bits.
Lulu wears a sweater
To cover up her

Al Levy, a transplanted North Carolinian, sang it over the telephone at the editor's request in Los Angeles in 1964. Levy fitted it to the melody printed for "Bang Away, Lulu I" by dropping the eighth bar of the tune for the verse.

Reuss (p. 268) has a version of this that borrows the tune of a teasing song; this textual type of "Lulu" is, of course, one of that group. Getz 2 (p. TT-14) has a similar teasing variant.

To the tune of "Bell Bottom Trousers," Barbara Rogers in Los Angeles in 1967 sang one stanza as learned in college in Salinas, California, circa 1951:

Lulu had a boy friend.
He drives a big red truck,
Takes her down an alley
And teaches her to ----
Flang dang, Lulu . . .

Miss Rogers set this barely recalled fragment of the teasing form of the song to a note-for-note repetition of the "Bell Bottom Trousers" tune, learned from a popular recording. Apparently, she refurbished her tune by relying on a known melody closest to the tune she could only imperfectly recall. To the extent this occurs, it can be argued that popular records actually aid oral tradition. See too the editor's article, "Barbara Allen in America: Cheap Print and Reprint" (pp. 41-50) on the folk use of songsters to refresh Child 84 in oral tradition.

Bang Away, Lulu III

This third version of "Bang Away, Lulu" is something of a compromise between the uninhibited and the teasing forms of "Lulu."

Lulu gave a party.
Lulu gave a tea.
Then she left the table
To watch her chicken peck.

Chorus:
Bang, bang, Lulu.
Bang away all day.
Who we gonna bang on
When Lulu goes away?

Lulu was astonished,
Lulu gave a start,
For right upon the table,
She watched her ducky fly.

Lulu had a chicken.
Lulu had a duck.
She'd put 'em on the table
And then she'd watch 'em fight.

This unusual variant was sent to the editor by Debbie Bonetti of Los Angeles in 1967.

The Ring-Dang-Doo

Sometime around the age of puberty, boys seem to learn this song, just as their fathers did before them, and their fathers before that. From generation to generation, the song has changed, but the various versions will almost invariably contain the description of the ring-dang-doo (here called the "ring-a-rang-roo") as being "soft and round like a pussy cat."

[A]

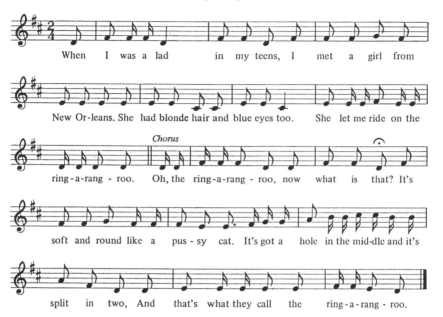

When I was a lad in my teens,
I met a gal from New Orleans.
She had blond hair and blue eyes too.
She let me ride on the ring-a-rang-roo.

Chorus:
Oh, the ring-a-rang-roo, now what is that?
It's soft and round like a pussy cat.
It's got a hole in the middle and split in two,
And that's what they call the ring-a-rang-roo.

She took me down into her cellar,
And said that I was a mighty fine feller.
She fed me wine and whiskey too.
She let me ride the ring-a-rang-roo.

Her father came and angrily said,
"You have lost your maidenhead.
Well, pack your bags and your Kotex too,
And make your living off your ring-a-rang-roo."

So she went off to be a whore,
And hung this sign above her door:

"One dollar each and three for two
To take a crack at my ring-a-rang-roo."

They came by twos, they came by fours,
Until at last they came in scores,
But she was glad when they were through
For they had ruined her ring-a-rang-roo.

[B]

When I was a young man in my teens
I met a girl from New Orleans.
She was young and pretty too,
And she let me ride her ring-dang-doo.

Chorus:
Oh, the ring-dang-doo, now what is that?
It's big and round like a pussy cat,
Covered with fur and split in two.
That's what they call the ring-dang-doo.

Now along came Pete, the son-of-a-bitch.
He had blue balls and the seven-year itch.
He had the clap and the syphilis too,
And he put them all in the ring-dang-doo.

And now she lies beneath the sod;
Her soul, they say, is gone to God,
But down in Hell, when Satan's blue,
He takes a slice of the ring-dang-doo.

[C]

When I was a young lad in my teens,
I knew a girl in New Orleans.
Oh, she was young and pretty too,
And said she had a ring-dang-doo.

Chorus:
What is that thing right over there,
So soft and smooth and covered with hair,
So round and firm and split in two?
Why, that there thing is the ring-dang-dooo.

This girl I knew, she had a feller.
She took him down into the cellar.
She fed him wine and whiskey too,
And she let him ride on her ring-dang-doo.

184

Her father cried from out the bed,
"Oh, daughter dear, have you lost your head?
Go pack your bag, and Kotex too,
And make your living on your ring-dang-doo."

So she went to town to become a whore.
She tacked a sign upon her door:
"Two dollars down, two bits will do,
And you can ride on my ring-dang-doo."

And they came by twos, and they came by fours,
And when they came, they came by scores.
And they brought their money and their rubbers too,
And she let them ride on her ring-dang-doo.

Well, the army came and the navy went.
The price went up to fifty cents.
But still they came to get their screw.
Oh, how they rode on the ring-dang-doo.

Now from the hills there came a son-of-a-bitch.
He had the clap and the seven-year itch.
He had the syph and the blue-balls too,
And she let him ride on the ring-dang-doo.

Well, our girl died in a year or two.
And the fellers mourned 'cause they missed their screw.
They fucked each other and their mothers too.
Oh, they wanted to ride her ring-dang-doo.

They tacked her tits to the courthouse wall.
They pickled her pussy in alcohol.
They buried it 'neath the avenue,
And now the busses ride on the ring-dang-doo.

This ballad has two endings, one in which the owner of the ring-dang-doo passes on what is known as a social disease to all those who visit her, the other ending when her career is cut short by a customer who gives her the pox. Hoffmann has assigned this motif number X712.5.2.

The song may not be very old. In the 1920s, Robert W. Gordon got an undated fragment from a sailor, sung to the tune of "How Dry I Am." Randolph has three versions, as "The Doo-Gee-Ma-Doo," among his "Unprintables" (pp. 119-22), the oldest attributed to a soldier who sang it in Argenta, Arkansas, in 1918. The tune for that is the chorus of "The Arkansas Traveler." For versions of that tune from oral tradition, see Bayard (pp. 267-71); and Rosenbaum (pp. 106-7).

A second text goes to a set of "The Irish Washerwoman." It is included in *Immortalia* (p. 68), firmly dating it to at least 1927; it is also in the 1968 reprint (p. 81). Larson has three "Barnyard" versions from Idaho, probably dating to the 1930s (pp. 13-14). D. K. Wilgus's Western Kentucky Folklore Archive housed at UCLA has a text said to have been learned from soldiers on a transport in the Pacific in 1943 or 1944. For "Washerwoman" tunes collected from oral tradition see, Bayard (pp. 415-20).

The Archive of American Folk Song contains two recordings of "Rang Dang Do" on AFS 1486.

Printed sources are not many. Logsdon (pp. 241-44) has a multi-stanza text and tune; it concludes with two unusual floating quatrains often linked to songs of faithless lovers or broken romances. Brand (pp. 80-81) has a variant of the "A" text here. Babab (p. 122) starts with Brand, then goes on to the second version. Both *Songs of Raunch and Ill-Repute* (p. 19) and *Songs of Roving and Raking* (p. 111) have the girl catch the pox. The song is included also on *Unexpurgated Folk Songs of Men;* and, with two variants, in Getz 2 (pp. RR-4, 5). Getz's second version, dating from the Vietnam conflict, is taken from the careful compilation of Air Force Lt. Col. James P. Durham ("Bull Durham's Songs of S.E.A." [1970]: 66-67).

Even though the song may be relatively new, it has spread far. It has been collected in Great Britain by MacColl and Seeger (pp. 159-60). Three Australian texts are in print: Morgan 1 (p. 26); Laycock (pp. 128-30); and Hogbotel and Ffuckes (p. 17). Cleveland (p. 95) reports it sung by New Zealand troops during World War II, and Hopkins (p. 140) by Canadian. Abrahams (p. 171) reports the song in recitation form, and has collected unpublished West Indies variants "from a number of women informants."

Still, the overwhelming currency of the song in the United States suggests it was born in the New World and migrated to the old.

The "A" text was contributed by Roy Torkington, of Los Angeles, who learned it in Rochester, New York, in 1956.

The "B" text and tune here are from the editor's youth, learned about 1948-49 in Los Angeles.

The "C" text is from Harry A. Taussig's collection made at the University of California, Berkeley, between 1958 and 1963.

The Chisholm Trail

John A. Lomax, who pioneered collecting folk song in the American west, judged this ballad close to being *the* cowboy epic. Stretched end to end, the verses reached from the Panhandle to the rail heads of Kansas, chronicling the hero's misfortunes as he drove the 2-U (or "goddam") herd up the trail.

[A]

Now gather 'round, boys, and listen to my tale,
And I'll tell you my troubles on the old Chisholm Trail.

Chorus:
Singing, ki-yi-yippy, yippy-yay, yippy-yay,
Singing, ki-yi-yippy, yippy-yay.

Alternate Chorus:
Gonna tie my pecker to my leg, to my leg,
Gonna tie my pecker to my leg.

My name's Bill Taylor and my love's a squaw,
Livin' on the banks of the muddy Washita.

I come from Texas with the longhorn cattle
On a ten-dollar horse and a forty-dollar saddle.

Sittin' in the saddle with my hand on my dong,
Shootin' jism on the cows as we go along.
(Alternate chorus)

We left Texas on October twenty-third,
And traveled up the trail with the 2-U herd.

187

We didn't reach town till winter, Eighty-two.
My ass was draggin' and my pecker was too.
(Alternate chorus)

I went huntin' tail from a parlor house whore,
But I didn't have enough, so they kicked me out the door.
(Alternate chorus)

With my ass in the saddle and my pecker all sore,
I spied a little lady in the whorehouse door.

I asked for tail and I gave her a quarter,
And she says, "Young man, I'm a minister's daughter."

I took out a dollar and I put it in her hand,
And she says, "Young man, will your long pecker stand?"

I grabbed right hold and I throwed her on the grass.
My toe-hold slipped and I rammed it in her ass.

I fucked her standin' and I fucked her lyin';
If she'd a-had wings, I'd a-fucked her flyin'.

Five days later, my prick turned blue.
I ran to the doctor and he didn't know what to do.

So I went to another and he said, "Cough."
I coughed so hard my balls dropped off.

I went to another 'cause my pecker was sore;
"By God," said the doctor, "It's that same damn whore."

So I sold my horse and I sold my saddle,
And I bid goodbye to the longhorn cattle.

The last time I seen her and I ain't seen her since,
She was scratchin' her cunt on a barbed wire fence.

[B]

Looking for a job, and I went broke flat.
Got a job riding on the Double-O flat.

Signs pinned up on the bunkhouse door,
"Punchers allowed at a quarter after four."

"Round up and saddle up some old pitching hoss,
If you can't ride him, you're fired by the boss."

As I come a-riding 'cross the Double-O range,
I was thinking of my sweetheart that I left on the ranch.

I rode on with the old man's daughter,
Guess I said a few words what I hadn't oughter.

188

I told her that I'd love her like I loved my life,
I asked her how she'd like to be a cowpuncher's wife.

Said she'd like it fine, but I better see her dad,
For he got the dough, and it might make him mad.

I went to the old man, as all lovers oughter,
I says, "Old Man, I'm in love with your daughter."

He grins and he points to the Double-O roan,
That's piled every puncher that ever rode alone.

Says, "If you can ride that horse, and not pull leather,
You and my daughter can throw your things together."

Went to the hoss, and slammed on my saddle,
Best damn rider that ever punched cattle.

All the punchers yelled, as all punchers oughter,
For they knew I was riding for the Old Man's daughter.

Jumped in the saddle and gave a little yell,
What's going to happen is damned hard to tell.

Spurred him on the shoulder, and hit him with my quirt,
Gave four jumps, and rolled me in the dirt.

Went to the Old Man to have a little chat,
Hit him in the face with my old felt hat.

Went to the girl, and offered her a quarter,
Says she, "Go to Hell! I'm a cowpuncher's daughter!"

Offered her a dollar, and she took it in her hand,
Punched me in the belly, says, "Well, I'll be damned!"

Threw my arms around her and laid her on the grass,
To show her the wiggle of a cowpuncher's --- [ass].

The hair on her belly was a strawberry brown,
The crabs on her m---- [mound] were jumping up and down.

Took my old jockey to the watering trough,
Washing him and I scrubbed him till his head fell off.

In about nine days, when I looked for to see,
Chancres on my p----- [pecker] were big as a pea.

She found it out, and called me a kid,
Told me to remember her, and by God, I did!

Wrote me a letter, don't think I lied,
Said, "I'm leaving Texas, fast as I can ride."

Know a little Injun, damn pretty squaw,
Guess I'll go and see her for I leave for Arkansas.

Going to leave Texas, going to head for home,
All on account of the Double-O roan.

Sheep man a-stealing of the Double-O grass,
Boss says, "Shoot him, but not in the --- [ass]."

So we pulled out our guns and we got him on the fly,
Crawled in the weeds, and I guess he's going to die.

Chased a bunch of hosses through the G-- [God] d----- [damned] sheep,
The scatterment they made, made the sheep men weep.

Camped overnight at the A Bar B's,
Got so damn cold I thought I would freeze.

Raining hard and muddy as hell,
Trailing through the bumbo sure is hell!

Hit Belle Fourche, and went on a spree,
Sheriff come a-running, and he picked on me.

Locked me up in lousy old jail.
Boss said he'd be damned if he went my bail.

Just because I worked for him wa'n't no sign
That a cowpoke's boss had got to pay his fine.

Met a girl and though I'd seen her before,
Tried her and I found she was a G-- [God] d----- [damned] whore.

Went to make a date as a cowpuncher oughter,
Found out the girl was that damn sheriff's daughter.

Sheriff on my trail, left town on the run.
If he catches up, have to use my gun.

Left Belle Fourche and left her on the lope,
To keep my neck from wearing out a scratchy old rope.

Going to leave Montana, and marry my squaw,
Going to settle down in Arkansas.

[C]

The first time I saw her she was floating down a stream
With a belly full of clabber and a cunt full of cream.

Chorus:
Come-a-ki-yi-yippy, yippy-yay, yippy-yay,
Come-a-ki-yi-yippy, yippy-yay.

Then the next time I saw her she was pulling off a hound,
And the jaws of her twat were a-drippin' on the ground.

Her tits hung down like a pair of wooden buckets,
And her cunt stunk so that a dog wouldn't fuck it.

The next time I saw her she was pulling off her brother.
The crabs on her ass were a-fuckin' one another.

She ripped and she roared, and she shit on the floor,
And she wiped her ass on the knob of the door.

Then the next time I saw her she was lyin' in her bed,
With a carrot in her cunt, and damn near dead.

Her cunt was so big that no man could screw it,
But an elephant saw it and went right to it.

And the next time I saw her she was lyin' on the floor,
And the breeze from her ass blew the cat out the door.

Oh, the moon shown down on the nipple of her tits,
And she washed her teeth in bluebird shit.

So I grabbed her by the neck and threw her on the grass.
Then I stretched her cunt from her navel to her ass.

The neighbors all thought that she couldn't take a fuck.
So she took on a horse and after that he couldn't buck.

The next time I saw her she was standin' in the door,
And the hair from her cunt hung down to the floor.

So I grabbed her by the waist and threw her on the floor,
But the wind from her ass blew me out the door.

Then I went downstairs to get some cider,
And there I saw a bedbug a jackin' off a spider.

When I came back, she was sittin' in the stream,
From her ass were blowin' bubbles, from her cunt was flowing cream.

The sun shown down on the end of her tits.
She knew she was a whore, but she didn't give a shit.

Well, the last time I saw her, and I haven't seen her since,
She was jackin' off a nigger through a barbed wire fence.

This odyssey has long had bawdy verses interwoven, though only a few have appeared in print: in the relatively scarce *Immortalia* ([1927]: 38-39); and its 1968 reprint (pp. 57-58); in Hart's *Immortalia*, 3 (pp. 96-99); in Babad (p. 131), reprinting the text in *Songs of Roving and Raking* (p. 118); and in Getz 2 (pp. KK-3 and TT-14, 15). Laycock (pp. 260-62) had a text from Australia. Randolph had five short versions or fragments in his "Unprintable" collection (pp. 169-73).

The most recent report is in Logsdon (pp. 66-69). The "A" text there is "Chisholm Trail" only by virtue of the melody and chorus. The verses seem borrowed from another bawdy song related to the seemingly lost "Bugaroo." (A worn version of this ballad recorded by Louis Winfield Moody on AFS 4971 on July 21, 1941, was furnished by James Leary of Mt. Horeb, Wisconsin.)

For references to other, non-bawdy texts of "Chisholm Trail," see Brown, 3 (p. 248); and Randolph, 2 (p. 174); to which may be added those in Lomax, *Folk Songs of North America* (pp. 370-71); and Moore (p. 285). John Lomax in *American Ballads and Folk Songs* (p. 376) notes there are "hundreds of unprintable stanzas."

The "A" text here was gathered by a former student in 1960 from a patron of a Los Angeles saddle shop. The informant was a rodeo cowboy with whom he had worked on a ranch in Colorado.

The "B" text, forwarded by J. Barre Toelken from the Gordon collection at the University of Oregon, was collected on August 25, 1930, from Charles E. Roe, with "additional verses from Slim Guyer, Montana." It is number 3781 in the Gordon collection.

The "C" text was collected at Stanford University on December 15, 1960, from Charles Petrone by Harry A. Taussig.

Gonna Tie My Pecker to My Leg

Fragments of the marathon "Chisholm Trail" have broken off and circulate by themselves, most often with the promise of the title sung as a chorus.

[A]

Chorus:
I'm going to tie my pecker to my leg, to my leg,
Going to tie my pecker to my leg.

Reached in my pocket for a dime.
She said, "Young man, you're wasting your time."

Reached in my pocket, pulled out a quarter,
She said, "Young man, I'm a rich man's daughter."

Reached in my pocket and pulled out six bits,
All she did was flip her tits.

Reached in my pocket, pulled out a buck,
She said, "Young man, you've bought a fuck."

Last time I saw her, haven't seen her since,
She was jacking off a Negro through a barb-wire fence.

[B]

When I was young and just a pup,
Fifty-two women did I fuck.
Forty-nine of them I knocked up.
If that's not fuckin', I'll give up.

Chorus:
Coma [sic] tie my pecker to my leg, to my leg.
Coma tie my pecker to my leg.

Jumped in the saddle and the saddle wasn't there,
And I rammed nine inches up the old gray mare.
Jumped off the horse and knocked on the door,
She said, "Come on in, I'm an old Injun whore."

Oh! I fucked her sittin' and I fucked her lyin'.
If I had wings, I'd fuck her flyin'.
Oh! the last time I seed her and I ain't seed her since,
She was jackin' off a nigger through a bob-wire fence.

[C]

Chorus:
Tie my pecker to my leg.
Tie my pecker to my leg.

The last time I seen her and I haven't seen her since,
She was jackin' off a nigger through a barbed wire fence.

The last time I seen her she was sittin' on the stern.
She was holdin' his'n and he was holdin' her'n.

This secondary form of "Chisholm Trail" is marked by the chorus that gives the song its name. In it, the narrative is compressed, usually to a meeting of the cowboy and a woman whose sexual favors he attempts to purchase. The only printed version is a thirteen-stanza effort dating from the Vietnam War era in which the narrator contracts a social disease and is reduced to:

And now you can see I'm a peckerless man.
I fuck 'em with my finger and fool 'em when I can.

It is in James P. Durham, "Bull Durham's Songs of S.E.A." ([c. 1970]: 54-55), and reprinted in Getz 2 (TT 14-15).

193

The "A" text was collected by Bill Strode at Western Kentucky State College, 1958, and deposited by D. K. Wilgus in the Western Kentucky Folklore Archive at UCLA. One wonders if Strode changed "nigger" to the less offensive "Negro."

The "B" text is also from the Western Kentucky Folklore Archive. It was collected in Lyndhurst, New Jersey, in the 1950s.

Attorney Ed Ulman in 1967 contributed the "C" text, which he dated to his Los Angeles high school days in the early 1950s.

While Hanging Around Town

Another warning to stay away from the flash girls. It is sung to the melody known as "The Strawberry Roan."

While hang-ing 'round town with cunt on my mind, And noth-ing to do, just wast-ing my time, I spied a young la-dy there on the walk, De-cid-ed to give her a line of my talk.

While hanging around town with cunt on my mind,
And nothing to do, just wasting my time,
I spied a young lady there on the walk,
Decided to give her a line of my talk.

I stepped up beside her and said, "I suppose
You're a hot number by the looks of your clothes."
"Yes, I'm a hot number, and a good one I claim.
There isn't a G.I. that I cannot tame."

I showed her a ten spot. She said, "You're my man.
There isn't a G.I. that I cannot stand."

She gave me a wink and I followed her there
To the hotel room at the head of the stair.
   Her dress slipped off and I saw at a glance
   That the strawberry blonde didn't wear any pants.

We pulled in the room about a quarter to nine.
There in the middle a-spilling my slime.
She fizzled and farted and let out a scream,
Kicked off the head of my fucking machine.

Nine days later I lay flat on my back,
My old pecker tied up in a sack.
So, come all you G.I.'s and listen to me,
Just crack your old fist and let all women be.

This was sung by a twenty-four-year-old informant in Mc-
Lemoresville, Tennessee, in 1947 to Virgil Adams, who contributed
it to the Western Kentucky Folklore Archive at UCLA. A second,
fragmentary text was collected by actor Robert Easton in Los Angeles
in 1960. For a history of "The Strawberry Roan," which lends its
tune to this, see Logsdon, *The Whorehouse Bells Were Ringing* (pp. 87-
91).

The Big Black Bull

Considering the fact that, until recently, the United States was
predominately rural, it is surprising that there are not more barnyard
epics such as this. "The Big Black Bull" is seemingly the only such
pastorale still in oral circulation.

[A]

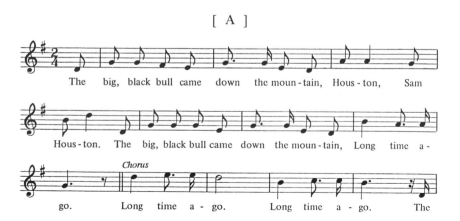

195

big, black bull came down   the moun-tain, Long   time   a - go.

The big, black bull came down from the mountain,
Houston, Sam Houston.
The big, black bull came down from the mountain
Long time ago.

Chorus:
Long time ago.
Long time ago.
The big, black bull came down from the mountain
Long time ago.

He spied a heifer in the pasture,
Houston, Sam Houston.
He spied a heifer in the pasture
Long time ago.

Chorus:
Long time ago.
Long time ago.
He spied a heifer in the pasture
Long time ago.

He jumped the fence and he jumped that heifer,
Houston, etc.

He missed his mark and *fffitt* in the pasture,
Houston, etc.

His tool ran dry and his balls grew hollow,
Houston, etc.

Wiped his cock on a hickory sapling,
Houston, etc.

The big black bull went back to the mountain,
Houston, etc.

[B]

Oh, the big black bull came down from the mountain,
You said, John, you said.
The big black bull came down from the mountain,
A long time ago.
    A long time ago.
    A long time ago, a long time ago.

196

> A big black bull came down from the mountain,
> A long time ago.
>
> He pawed the ground and pfft in the fountain,
> You said, John, you said.
> He pawed the ground and pfft in the fountain.
> A long time ago.
> > A long time ago.
> > A long time ago, a long time ago.
> > A big black bull came down from the mountain,
> A long time ago.

Similarly, subsequent stanzas insert these lines in the formula:

> He whetted his wang on a hickory sapling.
> Now, seven white cows were grazing in the pasture.
> The big black bull went back to the mountain.
> His balls hung low and his back was broken.
> Seven white calves were born next season.

This is a college song of some popularity, and in laundered versions is frequently sung as a camp and hiking song by Boy Scouts and such.

Sandburg (p. 164) has a version, which he dates to pre-Civil War years, that being the earliest report of the song. (D. K. Wilgus, in a review of this manuscript, recalled seeing a text in a now forgotten "gift book" that could be dated to 1841.)

It is possible, if not probable, that black chanteymen shipping out of Southern ports on the great sailing ships refashioned the song into the shanty, "A Long Time Ago." For a text of that shanty, see Colcord (pp. 65 ff.). See also the related "Leave Her Johnny, Leave Her" in Hugill (pp. 239 ff.) to which "Big Black Bull" has both rhythmic and textual similarities. (In a letter to the editor, Abrahams has suggested that "Leave Her, Johnny, Leave Her" merits temporal primacy and that "Big Black Bull" is *its* descendant. In either case, the interpreting agents would apparently be black chanteymen.)

The song has apparently circulated in military circles for some time. John Dos Passos' *Nineteen Nineteen* asserts that it was sung by American soldiers on the Italian front during World War I. Getz (p. S-3) prints a "Sam Houston" text from air force currency, though it may be originally from university currency. Laycock (pp. 169-70) has the song from an American source.

Peggy Seeger sings a version of "Big Black Bull" called "Great Big Dog" as a lullaby on *The Three Sisters* (Prestige 13029). Pete Seeger has recorded a sea variant as "Hoosen Johnny" on *Beasts, Birds, Bugs and Bigger Fishes* (Folkways FP711). Roberts and Agey (pp. 296-97) have it as "The Little Black Bull."

One of three in the editor's collection, the "A" variant is from Stuart Grayboyse, an insurance salesman, who learned the song in Los Angeles prior to 1952. His tune, sung for the editor in 1964, owes much to "The Old Gray Mare." The "B" text is from the Blaine Stubblefield collection at Utah State University.

The melody for the "The Old Gray Mare" hauls other bawdy songs, including the scatological "She Shit on the Whiffletree" in Randolph's "Unprintable" collection (p. 126). It also carries the local song "Sealer's Ball," in Peacock, 1 (p. 94).

The Lehigh Valley

How Victorian hearts fluttered when popular singers of the day sang of innocent maidens seduced from their proper parlors by dastardly villains. The immorality plays of the period presented their own prim estimate of crime and punishment. If the girl fell into sinful ways, she inevitably had to die repentant at the end of the piece. If she remained chaste and simple in spite of the temptations thrust upon her, the hero would just as inevitably arrive on the scene to save both the day and her virtue.

In the harsh light of reality, this sort of melodrama was not going to last very long. Once "The Tramp's Lament" left the overstuffed drawing rooms, the bathetic agonies were quickly trimmed away. In the original "Tramp's Lament," the narrator informs the listener that he was once a blacksmith, and having put aside his anvil, he is hammer and tongs after the city slicker who stole his innocent daughter Nellie from hearth and fireside.

> Well, it's the same old story,
> Common enough, you'll say,
> But he was a soft-tongued devil
> And got her to run away.
>
> More than a month, or later,
> We heard from the poor young thing.
> He had run away and left her
> Without any wedding ring.

Nellie returns home to die of a raging fever, and dad is off to hunt the scoundrel who ruined his daughter. No self-respecting hobo could resist such an easy target.

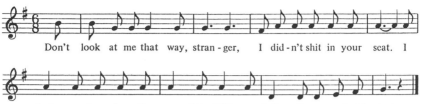

Don't look at me that way, stranger,
I didn't shit in your seat.
I just come down from the mountains
With my balls all covered with sleet.

I've been up in the Lehigh Valley,
Me and my old pal, Lou,
A-pimpin' for a whorehouse
And a God damned good one too.

It was there that I first fucked Nellie;
She was the village belle.
I was only a lowdown panderer
But I loved that girl like hell.

But along came a city slicker,
All handsome, gay and rich,
And he stole away my Nellie,
That stinking son-of-a-bitch.

I'm just restin' my ass a moment,
And then I'm on my way.
I'll hunt the runt that swiped my cunt
If it takes till Judgment Day.

There are three variants of this in the editor's collection, including the one here from Marvin Gelfman, who learned it in New York City in 1960.

Hoffmann has assigned this ballad motif number X724.5.2.1. Other versions are in Babab (p. 135) reprinted from *Songs of Roving and Raking* (p. 116); *Immortalia* ([1927]: 59, and the 1968 reprint, 75); and Hart's *Immortalia*, 2 (pp. 44-45). John Greenway sings an expurgated variant on *The Great American Bum* (Riverside 12-619). Laycock's Australian informants present this text as a recitation.

Randolph, 4 (pp. 369-70) has the original parlor song; his "Unprintable" anthology (p. 230) notes it is said to be by Edward Harrigan and used in his 1882 play *Squatter Sovereignity*. Randolph's raucous version is sung to the melody of "The Red River Valley" and dates to about 1912. The Gordon "Inferno" in the Library of Congress has a text, possibly from Cleveland, Ohio, dated March 3, 1918 (No. 3913).

Milburn (pp. 41-58) gives a thirteen-stanza text, calling it "an original poem," and a "pathetic recitation," seemingly unaware that the words were set to music. His second version he considers "the most brilliant item the Lehigh Valley school has produced"; the first and last of Milburn's verses run:

> Don't move over, stranger,
> I won't ---- on your seat,
> Nor ---- on the coat that's on your back,
> Nor the shoes that's on yer feet.
>
> Now, God be with you, stranger,
> And I'll be on my way.
> I'll hunt the runt that stole my ----
> If it takes till Judgment Day.

Abrahams, *Positively Black* (pp. 47 ff.) has a toast, "Toledo Slim," from this same tradition, with borrowings from "The Lehigh Valley." Unpublished texts are in Larson's Idaho "Barnyard" collection (p. 17); and the Indiana University Folklore Archives.

D. K. Wilgus has suggested that the bawdy recitation usually known as "Our Lil" may be related to this song in that some versions place the action "down in the Lehigh Valley." The recitation begins:

> Lil was the best our camp produced,
> And of all the gents that Lillian goosed,
> None had such goosing, and never will,
> Since the Lord took to his bosom our lady, Lil.

Legman discusses this recitation in his *Horn Book* (pp. 416-20); and in his pioneering "Bawdy Monologues and Rhymed Recitations" (*Southern Folklore Quarterly* 40 [1976]: 90, 98-102). There are texts too in *Immortalia* (both 1927 and 1968) credited to the Chicago newspaper man and sometime poet Eugene Field.

Hallelujah, I'm a Bum

Rightfully considered an American classic, this hobo-bum-tramp's song could not fairly be called "bawdy," but merely one with some off-color verses. The fourth stanza, however, does have a neat play-upon-words dependent upon the music and all but lost on the printed page.

Oh, why don't you work like other men do?
How the hell can I work when there's no work to do?

Chorus:
Hallelujah, I'm a bum,
Hallelujah, bum again.
Hallelujah, give us a handout
To revive us again.

Springtime is here and I'm just out of jail,
The whole winter in without any tail.

I went to a house and I knocked on the door,
My cock sticking straight out, my balls on the floor.

I asked for a piece of bread and some food.
The lady said, "Bum, you will eat when I'm screwed."

When I left that lady, my cock it was sore,
My belly was full, her ass it was tore.

I went to another and I asked her for bread.
She emptied the peepot all over my head.

Be happy and glad for the springtime has come.
We'll throw down our shovels and go on the bum.

Why don't you fuck like other men do?
How the hell can I fuck when there's no broads to screw?

Harry McClintock's song, having been expropriated by the public, has acquired innumerable stanzas, bawdy and otherwise. This version was collected by the editor from a retired postal worker in Los Angeles in 1966; he thought he might have learned the song during the late Depression while riding America's finest railroads *al fresco.* The editor's father, the late Max Cray of San Mateo, California, also knew some of these verses; he had learned them in Cleveland, Ohio, in the 1930s.

The melody borrowed by McClintock for his song is the hymn tune, "Revive Us Again." For a history of "Hallelujah, I'm a Bum," see Greenway (pp. 197 ff.). To his textual references, add Sandburg (p. 183); Leach (p. 108); and Lomax and Lomax, *American Ballads and Folk Songs* (pp. 26-28). Milburn (pp. 97-101) gives two variants.

The Winnipeg Whore

Lurking somewhere between the lines of this song may be a real woman, raised to mythic heights by lumberjacks. They borrowed a dance tune now known to school children as "Reuben, Reuben, I've Been Thinking" and to infants as "Ten Little Indians," hanging upon it an elegy in honor of the lady.

[A]

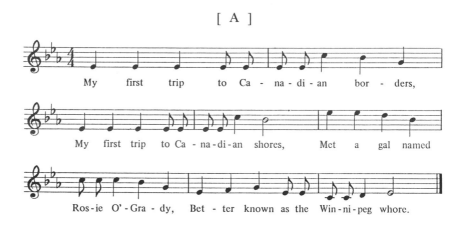

My first trip to Ca - na - di - an bor - ders,
My first trip to Ca - na - di - an shores, Met a gal named
Ros - ie O' - Gra - dy, Bet - ter known as the Win - ni - peg whore.

On my first trip to Canadian borders,
My first trip to Canadian shores,

Met a gal named Rosie O'Grady,
Better known as the Winnipeg whore.

Said, "My faith! you look familiar,"
Flopped her ass upon my knee,
Said she'd meet me in the northeast corner,
Dollar and a half would be her fee.

Some were fiddling, some were fie-deling,
Some were fucking on the bar room floor,
But I was up in the northeast corner
Putting it to the Winnipeg whore.

Fucked her once, fucked her twice,
Then I fucked her one time more.
She gave a shout, and then she fainted.
That was the end of the Winnipeg whore.

[B]

My first trip up the Saginaw River,
My first trip to the Canadian shore,
There I met sweet Rosie O'Grady,
Better known as the Winnepeg whore.

"Come right in. I'm glad to see you.
Slap your ass across my knee.
We will have some fun together.
Dollar and a half will be my fee."

Some were dancin', some were prancin',
Some lay drunk on the barroom floor,
But there I was in the northwest corner
Screwin' hell out of the Winnepeg whore.

Then, in there walked some [sono]bitches, [*sic*]
Must have been a score or more.
Oughta seen me shit my britches
Sliding' my ass on the barroom floor.

The melody, "Reuben, Reuben," was probably first borrowed by woodsmen from East Coast fishermen, who themselves used it for other bawdy songs. (See the endnote for "Caviar Comes from Virgin Sturgeon," below.)

Randolph ("Unprintable," 246) has one stanza of this from an Ozark informant, a parallel to the third here. Larson's "Barnyard" compilation from Idaho schoolchildren (p. 21) has a seven-stanza text localized to Denver.

Brand (pp. 60-61); *Songs of Raunch and Ill-Repute* (p. 21); *Songs of Roving and Raking* (p. 115 [reprinted in Babab, 123]); Laycock (p. 243); *Barely Alive* (Sault Antlers Records) and Hart's *Immortalia*, 3 (pp. 22-25), have variants of "The Winnipeg Whore" in which the girl lifts the narrator's watch and wallet. They conclude with something like:

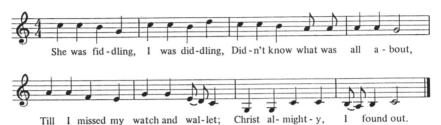

She was fid-dling, I was did-dling, Did-n't know what was all a-bout,

Till I missed my watch and wal-let; Christ al-might-y, I found out.

> She was fiddling; I was diddling,
> Didn't know what 'twas all about,
> Till I missed my watch and wallet,
> Christ almighty, I found out.
>
> Up jumped the whores and sons of bitches,
> Must have been a score or more.
> You'd have laughed to cream your britches
> To see my ass fly out the door.

The "A" version, one of two in the editor's collection, is from Los Angeles bookseller Ray Fisher, who sang it in 1964. Dean Burson had a one-stanza fragment from UCLA, collected in 1960. A third version is traceable to Brand's recorded series.

D. K. Wilgus sang the "B" text of this song heard in Columbus, Ohio, circa 1933, to "Reuben, Reuben." This is the earliest text recovered. Wilgus also contributed a 1951 text from Glasgow, Kentucky, to the Western Kentucky Folklore Archive.

Kathusalem

In the original song, published in 1866, the heroine falls in love with an infidel, much to the displeasure of her father, the Baba of Jerusalem. One night, when the lovers are together, papa Baba greases a cord with goozalem and garrotes the two. And now the ghosts of the pair float over Jerusalem's Wailing Wall.

By the First World War, "Kathusalem" had fallen upon evil ways.

[A]

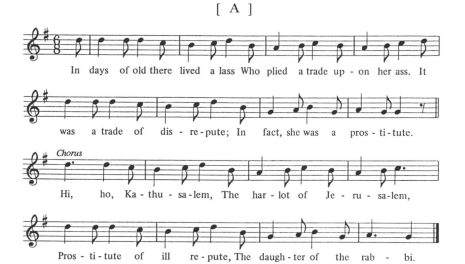

In days of old there lived a lass Who plied a trade up-on her ass. It was a trade of dis-re-pute; In fact, she was a pros-ti-tute.

Chorus

Hi, ho, Ka-thu-sa-lem, The har-lot of Je-ru-sa-lem,

Pros-ti-tute of ill re-pute, The daugh-ter of the rab - bi.

In days of old there lived a lass
Who plied a trade upon her ass.
It was a trade of disrepute;
In fact, she was a prostitute.

Chorus:
Hi, ho, Kathusalem,
The harlot of Jerusalem,
Prostitute of ill repute,
The daughter of the rabbi.

Kathusalem was a sly old witch,
A dirty whore, a fucking bitch,
Who maketh all the pricks to twitch,
This harlot of Jerusalem.

When the Jewish army came to town,
The price went up and she went down,
And took them on, white, black or brown,
This harlot of Jerusalem.

There was a priest within the walls
Whose mammoth cock and hairy balls
Alarmed the ladies one and all
Who lived in old Jerusalem.

She took him to a shady nook,
And from its hiding place she took

His penis curved into a hook,
The pride of all Jerusalem.

She was short and underslung;
He missed her cunt and hit her bung.
And planted the seed of many a son
In the butthole of Kathusalem.

Now the bastard's down in hell,
They say he's doing rather well,
And you can tell him by the smell
Of the asshole of Kathusalem.

[B]

In days of old there was a dame
Who plied a trade of ancient fame.
It was a trade of ill-repute;
In fact, she was a prostitute.

Chorus:
Hi, ho, Kathusalem,
The harlot of Jerusalem,
Prostitute of ill repute,
The daughter of the rabbi.

It was a fact: she had a crack
With hair so black, it could contract
To fit the tool of any fool
Who fucked in all Jerusalem.

And now within this city's wall
There dwelt a priest both lean and tall,
And he could fornicate them all,
The maidens of Jerusalem.

One night, returning from a spree,
His customary hard had he,
And on the street he chanced to meet
This harlot of Jerusalem.

He laid her down upon the grass,
Lifted her dress above her ass;
He grabbed his prick and made a pass
At the fuck-hole of Kathusalem.

But she was low and underslung;
He missed her twat and hit her bung,
Planting the seeds of many a son
In the asshole of Kathusalem.

Kathusalem, she knew her part;
She spread her legs; she blew a fart,
And blew the bastard all apart,
All o'er the walls of Jerusalem.

In days to come she bore a brat,
A son-of-a-bitch, a dirty rat,
Who masturbated with a cat,
The bastard of Kathusalem.

[C]

In olden days there was a maid
Who used to ply a thrifty trade,
A prostitute of ill repute,
The harlot of Jerusalem.

Chorus:
Hi, ho, Kafoozalum,
The harlot of Jerusalem.
The prostitute of ill-repute,
The daughter of the rabbi.

She was a wily witch,
A goddam, whorey son of a bitch,
And every dong it got the itch
That dangled in Jerusalem.

One day returning from a spree,
A high and mighty jubilee,
Kafoozalum he chanced to see,
Passing through Jerusalem.

He took her to a shady rock
And there uncoiled his precious cock,
Forty feet of precious cock
Into the bowels of Kafoozalum.

The son of a bitch was underslung.
He missed her hole and hit her bung
And drove his dong into her dung,
Down by Jerusalem.

Now Kafoozelum, she knew her part.
She cocked her ass and let a fart
And blew that bastard like a dart
High over Jerusalem.

And there he lay a broken mass,
His cock all filled with shit and gas,

> And Kafoozelum, she wiped her ass
> All over the walls of Jerusalem.

According to Spaeth (*History*, 166), this is a parody of a popular song published by Frederick Blume in New York in 1866 under the title of "Kafoozelum." The sheet music credits the song to one "S. Oxon." Whoever "S. Oxon" was—the abbreviation may stand for Bishop of Oxford or Son of Oxford—he intended his song to satirize the period's bathetic love songs as well as the then-current, pervasive influence of the exotic in the popular arts. For texts of the original song, see Spaeth, *Read 'Em and Weep* (pp. 148-49); Leach (pp. 86-87); or Lynn (pp. 34-35). It is recorded by Oscar Brand on *Laughing America* (Tradition 1014). By World War I, Spaeth says, a bawdy parody—Hoffmann has assigned to it motif number X733.1.2—was in circulation. The chorus, dated to 1919, is in Nettleingham (*More*, 66).

More recently, Brand presents a heavily edited version of the ribald redaction on *Bawdy Songs and Backroom Ballads*, 3 (Audio Fidelity 1824); the same is in his book (pp. 20-21), and recorded on *Barely Alive* (Sault Antlers Records). *Songs of Roving and Raking* (p. 113), *Songs of Raunch and Ill-Repute* (p. 26); Babab (p. 130); and Getz 2 (pp. KK-1, 2), are less inhibited.

A second form of the ballad, apparently of British currency, is closer in narrative to the original popular song. It tells the story of an outraged "Onanite, whose balls were melons made of shite," coming upon Kathusalem and a student amid their carnal capers.

> A tree supplied him [the intruder] with a stick,
> To which he fastened half a brick,
> And he took a swipe at the mighty prick.
> Of the student of Jerusalem.
>
> He seized the fucker by his hook,
> And such a mighty heave he took,
> He flung him over Kendron's brook,
> That babbles past Jerusalem. (Vicarion, n.p.)

Compare that to the original verse, given in Leach (p. 87):

> The pious Baba said no more
> Than twenty prayers, but went upstairs
> And took a bowstring from a draw'r
> And greased it well with goozalum.
> The maiden and the youth he took,
> And choked them both and little loth,
> Together pitched them in the brook
> Of Kedron, near Jerusalem.

In the bawdy British versions at hand, however, Kathusalem and her lover together best their attacker.

> And feeling full of rage and fight
> He pushed the bastard Onanite
> And rubbed his face in Kathy's shite,
> The foulest in Jerusalem.
>
> Kathusalem, she knew her part,
> She closed her cunt and blew a fart
> That sent him flying like a dart
> Right over old Jerusalem. (McGregor, p. 55)

Thus in British versions, it seems, it is the Onanite, the intruder, whose "asshole hangs from a tree outside of old Jerusalem." The American version is much more the story of a sexual contest between Kathusalem and "the priest both lean and tall" ending with the cleric blown over the walls.

The Gordon "Inferno" collection in the Library of Congress has an unidentified fragment dating from the 1920s, the only American text containing this element. The editor has not otherwise found the song in the United States but variants of it are in Vicarion's Book, No. 49; Hopkins (p. 171); Laycock (pp. 186-90); Hogbotel and Ffuckes (p. 33); Morgan 1 (pp. 75-78); and the identical text in MacGregor (pp. 52-55).

It seems likely that the British parody was the original bawdy version of the song, and the American version is a rewrite of that.

The Taussig collection, put together in northern California between 1958 and 1963, has three versions of "Daughter of the Rabbi" or "Kafoozalem." While still telling the American tale, two of the three share the "part-fart-dart" stanza.

The "A" version was collected by the editor in Los Angeles from an aerospace engineer who learned it at CCNY in 1950.

The "B" version here was collected by Dean Burson in Los Angeles from an informant who learned the song at Carnegie Tech in 1959.

The "C" text was collected by Harry A. Taussig in Berkeley, California, between 1958 and 1963.

The melody generally used for "Kathusalem" is the children's song "London Bridge Is Falling Down" disguised in triple time. The tune for the chorus in the original popular song strongly suggested a triple-time variant of "London Bridge" already in tradition — used as early as 1715 for "Will Ye Go to Sheriffmuir?" See Cazden, Haufrecht, and Studer (pp. 562-63) for a history, and their *Notes* (pp. 108-9) for citations to early occurrences of the melody. Fuld (p. 337) points out that the first printing of the familiar melody under the title "London Bridge" took place only in 1879, 135 years after the text first saw print. That is also thirteen years after Blume's "Ka Foozle-Um," which suggests that it was the popular song, reintroduced in oral tradition that ultimately resulted in the children's tune "London Bridge Is Falling Down."

Abdul the Bulbul

The Crimean War stimulated a good deal of interest in things oriental and pseudo-oriental during the middle of the nineteenth century. The influence was felt throughout the popular arts, and was even absorbed in the clothing styles and interior designs of the period.

The original "Abdul" concerned the fateful duel between Ivan and the Emir, the pair doing each other in, snick and snee. However, that light-hearted lampoon of Russo-Turkish relations became in oral tradition a contest of a different sort.

[A]

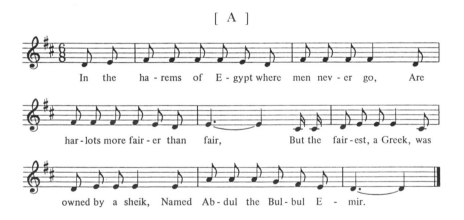

In the harems of Egypt where men never go
Are harlots more fairer than fair;
But the fairest, a Greek, was owned by a sheik
Named Abdul the Bulbul Emir.

A traveling brothel came into that town,
Having traveled the roads from afar.
It was run by a pimp with cock never limp,
Called Ivan Stavinsky Stavar.

[B]

In the harems of Egypt no infidels see
The women are fairer than fair;
But the fairest, a Greek, was owned by a sheik
Called Abdul the Bulbul Emir.

A traveling brothel came into the town,
Run by a pimp from afar
Whose great reputation had traveled the nation,
'Twas Ivan Skavinsky Skavar.

Abdul the Bulbul arrived with his bride,
A prize whose eyes shone like a star.
He claimed he could prong more cunts with his dong
Than Ivan Skavinsky Skavar.

A great fucking contest was set for the day
A visit was planned by the czar,
And the curbs were all lined with harlots reclined
In honor of Ivan Skavar.

They met on the track with their tools hanging slack,
Dressed only in shoes and a leer.
Both were fast on the rise, but they gasped at the size
Of Abdul the Bulbul Emir.

The cunts were all shorn and no rubber adorned
The prongs of the pimp and the peer,
But the pimp's steady stroke soon quickened and broke
The chance of the Bulbul Emir.

They worked through the night till the dawn's early light.
The clamor was heard from afar.
The multitudes came to applaud the ball game
Of Abdul and Ivan Skavar.

When Ivan had finished he turned to the Greek
And laughed when she shook with great fear.
She swallowed his pride; he buggered the bride
Of Abdul the Bulbul Emir.

When Ivan was done and wiping his gun,
He bent down to polish his gear.
He felt up his ass a hard pecker pass;
'Twas Abdul the Bulbul Emir.

The crowds looking on proclaimed who had won.
They were ordered to part by the czar,
But fast were they jammed; the pecker was crammed
In Ivan Skavinsky Skavar

Now the cream of the joke when apart they were broke
Was laughed at for years by the czar,
For Abdul the Bulbul left most of his tool
In Ivan Skavinsky Skavar.

The fair Grecian maiden a sad vigil keeps
With a husband whose tastes have turned queer.
She longs for the dong that once did belong
To Abdul the Bulbul Emir.

Fuld (p. 84) tracks the original song to "Abdulla Bulbul Ameer," with words and music by Percy French, composed at Trinity College, Dublin, in 1877. The bawdy parody cannot be so precisely fixed.

This ballad is relatively rare in urban circles today. The "A" text and the tune were furnished by a retired San Francisco contractor, in 1984. He learned the song in the army forty years earlier, and could recall only a few fragmentary lines after the first stanzas.

The "B" text here, sent without a tune, was furnished by a colleague who learned it while attending Harvard University in the 1940s. Its "pure" tradition may be questionable; the correspondent believes he had a hand in "filling out" or rewriting a then-current, shorter form of the ballad.

Though a more detailed narrative, the "B" text is similar to an unpublished version collected by Mrs. Edith Fowke; and to the refurbished (?) variant in Christopher Logue's *Count Vicarion's Book of Bawdy Ballads*. Other lusty variants from around the British Empire are in Morgan 1 (pp. 86-87) and McGregor (pp. 26 ff.); Hogbotel and Ffuckes (p. 35); and Cleveland (p. 95). Getz 2 (pp. AA-1, 2) has a conflation based upon a text sung by Australian pilots during the Korean conflict. An unpublished version close to "B" here was current among Indiana University rugby players in 1969.

Other tunes and texts of the ballad, presentable in polite company, are in Sandburg (pp. 344-46); Spaeth (pp. 145-48); and Dick and Beth Best, *Song Fest* (New York [1955]: 56-57).

Walking Down Canal Street

This is a curious thing. A formula song, it is sung to the first eight bars of the otherwise unrelated "Bell Bottom Trousers."

[A]

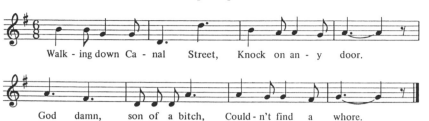

Walk-ing down Ca - nal Street, Knock on an - y door.

God damn, son of a bitch, Could - n't find a whore.

Walkin' down Canal Street, knock on any door;
God damn son-of-a-bitch, couldn't find a whore.

Finally found a whore and she was tall and thin;
God damn son-of-a-bitch, couldn't get it in.

Finally got it in and wiggled it about;
God damn son-of-a-bitch, couldn't get it out.

Finally got it out and it was red and sore.
The moral of this story is: Never fuck a whore.

[B]

I wandered down the street,
And I knocked on every door;
To save my life from hell, boys,
I couldn't find a whore!

At last I found a whore;
She was sitting on a rock;
To save myself from hell, boys,
I couldn't find my cock!

At last I found my cock,
In the center of my hand;
To save my life from hell, boys,
I couldn't make it stand.

At last I made it stand,
As stiff as any pin;
To save my life from hell, boys,
I couldn't get it in!

At last I got it in
And wiggled it about;

213

To save my life from hell, boys,
I couldn't get it out.

At last I got it out,
All mattery and sore.
To save your life from hell, boys,
Never fuck a whore.

Reuss (pp. 114-15) records a Marine Corps version of "Walking Down Canal Street," dated to 1963. The Reuss song borrows its introductory verse from "In Bohunkus, Tennessee," its chorus from "The Frigging Fusiliers," and the tune for these from "Tramp, Tramp, Tramp." The formulaic portion is sung to "Bell Bottom Trousers." *Songs of Raunch and Ill-Repute* (p. 30) has the formula versions too, but with no tune indicated.

UCLA college student Dean Burson collected the "A" version at that school in 1960.

The "B" text is reprinted from Larson's Idaho "Barnyard" store (p. 25).

Red Wing

This ballad of an Indian maiden began life, shortly after 1900, as a sentimental parlor song. It has taken on an entirely different character since.

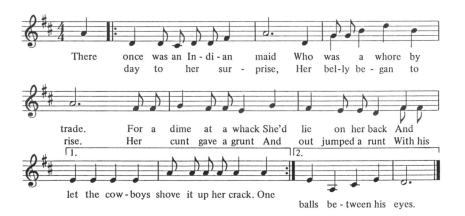

There once was an In-di-an maid Who was a whore by
day to her sur - prise, Her bel-ly be - gan to

trade. For a dime at a whack She'd lie on her back And
rise. Her cunt gave a grunt And out jumped a runt With his

1. let the cow-boys shove it up her crack. One

2. balls be - tween his eyes.

There once was an Indian maid
Who was a whore by trade.
For a dime at a whack,
She'd lie on her back
And let the cowboys shove it up her crack.
    One day, to her surprise,
    Her belly began to rise.
    Her cunt gave a grunt
    And out jumped a runt
    With his balls between his eyes.

This ballad is well-known, or, at least, its first stanzas are frequently encountered. There are six variants in the editor's collection.

The most extended text seen is in *Songs of Raunch and Ill-Repute* (p. 1); *Songs of Roving and Raking* (p. 61); and Babab (p. 78). All are probably from Brand, a version notable for its truly classic euphemism for a would-be rapist's emasculation:

Now he was an Indian wise.
He reached for Redwing's thighs.
With an old rubber boot on the end of his toot [root?],
He made poor Redwing open up her eyes.
    But when she came to life,
    She grabbed her Bowie knife;
    It flashed in the sky as she let it fly,
    And shortened his love life.

For other versions of the bawdy song, see Laycock (pp. 207-10) and the references there; Randolph, "Unprintable" (p. 620); Legman, *The Limerick* (p. 193, No. 939); *Raunch and Ill-Repute* (p. 30); Hart's *Immortalia* (pp. 44-49); and Laycock (pp. 199-200). Larson's "Barnyard" anthology (p. 31) has an Idaho text.

Other parodies exist concurrently in oral tradition. Greenway (p. 299) notes that the original title even faces the threat of displacement by Woody Guthrie's "Union Maid": "I have seen at least a half-dozen union songs written to the tune of 'Red Wing,' but all of them have the notation, 'Sung to the tune of Union Maid.' " Shaw (pp. 52-53) has a Liverpool children's parody. An air force parody, possibly expurgated, is in Wallrich (p. 164). Getz (p. L-8) has a World War II text to the tune.

The popular song is credited to Kerry Mills and Thurland Chattaway, and was published in 1907. Roger Abrahams has noted in a letter to the editor that "in the late 'Nineties and early part of this century, there were reams of songs written in praise of Indian maidens, the progenitor — 'Little Mohee.' "

The version printed here is from the singing of Norman Kaplan of New York City. He learned the song "in school" about 1940. He was then about eight years old.

I-Yi-Yi-Yi

For sheer length, this is the champion bawdy song of all time. At any song swap, this is likely enough to run on for twenty-five or thirty verses, and that barely scratches the surface. The standard collection of limericks contains 1739 entries, any one of which might turn up as a verse in "I-Yi-Yi-Yi."

The song also has a number of different choruses, each popular in its own locale; two of the best-known are included here. The first is set to a part of the chorus of "Cielito Lindo," a handsome complement to the music for the verses, known as "The Gay Caballero."

[A]

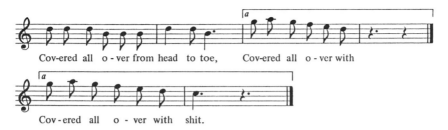

Cov-ered all o - ver from head to toe, Cov-ered all o - ver with

Cov-ered all o - ver with shit.

Chorus:
I-Yi-Yi-Yi,
In China, they never eat chili.
So here comes another verse worse than the other verse,
So waltz me around again, Willie.

There was a young man from Racine,
Who invented a fucking machine.
Concave or convex,
It would fit either sex,
And jack itself off in between.

There once was a whore from the Azores,
Whose cunt was all full of big sores.
The dogs in the street
Lapped up the green meat
That hung in festoons from her drawers.

A scholarly fellow from Duckingham
Wrote a treatise on women and fucking 'em.
But he was beat by a Turk
With a twelve-volume work
On cunts and the fine art of sucking 'em.

There was a young lady from Munich
Who was ravished one night by a eunuch.
At the height of her passion,
He slipped her a ration
From a squirt gun concealed in his tunic.

When she wanted a new way to futter,
He greased her behind with butter.
Then with a sock,
In went his jock,
And they carried her home on a shutter.

A mathematician named Fine
Always showed her classes a good time.

217

Instead of multiplication,
She taught fornication,
And never got past sixty-nine.

[B]

The tune for the verse remains the same. The chorus of "Sweet
Violets" is borrowed from a stage song of the nineteenth century.

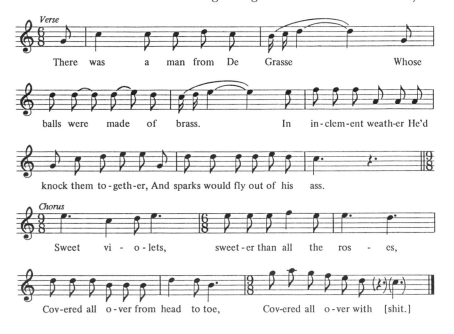

Chorus:
Sweet violets, sweeter than all the roses,
Covered all over from head to toe,
Covered all over with [shit]

There was a man from DeGrasse
Whose balls were made of brass.
In inclement weather,
He'd knock them together,
And sparks would fly out of his ass.

There once was a man from Blatz
Whose balls were constructed of glass.

218

When they clanked together,
They played "Stormy Weather,"
And lightning shot out of his ass.

There once was a man from Boston
Who drove around in an Austin.
There was room for his ass
And a gallon of gas,
So his balls hung out and he lost them.

There was a young girl named Myrtle
Who had an affair with a turtle.
Her swelling abdominal
Was considered phenomenal
Till they discovered the turtle was fertile.

An unfortunate fellow named Chase
Had an ass that was badly misplaced.
He showed indignation
When an investigation
Proved that few persons shit through their faces.

There was a young man named Hentzel
Who had a terrific long pencil.
He went through an actress,
Two sheets and a mattress,
And shattered the family utensil.

There once was a man from Nantuckett
With a cock so long he could suck it.
Said he, with a grin,
As he wiped off his chin,
"If my beard was a cunt, I would fuck it."

There once was a hermit named Dave
Who kept a dead whore in his cave.
He said, "I admit
I'm a bit of a shit,
But think of the money I save."

There was a young fellow from Kent
Whose dong was so long that it bent.
To save himself trouble,
He put it in double,
And instead of coming, he went.

There once was a maid from Cape Cod
Who thought babies came from God,

But it wasn't the Almighty
Who lifted her nighty,
But Roger the lodger, by God.

There once was a rabbi from Keith
Who circumcised men with his teeth.
It was not for the treasure,
Nor sexual pleasure,
But to get at the cheese underneath.

There once was a man from Iraq
Who had holes down the length of his cock.
When he got an erection
He would play a selection
From Johann Sebastian Bach.

There was a young lady from Dee
Whose hymen was split into three,
And when she was diddled,
The middle string fiddled
"Nearer My God to Thee."

There was a young man from Leeds
Who swallowed a package of seeds.
Great tufts of grass
Grew out of his ass,
And he couldn't sit down for the weeds.

While Titian was mixing rose madder,
He espied a nude girl on a ladder.
Her position to Titian
Suggested coition
So he climbed up the ladder and had 'er.

There was a lady named Wild
Who kept herself quite undefiled
By thinking of Jesus,
Contagious diseases,
And the bother of having a child.

There was a couple named Kelly.
They were stuck belly to belly
Because, in their haste,
They used library paste
Instead of petroleum jelly.

[C]

There once was a novice at Chichester
Whose form made the saints in their niches stir.

One morning at matins,
Her bosom 'neath satins
Made the Bishop of Chichester's britches stir.

There once was a lady named Alice
Who used a dynamite stick for a phallus.
They found her vagina
In North Carolina
And the rest of her body near Dallas.

A Roman who hailed from Gadondom
Used a fried hedgehog's hide for a condom.
His mistress did shout
As he pulled the thing out,
"*De gustibus non disputandum!*"
["There is no disputing taste!"—ed.]

There was a young lawyer named Rex
With diminutive organs of sex,
When hauled in for exposure,
He replied with composure,
"*De minimis non curat lex.*"
["The law does not concern itself with trivial things."—ed.]

There was a biologist named Reba
Who loved a sexy amoeba.
This primordial jelly
Would crawl on her belly
And murmur, *"Ich liebe. Ich liebe."*

On the breast of a lady named Gail
Was tatooed the price of her tail.
And on her behind,
For the sake of the blind,
Was the same information in Braille.

There was a young man named Adair
Who was fucking a girl on the stair.
The bannister broke
And by doubling his stroke,
He finished her off in mid-air.

An Argentine gaucho named Bruno
Said, "Fucking is one thing I do know.
All women are fine,
And sheep are divine,
But llamas are *numero uno.*"

[D]

A wealthy old maid from Twickenham
Had a butler without any prick on him.
On her knees every day,
To God she would pray
To lengthen and strengthen and thicken him.

There was a young lady named Ransom
Who was loved three times in a hansom.
When she asked for more,
Came a voice from the floor,
"My name is Simpson, not Sampson."

There once was a queer from Khartoum
Who invited a whore [dyke] to his room.
They argued all night
As to who had the right
To do what, and with which and to whom.

She wasn't what one would call pretty,
And other girls offered her pity.
So nobody guessed
That her Wasserman test
Involved half of Oklahoma City.

A lady astrologist in Vancouver
Once captured a man by maneuver.
Influenced by Venus,
She jumped on his penis,
And nothing on earth could remove her.

There was a young lady from France
Who decided to take just one chance.
For an hour or so,
She just let herself go,
And now all her sisters are aunts.

There was a young lady from Maine
Who enjoyed copulating on a train.
Not once, I maintain,
But again and again
And again and again and again.

An Eskimo on his vacation
Took a night off to succumb to temptation.
'Ere the night was half through,
The Eskimo was, too,
For their nights are of six months' duration.

Gershon Legman's comprehensive *The Limerick* established far beyond question that limericks are the products of the educated, and circulate largely in that group. Those included here—culled from approximately 100 in the editor's files—were gathered by Burson at Carnegie Tech and UCLA in 1959 and 1960 (the "A" version), by the editor in Los Angeles from 1960 to 1965 (the "B" text), by two of Abrahams's former students in Austin, Texas in 1963 (the "C" version) and by Robert Easton in Los Angeles in 1960 (the "D" version).

The first chorus, from the imported popular song, "Cielito Lindo," and the alternate chorus are both current in Los Angeles. "Cielito Lindo" was printed first in Mexico City in 1919, credited to Quirino Mendoza y Cortez. He secured a copyright in 1929. *Grove's Dictionary* says, however, the song is traditional, and dates it to 1850; Mendoza y Cortez merely arranged it. As well-known as the song is in the United States, it did not make its way to this country until 1923.

The second chorus is fashioned from the last three lines of the song "Sweet Violets" by J. K. Emmet as it was sung in his now-forgotten play of 1882, *Fritz Among the Gypsies*. (The bracketed word above, [shit], can be omitted.) Those lines run:

> Oh, sweet violets, sweeter than all the roses,
> Zillah, darling one, I plucked them
> And brought them to you.

Repopularized by a 1951 recording by Dinah Shore, with words and music credited to Cy Cohen and Charles Crean, that version was "adapted from a folk song," according to Jacobs (p. 226). See "Sweet Violets," an unrelated teasing song, below.

Leach (p. 101) has a melody for a song he calls, appropriately enough, "Limericks." Leach's tune is the same as that used for the verse here: "The Gay Caballero." He does not include a verse.

Reuss (p. 219) says the tune his informants used for the verses was also "The Gay Caballero." He prints four texts, a tune and twenty-four limericks. It may be that the inspiration to borrow the melody of "The Gay Caballero"—itself said to be a "Spanish tune"—came from "The Filipino Hombre," a Philippine insurrection song in Dolph (p. 188). That version, possibly expurgated, has its stanzas in limerick form:

> There once was a Filipino *hombre*,
> Who ate rice, *pescado y legumbre*.

> His trousers were wide,
> And his shirt hung outside,
> And this, I may say, was *costumbre*.

Since the first edition of this book, a number of other versions of "I-Yi-Yi-Yi" have been printed. Getz 2 (pp. SS-8 ff.) has a conflation of fifty verses. Morgan 1 (pp. 161 ff.) presents sixty limericks and a two-line chorus: "That was a jolly good song / Sing us another one do." Morgan 2 (pp. 151 ff.) has thirty more. Morgan 2 (p. 141) also prints an unrelated song that uses the "I-Yi-Yi-Yi" refrain. As "Waltz Me Around Again, Willie," a forty-stanza version appears in the dittographed "Scientific and Professional Personnel Songbook," circulated among Army Chemical Corps personnel in Maryland, circa 1959. Lydia Fish of Buffalo State University provided a copy.

The seemingly standard melody used here for the verses is another offshoot of the "Goodnight Irene" tune family. Hoffmann has assigned the motif number of Z19.4 for all limerick songs.

The Little Red Train

Neither its literary qualities nor its musical brilliance commend "The Little Red Train." Still, it perseveres in oral tradition, perhaps because it is so easy to learn and sing.

[A]

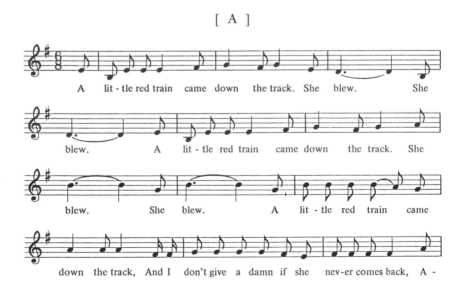

A lit-tle red train came down the track. She blew. She blew. A lit-tle red train came down the track. She blew. She blew. A lit-tle red train came down the track, And I don't give a damn if she nev-er comes back, A-

way she blew, oh, Je - sus, how she blew.

A little red train came down the track.
She blew. She blew.
A little red train came down the track.
She blew. She blew.
A little red train came down the track,
And I don't give a damn if she never comes back,
Away she blew, Jesus Christ, how she blew.

Subsequent verses follow the same pattern, substituting:

The engineer was at the throttle
Pissing into a whiskey bottle.

Hobo Bill was riding the rods
When ninety-nine cars rolled over his cods.

The railroad cop was in the yard,
Holding his billy and making it hard.

[B]

A little red train came down the track.
She blew. She blew.
A little red train came down the track.
She blew. She blew.
A little red train came down the track,
And I don't give a damn if she never comes back,
Away she blew, oh Jesus, how she blew.

The engineer was at the throttle,
A-jacking off in a whiskey bottle.

The fireman, he was shoveling coal
Right up the engineer's asshole.

The switchman, he was at the switch,
A-swishing away like a son-of-a-bitch.

A blonde was in the dining car,
A-puffing away on a black cigar.

A porter was waiting in the car,
To take the place of the black cigar.

The flagman he stood out in the grass,
The staff of the flag run up his ass.

In the first edition of this book, the editor styled "The Little Red Train" as a off-spring of "Snapoo." More reasoned consideration suggests that "Train" is of independent origin though it is sung to two tunes that also carry "Snapoo": "When Johnny Comes Marching Home" and "Mademoiselle from Armentieres."

There are three similar versions in the editor's collection, and a four-stanza variant in *Songs of Roving and Raking* (p. 117), all from a campus currency. Babab (p. 132) reprints the latter as "The Sixty-Nine Comes Down the Track." *Immortalia* ([1927]: 93, and [1967]: 108) also carries a variant. Randolph, "Unprintable" (pp. 223-26) has variants sung to both "Johnny" and "Mademoiselle."

Randolph's "Unprintable" (pp. 223-26) reports three versions, the earliest said to date to the early 1900s. Sandburg (p. 379) gives one stanza of "The Wind It Blew Up the Railroad Track," sung to "When Johnny Comes Marching Home." One suspects he had other, less presentable verses at hand. Milburn acknowledges that his " 'The Old 99' has a large number of stanzas too vigorous for pallid print." His tune too is "When Johnny."

Fuld (pp. 189, and 344-45) has histories of the two melodies in question. "Johnny" dates from the American Civil War, "Mademoiselle" from the First World War.

The "A" text, sung to "When Johnny," the editor heard at a party in Los Angeles in 1961. The "B" text is from Dean Burson, as it was sung at UCLA in 1960; his tune was "Mademoiselle from Armentieres."

The Woodpecker's Hole

A sea song come ashore, the bawdy element of this camp and college song has all but vanished. Just why American singers persist in abusing the woodpecker, to the tune of "Dixie," is not clear. English sailors preferred the first mate, which makes perverse sense.

I stuck my fin-ger in the wood - peck-er's hole, And the wood - peck - er said, "God damn your soul, Take it out, take it

out,   take it   out   re - move   it.

> I stuck my finger in the woodpecker's hole,
> And the woodpecker said, "God damn your soul!
> Take it out, take it out, take it out, remove it."
>
> I replaced my finger in the woodpecker's hole,
> And the woodpecker said, "God damn your soul!
> Wrong way, wrong way, wrong way, revolve it!"
>
> I revolved my finger in the woodpecker's hole,
> And the woodpecker said, "God damn your soul!
> Wrong way, wrong way, wrong way, reverse it!
>
> I reversed my finger in the woodpecker's hole,
> And the woodpecker said, "God damn your soul!
> Take it out, take it out, take it out, remove it!"
>
> I removed my finger from the woodpecker's hole,
> And the woodpecker said, "God damn your soul!
> Put it back, put it back, put it back, replace it!"

The record of this song is certainly incomplete. The tune is white minstrel Dan Emmett's "Dixie," composed about 1859. But why a woodpecker? In Randolph, the subject is a "peckerwood," a local name for what is known elsewhere as "white trash" or "redneck." Perhaps then the song is a lampoon or *blaison populaire*. Or, as Reuss suggests, that inane effort may be descended from a rhyme printed in the circa 1890 ephemeral publication called *The Stag Party*.

> A woodpecker flew to the school-house yard,
> And he pecked and he pecked for his pecker was hard.
> The woodpecker flew to the school house door.
> And he pecked and he pecked until his pecker was sore.
> After which he flew back to the yard again,
> And the woodpecker's pecker got over its pain.

Randolph's "Unprintable" has three variants from the Ozarks, sung to the melody of "Little Brown Jug."

The earliest indisputable "Woodpecker" fragment, dated to 1919, is in Nettleingham, (*More*, 66). Hugill (p. 424) has a British sailors' version, probably older. Getz 2, (pp. WW-9, 10) and Cleveland, (p. 95) report a World War II currency for the song.

Morgan 2 (pp. 56-57) is from England, presumably. Laycock (pp. 18-19) is Australian, and ends with this stanza:

227

> I withdrew my finger from the woodpecker's hole,
> The woodpecker said, "God bless my soul!
> Have a whiff, have a whiff, have a whiff. Re-volting!"

Collegiate and sometimes expurgated campers' versions are common, with or without tunes. It is included in the mimeographed "The One, The *Only* Baker House . . . Songbook," p. 18, from M.I.T. circa 1950. Forwarded by Lydia Fish of Buffalo State University, the dittographed "Scientific and Professional Personnel Songbook" (attributable to college men drafted into the Army Chemical Corps, circa 1959) offers a last stanza ending: "Take it out, take it out, I've had it." Reuss (pp. 258-60) has a text, like that used here, from Carnegie Tech, ultimately. Reuss also notes that Randolph had the song from the Ozarks, and cites various manuscript appearances.

The variant used here was gathered by Dean Burson from his Carnegie Tech informant in Los Angeles in 1960.

"The Woodpecker's Hole" echoes in the World War I mock sung to the bugle cry "Reveille." J. Barre Toelken forwarded it from the Oregon Gordon Collection where it is No. 150.

> There's a sailor in the grass with a soldier on his ass.
> Take it out, take it out, take it out, take it out.

The Pioneers

This is a far cry from the schoolboy's myth of the overlanders braving the savage land, fighting off the marauding Indians, turning the wilderness into a Garden of Eden. One suspects the tone of the song is a lot closer to the attitude of the overlanders themselves than school books would lead us to believe.

[A]

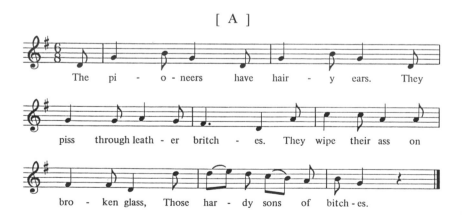

The pi - o - neers have hair - y ears. They piss through leath - er britch - es. They wipe their ass on bro - ken glass, Those har - dy sons of bitch - es.

228

The pioneers have hairy ears.
They piss through leather britches.
They wipe their ass on broken glass,
Those hardy sons-of-bitches.

When cunt is rare, they fuck a bear.
They knife him if he snitches.
They knock their cocks against the rocks,
Those hardy sons-of-bitches.

They take their ass upon the grass
In bushes or in ditches.
Their two-pound dinks are full of kinks,
Those hardy sons-of-bitches.

Without remorse, they fuck a horse,
And beat him if he twitches,
Their two-foot pricks are full of nicks,
Those hardy sons-of-bitches.

To make a mule stand for the tool,
They beat him with hickory switches.
They use their pricks for walking sticks,
Those hardy sons-of-bitches.

Great joy they reap from cornholing sheep
In barns, or bogs or ditches,
Nor give a damn if it be a ram,
Those hardy sons-of-bitches.

They walk around, prick to the ground,
And kick it if it itches,
And if it throbs, they scratch it with cobs,
Those hardy sons-of-bitches.

[B]

The cannoneers, they have no fears,
They piss through leather britches
And knock their cocks 'gainst jagged rocks,
Those hardy sons of bitches.

They masturbate from morn till late
Till their bloody foreskin twitches.
Next morn at ten they begin again,
Those hardy sons of bitches.

When tail is rare, they rape the bear
In dusky nooks and niches,

Nor give a care for sand or hair,
Those hardy sons of bitches.

They crawl and creep upon a sheep,
And fuck her while she pitches,
Nor give a damn if it be a ram,
Those hardy sons of bitches.

They scrounge a cow and care not how
The shit sticks to their breeches
And fergie a bull and fill him full,
Those hardy sons of bitches.

The cannoneers have hairy ears,
Nor care how much it itches,
To wipe their ass on broken glass,
Those hardy sons of bitches.

This is one of a group of parodies, generally sung to the tune of "Son of a Gambolier," that defame various occupations or branches of the military service. Leach (p. 115) has one entitled "The Infantry"; Dolph (p. 179) has "The M.P.s"; Wallrich (p. 195) has "The A.P.s"; and Legman, *The Limerick* (p. 420, n. 752) cites one entitled "The Engineers." Niles, Moore, and Wallgren, (pp. 29-42) have a spate of such slanders. The tune is in Dolph (pp. 125-26).

The late San Francisco lexicographer Peter Tamony has cited some evidence in *American Notes & Queries* (10 [1972]: 72) that the civilian "hairy-eared engineers" has entered oral tradition. Tamony recalled one verse of the song, to the tune of "Son of a Gambolier," heard about 1919:

The engineers have hairy ears,
And wear red-leather britches;
They knock their cocks against hard rocks,
The hardy sons-of-bitches.

A similar quatrain dated to 1929 from Michigan's Upper Peninsula is in the Indiana University Folklore Archives.

In his novel of pre-World War II China, *The Sand Pebbles*, Richard McKenna uses two verses of a song obviously from the same tradition that celebrates naval personnel assigned to China's Hunan Province:

Us Hunaneers, we got no fears,
We do not stop at trifles;
We hang our balls upon the walls
And shoot at them with rifles. (p. 68 of the Fawcett edition)

> Us Hunaneers, we shed no tears,
> We give no damn for riches;
> We prong our wives with butcher knives,
> Us hardy sons-of-bitches. (p. 70)

A variant of the first stanza circulates as a children's song. Shaw (p. 7) has it, and a similar text is sung by Los Angeles schoolchildren.

While the most common melody for the song is "Son of a Gambolier," the melody used here is "The Hearse Song." See Sandburg (p. 444) or Dolph (pp. 122-23) for versions set to "Hearse."

Fuld (p. 516) notes early appearances of the tune, citing its first printing in *Carmina Yalensia* in 1873. Within three years it had been borrowed by vaudevillian Ed Harrigan for a textually unrelated comic stage song, "Dunderbeck." Not until 1919, Fuld states, was the tune linked to the Rambling Wrecks of Georgia Institute of Technology. The Georgia Tech/wreck line seemingly inspired the cowboy song "Joe Williams," as given in Logsdon (pp. 182-85).

The "A" text and tune here was furnished by Dale Koby in 1961 and probably is derived from *Immortalia* (1927), a copy of which he owned. Koby's last verse is different, however. A similar text is in *Songs of Roving and Raking* (p. 80), credited to Gershon Legman with slight variations. Legman's text is apparently from *Immortalia* ([1927]: 27, reprinted in 1968, 45). Babab (p. 93) has the same text, with a tune added by the editor.

The "B" text is from a typescript in the Robert W. Gordon California collection in the Library of Congress. It is attributed only to a former artilleryman who sang it in Berkeley in 1923—presumably to the tune of "Son of a Gambolier."

The Gay Caballero

This song, under one or another title, was known on various college campuses well before Ohio State University student Frank Crumit edited and then recorded it. That record sold very well before falling into virtual oblivion. Meanwhile, the original bawdy song lives on.

[A]

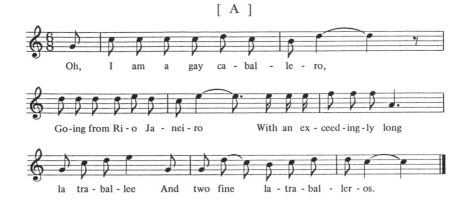

Oh, I am a gay caballero,
Going from Rio de Janeiro
With an exceedingly long latraballee
And two fine latraballeros.

I went down to Tijuana,
Exceedingly fine Tijuana,
With my exceedingly long latraballee
And my two fine latraballeros.

I met a gay senorita,
Exceedingly gay senorita.
She wanted to play with my latraballee,
And with one of my latraballeros.

Oh, now I've got the clapito,
Exceedingly painful clapito,
Right on the end of my latraballee,
And on one of my latraballeros.

I went to see a medico,
Exceedingly fine medico.
He looked at the end of my latraballee
And at one of my latraballeros.

He took out a long stiletto,
Exceedingly long stiletto.
He cut off the end of my latraballee
And one of my latraballeros.

And now I'm a sad caballero,
Returning to Rio de Janiero,

Minus the end of my latraballee
And one of my latraballeros.

At night I lay on my pillow
Seeking to finger my willow.
All I find there is a handful of hair
And one dried-up latraballero.

[B]

There once was a gay Don d'Ilio,
Who lived in a high white castilio
And he played with his trototoilio
And the works of his raggle de bam, bam! bam!

One day to that high white castilio
There came a gay young senorio [sic]
And she played with trototoilio
And the works of his raggle de bam, bam! bam!

Next day that gay Don d'Ilio
Laid her down on a soft sofailio
And he eased in his trototoilio
And the works of his raggle de bam, bam! bam!

Nine days later that gay Don d'Ilio
Gnashed his teeth with rage at the senorio
And gazed with sorrow on his trototoilio
And the works of his raggle de bam, bam! bam!

He went to see Dr. Gonzalio
Who told him he had the clapilio
And he gave him a bottle of castorio
For the works of his raggle de bam, bam! bam!

The "A" version, one of five in the editor's files, was gathered by
Dean Burson from his Carnegie Tech informant who learned it about
1959. The oldest version of this "exceedingly" text is in Nettleingham's *More* (p. 81) expurgated, but of World War I military currency.

The "B" text is No. 448 in the Robert W. Gordon Collection of
American Folk Song at the University of Oregon, dated December,
1927, and was forwarded by J. Barre Toelken. Randolph's "Unprintable" (pp. 519-21) has the familiar melody with a similar, if fragmentary text his informant said she first heard about 1912. These
are seemingly incomplete versions of the song later adapted, then
copyrighted by Lou Klein and Frank Crumit, and released as RCA
Victor V-21735 in 1929. (David Ewen, *Life and Death of Tin Pan Alley*

[New York, 1964]: 302, states that Crumit's record sold almost two million copies.)

The college song may also be responsible for this limerick—or vice versa:

> There once was a Spanish nobilio
> Who lived in a Spanish castilio.
> His *cojones* grew hot
> More often than not
> At the thought of a Spanish jazzilio.

Whatever the original song—and the record is too fragmentary to permit definitive statements—the limericks of "I-Yi-Yi-Yi" *are* sung to the tune used for "The Gay Caballero." The Crumit tune serves too as the vehicle for "The Gun Canecutter" in Matthews and Anderson (p. 106); and "Brown Flour," a local Newfoundland song written shortly after the Crumit record was released. "Flour" is in Peacock 1 (p. 46). The first four bars of "Caballero" also bear the quatrain "Sally McWhorter" in Randolph's banned materials (pp. 163-64). Wallrich (p. 132) has another text entirely, "The Ten Thousand-Mile Bomber," set to it.

Though American in origin, this song has traveled widely. Morgan 2 (pp. 29-31) has it from British rugby circles. Laycock's (pp. 224-25) is from 1960 and Canberra. His text offers the moral:

> Now listen you filthy backstreeters,
> If you want to go fuck senoritas,
> And you don't want the pox,
> Shove socks on the tops
> Of your roto-roto-maree-os.

American versions of the song are in *Immortalia* ([1927]: 128; the reprint of 1968, 45); and Hart's *Immortalia*, 3 (pp. 40 ff.), with this tune. Getz 2 (pp. GG2) prints two versions from air force songbooks. Reuss (pp. 261-62) has a seven-stanza variant, from Michigan State University, collected in 1953. Legman, *The Horn Book* (p. 228) gives one stanza. The bawdy song continues to circulate, witness two variants from the same singer, cowboy Riley Neal, in Logsdon (pp. 169-72).

The editor remembered from his youth, prior to 1948, a similar parody sung to the melody of "Alla en el Rancho Grande," a 1934 Mexican import that achieved great popularity in the United States. The ribald rewrite runs:

My name is Pancho Villa.
I got the gonorrhea.
I got from Maria,
She gave it to me free-a.
Ha-ha-ha-ha.

I took her to my castle,
And laid her for a peso.
I fucked her in the asshole,
And fucked her in the face-o.
Ha-ha-ha-ha.

Reuss (p. 263) had a four-line fragment of this from Phoenix, Arizona, circa 1959.

Humoresque

This is atypical of American bawdy song. First of all, the tune is borrowed from the familiar piano composition by Antonín Dvořák. Second, it makes no real sense; the last two stanzas bear no relation to the first two. Finally, co-authorship of it is claimed by no less a figure than the late Associate Justice of the Supreme Court William O. Douglas.

Pas - sen-gers will please re-frain From flush - ing toi - lets while the train Is stand - ing in the sta - tion. I love you. We en-cour - age con - sti-pa - tion While the train is in the sta - tion. Moon-light al-ways makes me think of you.

[A]

Passengers will please refrain
From flushing toilets while the train
Is standing in the station. I love you.
We encourage constipation
While the train is in the station.
Moonlight always makes me think of you.

If you simply have to go
When other people are too slow,
There is only one thing you can do.
You'll just have to take a chance,
Be brave and do it in your pants,
But I'll forgive you, darling. I love you.

[B]

Every evening after dark
We goose the statues in the park;
If Sherman's horse can stand it, so can you.
Washington was very firm
And Lincoln didn't even squirm.
Darling, that's why I'm in love with you.

[C]

Mabel, Mabel, strong and able,
Get your big ass off the table.
Don't you know the quarter is for beer?
You can always earn your pay,
But make your tips another way,
And I'll forgive you, darling. I love you.

[D]

I love to go out after dark
And goose the statues in the park,
A lovely pastime at the close of day!
Unperturbed they stand so still,
While WHOOPS! it's me that gets the thrill.
It really is a lovely way to play.

I've noticed lately
They stand so stately
Out there in the dark when dew is on the ground.

I sometimes tease them
And do displease them,
If I fail to show up as the sun goes down.

The Thinker is the only one
With whom I can have no fun.
He sits upon a boulder, rough and coarse.
Napoleon sits upon his steed.
I cannot goose him, no indeed,
And so instead I goose his horse.

Passengers will please refrain
From flushing toilets while the train
Is standing in the station. I love you.
Prostitutes and lovely ladies
Have to douche or they'll have babies.
If Sherman's horse can take it, why can't you?

Ever since you met our Nelly,
She's had trouble with her belly,
Wish you'd never seen our little town!
Ever since I met your Venus
I've had trouble with my penis.
Wish I'd never seen your little town.

This is another of the more frequently encountered bawdy songs, though most informants seem to know only one or two verses. The song is unusual in that it is one of the very few with a genuine oral currency set to melodies drawn from what is known as "art" or "classical" music.

Dvořák published his set of six *Humoresques,* Op. 101, in 1894. Sometime in the early 1930s, according to his autobiography, *Go East, Young Man* (pp. 171-72), William O. Douglas and fellow Yale law school professor Thurman Arnold were riding the New Haven Railroad and were inspired by a sign in the toilet:

Thurman and I got the idea of putting these memorable words to music, and Thurman quickly came up with the musical refrain from *Humoresque:*

Passengers will please refrain
from flushing toilets while the train
is standing in
or passing through
a station.

Thurman at once addressed the passengers in the parlor car and taught them to sing this song in unison. After many attempts, they were

237

able to make a perfect rendition. Thereafter, it was common on the New Haven to hear people singing the song.

If Arnold and Douglas are to be credited with the composition, the song certainly spread quickly. Wallrich (p. 166), in presenting a World War II air force version in three verses, says that he first heard the song on college campuses in the early 1930s. Legman (*The Limerick,* 465, n. 1676) dates his version to 1944. Brand's text (pp. 48-49, reprinted in Babab, 73); Getz 1 (p. S-9); and Getz 2 (p. HH-10) are undated.

Other versions are in *Songs of Roving and Raking* (pp. 64-65) and *Songs of Raunch and Ill-Repute* (p. 2). Morgan 1 (pp. 73-74) has a British text. Hogbotel and Ffuckes (pp. 62-63); and Laycock (pp. 162-63) have Australian texts.

The "A" version here is from the editor's youth in Los Angeles, circa 1945. It was considered very risque at the time.

The "B" text is from Robert Leventhal of Los Angeles and dates from approximately the same time.

The "C" text is from Marjorie Cray and was learned in San Diego about 1960.

The "D" version is from the Harry A. Taussig Collection, compiled at Berkeley, California, between 1958 and 1963.

Others of these impertinent art songs have achieved oral currency. Children carol, to the melody of Bizet's "Toreodor Song":

> Toreodor-a, don't spit on the floor-a,
> Use the cuspidor-a, that's what it's for-a.

Less well known are these two children's ditties sung to "The Soldier's Chorus" from Gounod's *Faust*:

> My father murdered a kangaroo,
> Gave me the grisily part to chew.
> Wasn't that a helluva thing to do,
> To give me to chew the grisily part of a dead kangaroo?

That from Roger D. Abrahams of Philadelphia. Marjorie Morris of Los Angeles remembered this from her youth to the same melody:

> Hey, Aunt Jemima, look at your Uncle Jim.
> He's in the bathtub learning how to swim.
> First he does the backstroke, then he does the crawl,
> Now he's under water doing nothing at all.

Christopher Logue, as Count Vicarion, offers this to the tune of "La Dona E Mobile":

> Arseholes are cheap today,
> Cheaper than yesterday,
> Small boys are half-a-crown,
> Standing up or lying down,
> Big ones for bigger pricks,
> Biggest ones cost three-and-six,
>
> Get yours before they're gone,
> Come now and try one. (No. 40)

The same is in Morgan 1 (p. 136) and Getz 2 (p. AA-11).

Christian Gunning's copy of The USC Marching Band's unofficial songbook, "Hymenal," contains these lines to be sung to the "Hallelujah Chorus" of Handel's *Messiah*. Their oral currency beyond USC has not been established:

> Chorus:
> Eat my butt out.
> Eat my butt out.
> Eat my butt out, eat my butt out.
> Eat my butt out.
>
> Please lick my sweaty balls,
> They're so dirty.
> They're so dirty. They're so dirty.
> They're so dirty. They're so dirty.
>
> Please eat my crusty ass,
> It's so mushy.
> It's so mushy. It's so mushy.
> It's so mushy. It's so mushy.

To all these notices of classical tunes in oral currency may be added Bronson's citation of a portion of a Gluck melody used to carry a Kentucky text of "The Two Brothers" (Child 49). See his first volume (p. 387).

Footprints on the Dashboard

Another poem set to "Humoresque," this sometimes travels as part of the longer song.

> Was it you who did the pushin',
> Put the stains upon the cushion,
> Footprints on the dashboard upside down?

239

Was it your sly woodpecker
That got into my girl Rebecca?
If it was, you better leave this town.

It was I who did the pushin',
Put the stains upon the cushion,
Footprints on the dashboard upside down.
But since I got into your daughter,
I've had trouble passing water,
Now I guess we're even all around.

There have been five other reports of this song. Getz 2 (p. HH-10) has it from an air force songbook, perhaps James P. Durham's "Bull Durham's Songs of S.E.A." ([1970]: 4). It is also included in the undated, mimeographed "Shitty Songs of SX [Sigma Chi]," a copy of which was furnished by Guy Logsdon. Laycock (pp. 140-41) has a presumably Australian version.

Collected by Kenneth M. Moss, 1964, from a member of Acacia fraternity, UCLA, this text was deposited in the UCLA Folklore Archives. F. M. Rivinus forwarded to the editor a second text, from Philadelphia, circa 1945.

Caviar Comes from Virgin Sturgeon

Some years ago actor-folksinger Burl Ives recorded a song that he called "The Eddystone Lighthouse," happily caroling for children an innocent fragment of a longer piece of bawdry. This is a larger portion of that song, sung to the familiar tune of "Reuben, Reuben, I've Been Thinking."

[A]

Cav-i-ar comes from vir-gin stur-geon.
Vir-gin stur-geon's a ver-y fine dish. Ver-y few stur-geon
are ev-er vir-gin, That's why cav-i-ar's a ver-y rare dish.

Caviar comes from virgin sturgeon;
Virgin sturgeon's a very fine dish.
Very few sturgeon are ever virgin,
That's why caviar's a very rare dish.

Caviar comes from virgin sturgeon;
Virgin sturgeon's a very fine fish.
Virgin sturgeon needs no urgin';
That's why caviar is my dish.

I fed caviar to my girlfriend;
She was a virgin tried and true.
Now my girlfriend needs no urgin',
There isn't anything that she won't do.

I fed caviar to my grandpa;
He was a gent of ninety-three.
Shrieks and squeals revealed that grandpa
Had chased grandma up a tree.

Father was the keeper of the Eddystone light,
And he slept with a mermaid one fine night.
Results of this were offspring three;
Two were fishes and the other was me.

The postman came on the first of May;
The policeman came on the very next day.
Nine months later there was hell to pay:
Who fired that first shot, the blue or the gray?

Little Mary went a-sledding,
And her sled turned upside down.
Now little Mary's singing,
"M'ass is in the cold, cold ground."

[B]

Shad roe comes from scarlet shad fish.
Shad fish have a very sorry fate.
Pregnant shad fish is a sad fish,
Got that way without a mate.

The green sea turtle's mate is happy
With her lover's winning ways.
First he grips her with his flippers,
Then he grips and flips for days.

Mrs. Clam is optimistic,
Shoots her eggs out in the sea,

241

Hopes her suitor is a shooter,
With the self-same shot as she.

Give a thought to the happy codfish,
Always there when duty calls.
Female codfish is an odd fish;
From them come codfish balls.

[C]

Caviar comes from virgin sturgeon.
Virgin sturgeon's a very fine fish.
Virgin sturgeon need no urgin'.
That's why caviar is my dish.

Oysters they are fleshy bivalves.
They have youngsters in their shell.
How they diddle is a riddle,
But they do, so what the hell.

The content and vocabulary of this song would indicate its origins and development lie among a group not usually thought of as "folk" — educated urbanites. Its preservation in oral tradition since the First World War (it may well be older) indicates that, despite higher education and increasing urbanization, oral tradition persists.

The first firm date of this song is in 1934 when L. T. Jack Shoemaker heard Bill Comer of Orlando, Florida, sing one stanza, apparently the first here, at the annual "Promenade" of the American Legion's 40 and 8. (This would suggest the song dates from perhaps World War I.) See *Bawdy Ballads and Lusty Lyrics* (Indianapolis: Drake House Publishers [c. 1935, c. 1950]: 124).

"Caviar" is invariably sung to the tune "Reuben, Reuben." That song is dated at least to 1871, according to Fuld. Levy's *Flashes* (p. 109) reprints the cover of an 1878 Boston imprint, and a transcription of the original song.

"Reuben" has been used too for other songs. Fiddlin' John Carson recorded the comic number "Papa's Billy Goat" in 1923 for Okeh Records, according to Cohen (p. 290). It has also been used for other bawdy songs. Ed McCurdy sings a variant of one such, "Fellow From Fortune," which he calls "Sally Brown" on his recording *Songs of the Sea* (Cambridge 11):

Sally Brown she had a baby.
Father said that he don't care.

242

It belongs to a fellow from Fortune
What was fishing up here last year.

Sally goes to church on Sunday,
Not to sing and pray, I fear.
But to see that fellow from Fortune
What was fishing up here last year.

Another maritime song, "Lots of Fish in Bonavist Harbor," uses the same melody and has ribald verses. Alan Mills sings a variant with a hint of ribaldry on *Songs, Fiddle Tunes and a Folktale from Canada* (Folkways FG 3532). The tune also carries "The Raw Recruit," in Dolph (pp. 17-18) with a seemingly expurgated text. Randolph's "Unprintable" (p. 344) has another he titles "Mistress Murphy."

Reuss (pp. 200-201) offers extensive citations to underground printings and offers three versions of "Caviar" from college sources. Other texts of the song may be found in Leach (p. 118); Lynn (p. 33); *New Locker Room Humor* (pp. 60-61); *Songs of Roving and Raking* (p. 79); *Songs of Raunch and Ill-Repute* (p. 17, reprinted in Babab, 99); and Getz (p. UV-3). It is recorded on *Barely Alive* (Sault Antlers Records).

For British Empire currency, see Logue-Vicarion, No. 25; Morgan 1 (pp. 130, and p. 129), where six "Caviar" stanzas have been tacked by a printer's error to the end of another song. Laycock (pp. 271-73) has an Australian text, Hopkins (p. 172) a Canadian.

There are five versions of varying length and ingenuity—as well as zoological accuracy—in the editor's collection. The "A" version here is from the Dean Burson collection, as sung at Carnegie Tech in 1959. The "B" text was collected by James W. Kellogg in 1963 in Texas and was forwarded through the courtesy of Roger D. Abrahams; the stanzas entered at "C" were collected by the editor in Santa Barbara in 1962 from an employee of the Center for the Study of Democratic Institutions.

The Sexual Life of the Camel

The Sphinx is one of the seven wonders of the world. This commonly found American ditty does not rank quite so high.

[A]

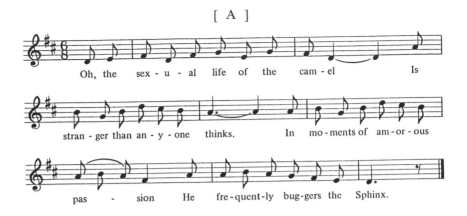

Oh, the sex - u - al life of the cam - el Is stran - ger than an - y - one thinks. In mo - ments of am - or - ous pas - sion He fre - quent - ly bug - gers the Sphinx.

Oh, the sexual life of the camel
Is stranger than anyone thinks.
In moments of amorous passion,
He frequently buggers the Sphinx.

But the Sphinx's posterior passage
Is clogged with the sands of the Nile,
Which accounts for the hump on the camel,
And the Sphinx's inscrutable smile.

[B]

The sexual life of the camel
Is stranger than anyone thinks.
At the height of the mating season,
He tries to bugger the sphinx.
But the sphinx's posterior sphincter
Is clogged by the sands of the Nile,
Which accounts for the hump on the camel
And the sphinx's inscrutable smile.

In the process of syphilization
From the anthropoid ape down to man,
It is generally held that the Navy
Has buggered whatever it can.
Yet recent extensive researches
By Darwin and Huxley and Hall
Conclusively prove that the hedgehog
Has never been buggered at all.

244

We therefore believe our conclusion
Is incontrovertibly shown
That comparative safety on shipboard
Is enjoyed by the hedgehog alone.
Why haven't they done it at Spithead
As they've done it at Harvard and Yale
And also at Oxford and Cambridge
By shaving the spines off its tail?

This sophisticated ditty is one of the more popular songs in the urban singing tradition, judging from the editor's collection. It is a good example, too, of the sort of song most likely to be retained by educated urban singers. By no means do they eschew the obscene, but they seem to appreciate it the more if it is clever, literate and, like the limerick, dependent upon some specialized information. Hoffmann has affixed to the song motif number X734.5.2, "hedgehog cannot be buggered."

Songs of Roving and Raking (p. 101) has the two stanzas of "A" embedded in a longer song set to the traditional Irish street ballad tune "Mush, Mush, Mush Tour-a-li-ady." The same is in *Songs of Raunch and Ill-Repute* (p. 3). Reuss (pp. 273-74) includes a variant from Michigan State University credited ultimately to military currency. He also has a two-stanza text from Indiana University, collected in 1964, with no tune indicated. Reuss cites no less than forty-six variants from three midwestern institutions now housed in the Indiana University Folklore Archives, and references to the song in ephemeral collections. Getz 1 (pp. S-7, 8) also has it.

Reisner (p. 58) prints two versions without music, garnered from lavatory walls. He adds cryptically, "Quite common in England and has been set to music." Other "British" texts are in Morgan 1 (p. 137); Morgan 2 (p. 36). Laycock (pp. 125-26) says his version is to be sung to "The Eton Boating Song."

The "A" version here, one of three nearly identical texts in the editor's files, was contributed by Robert Easton, an actor and voice coach, who collected it in Los Angeles in 1960. The poem is also sung to "My Bonnie Lies Over the Ocean."

The "B" text is from Indiana University's rugby team, circa 1966, as collected by Bill Zimmerman at that school.

I Used to Work in Chicago

The plays-upon-words in this product of urban America are either the best, or the worst, depending upon your point of view, in bawdy songlore. The song was most popular among high school students prior to 1960; a generation later, students of that age are doing it, not singing about it.

[A]

Chorus:
I used to work in Chicago
In a department store.
I used to work in Chicago.
I did but I don't anymore.

A lady came in for some gloves one day.
"What will you have?" I said.
"Rubber," she said, and rub her I did.
I did but I don't anymore.

A lady came in for a hat one day.
"What will you have?" I said.
"Felt," she said, and feel her I did.
I did but I don't anymore.

The following verses substitute these products and reactions:

Cake . . . layer . . . lay her I did
Dress . . . jumper . . . jump her I did
Shoe . . . pump . . . pump her I did

[B]

Chorus:
I used to work in Chicago
In a department store.
I used to work in Chicago.
I did but I don't anymore.

A lady came in for a dress one day.
"What'll it be," I said.
"Jumper," she said and jumper I did.
I did but I don't any more.

Poultry . . . goose . . . goose her I did
Meat . . . neck . . . neck her I did

[C]

A lady came in for some fruit one day.
"What will you have?" said I.
"Plums," she said, and plumb her I did.
I did but I don't anymore.

Cake . . . layer . . . lay her I did
Hardware . . . nails . . . nail her I did
Cinnamon . . . sticks . . . stick her I did
Pea soup . . . split . . . split her I did
Milk . . . cream . . . cream her I did
Booze . . . liquor . . . lick her I did
Covers . . . spread . . . spread her I did
Banana . . . peeled . . . peel her I did
Some rope . . . jump . . . jump her I did
Dress . . . jumper . . . jump her I did

There are a number of leads to the possible origin of the song. In a variant the editor sang circa 1950, the last line of each verse, "I'll never go there anymore," and that portion of the melody are identical to the last line of the chorus of "The Bowery," the popular song written in 1892 by Percy Gaunt and Charles H. Hoyt and published by T. B. Harms, New York City. There is no other similarity, either

247

in tune or text. In the present form then, "I Used to Work in Chicago" would seem to postdate the publication of "The Bowery."

The first phrases of the melody are those of the all-too-familiar "The Bear Went Over the Mountain," "Pig in the Parlor," or "Marbrough s'en va-t-en guerre." Spaeth *(History,* 31) summarizes the appearances of "Marbrough." Botkin (p. 290) locates a fragment of what may be the forerunner of the play-party "Pig in the Parlor," a single stanza that hints of the same Scots-Irish tinkers' song that gave rise to "My God, How the Money Rolls in."

That tinkers' song appears on Arthur Argo's *A Wee Thread o' Blue* (Prestige 13048) as "Haben Aboo an a Banner" with this verse:

> Then I was a draper in London.
> A lady cam' into my shop.
> Oh, she asked for three yards o' my linen.
> I gave her three yards o' my
> > Haben aboo an' a banner,
> > Haben aboo an' a bay,
> > My haben aboo an' a banner
> > Mish-a-toodle-i-toodle-i-ay.

(Argo's tune is unrelated, a set of "Mush, Mush, Mush Tour-a-li-ady.")

"The Jolly Tradesmen," from D'Urfey's *Pills to Purge Melancholy,* 6 (pp. 91 ff.) uses the same formulaic wordplay of "I Used to Work in Chicago" and the shop verse of Argo's tinkers' song. The second, fourth, and eighth stanzas of "The Jolly Tradesmen" are example enough of the *double entendre*:

> Sometimes I am a Butcher,
> And then I feel fat Ware, Sir;
> And if the Flank be fleshed well,
> I take no farther care, Sir;
> But in I thrust my Slaughtering-Knife,
> Up to the Haft with speed, Sir;
> For all that ever I can do,
> I cannot make it bleed, Sir.

> Sometimes I am a Glover,
> And can do passing well, Sir;
> In dressing of a Doe-skin,
> I know I do excel, Sir.
> But if by chance a Flaw I find,
> In dressing of the Leather;
> I straightway whip my needle out,
> And I tack 'em close together.

> The Tanner's Trade I practice,
> Sometimes amongst the rest, Sir;
> Yet I could never get a Hair,
> Of any Hide I dress'd, Sir;
> For I have been tanning of a Hide,
> This long seven Years and more, Sir;
> And yet it is as hairy still,
> As ever it was before, Sir.

Were the wordplay of "The Jolly Tradesmen" fitted to the satirical quatrains of "Have You Heard of a Frolicksome Ditty?," the result might well be something close to the "shop" stanza in the tinkers' song. As "Song CCXXXIX" in *The Vocal Miscellany* (3d ed., London [1738]: 1, 214-15), the satirical stage song "Have You Heard" runs:

> 1 Man.   I once was a Poet at *London*,
>   I kept my Heart still full of Glee;
>   There's no Man can say that I'm undone,
>   For begging's no new Trade to me.
>   *Tol derol*, &c.

> 2 Man.   I once was an Attorney at Law,
>   And after a Knight of the Post:
>   Give me a brisk Wench of clean Straw,
>   And I value not who rules the Roast.
>   *Tol derol*, &c.

> 3 Man.   Make room for a Solider in Buff,
>   Who valiantly strutted about,
>   Till he fancy'd the Peace breaking off,
>   And then he most wisely—sold out.
>   *Tol derol*, &c.

> 4 Man.   Here comes a Courtier polite, Sir,
>   Who flatter'd my Lord to his Face;
>   Now railing is all his Delight, Sir,
>   Because he miss'd getting a Place,
>   *Tol derol*, &c.

> 5 Man.   I still am a merry Gut-Scraper,
>   My Heart never yet felt a Qualm;
>   Tho' poor, I can frolick and vapour,
>   And sing any Tune, but a Psalm.
>   *Tol derol*, &c.

6 Man.   I was a fanatical Preacher,
          I turn'd up my Eyes when I pray'd;
          But my Hearers half starved their Teacher,
          For they believ'd not one Word that I said.
          Tol derol, &c.

1 Man.   Whoe'er would be merry and free,
          Let him list, and from us he may learn:
          In Palaces who shall you see,
          Half so happy as we in a Barn?
          Tol derol, &c.

    CHORUS of all.

Whoe'er would be merry and free,
Let him list, and from us he may learn:
In Palaces who shall you see,
Half so happy as we in a Barn?
    Tol derol, &c.

This song, too, is set to the tune of "Old Hewson the Cobbler," the "scurrilous and indecent" ditty that led eventually to "My God, How the Money Rolls In." Thus, early in its life—in 1731, according to James C. Dick's edition of *The Songs of Robert Burns* (p. 415)— when it was sung in the ballad opera *The Jovial Crew,* "Old Hewson" is carrying the stanzaic kernels of "I Used to Work in Chicago." From that would come "Pig in the Parlor," "I Used to Work in Chicago," and "My God, How the Money Rolls In." The line of descent would stem from the tinkers' song, lead to an unrecovered version of a game or play-party song set to the tune of "Marbrough" and containing something close to the "store-shop" verses in some texts of the tinkers' song.

The game or play-party song would, in turn, spawn both "Pig in the Parlor," with its "Marbrough" tune, and "I Used to Work in Chicago," set to the same tune—until warped a bit by the later "The Bowery."

The editor first heard "I Used to Work in Chicago" while in high school in 1948 in Los Angeles. Memory of that version coincided closely with the two collected by Anne Smith in 1960 and Sandra Stolz the following year. The "A" text is from Ms. Smith. The "B" text is from Ms. Stolz, the "C" from the editor's memory. Three other versions are in the editor's collection.

In a letter of May 13, 1971, Oscar Brand claimed he wrote additional verses to "Chicago," and is responsible for its currency. His version was copyrighted in 1951.

The earliest recovery of "Chicago" is in Larson's unpublished "Barnyard" collection, compiled in 1952 from material collected in Idaho as much as two decades before. Number 40 there reads:

> When I was in Chicago,
> I worked in a department store;
> I worked in a hosiery department—
> I did but I don't anymore.
>> A lady came asking for garters;
>> I asked her what kind she wore.
>> She pulled up her dress and said, "Rubber."
>> I did but I don't anymore.

Other printed variants are in *Songs of Raunch and Ill-Repute* (p. 14); and Getz 1 (p. I-10, from an air force songbook). Hart's *Immortalia*, 3 (pp. 16 ff.) has a virtually identical tune to that here. Morgan 2 (pp. 52-53) is from Great Britain, and Laycock (pp. 262-64) from Australia.

I Want to Play Piano in a Whorehouse

Sung broadly, in a whiskey tenor, this thumb-to-the-nose ditty makes mock of the bathetic laments of an earlier, more innocent time.

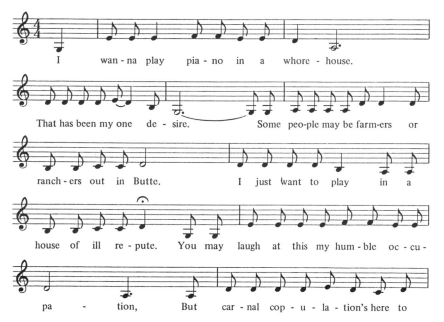

I wan-na play pia-no in a whore - house.
That has been my one de - sire. Some peo-ple may be farm-ers or
ranch-ers out in Butte. I just want to play in a
house of ill re - pute. You may laugh at this my hum - ble oc - cu -
pa - tion, But car - nal cop - u - la - tion's here to

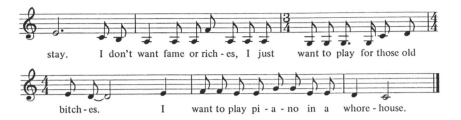

stay. I don't want fame or rich - es, I just want to play for those old

bitch - es. I want to play pi - a - no in a whore - house.

I wanna play piano in a whorehouse,
That has been my one desire.
Some people may be farmers or ranchers out in Butte,
I just want to play piano in a house of ill-repute.

You may laugh at this, my humble occupation,
But carnal copulation is here to stay.
I don't want fame or riches.
I just want to play for those old bitches.
I wanna play piano in a whorehouse.

Sung by Wally Fey, an air force veteran of the Vietnam Era, on a tape furnished by Bill Getz. Fey considered it "sort of a classic."
Getz 2 (p. II-8) prints a slightly different version.

Schnooglin'

In one or another form, this warning in rhyme is known in hundreds of girls' schools and summer camps. This version happens to come from a B'nai B'rith Girls' camp in Southern California — AZA is the organization for Jewish boys. It could have easily come from a YWCA, a Girl Scout, or a Catholic Youth Organization camp.

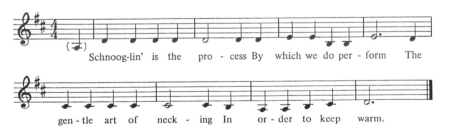

Schnoog-lin' is the pro - cess By which we do per - form The

gen - tle art of neck - ing In or - der to keep warm.

Schnooglin' is the process
By which we do perform

252

The gentle art of necking
In order to keep warm.

There's schnooglin' on the beaches,
Schnooglin' in the park.
An AZA can teach you
How to schnoogle in the dark.

Now gather round me, girlies,
And listen to my plea:
Don't ever trust an AZA
An inch above your knee.

I know a girl who tried it,
And dearly did she pay.
The son-of-a-gun, he left her
With the son of an AZA.

This little AZA boy,
He grew up one day,
And met a BBG girl
In the same old-fashioned way.

This little BBG girl,
She did not hear our plea,
And now they have between them
Another BBG.

The moral of this story
Is very plain to see:
Don't ever trust an AZA
An inch above the knee.

This was furnished by Marilyn Eisenberg Herzog who reported it sung by B'nai B'rith campers in Los Angeles about 1958. Her melody is a flattened out set of "Solomon Levi."

Harry A. Taussig caught a four-stanza version of the song in Berkeley between 1958 and 1963.

There Was an Old Lady

This is a constantly shifting aggregation of verses sung to the familiar "Turkey in the Straw" fiddle tune.

Oh, there was an old lady at the age of sixty-three.
She said, "Please, sonny, won't you stick it into me,
With your long-tailed Studebaker, asshole-belly-shaker,
Hi-ho lady-maker hangin' to your knee."

Chorus:
Come on you bastards, come on you whores.
Pull up your dresses, pull down your drawers.

254

First lady up and the second lady back,
Third lady's finger in the fourth lady's crack.

Oh, little Tommy Tucker, he came from France.
He played his fiddle at the fiddle-fucker's dance,
With his long-tailed Studebaker, asshole-belly-shaker,
Hi-ho lady-maker hangin' to his knee.

Oh, a fly flew into the grocery store.
He shit on the counter and he pissed on the floor.
He farted in the coffee and he barfed in the tea.
It splashed on the counter and it got on me.

Oh, she ripped and she tore and she shit on the floor,
She wiped her ass on the knob of the door.
And the moon shone bright on the nipple of her tit
Blue bird singing, "Sweet chicken shit."

Chorus:
Come on you bastards, come on you whores.
Pull up your dresses, pull down your drawers.
First lady up and the second lady back,
Third lady's finger in the fourth lady's crack.
        Sung by the whorehouse quartet.

This is a collection of fragments from other songs ("long tailed Studebaker" stems from "The Tinker," the name of an automobile substituting for "kidney-wiper" and "baby-maker" becoming "lady-maker"); a fiddle tune mnemonic ("First lady . . ."); and quatrains that circulate by themselves.

Randolph's "Unprintable" manuscript offers other verses to the melody (pp. 440-43). He also has (pp. 496-99) stanzas to a song in which a lady comes from France to "fiddle, fuck and dance." The "first lady up" chorus appears too in Randolph, set to several other fiddle tunes.

Cazden, Haufrecht, Studer (pp. 612-14) present a history of the melody. Fuld (pp. 107-8) offers an extended discussion of variant editions and origins, crediting stage and minstrel performer Mose Case with the 1858 composition of the tune. Bayard (pp. 276-80) has a clutch of variant tunes from Pennsylvania fiddling tradition.

The first two stanzas printed here are from Boulder, Colorado, deposited in the Indiana University Folklore Archive by Phil Savage in 1953. Robert Easton gathered the fly quatrain in Los Angeles in 1958. Alice O'Brien collected the ripped-and-tore verse in Los Angeles two years later.

Teasing Songs

There are any number of these songs, which stanza after stanza rush right up to the brink of the tabooed word, then do a hasty about-face. They are especially popular with children, though an occasional adult will remember one from childhood.

Suzanne Was a Lady

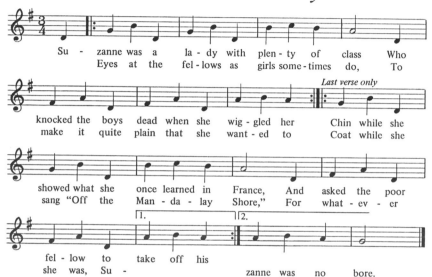

Suzanne was a lady with plenty of class
Who knocked the boys dead when she wiggled her

Eyes at the fellows as girls sometimes do
To make it quite plain that she wanted to

Go for a walk or a stroll through the grass,
Then hurry back home for a nice piece of

Ice cream and cake and piece of roast duck,
And after each meal she was ready to

Go for a walk or a stroll on the dock
With any young man with a sizeable

Roll of green bills and a pretty good front,
And if he talked fast enough, she would show him her

Little pet dog who's subject to fits,
And maybe let him grab hold of her

Little white hand with a movement so quick.
Then she'd lean over and tickle his

Chin while she showed what she once learned in France,
And asked the poor fellow to take off his

Coat while she sang "Off Mandalay Shore,"
For whatever she was, Suzanne was no bore.

A number of these teasing songs have been reported from oral tradition. Hoffmann has assigned to them two motif numbers: X749.5.1, teasing songs with word omitted; and X749.5.1.2, "teasing songs with homonyms."

The form itself has respectable antiquity. The *Percy Folio Manuscript*, dating to perhaps 1615, contains a poem entitled "A Friend of Mine" with three introductory stanzas tacked on to what would appear to be an even older folk song. (The first two of those stanzas are omitted here.)

It was my chance, not long ago,
By a pleasant wood to walk,
Where I unseen of any one
Did hear two lovers talk.

And as these lovers forth did pass
Hard by a pleasant shade,
Hard by a mighty pine tree there,
Their resting place they made.

"In sooth," then did this young man say,
"I think this fragrant place
Was only made for lovers true
Each other to embrace."

He took her by the middle small—
Good sooth I do not mock—
Not meaning to do any thing
But to pull up her [smock]

Block whereon she sat, poor silly soul,
To rest her weary bones.
This maid she was no whit afraid,
But she caught him fast by the [stones]

Thumbs, whereat he vexed and grieved was,
So that his flesh did wrinkle.

257

The maid she was no whit afraid,
But caught him fast hold by the [pintle]

Pimple which he had on his chin likewise.
(But let the pimple pass.)
There is no man here but he may suppose
She were a merry lass.

He boldly ventured, being tall,
Yet in his speech but blunt
He never ceased, but took up all
And catch'd her by the [cunt]

Plump and red rose lips he kissed full sweet.
Quoth she, "I crave no succor."
Which made him to have a mighty mind
To clip, kiss, and to [fuck her]

Pluck her into his arms. "Nay, soft," quoth she,
"What needeth all this doing?
"For if you will be ruled by me,
You shall use small time in wooing."

"For I will lay me down," quoth she,
"Upon the slippery seggs, (marsh plants)
And all my clothes I'll truss up round,
And spread abroad my [legs]

"Eggs which I have in my apron here
Under my girdle tucked;
So shall I be most fine and brave,
Most ready to be [fucked]

"Ducked unto some pleasant springing well,
For now it's time of the year
To deck, and bathe, and trim ourselves,
Both head, hands, feet, and gear."

These teasing songs have gained wide distribution. The Opies have three from English school children (pp. 94, 97). Other English rhymes of the type are in Shaw (pp. 99, 105, 109-10 and 112); and in Logue-Vicarion, "A Clean Story," No. 7. Laycock (pp. 32-33) and Winnan (p. 93) have others from Australia.

American recoveries are even more numerous. Nancy Leventhal collected a similar teasing rhyme from Hawthorne, California, children. See *Western Folklore* (22 [1963]: 245) and the references there. To those, add no less than six contained in the Randolph "Unprintable" manuscript: "Peter Murphy's Dog" (pp. 183-85); "The Handsome Young Farmer" (pp. 186-192); "There's Fun in the Country" (pp. 193-98); "Down on the Farm" (pp. 199-200); "A Soldier I Would Be" (p. 203-5); and "I Saw Her Snatch" (pp. 206-9). In addition Brand has two on *Bawdy Western Songs* (Audio Fidelity 1920) under the title "Pinto Pony" and "The Clean Song," also recorded on *Bawdy Sea Chanties* (Audio Fidelity 1884). Lynn's *Housemothers* (p. 28) has another. Francis Very reported yet another in the *Journal of American Folklore* (75 [1962]: 262). Getz 2 (pp. CC-5, 6; II-6; and NN-1, 2) has three more. Reuss (pp. 269-72) has two, as well as ephemeral references. The tune he prints is close to that printed here.

"Suzanne Was a Lady" is from the singing of Donald Naftulin, M.D., in Los Angeles in 1964. He learned the song some twenty years before as a boy in Toledo, Ohio. This version was recorded on *Barely Alive* (Sault Antlers Records). The Indiana University Folklore Archives contain two analogues.

The Ship's in the Harbor

The next two songs are sung to the same tune as "Suzanne."

The ship's in the harbor; she lies by the dock
Like a young man with a stiff standing

Backbone to brace when he stands and salutes,
Backbone to brace when he stands and salutes.

And there was young Johnny, the pride of the crew,
Who liked to drink whiskey and also to

Water the garden when he was at home,
Water the garden when he was at home.

He could swim like a fish and could swim like a duck.
He could show the young ladies a new way to

Save their sweet souls if they should have a cramp,
Save their sweet souls if they should have a cramp.

But then we put in at a far northern port,
And he froze it one morning and broke it off

Halfway to Juneau and halfway to Nome,
Halfway to Juneau and halfway to Nome.

The ship's in the harbor; she lies by the dock,
But, alas for poor Johnny, he has no more

Yardarm to splice with, or topmast to brace,
Yardarm to splice with, or topmast to brace.

The first six stanzas of this were sung by then-eight-year-old Virginia Newbold in 1958 in Santa Monica, California. The balance is from a version from Northern California furnished by Dale Koby. Koby's text is probably traceable to *Immortalia*, the 1927 edition of which has it on pages 62-63, the 1968 edition on page 79.

There Once Was a Farmer

There once was a farmer who lived by the crick.
For pleasure and pastime he played with his

Horses and cattle. In the days of his yore
He married a young lady he thought was a

Very nice young lady who rolled in the grass.
When she rolled over she showed him her

Hose and stockings. They fit like a duck.
She thought she had found a new way to

Raise up the children and teach them to knit,
While the boys in the barnyard shoveled up

Contents of the stable. They did it for fun.
If you think I composed this, you're a liar, by gum.

This is from the Western Kentucky Folklore Archive at UCLA, collected by Delane Simpson in Bowling Green, Kentucky, in 1957. It is a longer version than that from the editor's youth, learned about 1940 in either Cleveland or Los Angeles, and printed in the first edition of this book. Abrahams has forwarded a similar song from Texas. *Immortalia* (1927) and the 1968 reprint (p. 122) have an analogous recitation:

There was an old man sitting on a rock,
Watching little boys playing with their
Agates and marbles in springtime of yore;
While over in the bushes they watched a fat
Brunette young lady sitting in the grass;
When she rolled over you could see her shapely
Shoes and stockings that fit like a duck;
She said she was learning a new way to
Bring up her children and and teach them to knit;
As over in the bushes they were taking a
Little companion down to the docks;

260

And said they would show him the length of their—
You may think this is bull-shit,
But it isn't, by God!

Rather similar to that is "There Was a Rich Merchant," collected
in 1932 by Robert W. Gordon. It was forwarded by J. Barre Toelken
from the Gordon collection at the University of Oregon where it is
number 3853.

There was a rich merchant who sat on a rock
Amusing some women by shaking his

Stick at some ladies in front of a store.
Along came a lady who looked like a

Perfect young lady. She sat on the grass
And when she sat down I could see all her

Ruffles and flounces and each little tuck.
She said she was learning a new way to

Bring up her daughters to sew and to knit.
The boys in the the stable were shoveling

The stuff in the stable all over the sod.
And if you don't think so, just smell it, by God!

Two Irishmen, Two Irishmen

The most aggressive of these teasing songs, and perhaps the most
popular, finally plunges over the brink.

Two Irishmen, two Irishmen were digging in a ditch.
One called the other a dirty sonova-----

Peter Murphy had a dog, a very fine dog was he.
He gave it to a lady to keep her company.

She taught it, she taught it, she taught it how to jump.
He jumped right up her petticoat and bit her in the ----

Country boy, country boy sitting on a rock.
Along came a bumble bee and stung him on the ----

Cocktail, ginger ale, five cents a glass.
If you don't believe me, you can shove it up your ---

Ask me no questions; I'll tell you no lies.
If you ever get hit with a pail of shit, be sure to close your eyes.

Sung by Dick Bakken in Los Angeles in 1988. Bakken learned the song from a schoolmate, Donnie Zolman, in Spokane, Washington, about 1950. "Donnie always stressed whenever he did that song that it only had one dirty word in it, and it's not that bad of a one either," Bakken added. Laycock (pp. 192-93) has a variant of this from Australia.

Sweet Violets

My sister went out in the garden,
She went in the garden to sit, sit, sit, sit,
And when we looked out in the garden,
The ground was all covered with

Chorus:
Sweet violets,
Sweeter than all the roses,
Covered all over from head to toe,
Covered all over with

My baby, she swallowed a cherry.
She died from having a fit,
And while examining the diapers,
My fingers were covered with

My uncle went up in an airplane.
They strapped him down in the pit,
And when he walked out of the airplane,
The cabin was covered with

My sister, she married a sailor.
That fellow was really a wit,
But when he'd come home in the evening,
His pants were all covered with

And now that my story is ended,
I make my sudden ex-it.
If someone didn't like my story,
They can shower me with a bouquet of

For their popular song of 1951, Cy Coben and Charles Grean
actually adapted a folk song, according to Jacobs (p. 226). The model
was probably the bawdy "Sweet Violets," which is, fittingly enough,
itself a folk redaction of an earlier popular song.

This version is one of two in the Indiana University Folkore Archives. It was recovered in Chicago, Illinois, in 1948. Morgan 1 (p.
132-33); Getz (p. S-25); and Hopkins (p. 154) have other versions,
from Great Britain, United States Air Force, and Canadian military
currency. Hopkins also has the "Sweet Violets" melody.

Finally, we have two teasing recitations by school children, the first
a thumb-to-the-nose parody of Longfellow's "The Midnight Ride of
Paul Revere."

Listen, my children, and you shall hear
Of the midnight ride of Paul Revere.
He jumped in the car, stepped on the gas.
The bottom fell out and he fell on his

> Now don't get excited and don't be alarmed.
> I was going to say he fell on his arm.

And the second, a parody of a parody, no less:

> Listen, my children, and you shall hear
> Of the midnight ride of a glass of beer.
> Out of the icebox and into a glass,
> Down the stomach and out of your
>
> Don't get excited and don't get sore.
> Down the stomach and out to the floor.

Ditties

In the course of one's field work, a folk song collector is certain to turn up any number of short songs, or fragments of longer songs. Frequently, these do not see print unless the fragment is a survival of a rare song or ballad. These ditties are not necessarily rare at all.

To the tune of "The Irish Washerwoman":

> Oh, Binnie, oh, Binnie, oh come ye quick
> And see the wild Irishman handle his prick.
> 'Tis as long as your arm and as thick as your wrist
> With a knob on the end as big as your fist.

To the much-used melody of "Sweet Betsy from Pike":

> You can talk about fucking; well, fuckin's all right.
> I fucked with a whore twenty times in one night,
> And each time I fucked her, I came out a quart.
> If you don't think that's fucking, well, you fucking well ort.

The tune of the verse of the Civil War classic "Tramp, Tramp, Tramp" carries this burden:

> He was sitting in the prison with his head between his hands,
> And the shadow of his prick against the wall,
> And the hairs grew thick from his knees up to his prick,
> And the rats were playing billiards with his balls.

A number of quatrains borrow the tune of "Turkey in the Straw":

[A]

> Oh, I had a girl friend, she liked to sport and play,
> Cutest little girl friend that ever hit the hay.

The skin on her belly was tight as a drum,
And every time we fucked it went rub-a-dum-dum.

[B]

Shmendrick had a horse and he thought it was a cow,
And he went out to milk it and he didn't know how,
And the night was dark and dreary and Shmendrick couldn't see,
And the darned little horsey went a-wee, wee, wee.

[C]

She ripped and she tore, and she shit on the floor,
Wiped her ass on the knob on the door,
And the moon shone bright on the nipple of her teat.
Bluebird singing, "Sweet chicken shit."

A variant on this is somewhat more coherent:

Oh, the moon shone bright on the nipple of her teat
As she went to the outhouse to take a little shit,
But her ass gave a grunt and she shit on the floor,
And the smell of her farts drove the cat out the door.

To the melody of "Goodnight, Irene," a fashion note:

Sometimes Irene wears pajamas.
Sometimes Irene wears a gown.
Sometimes Irene wears nothing,
And shocks all the people in town.

The much-used melody of "The Girl I Left Behind Me" serves for these two songs:

The wind blew free and she couldn't see,
And the wind blew up her nightie.
You should have seen those great big teats,
Well, Jesus Christ almighty!
Oh, I pumped her once and I pumped her twice,
And I pumped her once too often,
And I broke the mainspring in her back,
And now she's in her coffin.

And:

Oh, there's hair on this and there's hair on that,
And there's hair on my dog, Fido.

265

> But there's far more hair, and I won't say where,
> On the girl I left behind me.

Yet another quatrain, collected by in 1956 in Kentucky, is set to the same melody:

> Oh, she wiggles and she wobbles and she shits on the floor.
> The blast from her ass blew the cat out the door.
> The moon shines bright on the nipple of her tit
> As she washes her teeth with canary bird shit.

To the saccharine strains of "If I Had the Wings of an Angel":

> Oh, if I had the wings of an angel
> And the ass of a hairy baboon,
> I would fly to the end of creation
> And cornhole the man in the moon.

And to the familiar "Red River Valley":

> Come and sit on my face if you love me.
> Come and sit on my face if you care.
> Let me eat out your red river valley.
> Let me tangle my teeth in your hair!

The melody of the longtime favorite "The Wreck of the Old Ninety-Seven" shoulders this burlesque:

> She was goin' down the grade makin' ninety miles an hour
> When the wheel on her bicycle broke.
> She was found in the grass with a sprocket up her ass
> And her titty was punctured by a spoke.

"Oh Binnie" was sung to the editor by management consultant Robert Leventhal in Los Angeles in 1955. Larson's "Barnyard" (p. 43) has it from Idaho. Getz 1 (p. I-8) presents another set of words to the tune. Randolph's "Unprintable" (pp. 465-46), has a variant of the stanza here and other quatrains to "The Irish Washerwoman." A variant on the last two lines runs:

> It's thick and it's hard and it spits at the end,
> And it's stronger than iron so it will not bend.

Frank M. Warner, "Folk Songs and Ballads from the Eastern Seaboard" (p. 2) has yet another quatrain hung on the tune:

> Oh, MacTavish is dead and his brother don't know it.
> His brother is dead, and MacTavish don't know it.
> They're both of them dead, and they're both in one bed,
> And neither one knows that the other is dead!

The editor recalls this anti-Gaelic screed from a misspent youth with the butt of the humor renamed Riley.

Folklorist Roger Abrahams forwarded "You Can Talk About Fucking" with the comment that it was a personal favorite. It turns up as the first stanza of three in what may be a British army song in Morgan 2 (p. 71).

"Shmendrick" served as a lullaby for Donald Naftulin, M.D., when his grandmother sang him to sleep in Toledo, Ohio, in the middle 1930s. Naftulin sang it for the editor in Los Angeles in 1964.

Off-color lullabies turn up now and again. Southern mountain children, the editor has been told, were lulled to sleep with:

> Daddy shot a bear, daddy shot a bear,
> Shot him through the asshole, never touched a hair.

(A tune for this is in Seeger, *Animal Folk Songs,* 78.) Bayard (p. 131) prints the couplet as sung in Pennsylvania.

Eminger Stewart of San Francisco reported a sly lullaby from eastern Oregon as current about 1932:

> Today is the day they give babies away
> With every pound of tea.
> If you know any ladies who want any babies,
> Just send them around to me.

Rosalie Sorrels has collected a variant from Utah singers; she has recorded it on *Rosalie's Songbag* (Prestige 13025). Combs, No. 15C, prints a Southern Mountain text. Reuss (p. 90) has it from Indiana's folklore archives as sung by college students, and Abrahams, in a letter to the editor, has identified it as "part of a farcical circus routine which was common in my adolescence." Shaw (p. 116) has a two-line fragment from Liverpool: "If any young lady wants a baby, / Come to the Cock of the North."

Bess Lomax Hawes furnished the "Goodnight, Irene" mock and the first of the quatrains sung to the melody of "The Girl I Left Behind Me." Getz 2 (p. SS-5, and WW-6, 7) has fuller versions of "The Girl," without tunes.

Abrahams forwarded both the second verse to "The Girl" and "She Ripped and She Tore" as collected by a former student. Of the latter, it might be noted that Laycock (p. 127) prints yet another quatrain, from an American graduate student in 1961:

> Oh, the moon shone bright on the nipple of her tit
> As she greased up her fanny with billygoat shit,

267

> And she wiggled and she giggled and she said with a roar,
> "Never have I seen such a tool before."

"The Girl I Left Behind Me" also carries "Two Ruby Red Lips," in Randolph ("Unprintable," 117) as well as other stanzas similar to that here (pp. 458-61).

"Oh, I Had a Girl Friend" is from the editor's imperfectly remembered boyhood in Los Angeles, about 1945. Lynn (p. 141) has a similar song, "I Had a Little Duck," less the bawdry. Randolph's "Unprintable" collection contains other poems set to "Turkey in the Straw" (pp. 217-18, 219-20, 373-74, and 440-43). Ford, *Traditional Music*, offers three others (pp. 435-37, and the tune itself at p. 59).

"He Was Sitting in the Prison" is from the editor's youth also, as is "If I Had the Wings of an Angel." "Prison" is often attached to the ballad "Ball of Yarn." Randolph ("Unprintable," 557-58), has a fragment said to date from the early 1900s. Laycock (p. 194) has another. The melody is invariably the verse to Geroge F. Root's "Tramp, Tramp, Tramp," copyrighted in 1864.

Larson's pioneering "Barnyard" collection from Idaho schoolchildren during the 1930s and 1940s contains a longer version. The two stanzas under the title of "The Jailer's Song" there have no tune indicated.

> In the prison cell I sit,
> With my fingers dipped in shit,
> > While the mice shoot craps upon the floor!
> If you want to hear them fart,
> You just spread their legs apart,
> > And they'll blow you through the keyhole in the door!
>
> In the prison cell I sit,
> With my shirttail soaked with shit,
> > And my balls a-hanging loose upon the floor!
> And the women, as they pass,
> Shoot peanuts at my ass.
> > I don't wanna go to prison any more!

"Come and Sit on My Face" was contained in the USC marching band's Xeroxed "Hymenal," furnished by Christian Gunning in 1988.

"The Old Ninety-Seven" parody is from the Western Kentucky Folklore Archive at UCLA, learned in Tomkinsville by John F. Newport about 1948.

The Second-Hand Muse

PARODY is a wicked weapon, laying mock not only to social values but to the very vehicles that carried the original work. It is one thing to borrow a tune. Folksingers do that all the time. It is quite another to set a parody to another tune, for parody deliberately shocks by imitation. It also satirizes the original, frequently borrowing a line or two so the comparison cannot be missed.

The authors of the songs that inspired these lampoons have suffered the ultimate contempt, not only the piracy of their song, but the scorn of the sentiment.

Born in a Whorehouse

> Born in a whorehouse, raised like a slave,
> Drinking and fucking are all that I crave,
> Smashing in windows, breaking down doors,
> Calling old ladies chicken-shit whores.
> Little old lady, bring me a toddy.
> I want to go out and fuck everybody.

Dean Burson collected this parody of Stephen Foster's 1864 "Beautiful Dreamer" at UCLA in 1960. A variant is in Linton (p. 43). Harry A. Taussig also learned it in Berkeley between 1958 and 1963; Taussig's version appends this *spoken* toast:

> Here's to Madge, that filthy bitch.
> Her cunt is lined with the seven-year itch.
> Between her toes green matter grows
> And bloody corruption flows from her nose.
>
> Rather than climb those scaly legs
> Or suck those festering tits,
> I'd drink a quart of dead man's blood
> Or bathe in liquid shit.

> Cunt, thou deep and bottomless pit,
> All matted with hair and covered with shit,
> Like a polecat's ass, thou smellest bad.
> But cunt, oh, cunt, thou must be had.

A variant collected by Ronald DeLong at UCLA in 1963 has these quatrains as part of the spoken toast:

> When your balls hang low and your cock hangs lower,
> And the end of your pecker turns blue,
> When it bends in the middle when you try to diddle,
> You're through, you bastard, you're through.
>
> Now I've fucked in France and I've fucked in Spain
> And I was the chief fucker on the battleship *Maine,*
> And when I'm dead let my tombstone be seen,
> "Here lies the human fucking machine."

My Grandfather's Cock

> My grandfather's cock was too large for his jock,
> So it hung ninety years on the floor.
> It was larger by half than the old man himself
> Though it weighed not a pennyweight more.
>> It was bought on the morn of the day that he was born,
>> And was always his treasure and pride.
>> But it stopped, short, never to come again
>> When the old man died.

This parody of the venerable song by Henry Clay Work, was contributed by Harry A. Taussig as sung in Berkeley, California, between 1958 and 1963.

Morgan 2 (p. 58) has a variant from British currency. Hogbotel and Ffuckes (p. 33) print an Australian version. McGregor (pp. 66-67) has this second stanza and chorus:

> My grandfather's cock was too long for his strides
> So he lent it to the woman next door,
> She grabbed it by the point, and pulled it out of joint,
> So he swore he'd never lend it any more.
>> He'd a horn on the morn on [of?] the day he was born,
>> It was always his pleasure and pride,
>> But it dropped, shrank, never to rise again
>> When the old man died.

Chorus:
Ninety years without cracking it,
What a cock! What a cock!
He spent his life whacking it,
What a cock! What a cock!
But it dropped, shrank,
Never to rise again,
When the old man died.

Henry Clay Work wrote the original "Grandfather's Clock," published in 1876 by C. M. Cady, New York City. That popular song's sheet music is reprinted in Jackson (pp. 76-79).

Ta-Ra-Ra Boom De Ay

[A]

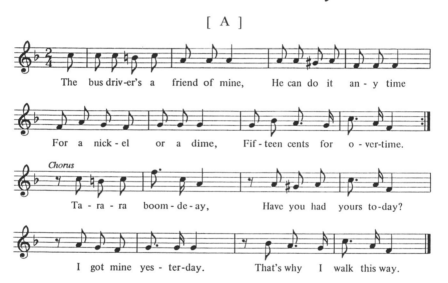

The bus driv-er's a friend of mine, He can do it an - y time
For a nick - el or a dime, Fif - teen cents for o - ver-time.

Chorus
Ta - ra - ra boom - de - ay, Have you had yours to-day?
I got mine yes - ter-day. That's why I walk this way.

The bus driver's a friend of mine.
He can do it anytime.
For a nickel or a dime,
Fifteen cents for overtime.

Chorus:
Ta-ra-ra boom de ay,
Have you had yours today?
I got mine yesterday.
That's why I walk this way.

271

Homosexuality
Fits her personality.
But my cock sticks out in front
So she takes it in her cunt.

[B]

Chorus:
Tra-la-la boom dee ay,
How did I get this way?
It was the boy next door.
He laid me on the floor.

My mommy was surprised
To see my belly rise,
And now my baby cries,
"Tra-la-la boom de ay!"

[C]

I don't want a Ford V-8.
I want a guy I can date.
I don't want an Oldsmobile.
I want a guy I can feel.

I don't want a Chevrolet.
I want a guy I can lay.
I don't want an old Mack truck.
I want a guy I can ----

Chorus:
Ta-ra-ra boom de ay,
Have you had yours today?
I had mine yesterday.
That's why I walk this way.

[D]

As a freshman she was shy,
When the boys gave her the eye.
When they asked her if she'd fuck,
She would say, "You're out of luck."

Chorus:
Ta-ra-ra boom de ay.
Have you had yours today?

I got mine yesterday.
That's why I walk this way.

As a sophomore she was told,
She would have to be more bold.
So at the sophomore dance she wore
The costume of a two-bit whore.

As a junior she was cherry.
Then one night when she got merry,
Drank too much whiskey and gin,
And her boy friend slipped it in.

As a senior she surprised
Her boy friend with a little prize.
He took one look and did agree
"The bastard looks a lot like me!"

There seem to be a fair number of differing songs and/or parodies sung to this tune. In addition to those here, Randolph's "Unprintable" anthology has three (pp. 222, 242, and 539). Lowenstein (p. 40) has two Australian versions. Norman Cazden has sketched an imposing history of this song, concluding that it was written by a black musician, Babe Connor, in a St. Louis bawdyhouse in 1888. Cazden cites a number of differing versions, all copyrighted, each attempting to capitalize on the unprecedented popularity of the first copyrighted version adapted by Henry J. Sayers in 1890 and published the following year. Bayard (p. 139) on the other hand concludes "My guess is that this tune was originally German, though I have not found it in available German sources." Fuld too seems to hint at a German forebearer (pp. 571-72).

The "A" version here is from the editor's misspent youth in Los Angeles, circa 1948. Harry A. Taussig had a similar text from Berkeley, California, 1958-63.

The "B" text is from a text deposited by a young woman in the Indiana University Folklore Archives in 1950. An undated but contemporaneous variant is in the Western Kentucky Folklore Archives at UCLA.

The "C" text is from the singing of a nurse in Cambridge, Massachusetts, in 1948. It is one of two similar texts deposited in the Michigan State collection at the Indiana University Folklore Archives.

Collected in 1961 from Los Angeles attorney Ed Ulman, "D" is similar to another deposited in the MSU-Indiana archive in 1950.

273

Casey Got Hit with a Bucket of Shit

Casey got hit with a bucket of shit
And the band played on.
He waltzed 'round the floor and got hit with some more
And the band played on.
    His balls were so loaded, he nearly exploded.
    The poor girl shook with alarm.
    He married the bitch with the seven-year itch
    And the band played on.

Only the familiar chorus of "The Band Played On," by John F. Palmer and Charles P. Ward, is used in this parody. According to Fuld (p. 123) the popular song was first printed in Joseph Pulitzer's *Sunday World* of June 30, 1895. There are two versions in the editor's files, this through the courtesy of Roger Abrahams. It was current on American college campuses circa 1960.

Old Aunt Sally

One dark night when the neighbors were in bed,
Old Aunt Sally sneaked out into the shed.
Her beau pushed her over among the straw and said:
"There'll be a hot time in the old town tonight!"

The first three months, she liked it very well;
The second three months her belly began to swell;
The third three months, and her kid began to yell:
"There'll be a hot time in the old town tonight!"

Set to the tune of "There'll Be a Hot Time in the Old Town Tonight," this is from the Larson "Barnyard" collection. Schoolchildren in Los Angeles sing the first stanza alone.

The original song with words by Joseph Hayden and music by Theodore M. Metz was published in 1896, according to Jacobs (p. 97). Fuld (p. 278) credits the song solely to Cad. [*sic*] L. Mays, stating it was published by Theodore A. Metz, New York City, in 1896.

In the Good Old Summer Time

In the cottage next to mine, in the cottage next to mine,
There lives a married couple and they do it all the time.

They go to bed at seven o'clock and they don't get up till nine.
There must be something doing in the cottage next to mine.

In the good old summer time, in the good old summer time,
Mary went to bed one night and forgot to pull the blind.
Johnnie climbed an apple tree and got there just in time
To see her pussy wussy in the good old summer time.

Guy Logsdon retrieved this, No. 3912, from the Gordon "Inferno" in the Library of Congress. Published in 1902, the original "In the Good Old Summer Time" is credited to Ren Shields and George Evans.

Sweet Adeline

Sweet Antoinette,
Your pants are wet.
You say it's sweat.
It's piss, I'll bet.
In all my dreams,
Your bare ass gleams.
You're the wrecker
Of my pecker,
Antoinette.

Dean Burson learned this in Los Angeles in 1960. Harry Taussig's version from Berkeley about this same time substitutes for the fourth line, "It's come I'll bet." Another version is in Linton (p. 137).

Jacobs credits the Peerless Quartet with first popularizing "Sweet Adeline," written in 1903 by Richard H. Gerard and Henry W. Armstrong.

St. Louis Woman

St. Louis woman, she had a yen for men;
She went to bed with a fountain pen.
The rubber busted and the ink ran wild.
St. Louis woman, she had a blue-black child.

Dean Burson collected this parody of W. C. Handy's 1914 "St. Louis Blues" in Los Angeles in 1960. Morgan 1 (p. 92) has an unrelated English song, "The Maid of the Mountain Glen," that borrows this.

Mother

M is for the many times you made me.
O is for the other times you've tried.
T is for the tourist cabin weekends.
H is is for the hell you raised inside.
E is for the everlasting passion.
R is for the 'reck you made of me.
Put them all together, they spell "Mother,"
And that is what you made of me.

This sentimental favorite by Theodore Morse and Howard Johnson was published in 1915.

The parody is common on college campuses, and a sequel on "father" sometimes turns up. Lynn (p. 71) has both mother and father stanzas.

This version, learned at UCLA in the 1950s, is one of four in the editor's files.

The Motherfucker's Ball

Oh, there's going to be a ball at the motherfuckers' hall.
The witches and the bitches gonna be there all.
Now, honey, don't be late,
'Cause they're passing out pussy 'bout half-past eight.
Oh, I've fucked in France and I've fucked in Spain,
I even got a piece on the coast of Maine,
But the best damned piece of all
Was when I got my mother-in-law
Last Saturday night at the motherfuckers' ball.

This was collected by Dean Burson from a former Carnegie Tech student in 1960.

Abrahams (pp. 169-70) has a recitation entitled "The Freak's Ball" modeled upon "Darktown Strutters' Ball" and inspired by a so-called race record of the 1930s.

Other sung parodies of the original song, written in 1915 by Shelton Brooks, are in Dolph (pp. 160-61); Hopkins (p. 134); and Wallrich (p. 11). All are from military informants; none are bawdy.

In the Shade of the Old Apple Tree

[A]

In the shade of the old apple tree,
A pair of fine legs I can see,
A little red dot,
With a hole on top,
It looked like a tarbrush to me.

In the shade of the old apple tree,
That's where Zelda first showed it to me.
It was hairy and black,
And she called it her crack,
But it looked like a subway to me.

So I pulled out my pride of New York.
It fitted in just like a cork.
And I said, "Oh, lady, don't scream,
While I dish out the cream,
In the shade of an old apple tree."

[B]

In the shade of the old apple tree,
That's where Mary first showed it to me.
It was hairy and black,
And she called it her crack,
But it looked like a subway to me.

Oh, I took out my forty-foot pole,
And shoved it right down that dark hole.
I bounced once or twice;
It really felt nice
In the shade of the old apple tree.

Claire Biane collected the "A" text in Los Angeles in 1960 from Eric Firth, who learned the song as a boy in Hull, England, about 1936. Morgan 1 (p. 151) is close, and like Firth, from England.

The "B" text was sung by Kenneth Potter, then of Sonoma county, California, to the editor in 1960.

Reuss (pp. 252-54) includes five parodies of varying faithfulness to those printed here. Seemingly, traditional singers have been more free in remaking this song than they have with most parodies. Reuss also includes references to ephemeral collections archived in the Kinsey Institute, Indiana University. Legman (*The Limerick*, 23, No. 110) has

277

another version, as do Count Vicarion, No. 9, Laycock (pp. 193-94), and Randolph's "Unprintable" collation (p. 603), which assigns his text to 1915 and Springfield, Missouri. Lynn (p. 5) has an inoffensive parody. Hart's *Immortalia*, 3 (pp. 26 ff.) runs:

> In the shade of the old apple tree,
> I got all that was coming to me.
> In the soft dewy grass,
> I had my piece of ass
> From a maiden that was fine to see.
>
> I could hear the dull buzz of the bee
> As it sunk its grub hooks into me.
> Her ass it was fine,
> But you should have seen mine
> In the shade of the old apple tree.

DeWitt (p. 55) has these and two more stanzas in his British barracks version.

The original song was written in the United States by Harry Williams and Egbert Van Alstyne in 1905. It was popularized by the Empire Quartet, according to Stillman (p. 163).

By the Light of a Flickering Match

> By the light of a flickering match,
> I saw her snatch,
> By the light of the match, well natch.
> By the light of the flickering match,
> I heard her scream, I saw it steam.
> I burned her snatch with my flickering match.

Harry Taussig gathered this in Berkeley, California, sometime between 1958 and 1963. Another text is in the mimeographed "Shitty Songs of Sigma Chi," forwarded by Guy Logsdon.

Introduced in *The Ziegfeld Follies of 1909*, the now-standard "By the Light of the Silvery Moon" was written by Edward Madden and Gus Edwards. At least three early recordings helped to popularize it.

Put on Your Old Gray Bustle

> Put on your old gray bustle and get out and hustle
> For tomorrow there's a mortgage coming due.

Just put your ass in clover, let the boys look it over,
If you can't get five, take two.

Put on that old blue ointment, the crabs' disappointment,
And we'll kill the bastards where they lay.
Though it scratches and itches, it will kill the sons-of-bitches
In the good old fashioned way.

Put on those old red panties that once were your auntie's
And let's go play in the hay,
And while they're out there hayin', we'll be in here layin'
In the good old-fashioned way.

This was learned "sometime after adolescence and sometime before maturity," about 1950, according to the businessman who sang it for the editor in 1963 in Los Angeles. A close variant is in Getz 2 (p. OO-10).

Brand—who claimed in a letter to the editor on May 13, 1971—to have written a number of the verses now in oral currency—has a fuller parody on *Bawdy Western Songs* (Audio Fidelity 1920).

Laycock (pp. 285-86) has another, from Australia. Cleveland (p. 94) states that "Put on that Old Blue Ointment" was sung by New Zealand troops in World War II, but gives no text. Morgan 1 (pp. 128-29) has a text of five stanzas presumably from British singers; by a printer's error six verses to "Caviar Comes from Virgin Sturgeon" are accidentally appended.

Wallrich (p. 157) and Getz 1 (p. YZ-2) have another parody entirely. So too Reuss (pp. 160 ff.), from various midwestern colleges. The closest version in Reuss to that used here was collected at Michigan State University in 1947:

Put on your old gray bustle; get your fanny in a tussle,
And we'll drink another glass of beer.
For it ain't for knowledge that I came to college,
But to raise hell while I'm here.

The original song, published in 1909, was written by Stanley Murphy and Percy Wenrich.

Let Me Ball You Sweetheart

[A]

Let me ball you, sweetheart; I'm in bed with you.
Let me hear you whisper that it's time to screw.

279

Make your body wiggle in the same old way,
And I'll be back to see you on my next pay day.

[B]

Let me call you sweetheart; I'm in bed with you.
Let me pinch your boobies till they're black and blue.
Let me stroke your vulva till it's filled with goo.
Let's play hide the weenie up your old wazoo.

Bethel Morgan sang the "A" text to the editor in Los Angeles in 1964. Linton (p. 136) had it.

The "B" text is from the UCLA Folklore Archive, collected in 1962 from the Tau Delta Tau fraternity members.

The original song, "Let Me Call You Sweetheart," was written by Beth Slater Whitson and Leo Friedman, and published in 1910. It was widely popularized by a recording made by the Peerless Quartet.

John Saw a Tulip

[A]

Oh, John saw a tulip, a big yellow tulip
When Mary took off her clothes.
She dared him to take it as she lay stripped naked
And he did as everyone knows.
Oh, she laid a-dreaming while he laid a-creaming;
'Twas down where the black hairs grow.
His cock was stiffer than julep when he saw her tulip
For it looked like a big red rose.

[B]

She wore her panties, her pretty pink panties
And I wore my BVD's.
First I caressed her, and then I undressed her
What a thrill she gave to me.
I played with her bubbies, her great big white bubbies,
And down where the short hair grows.
What could be sweeter as I played with my peter
And white-washed her big red rose?

J. Barre Toelken culled the first of these parodies of "When You Wore a Tulip" from the Robert W. Gordon Collection of American

Folk Song, University of Oregon (No. 2377). Gordon's informant said he learned the song about 1915, which suggests that parodies follow hard on the popularity of the original. A recording by the American Quartet did much to popularize the 1914 song by Jack Mahoney and Percy Wenrich, according to Jacobs (p. 257).

Harry Taussig contributed the "B" version, learned in Berkeley, California, sometime between 1958 and 1963.

Morgan 1 (p. 23); and 2 (p. 124) have other parodies to this melody.

Jada

[A]

Scrotum. Scrotum.
S-C-R-O-T-U-M.
Mangy, scrungy,
S-C-R-O-T-U-M.
    Scrotum, scrotum,
    Covered with hair.
    What would you do
    If it wasn't there?
Scrotum, scrotum,
It's what we keep our gonads in!

[B]

She had 'em, yeah, she had 'em.
She had a pair of BVD's.
She wore 'em, she wore 'em.
She wore them right below her knees.
    She wore 'em in the springtime
    And she wore 'em in the fall.
    And when she had a date
    She never wore 'em at all.
But she had 'em. She had 'em.
She had a pair of BVD's.

The "A" parody of the 1918 song "Jada" came from one of Bess Lomax Hawes's students at San Fernando Valley Sate College in 1965.

The "B" version comes from Harry Taussig's collection, gathered at Berkeley between 1958 and 1963.

Introduced by Beatrice Lillie in the musical *Bean Pie,* the original song is credited to Bob Carleton.

In That Little Pink Nightie

In that little pink nightie of mine,
When I wear it, I always feel fine.
I remember the night; I was too tight to fight.
He said that he loved me. He loved me all right.
It's been six months tonight since that night,
And that little pink nightie's too tight.
I wore it; he tore it; I'll always adore it,
That little pink nightie of mine.

Barbara Rogers learned this parody of "Alice Blue Gown" in college in Salinas, California, in 1951. She sang it for the editor in 1967.

Hart's *Immortalia*, 3 (pp. 74 ff.) and Getz 2 (p. AA-6) have variants of a different parody on this song. Hopkins (p. 134) has another.

Joseph McCarthy and Harry Tierney wrote this now familiar song for the 1919 Broadway musical *Irene*.

Carolina in the Morning

Anything would be finer
Than to see my Carolina
In the morning.
Falsies lying on the floor
Next to teeth bought in a store
At dawning.
She looks like Mischa Auer
When she splashes in the shower.
Masochists come by the score
Just to see her strip once more
At dawning.

[B]

Nothin' could be finer
Than to be in her vagina
In the morning!
Nothin' could be sweeter
Than her lips around my peter
In the morning!
If I had Alladin's lamp
For only a day,
I'd have her sit upon my face

282

And this is what I'd say:
"Nothin' could be fine-ah
Than to be in her vagina
In the morning!"

The original song, written by Gus Kahn and Walter Donaldson, was published in 1922. Introduced on the vaudeville stage by William Frawley, it was popularized by a recording made by the duo of Van and Schenck.

A parody apparently first appeared in the original *Immortalia* ([1927]: 70). Contained also in the 1968 reprint (p. 86), it begins:

Nothing could be finer
Than to climb your Carolina,
In the morning.
Then's the time that she is best,
When she's had a little rest,
At dawning.

The "A" text is from Robert Easton, who noted it from a motion picture stuntman in 1960. "Mischa Auer" was a dapper, slender character actor of the 1930s and 1940s. The "B" text is from the USC Marching Band's unofficial Xerographed songbook, "Hymenal," given to to the editor by Christian Gunning in 1988. Taussig had the first half of it from Berkeley, 1958-63.

This is commonly collected on college campuses.

My Blue Bedroom

When evening is nigh,
And passion runs high,
I'll lead you to my blue bedroom.
Take a turn to the right,
There's a little red light.
It'll lead you to my blue bedroom.
    There's a smiling face
    On the pillow case,
    With a form divine.
    It's the same old line
    She's been had before,
    But tonight she's mine.
Just Molly and me.
There'll never be three,
'Cause we were careful in my blue bedroom.

Harry Taussig learned this take-off on "My Blue Heaven" in Berkeley between 1958 and 1963.

Written by George Whiting and Walter Donaldson in 1924, this song was used in Whiting's vaudeville act. It was popularized by a 1928 recording made by Gene Austin.

Doodle-De-Doo

Do it to me, like you did to Marie,
Last Saturday night on the davenport couch.
First you caressed her, and then you undressed her,
Last Saturday night on the davenport couch.
    Roses are red and ready for pluckin',
    I am sixteen and ready for high school.
    Doodle-de-doo, doodle-de-doo,
    Doodle-de-doddle-de-doo.

Showed it to me, her lily-white knee
And her doodle-de-doo, her doodle-de-doo.
She showed me her chest but the part I liked best
Was her doodle-de-doo, her doodle-de-doo.
    Under the cover, she'll shake it and shake it,
    With all of her shaking it's a wonder she don't break it.
    Doodle-de-doo, doodle-de-doo,
    Doodle-de-doodle-de-doo.

This parody was sent to the editor after a radio appeal for bawdy songs. The anonymous listener did not indicate where the song was learned, though something similar was current in Southern California high schools circa 1955.

Songs of Raunch and Ill-Repute (p. 23) has this variant as sung at Caltech in 1960:

Now won't you do it to me like you did to Marie
Last Saturday night, Saturday night?
First you caressed her and then you undressed her
Last Saturday night, Saturday night.

Cherries are ripe and ready for plucking
A girl sixteen is ready for high school.
Oh, won't you do it to me like you did to Marie
Late last Saturday night?

Now won't you do it to me like you did to Marie
Last Saturday night, Saturday [night]?

I know it's real because I heard her squeal
Last Saturday night, Saturday night.

It's really easy; there's nothing to it,
A dollar down and the rest when you do it.
Oh, do it to me like you did to Marie,
Late last Saturday night.

Paul Fussell's *Wartime* (New York: Oxford University Press [1989]:
262) quotes a bit of World War II graffiti that echoes these parodies:

When apples are ripe
And ready for plucking,
Girls of sixteen are ready for
NOT WHAT YOU THINK THEY'RE READY FOR,
YOU FILTHY-MINDED FUCKERS.

The original "Doodle-Doo-Doo" was written by Art Kassel and Mel
Stitzel in 1924 (Jacobs, 61). Kassel used it as a theme song for his
then-popular orchestra.

Pubic Hair

[A]

Pubic hair.
You've got the cutest little pubic hair.
There is no finer anywhere, pubic hair.
Penis or vagina, nothing could be finer.
Pubic hair.
I'm in heaven when I'm in your underwear.
I don't need a shove; I got a taste of love
From your pretty pubic hair.

[B]

Pubic hair,
You got the cutest patch of pubic hair.
I say no other can hope to compare to your pubic hair.
Penis or vagina, nothing could be finer
Than your pubic hair.
Oh, I'm in heaven when I'm in your underwear.
I never need a shove to get a mouthful of
Your delicious pubic hair.

The "A" text was forwarded by Bess Lomax Hawes from a collection made by one of her students at then San Fernando Valley State College in 1965. The "B" text, demonstrating the stability of oral tradition, is from "Hymenal," a 1987 Xeroxed songbook of the University of Southern California Marching Band.

The original song of 1926, "Baby Face," was written by Benny Davis and Harry Akst. It was popularized by vaudevillian Eddie Cantor.

Bye Bye Cherry

[A]

Back your ass against the wall.
Here I come, balls and all.
　　Bye, bye, cherry.
I may not have a helluva lot,
But what I got will fill your twat.
　　Bye, bye, cherry.
First you took me out into the wildwood,
Then you took advantage of my childhood.
Hoist your ass and shake a teat.
Guide my prick into your slit.
　　Cherry, bye, bye.

[B]

Back your ass against the wall,
Here I come, balls and all,
　　Bye bye cherry.

Wiggle your ass and flap your tits.
I'll pull it out before it spits.
　　Bye bye cherry.

Thrice twenty-three makes sixty-nine.
I'll eat yours if you suck mine.
　　Bye bye cherry.

Won't your mother be surprised
When she sees your belly rise?
　　Bye bye cherry.

Won't your father be disgusted
When he finds your cherry's busted?
　　Bye bye cherry.

Won't your brother laugh like hell
When he sees your belly swell.
　　Bye bye cherry.

Reuss (p. 255) notes a parody of the original popular song, "Bye, Bye Blackbird," in the under-the-counter "Dave E. Jones," *A Collection of Sea Songs and Ditties* ([ca. 1928]: 22-23). The original song, by Mort Dixon and Ray Henderson, published in 1926, was thus parodied early on.

Reuss prints a version collected in Chicago in 1951 that differs from Dave E. Jones only in the last three lines of the first verse: ". . . He came once, I came twice,/Holy jumping Jesus Christ!/Blackbird, goodbye."

> Take off all your underwear,
> I don't care if you're bare.
>> Bye, bye, blackbird.
> You learned me how to dance and sing
> And even how to shake that thing.
>> Bye, bye, blackbird.
> You took me to your bungalow in the wildwood
> And there you took advantage of my childhood.
> You put your hand beneath my dress,
> And there you found a blackbird nest.
>> Boy friend, bye, bye.
>
> Back your ass against the wall,
> Here I come, balls and all.
>> Bye, bye, blackbird.
> I know I haven't got a lot,
> But what I've got will fill you[r] twat.
>> Bye, bye, blackbird.
> Put your legs around me tighter, honey,
> Now my prick is starting to feel funny.
> Hoist your ass and wiggle your tits
> Till the great big snapper spits.
>> Cherry, bye, bye.

The "A" text is composed of half of each of the two verses in Jones, and with the Reuss text establishes that a humorous parody can retain its form over considerable time—even if the original song fades somewhat in popularity and familiarity. (Should the original disappear entirely while the parody continues in oral tradition, the burlesque aspect is lost, of course. The song then must persist on its own strength as a humorous song.)

Other versions of this are in Morgan 1 (p. 184); *Songs of Raunch and Ill-Repute* (p. 24, an incomplete stanza); and Getz 2 (pp. BB-21, 22), with two air force versions, one bawdy. Hopkins (p. 141) has another. Wallrich (p. 111) offers a fourth air force parody to this tune.

F. M. Rivinus of Philadelphia forwarded yet another set of words to the melody:

> Make me happy, make me gay.
> I can come twice a day.
> I'm your mailman.
> Lift the knocker, ring the bell.
> I can make you feel swell.
> I'm your mailman.
> > I can come in any kind of weather.
> > Don't you know my bags are made of leather?
> I don't mess with keys or locks.
> I'll slip it right in the box.
> I'm your mailman.

The "A" version is from a manuscript collection made by the mother of one of Bess Lomax Hawes's former pupils at then San Fernando Valley State College.

The "B" text is from the collection made by Harry A. Taussig in Berkeley, California between 1958 and 1963.

I've Got a Start on a Twelve-Inch Hard-on

> I've got a start on a twelve-inch hard-on
> That I've had all afternoon.
> Went to the doctor, he told me to cough
> I wish that he would have whacked it right off!
> Come to me, Venus, massage my penis
> And shrivel it like a prune
> 'Cause I've got a start on a twelve-inch hard-on
> I'll probably have till June, till June.
> I'll probably have till June.

This parody of "I'm Looking Over a Four-Leaf Clover" is contained in the USC Marching Band's unofficial "Hymenal," dated 1987, passed on by Christian Gunning.

Published by Mort Dixon and Harry Woods in 1927, the popular song was first publicized by Nick Lucas, according to Jacobs (p. 121). It then enjoyed a revival in 1948 with a number-one hit record by Art Mooney and his orchestra; followed by the 1949 motion picture, *Jolson Sings Again*, and a 1953 film, a remake of *The Jazz Singer*.

Minnie the Mermaid

Oh, what a time I had with Minnie the Mermaid
Down at the bottom of the sea.
Down amongst the corals where she lost her morals,
My, but she was good to me.
Oh, what a time I had with Minnie the Mermaid
Down in her seaweed bungalow.
Ashes to ashes, dust to dust;
Two twin beds and only one of them mussed.
Oh, what a gal was my Minnie the Mermaid,
Down at the bottom of the sea.

The inspiration for this bawdy parody was recorded first in 1930 by the Bernie Cummins Orchestra and released on Victor 22355, according to popular music scholar Lou Curtiss of Folk Arts Rare Records in San Diego, California. The parody was collected by Anne Smith from a woman who learned it at then Oregon State College (now University) in 1945.

Reuss (pp. 324-27) has a variant and references, noting that the folklore archives at Indiana University contain no less than eighty-eight versions of the song from high school and college students in the midwest

The Object of My Affection

The object of my affection makes my erection
Turn from pink to rosy red.
Every time she touches its head,
It points the way to bed.

From the singing of Ken Potter in Oakland, California, in 1964. It is based on the 1934 popular song by Pinky Tomlin, Coy Poe and Jimmy Grier.

These Foolish Things

Ten pounds of boobie in a loose brassiere,
A twat that twitches like a moose's ear,
A dried up cum drop in my bottle of beer,
These foolish things remind me of you.

289

An old dead fetus on a marble slab,
A toothless blowjob in a taxi cab,
A great big hard-on with a syphilitic scab,
These foolish things remind me of you.

Collected by Kenneth M. Moss in 1964 from a UCLA fraternity member, this was deposited in the UCLA Folklore Archives.

The original song, first published in Great Britain in 1936, is by Holt Marvell, Jack Strachey and Harry Link.

Hot Vagina

Hot vagina for your breakfast,
Hot vagina for your lunch,
Hot vagina for your dinner,
Just munch, munch, munch, munch, munch.
It's so speedy and nutritious,
Bite-size and ready to eat,
So take a tip from Tom, go eat your mom;
Hot vagina can't be beat.

This is seemingly the first parody of a singing commercial—the original was used on the Tom Mix radio serial of the late 1930s to advertise a breakfast cereal—and as such deserves preservation. Because of possible copyright infringement, only the first four bars of the melody for the breakfast food's singing commercial are given.

Dean Burson gathered this at UCLA in 1960. An identical version was collected in Berkeley by Harry Taussig between 1958 and 1963. F. M. Rivinius of Philadelphia had a text beginning "Hot vagina for your breakfast / Starts your day off shining bright."

The Last Time I Saw Paris

I'll ne'er forget that wedding night.
Her figure round and neat
Came off like icing on a cake
And landed at her feet.

The last time I saw cotton
Was on the floor that night.
It might look good in fancy clothes
But it's not much fun to bite.

Another of Robert Easton's snatches from motion picture professionals, this was collected in Los Angeles in 1960.

Written in 1940 by Oscar Hammerstein II and Jerome Kern to commemorate the fall of Paris to the Nazis, the song was introduced in the film *Lady, Be Good*. A Kate Smith recording ensured its popularity even before the song won an Academy Award that year.

You Are My Sunshine

The other night, dear, as we lay sleeping,
I could not help it. I lost control.
And now you wonder, just why I'm leaving;
You will find out in nine months or so.

Dale Koby contributed this, as learned in Northern California in 1961.

Written by Louisiana gubernatorial candidate Jimmie Davis with Charles Mitchell in 1940, "You Are My Sunshine" became Davis's campaign song. It was later popularized by Tex Ritter in the film *Take Me Back to Oklahoma* and in a later Bing Crosby recording (Jacobs, 268).

Sunday, Monday and Always

Oh, won't you tell me, dear,
The size of your brassiere?
Twenty? Thirty? Forty?
If it's forty-two,
I'll be in love with you,
Sunday, Monday and always.

Robert Easton gathered this from fellow professionals in the motion picture industry in 1960.

Johnnie Burke and Jimmie Van Heusen wrote the original song for Bing Crosby's 1943 motion picture *Dixie*.

On Top of Old Smoky

On top of old Sophie, all covered with sweat,
I've used fourteen rubbers, and she hasn't come yet.
For fuckin's a pleasure, and fartin's relief,
But a long-winded lover will bring nothing but grief.
She'll kiss you and hug you, and say it won't be long,
But two hours later, she's still going strong.

So come all you young lovers, and listen to me,
Don't waste your erection on a long-winded she.
For your root will just wither, and your passion will die,
And she will forsake you and you'll never know why.

According to Fuld (p. 416) this folk song first appeared in print in 1915 in an article by E. C. Perrow in the *Journal of American Folklore* (p. 159). The song gained no great popularity beyond the southern mountains until 1951.

In that year, a recording of this song by the folk-singing group The Weavers introduced the melody to urban parodists. They have taken repeated advantage ever since.

The first appearance of "Sophie" seems to have been in a songsheet said to have been compiled at Massachusetts Institute of Technology, circa 1957-60. The variant here is from a collection made in Los Angeles by Alice O'Brien in 1960. Shorter versions of this, and other parodies of "Smoky" are also sung by Los Angeles schoolchildren.

Secret Love

Once I had a secret love,
That lived within the heart of me.
When I asked my love her fee,
She said for me the fee was free.
When I asked why it was free,
She said, "Seeley Mattress sponsors me.
Last night, we were on Channel Four."
Now my secret love's no secret anymore.

Anne Smith gathered this from sorority sisters at UCLA in 1960. The original song, written by Paul Francis Webster and Sammy Fain for the 1953 motion picture *Calamity Jane,* was popularized by Doris Day.

Hey, Roll Me Over

Hey, roll me over,
Pull up my dress,
Now that I'm an A.O.Pi
I always will say yes.

Down with virginity,
Up with the vice.
I figure whenever he's got you down
You oughta give him a slice.

So I'll be up in just a minute,
Feelin' satisfied.
Then down upon the bed again
With my legs spread wide.

My reputation will be shot
But I'll look 'em in the eye.
For I'm an Alpha Omicron Pi,
Yes sir, I'm an Alpha Omicron Pi.

Collected by Debbie Bonetti of Los Angeles in 1960, this is the only parody of "Hey, Look Me Over" in the editor's collection. The original song was written by Carolyn Leigh and Cy Coleman for the 1960 musical *Wildcat.* It was introduced by Lucille Ball and Paula Stewart (Jacob, 94).

Foam Rubber Pads

Foam rubber pads, foam rubber pads,
Now we can tell the girls from the lads.
You've made our girls so fully packed;
They now have curves where once they lacked.
You've given each and every one
A silhouette where they had none.
Now every girl can [look] like Jane
And rustle forth for fun and gain.

Yet another of actor Robert Easton's collection of folklore from motion picture professionals, circa 1960, this borrows the melody of "O Tannenbaum." "Jane" here refers to Jane Russell.

Undergraduates Coarse

FRATERNITY and sorority houses, dormitories and living groups, are veritable hotbeds of bawdy song. And each year a new freshman class shows up on campus, to be indoctrinated into local ritual and ceremony, to learn the legends of fabled professors and celebrated students, to grow proficient at "quarters" or other drinking games, and to learn some of the more raucous songs.

So are the old ways preserved.

We Go to College

This has been one of the more widely sung of college songs over the years, adapted to various institutions of higher education.

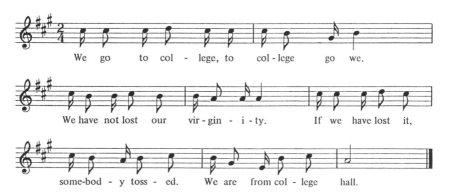

We go to col - lege, to col - lege go we.

We have not lost our vir - gin - i - ty. If we have lost it,

some-bod - y toss - ed. We are from col - lege hall.

[A]

We go to college, to college go we.
We have not lost our virginity.
If we have lost it, somebody tossed it.
We are from College Hall.

295

And once a week at the college dance,
We don't wear bras and we don't wear pants.
We always give the freshmen a chance.
We are from College Hall.

We go to college. Don't we have fun?
We know exactly how it is done.
We saw the movies in Hygiene A-1.
We are from College Hall.

We go to college and we can be had.
Don't take our word for it; just ask dear old dad.
He brings his buddies for graduate studies.
We are from College Hall.

[B]

We go to college, we're oversexed.
Just get in line, boys, you may be next.
We're highly rated, we're educated.
We are from Campus Hall.

We go to college, don't we have fun?
If we haven't done it, it can't be done.
We know hundreds of ways to get plundered.
We are from Campus Hall.

We go to college, we major in bed,
Ten to a dorm, not one maidenhead.
We could have saved it, but, oh, how we craved it.
We are from Campus Hall.

We go to college, each Christmas dance.
We don't wear bras and we don't wear pants.
We like to give the freshmen a chance.
We are from Campus Hall.

Yes, we go to college, we can be had.
If you don't believe us, just ask dear ole' dad.
He brings his buddies for graduate studies.
We are from Campus Hall.

Hey, we go to college, we fly this flag:
"Down with the shy boys, down with the drag.
We want a man who wants to and can."
We are from Campus Hall.

We go to college. Oil up your gun.
We'll show you how it ought to be done.

We saw the movies in Hygiene A-1.
We are from Campus Hall.

[C]

We are Whoredean, good girls are we.
We take no pride in our virginity.
We take precautions and avoid abortions,
For we are from Whoredean School.

Chorus:
Up school, up school,
Up school, up school,
Hey, up school - shit.
La, la, la, la, la, la, la, la,
La, la, la, la, la, la, la, la.

Our house mistress you cannot beat.
She lets us go walking in the street.
We sell our titties for three-penny bitties
Right outside of Whoredean School.

Our school doctor, she is a beaut,
Teaches us to swerve when our boyfriends shoot.
It saves many marriages and forced miscarriages
For we are from Whoredean School.

Our head prefect, her name is Jane.
She only likes it now and again,
And again, and again,
And again, and again,
And again, and again, and again.

We go to Whoredean, don't we have pluck.
We go to bed without asking a buck.
Try us sometimes, boys; you may be in luck
For we are from Whoredean School.

Our sports mistress, she is the best.
She teaches us to develop our chests.
So we wear tight sweaters and carry French letters
For we are from Whoredean School.

We are at Whoredean each all-school dance.
We don't wear bras and we don't wear pants.
We like to give our boyfriends a chance
For we are from Whoredean School.

Our school porter, he is a fool.
He's only got a teeny-weeny tool.

It's all right for keyholes and little girlies' peeholes,
But not good for Whoredean School.

Our school gardener, he makes us drool.
He's got a great, big, whopping, dirty tool.
All right for tunnels and Queen Mary funnels,
And just right for Whoredean School.

We got [*sic*] to Whoredean. Don't we have fun?
We know exactly how it's done.
When we lie down we hole it in one
For we are from Whoredean School.

These girls from Cheltenham, they are just sissies.
They get worked up from one or two kisses.
It takes wax candles and long broom handles
To rouse the girls from Whoredean School.

We go to Whoredean. We can be had.
Don't take our word, boy, ask your old dad.
He brings his friends for breathtaking trends
For we are from Whoredean School.

When we go down to the sea for a swim,
People remark at the size of our quim.
You can bet your bottom dollar
It's big as a horse's collar
For we are from Whoredean School.

This is widely known. Reuss (pp. 70-75) reports texts dated to the
1930s from Ohio State and Arkansas universities and cites references
to underground song collections. In the midwest, he reports, it is
sung either to the gospel song "We Shall Not be Moved" or to "the
familiar college tune known under many names, for example, 'Cheer,
Cincinnati.'. . ." As he gives it, that latter runs:

Reuss's fifth version of the song contains stanzas the editor has not found on the West Coast. (Block's is a Bloomington, Indiana, department store.):

> And after school when we go to Block's,
> We pick up bags of big woolly socks (oh, horse shit).
> We like the way they tickle our box.
> We are the Pi Phi girls.
>> Balls, balls, balls.

> And on the days when we got to school,
> We watch the teacher play pocket pool (oh, horse shit).
> We like the way he handles his tool.
> We are the Pi Phi girls.
>> Balls, balls!

Students at Caltech, according to *Songs of Raunch and Ill- Repute* (p. 9) sang these. (P.C.C. is "Pasadena City College, two blocks away from Caltech, with plenty of WASP ingenues," according to the computer scientist who loaned the editor a copy of the collection.):

> We go to collage [*sic*], t'collage go we,
> We never lost our virginity,

> We might have lost it, only they forced it.
> We are from P.C.C.

> We go to collage, don't we have pluck,
> We never work, and we allways [*sic*] fuck.
> Come on over, boys, you may be in luck.
> We are from P.C.C.

The *Raunch* collection (p. 29) has a variant, "The Girls from Sidney" with couplets. The first two run:

> We are from Sidney, from Sidney are we.
> We never lost our virginity. (Oh, bullshit)

> We use the very best candles you see,
> We are from Sidney we. (Balls, balls)

Another variant in the editor's files contains these additional stanzas:

> And every evening at one o'clock,
> We watch the watchman piss off the dock.
> We like the way he handles his cock.
> We go to N.Y.U.

> If we go riding in a canoe,
> We like to take on more than one or two.

> Sometimes we take on the whole goddam crew.
> We go to N.Y.U.

Still another, lampooning the college sorority, has these:

> We are the Pi Phis, happy are we,
> Happy go lucky, bare-ass and free.
> We'd like to share our virginity.
> We are the Pi Phi girls.
>
> And every month when our time is due,
> We save the rags for you boys to chew.
> We like to save the flavor for you.
> We are the Pi Phi girls.

Jacques Vidicam, a Los Angeles hairdresser, learned a fragment of the "C" version here from an English friend while Vidicam was serving at Fort Sam Houston, Texas, in 1964. He recalled two stanzas:

> We have a new girl; her name is Jane.
> She only does it now and again,
> And again and again and again and again.
> We are from Rodeen School.
>
> We have a new girl; her name is Flo.
> We never thought that she'd ever go,
> But she surprised the master by jacking him off faster
> Than any other girl in school.

Variants of this from British or rugby tradition, such as the "C" text, tend to place the ladies at fictional Whoredean or actual Roedean School. They also exhibit a leaning for verses with an AA[B]BC rhyme scheme.

A handful of other versions of the song have been located. The Opies (*Lore and Language*, 355) have one from English school girls. Morgan 1 (pp. 172-74) is fourteen stanzas long, and titled "Whoredean School." Laycock has it from Australia (pp. 268-71).

American versions are more plentiful. The oldest text seen, dating to 1927, is in *Anecdota Americana* 1 (p. 165), with the first verse here. Randolph's "Unprintable" (pp. 549-50) has three stanzas from the University of Arkansas dated to the early 1930s. Oscar Brand sings another variant on Volume 3 of his recorded collection (Audio Fidelity 1824) and on *Bawdy Songs Goes to College* (Audio Fidelity 1952). *Songs of Roving and Raking* (p. 116) has another. Babab (p. 135) is probably from Illinois currency. Getz 2 (p. TT-1) has a three-stanza fragment dating from the Korean War era. F. M. Rivinus reports the song from

Philadelphia, circa 1945. The AAAB rhyme scheme may be somewhat more prevalent in the New World.

The "A" text and tune for the version used here were contributed by a former UCLA student as sung at that institution about 1961. Taussig had another from northern California dating from the same period.

The "B" text was collected by Shirley Hay and Terry Black, in the fall of 1964 at Campbellsville College, Kentucky. It is deposited in the Western Kentucky Folklore Archive at UCLA.

The "C" text is one of a group of rugby songs in the Indiana University Folklore Collection, this deposited by Joe Storey in 1975. Two variants dating from 1967 and 1970 are somewhat shorter.

Roll Your Leg Over

This is the champion college song, sung the length and breadth of the land. Few who sing it, however, realize that the song is ultimately derived from an English ballad in which a male magician, a warlock, pursues a female magician, a witch, with something other than honorable intentions. To escape his intentions, she successively changes herself into a dove, an eel, a duck, a hare, a mare, a hot griddle, a ship, and finally a silken blanket. Nothing daunted, the warlock matches her dove for dove, trout for eel, drake for duck, hound for hare, saddle for mare, cake for griddle, and with neat euphemistic significance, a nail in the bow of the ship. In the last stanza

> Then she became a silken plaid,
> And stretched upon a bed,
> And he became a green covering,
> And gained her maidenhead.

In one or another form, the theme of the ballad is known throughout Europe. In the United States, the story is gone. Singers now rack their memories only to see who can come up with the most clever hypotheses.

[A]

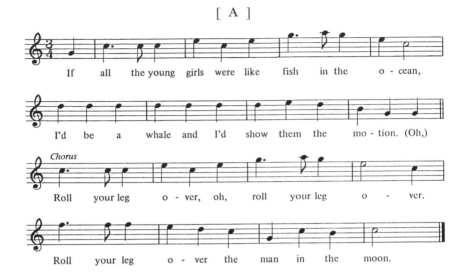

If all the young girls were like fish in the o - cean,

I'd be a whale and I'd show them the mo - tion. (Oh,)

Chorus

Roll your leg o - ver, oh, roll your leg o - ver.

Roll your leg o - ver the man in the moon.

If all the young girls were like fish in the ocean,
I'd be a whale and I'd show them the motion.

Chorus:
Oh, roll your leg over, oh, roll your leg over,
Roll your leg over the man in the moon.

If all the young girls were like fish in a pool,
I'd be a shark with a waterproof tool.

If all the young girls were like fish in the brookie,
I'd be a trout and I'd get me some nookie.

If all the young girls were like winds on the sea,
I'd be a sail and I'd have them blow me.

If all the young girls were like cows in the pasture,
I'd be a bull and I'd fill them with rapture.

If all the young girls were like mares in the stable,
I'd be a stallion and show them I'm able.

If all the young girls were like bricks in a pile,
I'd be a mason and lay them in style.

If all little girls were like bells in a tower,
I'd be a clapper and bang them each hour.

If all the young girls were like telephone poles,
I'd be a squirrel and stuff nuts in their holes.

302

If all the young girls were like gals down in Sydney,
I ain't got much left but I still got one kidney.

If all the young girls were like B-29's,
I'd be a jet fighter and buzz their behinds.

If all the young girls were like coals in a stoker,
I'd be a fireman and shove in my poker.

I wish all the girls were like statues of Venus,
And I were equipped with a petrified penis.

If all the young girls were like Gypsy Rose Lee,
I'd be a G-string; oh boy, what I'd see.

If all the young girls were like sheep in the clover,
I'd be a ram and I'd ram them all over.

If all the young girls were pancakes in Texas,
I'd be a Texan and eat them for breakfast.

If all the young girls were grapes on a vine,
I'd be a plucker and have me a time.

[B]

Chorus:
Roll your leg over, roll your leg over,
Roll your leg over the man in the moon.

If all little girls were little white rabbits,
And I were a hare, I would teach them bad habits.

If all little girls were like bats in a steeple,
And I were a bat, there'd be more bats than people.

If all little girls were like little red foxes,
And I were a hunter, I'd shoot up their boxes.

If all the young girls were like trees in the forest,
And I were a woodsman, I'd split their clitoris.

[C]

Chorus:
Roll your leg over, roll your leg over,
Roll your leg over the man in the moon.

If all the young ladies were rushes a-growin',
And I were a scythe, I would set out a-mowin'.

If all the young ladies were fish in the ocean,
And I were a shark, I would raise a commotion.

If all the young ladies were sheep in the clover,
And I were a ram, I would ram them all over.

If all the young ladies were singing this song,
It would be three times as dirty and five times as long.

If all the young ladies were little white vixens,
And I were a fox, I would chase them and fix 'em.

If all the young ladies were grapes on the vine,
And I were a plucker, I'd have me a time.

If all the young ladies were bells in the tower,
And I were the sexton, I'd bang on the hour.

If all the young ladies were bricks in a pile,
And I were a mason, I'd lay them in style.

If all the young ladies were fish in a pool,
Then I'd be a shark with a waterproof tool.

If all the young ladies were B-29's,
And I were a fighter, I'd buzz their behinds.

If all the young ladies were trees in a forest,
And I were a woodsman, I'd split their clitoris.

If all the young ladies were flowers in a pasture,
And I were a bee, I'd leave them in rapture.

If all the young ladies were bats in a steeple,
And I were a bat, there'd be more bats than people.

[D]

If all the young ladies were up for improvement,
I'd give them some help with a ball bearing movement.

If all the young ladies were little white kittens,
And I were a tomcat, I'd make them new fittin's.

If all the young ladies were wheels on a car,
I'd be a piston and I'd go twice as far.

If all the young ladies were little blind moles,
I'd find their burrows; I'd fill in the holes.

If all the young ladies were mares in a stable,
I'd be the groom, mounting all I was able.

If all the young ladies were diamonds and rubies,
And I were a jeweler, I'd polish their bubbies.

[E]

If all the young ladies were cows in the pasture,
And I were a bull, I'd make them run faster.

If all the young ladies were little white chickens,
And I were a rooster, I'd give them the dickens.

If all the young ladies were little white lambs,
And I were a ram, I'd ram all I can.

If all the young ladies were little white flowers,
And I were a bee, I would suck them for hours.

If all the young ladies were linear spaces,
And I were a vector, I'd aim at their bases.

If all the young ladies were answers to find,
And I were a frosh, I'd plug in and grind.

If all the young ladies were dx/dt,
I would integrate them d/me.

If all the young ladies were wrecks on the shoals,
I'd be a shipwright and plug up their holes.

If all the young ladies were vessels of clay,
And I were a potter, I'd make them all day.

If all the young ladies were pages in a book,
I'd turn them all over in some shady nook.

If all the young ladies were gigantic whales,
And I were a barnacle, I'd set on their tails.

If all the young ladies were bullets of lead,
And I were a gun, I'd bang till they're dead.

If all the young ladies were little red foxes,
And I were a hunter, I'd shoot at their boxes.

If all the young ladies were telephone poles,
Then I'd be a squirrel and shove nuts in their holes.

If all the young ladies were statues of Venus,
Then I'd be a sphinx with a petrified penis.

If all the young ladies wore dresses with patches,
I'd grab at the patches to get at their snatches.

If all the young ladies were mares in a corral,
I'd be a stallion and make them immoral.

If all the young ladies were wheat in the field
Then I'd be a scythe; I'd make them all yield.

If all the young ladies were big toy balloons,
I'd take out my pin and make them go boom.

If all the young ladies were bushes of berries,
I'd be a plucker; I'd take all their cherries.

If all the young ladies did not know the rules,
I'd have a great time just using my jewels.

If all the young ladies hid in the halls,
I'd go after them, swinging my balls.

If all the young ladies liked to hop,
I'd hang around and watch their tits flop.

I wish all them ladies was singing this song,
It'd be twice as dirty and ten times as long.

At least five workers—Kenneth S. Goldstein, Gershon Legman, Richard Reuss, D. K. Wilgus and the editor—have independently concluded that the rowdy "Roll Your Leg Over" can be ultimately traced to Child 44, "The Twa Magicians." While that ballad has not survived in oral tradition, its offspring are numerous. Hoffmann has assigned to it motif number X749.9.1.

The American college song is seemingly derived from an English love song, "Hares on the Mountain," which in turn owes much to "Oh, Sally, My Dear," a descendant of the Child ballad. If there are intermediaries between "Oh, Sally" and "The Twa Magicians," they do not seem to have survived.

Child's headnotes to the parent song suggest that the ballad is worth considerable study, embodying as it does a host of popular beliefs concerning witches and warlocks. The motif of successive transformations to aid flight from pursuers (D671) is the core of MT 313, and occurs too in other tales. (See the references at the related motifs, D 615.3; 630; 641.1.2; 642.3; and elsewhere.) The theme of the transformation combat figures also in MT 325 in which a youth bests a magician. Richard M. Dorson (*American Negro Folktales* [New York, 1967]: 141) has notes supplementing those in Aarne-Thompson (pp. 113-14).

Related too are the riddling contests and challenges in Child 1, 2, and 46. See J. Barre Toelken, "Riddles Wisely Expounded" (*Western Folklore* 25 [1966]: 1-16), on the sexual implications of riddles and riddling; and Tristram Potter Coffin, "Four Black Sheep Among the 305" in Porter, *The Ballad Image*. In all, the magical elements in tale and song are considerable.

For references to texts of both "Hares on the Mountain" and "Oh,

Sally, My Dear," see Dean-Smith. Add to those the entries in Bronson, 1 (pp. 348-53); Kennedy (pp. 395, 425); Karpeles, *Sharp's*, 1 (pp. 430-36); Sedley (p. 87); and McCarthy (pp. 99-100). Pete Seeger sings a version of "Oh Sally" on *Love Songs for Friends and Foes* (Folkways FA 2453), and Ewan MacColl another on *English and Scottish Love Songs* (Riverside 12-656).

The song seems to have lost its moorings, and is floating freely. An analogue to the first verse and the "roll your leg over" chorus used in the United States appears too in the otherwise unrelated British bawdy song "Creepin' and Crawlin' " or "The Knife in the Window." See both *Sharp's* D text and Kennedy's "Knife" (p. 406), which borrow the "Hares on the Mountain" tune, as well as a chorus from "The Jolly Tinker": "With his long fol-the-riddle-i-do right down to his knee." The melody, first verse and chorus of "Creep and Crawl" from East Anglia on A. L. Lloyd's record *The Bird in the Bush* (Topic 12T135) are from "Oh Sally":

Pretty Polly, pretty Polly, it's I've come a-wooin'.
Pretty Polly, pretty Polly, it's I've come a-wooin'.
She says, "Creep and crawl through the window then let's get a-doin'.
And lay your leg over me, over me, do.

O Lochlainn's "Blackbirds and Thrushes" in *More Irish Street Ballads* (p. 100) is sung to the worn down "English" melody. That tune was borrowed by Peadar Kearney for his otherwise unrelated "Down by the Glenside."

American college versions of "Roll Your Leg Over" abound, though the earliest firm date for the song, 1943, is attached to a Marine Corps version deposited in the Library of Congress's Archive of American Folk Song by H. L. Goodwin. Hopkins (p. 167) has a roughly contemporaneous version from Canadian sources.

Brand (pp. 72-73) presents a version, also included on his first volume of *Bawdy Songs and Backroom Ballads* (Audio Fidelity 906 or 1906), released about 1955. Dated to approximately 1960, *Songs of Roving and Raking* (pp. 99-100) has a twenty-two-stanza version, reprinted in Babab (p. 111). Getz 2 (pp. RR-5, 6) gives two versions from air force currency, but ultimately traceable to college circulation; so too the dittographed "Scientific and Professional Personnel Songbook," dating from 1959 and attributable to Army Chemical Corps draftees. (Lydia Fish of Buffalo State University furnished a copy.) Laycock (pp. 166-69) says his thirty stanzas are from an American student.

Songs of Raunch and Ill-Repute (pp. 10-11) sports an impressive forty-nine stanzas. In the first edition of this work, the editor suggested a number of those verses "were tossed off by the 'Ricketts Rowdies' at Caltech who compiled the collection." If so, they seem to have entered oral tradition; numbers five, six, and seven of the Caltech verses were gathered by Harry Taussig in Berkeley between 1958 and 1963. (See the "E" text.)

Reuss (pp. 236-39) has three texts from college students in Ohio and Indiana. The one tune Reuss includes is a set of the melody used here. He adds (p. 234) a stanza that, he claims, "accurately analyzes the purpose and psychological outlet behind the singing of this and a great many other college songs":

> We laugh and we sing and we joke all about it.
> It's only because we are doing without it.

The tune used here—generally the vehicle for the song—is apparently an elaboration of the last four bars of the melody collected by Cecil Sharp for "Oh, Sally, My Dear," and reprinted in Bronson, 1 (p. 352, No. 11). It is also borrowed, then simplified, for "The Sheep-Washer's Lament" in Anderson (p. 102). See too "The Friar in the Well's" first phrases in *Marrow Bones* (p. 33).

There are ten variants of "Roll Your Leg Over" in the editor's collection. Dean Burson provided the "A" text, as sung at UCLA in 1960. Anne Smith sang the "B" text, learned at that same school and in that same year. The "C," "D," and "E" texts were gathered by Harry Taussig in the San Francisco Bay area between 1958 and 1963.

Christopher Columbo

A sea song come ashore, or a landsman's ballad gone to sea—the evidence is contradictory—this is a detailed, highly inaccurate account of Colombo's voyage of discovery in 1492.

[A]

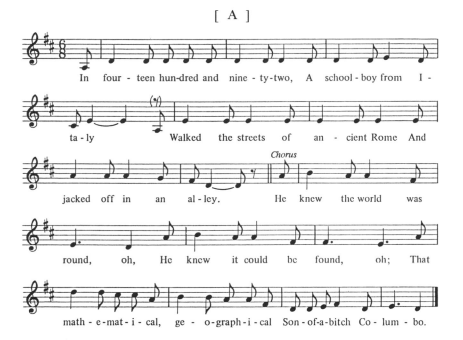

In four-teen hun-dred and nine-ty-two, A school-boy from I-ta-ly Walked the streets of an-cient Rome And jacked off in an al-ley. He knew the world was round, oh, He knew it could be found, oh; That math-e-mat-i-cal, ge-o-graph-i-cal Son-of-a-bitch Co-lum-bo.

Chorus:
He knew the world was round, oh,
He knew it could be found, oh,
That mathematical, geographical
Son-of-a-bitch Columbo.

In fourteen hundred and ninety-two,
A schoolboy from I-taly
Walked the streets of ancient Rome
And jacked off in the alley.

Columbo went to the Queen of Spain
And asked for ships and cargo.
He said he'd kiss the royal ass
If he didn't bring back Chicago.

Now three slick ships set out to sea,
Each one a double-decker.
The queen she waved her handkerchief,
Columbo waved his pecker.

Columbo came upon the deck,
His cock was like a flagpole.

309

He grabbed the bo'sun by the neck,
And shoved it up his asshole.

Columbo had a first mate.
He loved him like a brother,
And every night they went to bed,
And buggered one another.

Columbo had a cabin boy,
A dirty little nipper.
He stuffed his ass with broken glass,
And circumcised the skipper.

Columbo had a stowaway,
A bonnie little lassie.
He took her down below the deck,
And shoved it up her ass-ie.

For forty days and forty nights,
They sailed the broad Atlantic.
They saw a whore upon the shore.
By, God, she drove them frantic.

All the men jumped overboard,
Shedding coats and collars.
In fifteen minutes by the clock,
She made ten thousand dollars.

[B]

In fourteen hundred ninety-two,
A dago from I-taly
Was walking down the streets of Rome
A-selling hot tamales.

Chorus:
Christopher Columbo,
He knew the world was round O!
That masturbating, fornicating
Son of a bitch Columbo!

He went up to the Queen of Spain,
And asked for ships and cargo,
And "I'll be a son of a son of a bitch,
If I don't bring back Chicago!"

Columbo piped all hands on deck,
And tied them to the mast O!
And then he took their panties down,
And screwed them in the ass O!

The cabin girl ran down the deck.
The villain he pursued her.
The white of an egg ran down her leg.
Columbo, he had screwed her!

Columbo had a one-eyed mate.
He loved him like a brother,
And every night at seven bells,
They hopped upon each other!

And when at last they spied the shore,
It was the coast of Cub-y.
Upon the shore there stood a whore.
By God, she was a beauty!

Columbo, he jumped overboard.
The crew shed coats and collars.
In fifteen minutes by the clock,
She made nine hundred dollars.

Back to the ship Columbo went,
His prick was red and fiery.
He wiped it on the tablecloth
And logged it in his diary!

Of all the doctors in Cadiz,
There weren't so very many.
The only one Columbo knew
Was a goddam Jew named Benny.

So to this doc Columbo went,
His face was calm and placid,
But the goddam fool filled up his tool
With muriatic acid!

[C]

In fourteen hundred and ninety-two,
A dago from I-taly
Walked the streets of sunny Spain
A-shouting, "Hot tamale!"

Chorus: He knew the world was round, oh.
His balls hung to the ground, oh.
That masturbatin', navigatin'
Son-of-a-bitch Columbo.

Alternate chorus:
His balls were big and round, oh.
They nearly reached the ground, oh.

311

That fornicatin', masturbatin'
Son-of-a-bitch Columbo.

Columbo went unto the Queen
And asked for ships and cargo,
And said, "I'm a dirty son-of-a-bitch
If I don't bring back Chicago."

Columbo paced upon the deck.
He knew it was his duty.
He laid his whang into his hand,
And said, "Ain't that a beauty."

A little girl walked up on deck,
And peeked in through the keyhole.
He knocked her down upon her brown,
And shoved it in her peehole.

She sprang aloft, her pants fell off,
Columbo still pursued here.
The white of an egg ran down her leg,
The son-of-a-bitch had screwed her.

The sailors on Columbo's ship
Had each his private knothole,
But Columbo was a superman,
He used a padded porthole.

Columbo had a cabin boy.
He loved him like a brother,
And every night they went to bed
And laid upon each other.

For forty days and forty nights
They sailed in search of booty.
They spied a whore upon the shore.
My God, she was a beauty!

All the men jumped overboard,
A-shedding coats and collars.
In fifteen minutes by the clock,
She made ten thousand dollars.

Those were the days of no clap cure.
The doctors were not many.
The only doc' that he could find
Was a son-of-a-bitch named Benny.

Columbo strode up to the doc'.
His smile serene and placid.

312

The God damned doc' burned off his cock
With hydrochloric acid.

The history of this song is hard to draw, involving questions of folk or commercial origins. Harlow (pp. 55-58) dates a bawdy folk redaction of this song to 1876 when, he says, it was sung on board a sailing ship as both a fo'csle song and chanty. Harlow's printed text, however, is expurgated and much of it dwells upon the contrived adventures of a larcenous monkey; it bears no relationship to our "Columbo."

However, according to Leach (pp. 80-81) both words and music of "Christofo Columbo" are by one Francis J. Bryant. Leach gives no date for the song's creation, but is at pains to note that only his musical arrangement is copyrighted. This would suggest that Bryant secured his original copyright sometime after 1877 since Leach's anthology, published in 1933, respects Bryant's earlier copyright. (The maximum copyright was then for twenty-eight years to which might be added a twenty-eight-year renewal.) The Bryant/Leach text is a series of heavy-handed plays-upon-words, none of which are even remotely suggestive.

Levy (*Flashes of Merriment*, 192-94) similarly gives primacy to Bryant. Levy reprints the sheet music cover of the undated New York imprint by M. Witmark & Sons; he dates the song to 1893 and the Columbian Exposition.

Bryant's third verse and chorus suggest the inspiration for what Levy complains is the coarsening of the original:

In Fourteen Hundred and Ninety-two, 'twas then Columbus started.
From Palos on the coast of Spain to the westward he departed.
His object was to find a route, a short one to East Indy.
Columbus wore no whiskers and the wind it blew quite windy.

Refrain:
He knew the earth was round, ho!
That land it could be found, ho!
This geographic, hard and hoary,
Navigator gyratory,
Christofo Columbo.

If Harlow's date is to be trusted, on the other hand, it suggests that Bryant's copyrighted version was inspired by a bawdy song already in oral tradition. The record is spotty, but by 1933, when Leach reprinted much of Bryant's original, Leach felt compelled to state that this is "the original version. Of the others, some are clean and some . . . [sic]" In short, Leach was familiar with bawdy versions of the song.

313

But the trail of "Columbo" is far more convoluted. Legman's unpublished "Unexpurgated Folk-Balladry," Part 2 (p. 6) states that Walter Klinefelter's *Preface to an Unprintable Opus* also traces the origin of "Columbo" to the Columbian Exhibition of 1892 in Chicago. Klinefelter asserts the bawdy song was deliberately modeled on Gilbert and Sullivan's song, "In Enterprise of Martial Kind," sung by the Duke of Plaza Toro in *The Gondoliers.*

The Gondoliers was first presented on December 7, 1889, fully twelve years after Harlow dates the song, and some three years before the exhibition opened. If Harlow's date is to be trusted, he would seemingly call into question Klinefelter's account. However, it is possible that an older version (Harlow's) was recast at the Exposition (Bryant/Klinefelter's), or, even more titillating, that W. S. Gilbert *deliberately* used a then-current bawdy song as his model for the words of the famous song of the Duke of Plaza Toro.

Gilbert was a Rabelaisian fellow, constantly feuding with the more restrained Sullivan, the composer of the music for that model of Victorian romanticism "The Lost Chord" and for the exemplar of the church militant, "Onward, Christian Soldiers." It would not be impossible that Gilbert could succumb to the delicious joke of sending his antagonist-collaborator a poem deliberately modeled upon a bawdy song in oral tradition. (Sullivan did write the melodies after Gilbert presented him with the poems. For some years, they rarely met and barely spoke, their only tie a mutual appreciation of the financial success of their joint works.)

At any rate, Klinefelter's theory may be subsumed in this speculation. At the Columbian Exposition, matters turned full circle: the older bawdy song, perhaps something like Harlow's, was reset to the tune the unwary Sullivan had composed for Gilbert's cleaned up text inspired by the bawdy sea song.

There are three tunes used currently for the song: Sullivan's; a duple time similar to Harlow's; and the more frequently encountered triple-time melody such as that in Brand (pp. 70-71), or here. A set of this has also served as a vehicle for the unrelated "No More Booze" on Brand's *American Drinking Songs* (Riverside 12-630).

A number of versions of the song—to which Hoffmann has assigned motif number X749.4.1.2—have stanzas from "Frigging in the Rigging/The Good Ship Venus" intruding. The interlopers are identifiable by their limerick form.

Earlier reports of British and Empire versions are in Ewan MacColl, *Bless 'Em All* (Riverside 12-642); Morgan 1 (pp. 109 ff.), as "The North Atlantic Squadron," a version from World War II, and another at pages 186-87. Laycock (pp. 255-57) offers a seventeen-stanza Australian text. Hopkins (pp. 152-53) prints it as sung by Canadian servicemen during the Second World War.

North American variants are in *Immortalia* ([1927]: 86-87); and the 1968 reprint (p. 101); *Songs of Roving and Raking* (pp. 112-13); and Babab (pp. 124-25), with interspersed verses in limerick form from "The Good Ship Venus"; *Songs of Raunch and Ill-Repute* (pp. 22-23), with more such intrusions; and Getz 2 (pp. CC-6, 7). *Unexpurgated Folk Songs of Men* has a recorded version. Larson's "Barnyard" (p. 8) has unpublished texts.

Additionally, two bowdlerized texts are in Shay, *American Sea Songs* (pp. 207 ff.) and in Niles-Moore-Wallgren (pp. 106-7). The latter, firmly dating the song to at least the First World War, has another song to the "Columbo" tune (pp. 107-8).

The "A" text and tune here is from the singing of Robert Leventhal in Los Angeles, circa 1957.

The "B" text is the oldest seen, dated to 1918. It is No. 3909 in the Gordon "Inferno" in the Library of Congress.

The "C" version here is from Dale Koby, reportedly collected in northern California. Aside from its chorus, the text is virtually identical to that in *Immortalia,* a copy of which Koby had in his possession.

The Good Ship Venus

"The Good Ship Venus," sometimes known as "Frigging in the Rigging," got its start in merry old England. American doughboys returning from the First World War carried it to the United States, where it quickly gravitated to the halls of ivy. Rarely has the limerick been put to such extended narrative use. The melody for the verse may seem familiar; it is an adaptation of "Yankee Doodle."

[A]

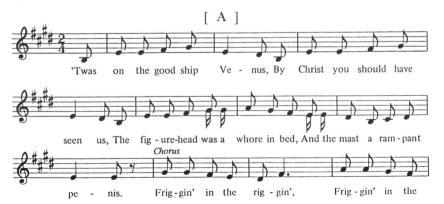

'Twas on the good ship Ve - nus, By Christ you should have seen us, The fig - ure-head was a whore in bed, And the mast a ram-pant pe - nis. Frig-gin' in the rig-gin', Frig-gin' in the

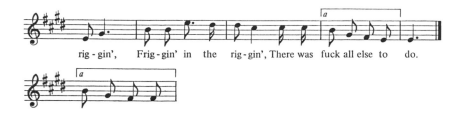

rig-gin', Frig-gin' in the rig-gin', There was fuck all else to do.

'Twas on the good ship Venus—
By Christ, you should have seen us—
The figurehead was a whore in bed,
And the mast was a rampant penis.

Chorus:
Friggin' in the riggin',
Friggin' in the riggin',
Friggin' in the riggin',
There was fuck all else to do.

The captain of this lugger,
He was a dirty bugger.
He wasn't fit to shovel shit
From one place to another.

The captain's name was Morgan
By Christ, he was a gorgon.
Ten times a day sweet tunes he'd play
On his reproductive organ.

The first mate's name was Cooper.
By Christ, he was a trooper.
He jerked and jerked until he worked
Himself into a stupor.

The second mate's name was Andy.
By Christ, he had a dandy,
Till they crushed his cock with jagged rock
For coming in the brandy.

The captain's wife was Mabel;
To fuck she wasn't able,
So the dirty shits, they nailed her tits
Across the barroom table.

The cabin boy was chipper,
Pernicious little nipper.
He stuffed his ass with broken glass
And circumcised the skipper.

316

The captain's daughter Mabel,
They laid her on the table,
And all the crew would come and screw
As oft as they were able.

The captain's daughter Mary
Had never lost her cherry.
The men grew bold and offered gold,
Now there's no virgin Mary.

The captain's other daughter
Fell in the deep sea water.
Delighted squeals revealed that eels
Had found her sexual quarter.

[B]

Twas on the good ship Venus,
My God! you should have seen us.
The figurehead was a maid in bed
Sucking the captain's penis.

Chorus:
Frigging in the rigging,
Wanking in the planking,
Masturbating in the grating,
'Cause there's fuck all else to do.

Oh, the wireless operator,
He was a masturbator.
With every jolt he shot his bolt
Across the oscillator.

Oh, the cabin boy was Kipper,
A dirty little nipper.
They stuffed his ass with broken glass,
And circumcised the skipper.

The first mate's name was Topper.
By God! he had a whopper,
Twice round the deck, once around his neck,
And up his ass the stopper.

Oh, the cookie's name was Freeman.
By God! he was a demon.
He served the crew a menstrual stew,
And foreskin fixed in semen.

There are five closely-related versions of this in the editor's files; the

317

longest has nine stanzas, though Legman describes the British form of the ballad in limerick form as "absolutely endless." He prints one version of seven stanzas in his limerick anthology (pp. 107-8).

Stanzas from "The Good Ship Venus" are frequently and freely intermixed with those from "Christopher Columbo." They are distinguished by the fact that "Venus's" verses are in limerick form. "Columbo's" need not be and usually are not.

British and colonial versions of the song include Morgan's eighteen-stanza version, 1 (pp. 68-71); Hopkins (pp. 58-59), and Cleveland (p. 95), who ascribe their variants to military sources. Laycock (p. 108) says his conflation of thirty-nine verses from Royal Navy currency is to be sung to "So Early in the Morning," also known as "Go In and Out the Window." The text in Vicarion, No. 18, has been doctored by an editor who apparently had no tune.

Randolph's "Unprintable" collection (pp. 529-34) has three versions from the Ozarks, and he dates it firmly to the 1890s. He also notes an article by Frederick Donaghey in *American Mercury* for June, 1926 (p. 243) attributing the original to Thomas Q. Seabrooke in an opera-bouffe *The Isle of Champagne.* Randolph's melody is lifted from the Duke of Plaza Toro's patter song. (See "Christopher Columbo," above.)

Other American texts, some with tunes, include those in Hart's *Immortalia* (pp. 92-95), and the mimeographed "One, the Only Baker House" songbook from M.I.T.; and Brand's desalinated version on *Bawdy Sea Songs* (Audio Fidelity 1884). Getz 2 (p. FF-6) has a seventeen-stanza version, noting that the song was popular among air men at least since World War II.

Six of the stanzas of "Columbo" in *Songs of Roving and Raking* (pp. 112-13), and Babab (p. 126) more properly belong to "The Good Ship Venus." Similarly, the editors of *Songs of Raunch and Ill-Repute* (pp. 22-23) offer a pastiche of the two songs, and give their entry both titles.

The "A" version here was learned by the editor from an unidentified 1st Cavalry Division song collection, mimeographed in Japan about 1950, but lacking a title page. The tune, a set of "Yankee Doodle," he added from his own childhood.

The "B" text is from the Indiana University Folklore Archives, deposited there in a collection of rugby songs by Drake Francescone in 1970.

Yo Ho, Yo Ho

This is one of a handful of bawdy formula songs still sung in urban America, hardy survivors of an ancient tradition in the Old World.

I put my hand upon her toe, yo ho, yo ho.
I put my hand upon her toe, yo ho, yo ho.
I put my hand upon her toe.
She said, "Little boy, you're much too low!
Get it in, get it out, quit fuckin' about!"
Yo ho, yo ho.

Similarly:
I put my hand upon her knee . . .
She said, "Little boy, you're teasin' me."

I put my hand upon her thigh . . .
She said, "Little boy, you're makin' me sigh."

I put my hand upon her breast . . .
She said, "Little boy, your missin' the best . . ."

I put my hand upon her twat . . .
She said, "Little boy, you're makin' me hot . . ."

Ribald and scatological formula songs are found in about the same frequency as they generally appear in Anglo-American folk song in general. In an unpublished survey, Joan Ruman Perkal and the editor located about one hundred examples of the genre. Most were children's songs; more than a few were hymns or gospel songs.

Despite this relative scarcity, the formula song generally and "I Put My Hand" in particular are of venerable lineage. The 1661 edition of *Merry Drollery* contains a cognate of "I Put My Hand"—if not a direct forebearer. "There Were Three Birds" was apparently a drinking song of traditional origin based on *double entendres.* ("Birds" were men, then as now, and "wimble" is an older name for an auger.)

> There were three birds that built very low,
> The first and the second cry'd, "Have at her toe."
> The third he went merrily in and in, in,
> And the third he went merrily in.
>> Oh, never went wimble in timber more nimble
>> With so little screwing and knocking on't in,
>> With so little knocking in.
>
> There were three birds that built on a pin.
> The first and the second cry'd, "Have at her shin."
> The third he went merrily in and in, in, (Etc.)
>
> There were three birds that built on a tree.
> The first and the second cry'd, "Have at her knee,"
> And the third he went merrily in and in, in, (Etc.)
>
> There were three birds that built very high.
> The first and the second cry'd, "Have at her thigh."
> The third he went merrily in and in, in, (Etc.)
>
> There were three birds that built on a stump.
> The first and the second cry'd, "Have at her rump."
> The third he went merrily in and in, in, (Etc.)

Rather closer in text to "Yo Ho" is "Billy Go Leary," as printed by one of the more disreputable of London's publishing houses in the early nineteenth century, J. Duncombe of 19, Little Queen Street, Holborne. His 1838 chapbook *The Fancy!: A Fanciful Collection of Fancy, Flash, and Amatory Songs* (pp. 9-11) gives the text of this *cumulative* formula song as:

Billy Go Leary
Or I Clapped My Hand on Her Thigh
A Very Celebrated Flash Song

> I clapp'd my hand on her toe, what's that my deary?
> That it [*sic*] my broad toe, Billy Go Leary.

Oh, as I kissed her, I cuddled her dearly.
Oh, as I kissed her, etc.

I clapp'd my hand on her shin, what's that my deary?
That is my sharp shin, Billy Go Leary,
Sharp shin, broad toe, etc.

I clapp'd my hand on her knee, what's that my deary?
That is my knocker knee, Billy Go Leary,
Knocker knee, sharp shin, broad toe, etc.

on her thigh . . . That is my thick a thigh
on her **** [muff?] . . . That is my p-g trough
on her belly . . . That is my grumble gut
on her chin . . . That is my chopper-chin
on her mouth . . . That is my chatter-box
on her eye . . . That is my window light
on her head . . . That is my louse cap
on her back . . . That is my hunchback
on her rump . . . That is my arse-tickle

Though the available text does not seem to be overtly sexual, "Matthew the Miller" in Purslow (*Wanton Seed*, 75) would appear to be related to this "Leary" formulaic family. The first verse there runs:

I clapped my hand upon her toe.
"What's this, my love, what's this, my dear?"
" 'Tis my toe-a-tap, I-go-leer."
Toe-a-tap, tit-a-tap-in,
Where Matthew the miller the malt grinds in.

Randolph's "Unprintable" has a similar formula song (pp. 87-88) dated to about 1890, but sung to an unrelated melody. The formulaic progression is also in "I Laid My Hand upon Her Knee" contained in Morgan 2, (p. 116).

"Yo Ho" has not often been reported. D. K. Wilgus noted that Josiah Combs had two variants of this in his Kentucky folk song collection. Cecil Sharp set it down as given by a Somerset singer, but the text "too coarse for publication," he recast the words into "Gently, Johnny, My Jingalo." See Reeves (*Idiom*, 114).

Only one other report of this has turned up. "Yoho" in Morgan 2 (pp. 64-65) has this stanzaic form:

He put his hand upon her toe, yoho, yoho,
He put his hand upon her toe, yoho, yoho,
He put his hand upon her toe,
She said, "Marine, you're might[y] slow.

> Get in, get out, quit ******* [fucking] about,"
> Yoho, yoho, yoho.

Randolph, 3 (pp. 89-91) has a modestly phrased, traditional variant entitled "He Kept A-Kissin' On" or "He Gave Her Kisses One." (See "Drive It Home," below.) Oscar Brand's *G.I.—American Army Songs* (Riverside 12-639) sports a more robust variant.

Hopkins (p. 135) has a version. He also prints (p. 133) a Canadian soldiers' formula song from the Second World War, "How Ashamed I Was," sung to a set of the related "Roll Me Over." Its last four stanzas run:

> I touched her on the thigh,
> How ashamed I was.
> I touched her on the thigh,
> How ashamed I was.
> I touched her on the thigh
> She said, "You're rather high."
> Oh, Gor Blimey, how ashamed I was.
>
> I touched her on the spot,
> She said, "You're getting hot."
>
> And then I shoved it in,
> She said, "It's awful thin."
>
> And when the baby came,
> The bastard had no name.

The formula in these songs lies in the steady progression from toe to rump, an external ordering to which the song is fitted. While most formula songs borrow some such external arrangement or ranking—numbers, letters of the alphabet, playing card values, and so on—Ms. Perkal and the editor have identified a second type of formula song, one which adopts an idiosyncratic, internal formula or chain of circumstances. The well-known lullaby "Hush, Little Baby" with its conditional offerings of gifts is one such. Another, forwarded by Rosalie Sorrels of Salt Lake City, as she collected it from children in 1963, is this scatologcal epistle:

> Annie Morier peed in the fire.
> The fire was so hot, she peed in the pot.
> The pot was so high, she peed in the sky.
> The sky was so blue, she peed right through.

The version of "Yo Ho, Yo Ho" printed here is unique in the editor's collection, one of a group contributed by Christian Gunning as sung informally by members of the University of Southern California marching band. The tune is "When Johnny Comes Marching Home."

Drive It On

This can hardly be considered inspired poetry. Nor does the tune, "She'll Be Comin' 'Round the Mountain," merit any great notice. Put the two together, however, and the result is a rollicking song.

I gave her inch-es one and drove it on.

I gave her inch-es one and drove it on.

I gave her inch-es one. She said, "Hon-ey, this is fun! Put your bel-ly close to mine and drive it on."

I gave her inches one and drove it on.
I gave her inches one and drove it on.
I gave her inches one. She said, "Honey, this is fun!
Put your belly close to mine and drive it on."

I gave her inches two and drove it on.
I gave her inches two and drove it on.
I gave her inches two. She said, "Honey, I love you!
Put your belly close to mine and drive it on."

Three . . . "Honey, please fuck me!"
Four . . . "Honey, give me more!"
Five . . . "Honey, I'm alive!"
Six . . . "Honey, this is kicks!"
Seven . . . "Honey, this is heaven!"
Eight . . . "Honey, this is great!"
Nine . . . "Honey, this is fine!"
Ten . . . "Honey, come again!"

"I Gave Her Inches One" is descended from a pumping chanty given by Hugill (p. 508) as "Put Your Shoulder Next to Mine and Pump Away." In turn it is the forerunner or progenitor of the more popular "Roll Me Over" (see below).

Songs of Roving and Raking (p. 118), and the reprint in Babab (p. 129) have a version entitled "Shove It Home" that stands between the sea chanty and the contemporary song. Credited to Gershon Legman, the melody of this version is a compressed set of Hugill's, lacking the repetitious, formulaic responses of the crew to the chantyman's lead. The stanzaic pattern is:

> I gave her inches one, shove it home, shove it home.
> I gave her inches one, shove it home.
> I gave her inches one; she said, "Johnny, ain't it fun?
> Put your belly close to mine and shove it home."

Tate has another variant (pp. 48-49) from Australia. Randolph's "Unprintable" manuscript (pp. 318-23) presents an Ozark variant, "He Kept A-Pushing on," the first version of which is sung to the otherwise unrelated "In Kansas."

Morgan 2 (pp. 129-30) offers a contemporary British text with this stanzaic form:

> Oh, once I had a girl, had a girl,
> Oh, once I had a girl, had a girl,
> Oh, once I had a girl, she put me in a whirl.
> Put your shoulder next to mine and pump away, pump away,
> Put your shoulder next to mine and pump away.

This song is less often encountered in oral tradition than the newer "Roll Me Over." The editor has seen seven versions of this song, the earliest collected in Michigan in 1952. A Texas variant forwarded by Abrahams furnished the tune here; the text was given by a resident of New York City, who said she learned it while attending Antioch College in the early 1950s. She could recall only a portion of the melody with certainty.

The tune here is a member of the very extended family of which "I Was Born About Ten Thousand Years Ago" and "She'll Be Comin' 'Round the Mountain" are a part.

Expurgated versions of this circulate as "I Gave Her Kisses One," a version of which is sung by Mrs. Hartley Minifie on *Ontario Ballads and Folksongs*, collected by Edith Fowke (Prestige 25014). Mrs. Minifie's tune is a set of the melody used for "They Had to Carry Harry to the Ferry" or "There's a Hole in the Bottom of the Sea," among

324

others. Randolph 3 (pp. 89-91) and the Brown collection 3 (pp. 368-69) also give innocuous "Kisses" texts. McCarthy (pp. 86-87) has "Pump Away" in which the singer "gave her presents one," and so forth. The tune there is another set of the "I Was Born About Ten Thousand Years Ago" family.

Roll Me Over

The printed page can be deceiving. "Roll Me Over" would seem to have little to commend it. Yet the song is easy to learn, easy to sing, and has a chorus wherein all may join at the appropriate moments. That explains why this is one of the more popular of bawdy songs on college campuses.

[A]

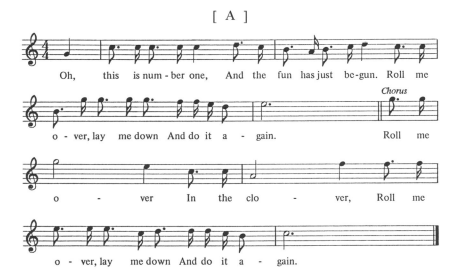

Oh, this is number one, and the fun has just begun.
Roll me over, lay me down and do it again.

Chorus:
Roll me over in the clover,
Roll me over, lay me down and do it again.

Oh, this is number two, and my hand is on her shoe.
Roll me over, lay me down and do it again.

325

Three . . . and my hand is on her knee.
Four . . . and I'm really hot for more.
Five . . . and my hand is on her thigh.
Six . . . and I'm really in a fix.
Seven . . . and I feel like I'm in heaven.
Eight . . . and the doctor's at the gate.
Nine . . . and the baby's doing fine.
Ten . . . and it's time to start again.

[B]

This is number one, and the fun had just begun.
Nelly, put your belly close to mine.
    Roll me over in the clover,
    Roll me over, lay me down and do it again.

This is number two, and my Nelly wants to screw.
Nelly, put your belly close to mine.
    Roll me over in the clover,
    Roll me over, lay me down and do it again.

This is number three, and it's time I had a pee.
This is number four, and I've got her on the floor.
This is number five; the bee is in the hive.
This is number six; the juices begin to mix.
This is number seven; could this really be heaven?
This is number eight, and I'm still feeling great.
This is number nine; now I'm feeling mighty fine.
This is number ten; let's start over again.

"Roll Me Over" may well be the most popular formula song in American oral tradition. There are six full versions in the editor's collection, and more might have been notated had they exhibited any variation from texts or tunes already in hand. In all, the editor has twenty-eight reports of the song.

Songs of Raunch and Ill-Repute (p. 20) adds "number 'leven, and it's just like number seven." Babab (p. 108) reprints it. Morgan 1 (pp. 123-24) has tortured rhymes for 11, 12, 20, 30, and 40 ("naughty"). Getz 1 (pp. R-4, 5) gives another variant. Reuss (pp. 244-49) presents three versions and references to appearances of the song in various manuscript holdings in the Kinsey Institute for Sex Research at Indiana University. The tune he gives (p. 247) is closer to "Put Your Shoulder/Belly Close to Mine and Pump Away" than that used here.

A fragment—"This is number two . . ." was sung in the 1976 motion picture *Stay Hungry*, directed by Bob Rafaelson.

326

There are three sightings of this in the Antipodes. Laycock (pp. 191-92) and Hogbotel and Ffuckes (p. 68) report it from Australia; Cleveland (p. 95) states the song was sung by New Zealand troops during World War II, but gives no text.

The "A" text and tune here were contributed by Stuart Grayboyse in Los Angeles in 1963. A virtually identical text appeared in the 1988 unofficial USC marching band songbook, "Hymenal."

The "B" version, the most radical in the editor's collection, is from former marine, now Los Angeles lawyer Alvin Tenner. Tenner is an indifferent singer, his tune a succession of doggedly rhythmic, indeterminate pitches over the compass of a fifth. For all its vagueness, it is clearly a set of the usual tune to which "Roll Me Over" is sung, and for that reason, the song is classed here rather than under "Shove It Home/Drive It On." It remains nonetheless, an obvious cross between the two songs, and may be a milestone on the road from "Shove It Home" to "Roll Me Over."

Son of a Gambolier

One imagines portions of this song have been attached to virtually every American university at one time or another. Georgia Tech might claim the tune for its fight song, "Rambling Wreck from Georgia Tech," but it has no lock on the lyrics. Stanford's Cardinals sang this version, sneering at the Gold and Blue of arch-rival California.

Oh, I wish I had an o-cean of rum, And su-gar a mil-lion pounds, The dear old quad to mix it in, And a chim-ney to stir it 'round; I'd drink to the Car-di-nal, so glo-ri-ous and so true, And I'd

Chorus

join the rol-lick-ing cho - rus: To hell with the Gold and Blue. I'm

Oh, I wish I had a ocean of rum, and sugar a million pounds,
The dear old quad to mix it in, and a chimney to stir it 'round.
I'd drink to the health of the Cardinal, so glorious and so true,
And I'd join the rollicking chorus: "To hell with the Gold and Blue."

Chorus:
I'm the sonuva, sonuva, sonuva, sonuva, sonuva gambolier,
The sonuva, sonuva, sonuva, sonuva, sonuva gambolier.
Like every honest fellow, I like my whiskey clear.
I'm a ramblin' wreck of poverty, the sonuva gambolier.

Oh, there's the road to Mayfield, as plain as plain can be.
And if you want to see a wreck, just take a look at me.
For I have been to Mayfield, and tasted of the beer,
And that is why my eyes are weak and I need to rest a year.

And here's to dear old Stanford, where the color of life is red,
We'll rise and give "The Varsity" from our coffins when we're dead.
And when we mount the Golden Stairs, we'll give St. Peter the cue
To join the rollicking chorus, "To hell with the Gold and Blue."

Listen all ye Roble maids, and harken unto me:
Never trust a Stanford man an inch above your knee.
I tried it once too often and now as you can see,
I have a little Stanford man a-trailing after me!

And here's the road to Roble, as plain as plain can be,
And if you want to see a wreck, just take a look at me!
For I have been to Roble, and screwed a Roble whore,
And that's why my balls are blue and the end of my cock is sore.

And here's to dear old Roble, where the color of life is red.
They'll have to use a candle when Stanford men are dead,
And when they get to heaven, they'll grab St. Peter's john,
And in a loud and ringing voice, they'll cry, "Shove on, shove on!"

Oh, gather round me girlies, and take a word from me:
Never trust a Stanford man an inch above your knee,
For he'll take you down to Mayfield and fill you full o' fizz,
And before the night is over, your maidenhead is his.

Oh, here's to prexy Wilbur, the medical horse's cock.
I hope he gets the syphilis, with a pimple on his jock!
He gives a talk to freshmen, the same one every year,
And he screws a dead canary, till its ass is out of gear.

328

And here's to old Professor Manning, the mathematical son of a bitch.
I hope he gets the syphilis, and dies with the seven-year itch.
We'll use his prick as a radius, and use his balls as base,
And prove by the theory of limits that his ass resembles his face.

The Berkeleyites be damned, boys, the Berkeleyites be damned.
The Berkeleyites be damned, boys, the Berkeleyites be damned.
If any Berkeley son of a bitch don't like this bit of sass,
He can take the Campanile and stuff it up his ass. ⁓

The Berkeleyites be damned, boys, the Berkeleyites be damned.
The Berkeleyites are a helluva crew, the assholes of the land.
Their cocks are striped with yellow and their guts are yellow too,
So we'll work by jerks and screw the works, and fuck the Gold and Blue.

And if we catch a Berkeley man within these sacred walls,
We'll take him down to Menlo and amputate his balls.
And then if that won't fix him, I'll tell you what we'll do:
We'll stuff his ass with broken glass, and seal it up with glue.

And if I had a condrum [*sic*] and a bottle of Vaseline,
I'd hie me up to Berkeley, and screw the Berkeley queen.
The Mills girls take three inches, at Stanford they take four,
But the Berkeley girls take all you've got, and yell like hell for more.

There was a young man named Riegels who performed a miraculous trick.
He greased his ass with butter, and inserted the head of his prick.
He did it not for pleasure, he did it not for wealth,
But he did it 'cause a Stanford man had told him to fuck himself.

* * * * * * * * *

His mother has the syphilis, his father has the itch.
His sister is a prostitute, and he's a bastard too,
And they're all loyal Berkeleyites, the pride of the Gold and Blue.

And if I had two balls of brass, and a john of a telephone pole,
I'd hie me to the northland, and breed with mare and foal.
I'd raise a race of stalwarts, so glorious and so true,
And I'd put them on the gridiron to whip the Gold and Blue.

But when we go to Hades, and after we are dead,
We'll paint the little devils a million shades of red.
We will make the rocks and caverns ring with the good old Stanford yell,
And we'll make the boys from Berkeley wish they'd never gone to hell.

Adam was the first man that the SAE's ever took in.
Solomon was the wisest who ever wore the pin.
Samson was the strongest, although he had the itch,
And when Julius Caesar came along, we dinged the son-of-a-bitch.

329

This extended version of "The Son of a Gambolier" was contributed by Harry A. Taussig, a former student at the University of California, Berkeley, who copied it from a collection made by Charles Petrone of Stanford on December 15, 1960. "Mayfield," "Roble," "Wilbur," "Manning," and "the Campanile" are local references.

The missing line of the fifteenth stanza is probably something like: "Here's to -------- ------------, that lousy son-of-a-bitch," with the name of the California football coach inserted.

The song is invariably sung to "The Son of a Gambolier," which has more than its share of bawdy songs to bear. (See "The Tinker," and "The Pioneers," in this work.) It has also served as a vehicle for "Fifty Thousand Lumberjacks," in *California Folklore Quarterly* (1[1942]: 376); "The Riddle Song," Bronson 1 (p. 379, No. 10); a marching song in praise of the Seventh Infantry Regiment in Dolph (pp. 550-52); "A Helluva Engineer," in Dolph (pp. 125-27); at least two air force songs in Wallrich (pp. 12, 84); and no less than seven not-unrelated songs cited by Reuss (p. 169). Oscar Brand uses it for a stage lampoon, "Dunderbeck," on *Laughing America* (Tradition 1014).

Joseph Hickerson, then an assistant archivist in the Archives of American Folksong in the Library of Congress, provided Reuss with an extensive text of a song that Reuss dubbed "Godiva." Hickerson's offering was taken from the anonymous collection, probably compiled at M.I.T. in the 1950s, "The *One* The *Only* Baker House Super-Duper Extra Crude Song Book." That omnibus song, to the "Gambolier" tune, runs:

Godiva was a lady who through Coventry did ride
To show the royal villagers her fine and pure white hide.
The most observant man of all, an engineer, of course,
Was the only man who noticed that Godiva rode a horse.

Chorus:
We are, we are, we are, we are, we are the engineers.
We can, we can, we can, we can demolish forty beers.
Drink rum, drink rum, drink rum, drink rum and come along with us,
For we don't give a damn for any damn man who don't give a damn for us.

She said, "I've come a long, long way and I will go as far
With the man who takes me from this horse and leads me to a bar."
The man who took her from her steed and led her to a bar [beer?]
Was a bleary-eyed survivor and a drunken engineer.

My father was a miner from the northern malamute [*sic*].
My mother was a mistress of a house of ill repute.
The last time that I saw them, these words rang in my ears,
"Go to MIT, you son of a bitch and join the engineers."

330

The Army and the Navy went out to have some fun.
They went down to the taverns where the fiery liquors run.
But all they found were empties, for the engineers had come
And traded all their instruments for gallon kegs of rum.

Sir Francis Drake and all his ships set out for Cazlais [*sic*] way.
They heard the Spanish rum fleet was headed out their way.
But the engineers had beat them by night and half a day
And though drunk as hooligans, you still could hear them say:

Venus was a statue made entirely of stone
Without a stitch upon her, she was naked as a bone.
On seeing that she had no clothes, an engineer discoursed,
"Why the damn thing's only concrete and should be reinforced."

Princeton's run by Wellesley, Wellesley's run by Yale,
Yale is run by Vassar, and Vassar's run by tail.
Harvard's run by stiff pricks, the kind you raise by hand,
But Tech is run by engineers, the finest in the land!!!!!

If we should find a Harvard man within our sacred walls,
We'll take him up to physics lab and amputate his balls.
And if he hollers "Uncle," I'll tell you what we'll do,
We'll stuff his ass with broken glass and seal it up with glue.

MIT was MIT when Harvard was a pup,
And MIT will be MIT when Harvard's busted up,
And any Harvard son of a bitch who thinks he's in our class
Can pucker up his rosy lips and kiss the Beaver's ass.

A maid and an engineer were sitting in the park.
The engineer was working on some research after dark.
His scientific method was a marvel to observe,
While his right hand wrote the figures, his left hand traced the curves.

Texts of the original song, "The Son of a Gambolier," from which the melody is borrowed, are in Sandburg (p. 44); Milburn (pp. 182-84); Leach (p. 115); and Spaeth (pp. 89-90), who describes it as "probably the most popular of all those melodies that are at the service of the parodist." He gives other songs set to the tune (pp. 90-91), then adds, "There are many other sets of words to this universal tune, some of them of an unprintable vulgarity, but widely circulated, nevertheless in the true folk-song style." One of these is "Old MacLelland" in Babab (p. 87), which used the first phrase of "Wreck."

Spaeth asserts an "obvious" Irish source for the tune. On *The First Hurrah!* (Columbia CL2165), the Clancy Brothers and Tommy Makem sing "The Gallant Forty-Twa," which the liner notes by Robert Sherman assign to "19th Century Ulster." Whatever the origin of the song, the tune was well known in the New World by the time of the Civil War.

It draws a fine line to distinguish this from the following song, "The Cardinals Be Damned." They are sung to the same tune, and they share verses. The major distinction is in the chorus, a faint recollection of the Irish folk song that may have originally inspired this.

The Cardinals Be Damned

Cal Berkeley responds. This bit of verbal violence upon the student body of Stanford University's Cardinals originated at the University of California's Berkeley campus but with a few names changed, it has probably been applied to most of the colleges and universities in the country. "The Rambling Wreck from Georgia Tech" melody also carries this screed.

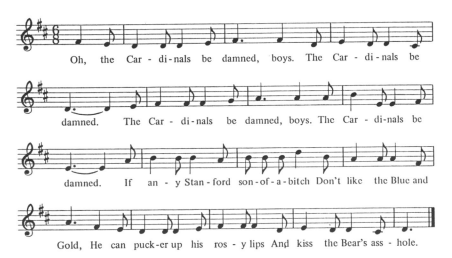

Oh, the Cardinals be damned, boys.
The Cardinals be damned.
The Cardinals be damned, boys.
The Cardinals be damned.
If any Stanford son-of-a-bitch
Don't like the Blue and Gold,
He can pucker up his rosy lips
And kiss the Bear's asshole.

Wellesley's run by Harvard,
And Harvard's run by Yale.
Yale is run by Vassar,
And Vassar's run by tail.
But Stanford is the only school
Entirely run by hand,
And those masturbating bastards
Are the blackest in the land.

Oh, I'm just a prostitute from Stanford
And I fuck for fifty cents.
I'll lay my ass upon the grass,
My pants upon the fence.
I'll lick you slimy belly;
I'll suck your cock with glee,
But get off me you son-of-a-bitch,
If you're from USC.

Oh, here's to ------ ---------, boys,
That Stanford son-of-a-bitch.
I hope he gets the syph and clap
And dies of the seven-year itch.
If you use his cock for a fulcrum,
And suspend his balls in space,
You can prove by the theory of limits
That his asshole is his face.

Oh, listen all you maidens
Oh, listen here to me.
Never trust a Stanford man
An inch above your knee.
He'll take you down to Menlo,
And he'll fill you full of fizz,
And in a half an hour
Your maidenhead is his.

If I had a little girl,
I'd dress her up in green,
And send her up to Stanford
Just to coach the Cardinal team.
If I had a little boy,
I'd dress him up in blue,
And he'd holler, "To hell with Stanford!"
Like his daddy used to do.

[B]

Oh, here's to "Cactus Jack," boys, the dirty son-of-a-bitch.
We hope he dies of syphilis combined with the seven-year itch.
If you take his prick as a radius and project his balls in space,
You can prove by the law of limits that his asshole is his face.

Chorus:
The Cardinals be damned, boys, the Cardinals be damned.
The Cardinals be damned, boys, the Cardinals be damned.
If any Stanford son-of-a-bitch don't like the Blue and Gold,
He can pucker up his rosy lips and kiss the Bear's asshole.

Harvard's run by Princeton and Princeton's run by Yale.
Yale is run by Vassar and Vassar's run by tail.
But from what I hear of Stanford, they run it off by hand.
Oh, the masturbating sons-of-bitches are the assholes of the land.

If I had a little girl, I'd dress her all in green,
And send her down to Menlo to coach the Stanford team.
But if I had a little boy, I'd dress him all in blue
And he'd yell, "To hell with Stanford!" like his daddy used to do.

Oh, listen all ye maidens, oh, listen well to me:
Don't ever trust a Stanford man an inch above your knee.
He'll take you down to Menlo and fill you full of fizz
And before the night is over, your maidenhead is his.

If we find a Stanford man within our sacred walls,
We'll take him down to Sather Gate and amputate his balls.
And if that doesn't fix him, I'll tell you what we'll do:
We will stuff his ass with broken glass and seal it up with glue.

If I had a prick of steel and balls of shiny brass,
I'd find a marble statue and ram it up her ass.
I'd breed a race of giants to roam throughout the land
Just to swell the mighty chorus of "The Cardinals Be Damned."

[C]

I wish I had a prick of steel
And balls made out of brass.
I'd find a marble statue,
And ram it up its ass,
And breed a race of giants
To rule throughout the land,
And sing another chorus of
"Cardinals Be Damned!"

Chorus:
Oh, Cardinals be damned, boys,
Cardinals be damned!
Cardinals, be damned, boys,
Cardinals be damned!
And any Stanford son-of-a-bitch
Who doesn't like the Trojan brass,
Can pucker up his rosy lips
And kiss my Trojan ass.

Oh, Harvard's run by Princeton
And Princeton's run by Yale.
Yale is run by Vassar
And Vassar's run by tail.
And Stanford's run on stud-horse piss
And if you think I lie,
We'll take a trip to Menlo
Where you'll see the same as I!

If I had a daughter,
I tell you what I'd do:
I'd send her off to Stanford
Where she'd never learn to screw!
But If I had a son,
It would be different then, you see.
I'd teach him how to drink and fuck
And send him to S.C.!

From texts in the New York State Historical Association Folklore
Archives, Reuss dates this "at least as far as the mid-1930's" (p. 62).
He footnotes one stanza, from a variant in the Indiana University
folklore archives, as sung at Rensselaer Polytechnic Institute, but gives
nothing more of the song called here "The Cardinals Be Damned":

R.P.I. was R.P.I. when Union was a pup.
And R.P.I. will be R.P.I. when Union's busted up.
And any Union son of a bitch we catch within our walls,
We'll nail him up against the wall and castrate his balls.

The version in *Immortalia* (p. 54) is but one stanza long, a variant
of the "A" text's second. That printing firmly places the song at least
as far back as 1927.

A less-localized version of "The Cardinals" from those included
here circulates as a camp song under the title of "Bill Braverman Be
Damned." A version of that song, collected in Philadelphia and forwarded by Roger D. Abrahams, contains these two verses:

If we catch a Quebec man within these hallowed walls,
We'll take him to the Rec Hall and amputate his balls.
And if he cries for mercy, I'll tell you what we'll do,
We'll stuff his ass with broken glass and seal it up with glue.

I wish I had a prick of steel, two balls of solid brass.
I'd find a marble statue and ram it up its ass.
I'd breed a race of giants to roam around the land
And to swell the mighty chorus of "Bill Braverman Be Damned."

There are nine texts of "The Cardinals Be Damned" in the editor's collection; they vary only in length. The "A" variant is from the singing of Stuart Grayboyse in Los Angeles in 1964. He learned it at UCLA in 1950.

The "B" version is from the collection of Harry Taussig, made in Berkeley between 1958 and 1963. Taussig notes it is to be sung to "Son of a Gambolier." The third stanza with its reference to dressing the girl in green suggests a much older, even English origin for this verse, and perhaps the song. As it happens, the colors of Stanford University are red and white. Dressing the girl in green is instead a traditional euphemism for describing the young girl as a virgin. The dashes in verse four indicate where the name of Stanford's football coach is to be inserted. "Cactus Jack" Curtis is the name of a former Stanford football coach.

The "C" version is from "Hymenal," the unofficial songbook of the University of Southern California Trojan Marching Band, a copy of which was given to the editor in 1988 by Christian Gunning.

Do Your Balls Hang Low?

A companion piece to "Four Old Whores," "Do Your Balls Hang Low?" peters out in the end, stretched from the ridiculous to the absurd.

Ting-a-ling, God damn, find a wo-man if you can. If you
Do your balls hang low? Do they swing to and fro? Can you

can't find a wo-man, find a clean old man. If you're
tie 'em in a knot, can you tie 'em in a bow? Can you

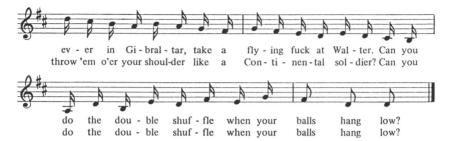

ev - er in Gi - bral - tar, take a   fly - ing fuck at Wal - ter. Can you
throw 'em o'er your shoul-der like a   Con - ti - nen - tal sol - dier? Can you

do the dou - ble shuf - fle when your balls hang low?
do the dou - ble shuf - fle when your balls hang low?

Chorus: Ting-a-ling, God damn, find a woman if you can.
If you can't find a woman, find a clean old man.
If you're ever in Gibraltar, take a flying fuck at Walter.
Can you do the double shuffle when your balls hang low?

Do your balls hang low? Do they swing to and fro?
Can you tie 'em in a knot? Can you tie 'em in a bow?
Can you throw 'em o'er your shoulder like a Continental soldier?
Can you do the double shuffle when your balls hang low?

Do your balls hang low? Do they swing to and fro?
Can you tie 'em in a knot? Can you tie 'em in a bow?
Do they make a lusty clamor when you hit them with a hammer?
Can you do the double shuffle when your balls hang low?

Successive verses substitute for the following for the third line of
the verse:

Can you bounce 'em off the wall like an Indian rubber ball?
Do they have a hollow sound when you drag 'em on the ground?
Do they have a mellow tingle when you hit 'em with a shingle?
Do they have a salty taste when you wrap 'em 'round your waist?
Do they chime like a gong when you pull upon your dong?

This inquiry is generally sung either to the tune of Leon Jessel's
"The Parade of the Wooden Soldiers," written in 1910, or the first
part of the traditional fiddle tune "Sailor's Hornpipe," known also as
"College Hornpipe." If the words are fitted to "The Parade of the
Wooden Soldiers," the last line is shortened to the question: "Do your
balls hang low?"

Copies of the fiddle tune are in most standard collections of jigs
and reels, including [Ira] *Ford's Old Time Fiddle Music*, No. 1 (Los
Angeles: Ford's Publications [c. 1931]: 26), from which it is reprinted
in his *Traditional Music* (p. 46). Fuld (p. 484) says the tune was first
printed in a violin tutor published in London circa 1775.

Apparently the fiddle tune's second part, or turn, is derived from,

or the inspiration of the seventeenth century ballad air "A-Begging
We Will Go." See Simpson (p. 41; and p. 291) for the musical phrases
used again in "Have at Thy Coat, Old Woman." "Sailor's Hornpipe"
also carries the unrelated "Mother Rackett's" as sung by Oscar Brand
on *American Drinking Songs* (Riverside 12-630). The anomalous tune
to which the version of "Do Your Balls" is sung in Babab (p. 84)—
identified as "Continental Soldiers"—is actually the entirely different
"Hoochie Coochie Dance."

There are six variants of "Do Your Balls" in the editor's collection,
including one sung at children's camps in Southern California that
substitutes "ears" for "balls." A text of that camp song is in Lynn
(*Swinging,* 30) with the indicium that it is to be sung to the melody
of "Turkey in the Straw."

The earliest report of this song is in Randolph's "Unprintable" (pp.
177-79), with a variant said to date from about 1900. His earliest
collected version, however, came in 1941.

The earliest version printed is from First World War British Army
currency and appears in Nettleingham's *More* (p. 47).

Other unblushing texts from Great Britain have appeared in Morgan 1 (p. 67); Morgan 2 (p. 120); and Shaw (p. 61). Laycock (pp.
267-68), and Lowenstein (p. 43) have Australian texts. Getz 2 (p. DE-
6) presents four stanzas, the first beginning, "In days of old, when
knights were bold . . ." *Songs of Raunch and Ill-Repute* (p. 25), and *Songs
of Roving and Raking,* p (65) offer four-stanza variants. Babab twice
reprints the latter (pp. 84 and 110). Hart's *Immortalia,* 3 (pp. 89 ff.)
also has it.

The tune and text here are from Peter Jaffee as he learned it at
Los Angeles City College in 1956. Dean Burson had the same from
a Carnegie Tech informant in 1960.

Balls to Mister Banglestein

As simple as it may be, this bit of nonsense retains its popularity
among younger singers. It is sung to the tune of "Ach, Du Lieber,
Augustin."

Balls to Mister Banglestein,
Banglestein, Banglestein.
Balls to Mister Banglestein,
Dirty old man.
For he keeps us waiting
While he's masturbating,
So balls to Mister Banglestein,
Dirty old man.

This was collected by Alice O'Brien in 1960. Other versions of this are in Abrahams; and Morgan 2 (p. 145).

Last Night I Stayed Up Late to Masturbate

Songwriters usually stay away from songs with tricky rhythms or complex rhyme schemes; it makes their work too difficult. "Last Night I Stayed Up" is a happy exception. Set to the tune of "Funiculi, Funicula," it sports one of the more felicitous meldings of tune and lyrics in this collection.

Last   night   I stayed up late to mas‐tur‐bate.
        night   I stayed up late to pull my pud.

It was   so   nice!   I   did   it twice.   Last
It felt   so   good!   I   knew it would.

You   should see me work‐ing   on   the short

strokes.   I   use my hand.   It's sim‐ply   grand.

You   should see   me work‐ing   on   the long   strokes.   I

use   my feet.   It's real‐ly   neat.   Smash   it!

Bash   it!   Beat   it on   the   floor.   Smite   it!

Bite   it!   Ram   it through the   door.   I have some friends who seem to

think   that   a   fuck   is sim‐ply   grand,   But   for

o‐ver‐all   en‐joy‐ment I   pre‐fer   it in   the hand.

340

Last night I stayed up late to masturbate.
It was so nice! I did it twice!
Last night I stayed up late to pull my pud.
It felt so good! I knew it would.
You should see me working on the short strokes;
I use my hand. It's simply grand!
You should see me working on the long strokes.
I use my feet. It's really neat.
Smash it! Bash it! Beat it on the floor.
Smite it! Bite it! Ram it through the door.
I have some friends who seem to think that a fuck is simply grand.
But for all around enjoyment I prefer it in the hand.

L. Denza's frisky "Funiculi Funicula" was written in 1880 to commemorate the opening of the Neapolitan funicular railway, but the parody is apparently of more recent vintage. See Fuld (p. 240).

There are three full variants in the editor's files, and two fragments. This is from Carnegie Tech, as sung to Dean Burson in Los Angeles in 1960. Reuss's "B" text (p. 214) is also from that school and little different from the Burson find.

Another is in *Songs of Roving and Raking* (p. 117, reprinted in Babab, 121, and credited to *Songs of Raunch and Ill-Repute* 20), which was compiled in 1960 at Cal Tech. Reuss (pp. 2111-14) also concludes the song is of recent vintage. Getz 2 (pp. FF-1,2) has two versions close to that here. It was also sung at USC by members of that school's marching band, according to a text in the unofficial songbook "Hymenal."

Two English versions have been reported. Vicarion. No. 31, is unsingable in its present form. Morgan 2 (p. 132) has one stanza. Shaw (p. 115) has a fragment of an entirely different song to the same tune.

Laycock's Australian text (p. 132) begins in an unusual fashion:

O My name is Antonio Agostini,
I pull-a da pud.
I feel-a good!

The Organ Grinder

This misogynic essay is another of those songs with nicely fitted text and tune, the melody here an echo of an organ grinder's aria.

Chorus: Re - o, re - o, bul-ly o re - o, Je - sus Christ how bul-ly I feel. Straight from the whore house peck-er like steel (with) my lit-tle or-gan grind - er. Verse Took my gal to cit - y hall, Spread her legs from wall to wall, Fucked her till I made her bawl With my lit - tle or - gan grind - er.

[A]

Chorus:
Rio, rio, bully o rio,
Jesus Christ, how bully I feel.
Straight from the whorehouse, pecker like steel,
My little organ grinder.

Laid my gal on her mother's bed,
Rubbed her tits until they bled,
Busted out her maidenhead
With my little organ grinder.

Laid her down upon the grass,
Aimed my pecker at her ass,
Missed her ass and mowed the grass
With my little organ grinder.

Laid her on her mother's bed,
Shoved it in up to her head,
Fucked her till she was dead
With my little organ grinder.

Followed her to the burial ground
Just to have another round,
Fucked her as they laid her down
With my little organ grinder.

Now she's dead and in her tomb,
Worms crawl in and out her womb.
I don't care if there's still room
For my little organ grinder.

Some folks say that I'm a knave;
Others say I can't behave
'Cause I jack off on her grave
With my little organ grinder.

[B]

Chorus:
Rio, rio, bully o rio,
Jesus Christ, how bully I feel.
Straight from the whorehouse, pecker like steel,
My little organ grinder.

Met my gal upon the street,
Shoved my pecker up her seat,
Stood there while she beat my meat
With my little organ grinder.

Took my gal to city hall,
Spread her legs from wall to wall,
Fucked her till I made her bawl
With my little organ grinder.

Took her to the city dump,
Placed her ass upon a stump,
Missed her rump and split the stump
With my little organ grinder.

Took her to the river side,
That was where she lost her pride.
For 'twas there I got inside
With my little organ grinder.

[C]

I fucked her living and I fucked her dying;
If I'd a-had wings I'd a-fucked her flying.

343

I threw her down into the chair and all I left was blood and hair.
The old folks knew that I'd been there with my old organ grinder.

I started for town with a heavy load and jacked off twice along the road
And then got hot and fucked a toad with my old organ grinder.

I backed her up ag'in a stump, took a hop, step, skip and a jump.
I missed her cunt and split the stump with my old organ grinder.

There are five versions of this in the editor's files, the earliest, in the Michigan State folklore archives at Indiana University, dated to 1954. The "A" text and tune is from Stanford University, circa 1960, collected by the editor. The "B" text is from a student collection, made at UCLA about the same time. The "C" version was recorded by Lou Curtiss of San Diego, California, as sung/chanted by a professional folksinger who explained he learned it in grade school.

F. M. Rivinus of Philadelphia has a three-stanza text dating from the 1940s beginning:

> I took my gal to the city hall,
> Spread her legs from wall to wall,
> Fucked her till I made her bawl,
> With my little organ grinder.
> Rio, Rio, bully, old Rio. . . .

Logsdon (p. 235 ff.) prints a different song, "Old Horny Kebri-O," whose scansion suggests it may be related to "Organ Grinder."

Hot Nuts

This folk song—it is that—was apparently inspired by a "race record" of 1936, a recording made by a black artist and sold largely to a black audience. In its current form, it knows no racial barriers.

> Chorus:
> Hot nuts. Hot nuts. Get 'em from the peanut man.
> Yeah, yeah, yeah, yeah, yeah.
> Nuts, hot nuts.
> Get 'em any way you can.
>
> Got it in the kitchen, got it in the hall.
> Got it on my finger, so I wiped it on the wall. Nuts.
>
> See that man dressed in brown.
> He's got the biggest nuts in town. Nuts.
>
> See that man dressed in black.
> He carries his nuts in a gunny sack. Nuts.

See that girl dressed in red.
She makes her living lying in bed. Nuts.

See that girl dressed in pink.
She's the one who makes my finger stink. Nuts.

See that girl sitting on his lap.
Bang with her and you'll get the clap. Nuts.

See that girl over there in slacks.
She shacks. Nuts.

Little red rooster, little black duck,
Put 'em on the table and watch them dance. Nuts.

See that man who walks like a duck.
He can't dance but he sure can fuck. Nuts.

See that girl dressed in blue.
She can't dance but she sure can screw. Nuts.

See that girl dressed in green.
She lost her quarter in the bathroom machine. Nuts.

See that cool guy named Harry.
He's got nuts, but he's still a fairy. Nuts.

Got some in a Cadillac, got some in a Ford,
But the best I got was on the running board. Nuts.

See that guy; he's a Phi Gam.
He's got nuts but they ain't worth a damn. Nuts.

Now there is a girl named Pearl.
She cracks so many nuts they call her "Squirrel." Nuts.

There is a girl named Jill.
She won't screw but her sister will. Nuts.

See that girl named Mary.
They call her "Dingleberry." Nuts.

See that girl in blue.
She'll polish your knob if you ask her to. Nuts.

See that man in back swinging a pick,
Missed one day and cut off his finger. Nuts.

That man over there goes to Texas Tech.
His nuts hang round his neck. Nuts.

Based on the available record, it is impossible to tell if "Hot Nuts" was first a traditional, then a popular song, or is a commercial song that has entered oral tradition. It remains that "Hot Nuts, Get 'Em

From the Peanut Man" was recorded by Chicago blues singer Lil Johnson on March 4, 1936, and released on Vocalion Record 03199. Seemingly popular, that song inspired blues singer Georgia White to record a "New Hot Nuts" on May 11, 1936 (Decca 7183), according to Lou Curtiss of Folk Arts Rare Records in San Diego. (On the interrelationship of the commercial music industry and oral tradition, see Norman Cohen, "Tin Pan Alley's Contribution to Folk Music," *Western Folklore* 29 [1970]: 9-20.)

Whatever its origins, "Hot Nuts" has become something of a portmanteau song, sharing verses with that complex of military cadences known as "The Jody Song" or "Sound Off."

The text here, collected by Judy Allred from University of Texas students, 1963, was forwarded by Roger Abrahams. Other versions dating from the early 1960s were collected at UCLA and Campbellsville College, Kentucky.

When the End of the Month Rolls Around

Set to the melody of "The Field Artillery Song," this is seemingly a relatively recent addition to the college student's repertoire.

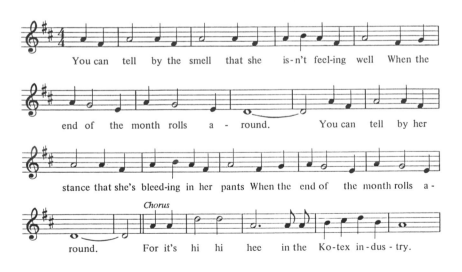

You can tell by the smell that she is-n't feel-ing well When the end of the month rolls a - round. You can tell by her stance that she's bleed-ing in her pants When the end of the month rolls a - round.

Chorus

For it's hi hi hee in the Ko-tex in-dus-try.

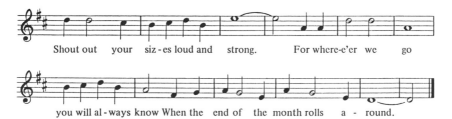

Shout out your siz-es loud and strong. For where-e'er we go

you will al-ways know When the end of the month rolls a - round.

[A]

You can tell by the smell that she isn't feeling well
When the end of the month rolls around.
You can tell by her stance that she's bleeding in her pants
When the end of the month rolls around.

Chorus:
For it's hi, hi, hee in the Kotex industry.
Shout out your sizes loud and strong.
[Shouted] Junior, regular, super-duper, bale of hay!
For where e're we go you will always know
When the end of the month rolls around.

You can tell by her walk that you'll sit around and talk
When the end of the month rolls around.
You can tell by the stench that she is a bloody wench
When the end of the month rolls around.

You can tell by her eyes that there is blood between her thighs
When the end of the month rolls around.
You can tell by her pout that her eggs are falling out
When the end of the month rolls around.

[B]

You can tell by the smell that she isn't feeling well
As the end of the month rolls around.
You can tell by the blotch that she's got a leaky crotch
As the end of the month rolls around.

Chorus:
So it's hi hi hee in the Kotex factory.
Shout out your sizes loud and clear:
Small, medium, large, extra absorbent, bale o' hay!
So it's hi hi hee in the Kotex factory
When the end of the month rolls around.
(Keep 'em bleeding!)
When the end of the month rolls around.

347

You can tell by the stain that she's in a lot of pain
As the end of the month rolls around.
You can tell by her stance she's got cotton in her pants
As the end of the month rolls around.

You can tell by her pain you'll be beating off again
As the end of the month rolls around.
You can tell by the string she's got something up her thing
As the end of the month rolls around.

You can tell by the flood that she's losing lots of blood
As the end of the month rolls around.
You can tell by her walk that tonight you'll only talk.
As the end of the month rolls around.

You can tell by the stench that she's a bloody wench
As the end of the month rolls around.
You can tell by her pout that her eggs are falling out
As the end of the month rolls around.

The oral currency of this was, until recently, in some doubt. Harry Taussig collected the "A" text in Berkeley, California, sometime between 1958 and 1963. Not until 1988, when Christian Gunning provided a copy of the unofficial USC Trojan Marching Band songbook, did a second version, the "B" text, turn up.

The song may be much more common than these reports would suggest. In any event, it seems to be of relatively recent origin.

The "Caisson Song," written by Edmund L. Gruber in 1907, was first published in 1918, according to Fuld (p. 156). Text and tune are in Dolph (pp. 40-42).

High Above a Theta's Garter

Poor Cornell. Never has a school's song suffered so much at the hands of so many as has that institution's Alma Mater. This is just one of a number of parodies set to that famous melody.

[A]

High a-bove a The-ta's gar-ter, High a-bove her knee,

Lies the key to The-ta suc-cess, Her vir-gin-i - ty.

Once she had it, now she's lost it. It is gone for good.
Lift her dress, oh, lift it gen - tly; Lay her on the grass.

She goes down for all the broth-ers, Like a The-ta should.
Of - ten are the times I've dreamed of A piece of The-ta ass.

High above a Theta's garter,
High above her knee,
Lies the key to Theta success,
Her virginity.
    Once she had it, now she's lost it.
    It is gone for good.
    She goes down for all the brothers,
    Like a Theta should.
    Lift her dress, oh, lift it gently;
    Lay her on the grass.
    Often are the times I've dreamed of
    A piece of Theta ass.

[B]

High above a Pi Phi's garter,
High above her knee,
Lies a Pi Phi's only honor,
Her virginity.
    So lift her dress up, raise it high, boys,
    Lay her on the grass.
    All I live for, all I die for
    Is good old Pi Phi ass.

349

High above a Pi Phi's garter,
Nestled near her lap,
Lies the thing we all dread,
Good old Pi Phi clap.
    So lift her dress up, raise it high, boys,
    So we all can see
    All a Pi Phi has to offer
    Our fraternity [dormitory].

The "A" text is one of two full versions in the editor's collection, from a member of a sorority (not the organization named) as it was sung in Los Angeles in 1955. The "B" text, from the UCLA Folklore Archives, was collected from a fraternity member in 1964.

At Michigan State and Indiana Universities, the sorority is usually the Pi Phi's. Reuss (p. 76) suggests that the attribution may be the result of that sorority's prestige, a prestige based in part upon the handsome physical endowments of the group's members. Reuss gives four versions, noting another eight from midwestern schools (pp. 76-80).

The editor learned another parody set to this tune, sung by men at Officers' Candidate School at Fort Benning, Georgia, in the early 1950s. As *Schadenfreude*, it was sung to satirize the plight of the newly commissioned infantry platoon leaders trained at that military post:

High above the Chattahoochie,
On the Upitoy,
Stands our noble alma mater,
Benning School for boys.
    Forward ever, backward never,
    Next of kin, goodbye.
    To the port of embarkation,
    Follow me and die.

The last line is especially pointed in that "Follow Me" is the motto of the Benning OCS.

Reuss has still other parodies of the Cornell Alma Mater (pp. 153 ff.).

To Thee, Hershey Hall

Dedicated in this version to a women's dormitory at UCLA, this grimly resolute vow is known and sung—especially by women, it would seem—at a number of centers of higher learning. Its tune is the saccharine wedding staple "My Wonderful One."

350

To thee, Hershey Hall,
We pledge our abortions,
The loss of our virginity,
To the friends we have made
And to those who have made us.
We linger through our pregnancy.
If I have a daughter,
I'll send her to college
As far from this place as can be,
Where the men will be truer
And not try to screw her.
To thee, Hershey Hall, to thee.

Questions about the oral currency of this song—collected by Anne Smith from a twenty-two-year-old male at UCLA in 1960—were dispelled by the Reuss dissertation. He noted "a remarkable currency among students in recent years, particularly among coeds" (p. 150) and cites fifty-four texts collected at Michigan State University between 1947 and 1956, nineteen more from Indiana University, and a scattering from high schools and universities from Ohio to Texas. D. K. Wilgus reported another text, from Murray State College, collected in 1948, contained in the Western Kentucky Folklore Archives at UCLA.

Reuss's tune is also that of "My Wonderful One." It was published by Dorothy Terris, Paul Whiteman, and Ferde Grofe in 1922.

We Are the Dirty Bitches

This is an example of what is known as a rasty-nasty among sorority women.

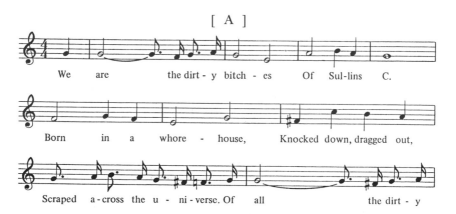

We are the dirt-y bitch-es Of Sul-lins C.

Born in a whore-house, Knocked down, dragged out,

Scraped a-cross the u-ni-verse. Of all the dirt-y

bitch - es, We are the worst. We hail from
Sul - lins C., The big - gest whore - house on earth.

> We are the dirty bitches
> Of Sullins C.,
> Born in a whorehouse,
> Knocked down, dragged out, scraped across the universe.
> Of all the dirty bitches,
> We are the worst.
> We hail from Sullins C.,
> The biggest whorehouse on earth.

[B]

> We're the dirty bastards,
> Scum of the earth,
> Born in a whorehouse,
> Shit on, spit on, kicked around the universe.
> Of all the dirty bastards,
> We are the worst.
> We're from ole M.S.C.
> The asshole of the earth.

Songs such as these demonstrate that women too share a good deal of bawdry, and have for generations. Folklorist Rayna Green notes her grandmother "continued to fill my big ears with a large and delightfully bawdy store of tales, songs, jokes, and sayings for the next thirty years. Grandmother was an unusually good storyteller, but her bawdiness was not remarkable in our family. Her sisters, my mother, my sisters, cousins, and aunts all engaged in the perpetuation of the bawdy tradition." Nor is Green's family that remarkable, she points out in her article "Magnolias Grow in Dirt, The Bawdy Lore of Southern Women" in *Southern Exposures* (4, No. 4 [1977]: 29).

One of five texts the editor has seen, the "A" version was contributed to the Western Kentucky Folksong Archive at UCLA by Daphne A. McCord of Bristol, Tennessee, in May 1957. It was sung by, or about, women at Sullins College in Bristol, Virginia.

The "B" text is one of two variants from Michigan State University,

352

collected by Margaret Rinehart in 1952 and deposited in the Indiana University Folklore Archive.

Fascinating Lady

This bit of fantasizing is common on college campuses, a parallel to the ubiquitous legends of the beautiful young woman who put herself through school as a high-priced call girl.

[A]

Wish I was a fas-ci-nat-ing la-dy With a past that's fast and a

Wish I was a fascinating lady
With a past that's fast and a future that is shady.
Sleep all day, work all night,
Live in a house with a little red light.
Once a month, I'd take a short vacation
And drive my customers wild.
Wish I was a fascinating lady
Instead of an innocent child.

[B]

Oh, I wish I were a fascinating bitch.
I'd never be poor, I'd always be rich.
I'd live in a house with a little red light,
And sleep all day and work all night.
And every once in a while I'd take a little rest,
Just to drive my customers wild.
Oh, I wish I were a fascinating bitch,
Instead of a legitimate child.

This is seemingly a parody of a popular song, though the original has not turned up. "Fascinating Bitch" enjoyed a burst of popularity in the 1960s; the Indiana University Folklore Archives contain no less than forty variants of this, and it was reported at UCLA and at Berkeley about the same time. Barre Toelken included a variant of "B," apparently of the same age, in "The Folklore of Academe," in

Brunvand, *The Study of American Folklore* (p. 379). "Fascinating Bitch," however, is said to be older; Cleveland (p. 95) states that it was sung by New Zealand troops in World War II, but gives no text.

The "A" version, plucked from the Indiana University Folklore Archive, dates from 1954 at Michigan State University; the "B" text is from the Taussig collection made in Berkeley between 1958 and 1963.

Take Your Man Around the Corner

And another rasty-nasty, this one to the melody of the popular song "Wake the Town and Tell the People."

> Take your man around the corner
> Where the lights are low.
> Put your arm around his shoulder,
> And the other down below.
>
> When he starts to shake and quiver
> And exclaim his glee,
> Tell him it's the secret handshake
> Of good ol' AGD.

This song from the women of Alpha Gamma Delta sorority was collected by Brookes Croonquist, and deposited in the UCLA Folklore Archive in 1979.

The original popular song, written by Sammy Gallop and Jerry Livingston, was published in 1955.

In Bohunkus, Tennessee

Bawdy songs tend to migrate, to be adapted to differing locales and groups. This is an exception, sung to the melody of "Tramp, Tramp Tramp"; almost invariably it falls down upon the head of Beta Theta Pi fraternity.

[A]

Verse

In Bo - hunk-us, Ten-nes-see There's a horse-'s ass. That's me. And my

fa - ther shov - eled horse - shit in the street. And when

I was ver - y young, he found dia - monds in the dung, And he

sent me off a Be - ta for to be.

Chorus

So stroke! stroke! stroke! you mas - tur - Be - tas!

Raise your foam - ing cocks on high. And we'll

drink an-oth - er glass to the per - fect horse - 's ass, The

sis - ter - hood of Be - ta The - ta Pi.

In Bohunkus, Tennessee,
There's a horse's ass. That's me.
And my father shoveled horseshit in the street.
And when I was very young,
He found diamonds in the dung
And he sent me off a Beta for to be.

Chorus:
So stroke! stroke! you master-Betas!
Raise your foaming cocks on high,
And we'll drink another glass
To the perfect horse's ass,
The sisterhood of Beta Theta Pi.

[B]

Down in Bohuggus, Tennessee,
Lived a half-assed family,
And the father shoveled horseshit in the street,
And one day when I was young,
He found a diamond in the dung
And a Beta I decided I would be.

[C]

Down in Nashville, Tennessee,
There's a girl who waits for me,
And her father shovels horseshit in the street,
And one day when she was young
Found a diamond in the dung,
So she pledged to Beta Omega Chi.

[D]

In my prison cell I stand, with my peter in my hand,
And my balls are dangling on the prison floor.
You can see the bloody snag where she hit me on the bag.
Oh, I'll never fuck a Beta anymore.

Hail, hail, you masturbators,
Raise your thundermugs on high,
And we'll drink another glass
To a perfect horse's ass,
To the sisterhood of Beta Omega Chi.

The history of this song is certainly not fully known. Legman (*Horn Book*, 251) notes its appearance in "a very rare collection of bawdy American college songs, *Lyra Ebriosa*," dated to 1930. He judges it to be a lampoon of "Ball of Yarn" (p. 421), apparently depending upon the fact that some versions of "Ball of Yarn" share something akin to the following stanza with "In Bohunkus":

In the prison cell I sit with my pecker dipped in shit,
And the shadow of my ass against the wall,
And the ladies as they pass stick their hatpins up my ass,
And the little mice play billiards with my balls.

The present editor is less certain of Legman's schema, preferring to consider the songs in question to be separate entities with the single shared stanza between them.

The "A" text and tune are from the Harry A. Taussig collection, made in Berkeley, California, between 1958 and 1963.

The "B" variant was contributed by an anonymous member of Beta Theta Pi to Kenneth Moss and deposited in the UCLA Folklore Archive in 1964.

The "C" text was collected by D. K. Wilgus at Western Kentucky State College in 1955. Wilgus noted that he heard a similar song at Ohio State between 1936 and 1941, adding that apparently the satirical song about the Betas (a fraternity) had been transferred to a local sorority.

"D" was contributed by Keith Martin of Ohio Co., Kentucky, in 1952 to the Western Kentucky Folklore Archive, now at UCLA.

My Girl's From USC

From USC or anywhere else. This is a sampling of the verses to this commonly sung parody of "My Best Girl's a New Yorker."

[A]

My girl's from U. S. C. She fights for chas - ti - ty,
And in my fu - ture life, She's going to be my wife.

Fights ev - 'ry - one but me. I love her so.
How the hell do I know that? She told me so.

My girl's from USC.
She fights for chastity,
Fights everyone but me.
I love her so.

Chorus:
And in my future life,
She's going to be my wife.
How the hell do I know that?
She told me so.

My girl's from Vassar,
None can surpass her.
She is a stroke on the
Varsity crew.

My girl's from Bennington,
Bangs like a Remington.
She's got that slight action
Finger control.

My girl's an Alpha Chi.
I feed her Spanish fly.
I am a horny guy.
I love her so.

My girl's a Kappa.
She chews tobacca,
Sits by the fireside and
Spits on the floor.

My girl's from Holyoke.
She lives on rum and coke.
She tells me dirty jokes.
I tell them too.

[B]

My girl's a Tri-Delt.
She knows just how it's felt.
She tickles me below the belt.
I love her so.

My girl's from SMU.
There's nothing she won't do,
If I should ask her to.
I love her so.

This multi-stanza parody of John Stromberg's 1895 song "My Best Girl's a New Yorker" was current at UCLA in 1960. The "A" version was collected by Anne Smith from a male informant at that time. The "B" stanzas were given to the editor four years later by Bethel Morgan in Los Angeles; she said there were more stanzas but could not recall them.

Lynn (*Swinging*, 32) has another, perhaps expurgated parody entitled "That's Where My Money Goes." The last verse of that hints of the bawdy song:

> My gal's a hullabaloo,
> She goes to (college) U.
> She wears the colors too.
> Love her, you bet I do.
> And in my later life,
> She's gonna be my wife.
> [Shouted] How the hell did you get that way?
> She told me so.

Getz 2 (pp. MM-8, 9) reports a version recalled from the 1930s at Indiana University. Lynn (*Swinging*, 17) and Best (pp. 55-56, 69) have other songs that borrow verses from "My Gal's a Corker."

Mary Ann Barnes

Marylou or Salome or Mary Ann Barnes or any of a dozen other names, the lady is formidable. This circulates both in collegiate and military circles.

[A]

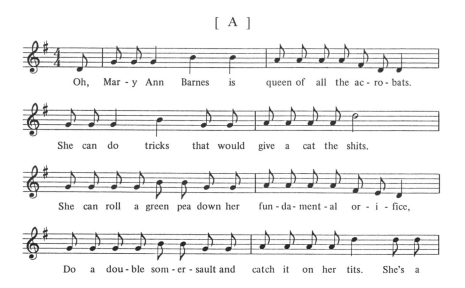

Oh, Mar - y Ann Barnes is queen of all the ac - ro - bats.

She can do tricks that would give a cat the shits.

She can roll a green pea down her fun - da - ment - al or - i - fice,

Do a dou - ble som - er - sault and catch it on her tits. She's a

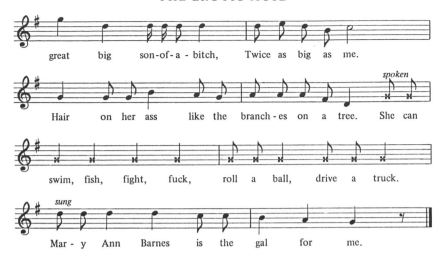

great   big   son-of-a-bitch,   Twice   as   big   as   me.

Hair   on   her   ass   like   the   branch-es   on   a   tree.   *spoken* She   can

swim,   fish,   fight,   fuck,   roll   a   ball,   drive   a   truck.

sung Mar-y   Ann   Barnes   is   the   gal   for   me.

Oh, Mary Ann Barnes is the queen of all the acrobats.
She can do tricks that would give a cat the shits.
She can roll a green pea down her fundamental orifice,
Do a double somersault and catch it on her tits.
    She's a great big sonovabitch, twice as big as me,
    Hair on her ass like the branches of a tree.
    She can swim, fish, fight, fuck,
    Roll a ball, drive a truck.
    Mary Ann Barnes is the gal for me.

[B]

My girl Marylou, queen of all the acrobats,
The things that she will do will drive a man to shit.
She can squirt green peas right out her dirty asshole,
Flip 'em in a somersault and catch them on her tit.
She is just a strapping girl, twice the size of me,
And the hairs around her twat are like the branches on a tree.
She can fuck, suck, jerk or screw, anything you want to do,
Just like the girl that's gonna marry you.

"A," under the title of "Mary Ann Barnes," was sung by Wally Fey
on a tape recording made for air force song collector and editor Bill
Getz. A similar item fixed to Purdue University and 1964 is in the
Indiana University Folklore Archive. F. M. Rivinus of Philadelphia
noted his text, like that here, is sung to the melody of the children's
song "Joshua Ebenezer Fry."

360

"B" is from Dean Burson's collecting at UCLA in 1960. Other versions are in Logue, No. 60, and Cleveland (p. 95), attributing it to New Zealand troops during World War II. Hopkins (p. 178) has an extended text and tune. Getz 2 (pp. SS-1, 2) has a celebration of "Salome," which borrows from "Marylou/Mary Ann."

Nelly Darling

This crapulous piece is, in effect, an anti-love song, a scathing mock of popular songs in praise of this or that girl.

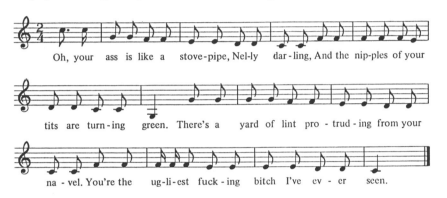

Oh, your ass is like a stovepipe, Nelly Darling,
And the nipples on your tits are turning green.
There's a yard of lint protruding from your navel.
You're the ugliest fucking bitch I've ever seen.

There's a lot[?] of blue ointment 'round your crotch, dear.
When you piss, you piss a stream as green as grass.
There's enough wax in your ears to make a candle.
So why not make one, dear, and shove it up your ass.

This was sung by former pilot Wally Fey on a tape recording for air force song collector and editor Bill Getz. Though not often reported, it apparently has wide campus currency.

I Love My Girl

This undergraduate essay on anal retentive behavior has but one purpose: to shock.

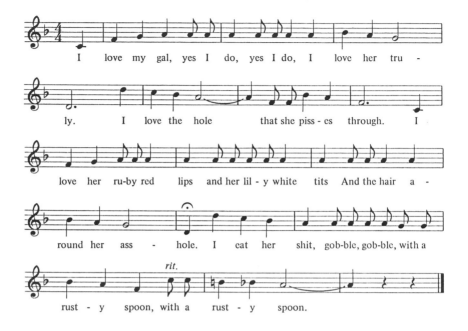

I love my gal, yes I do, yes I do, I love her tru-ly. I love the hole that she piss-es through. I love her ru-by red lips and her lil-y white tits And the hair a-round her ass-hole. I eat her shit, gob-ble, gob-ble, with a rust-y spoon, with a rust-y spoon.

I love my gal, yes, I do, yes, I do,
I love her truly.
I love the hole that she pisses through.
I love her ruby red lips and the lily white tits
And the hair around her asshole.
I eat her shit, gobble, gobble,
With a rusty spoon,
With a rusty spoon.

Multiple versions of this have been reported. Dean Burson collected it at UCLA in 1960. It turned up at California State University Northridge (then San Fernando State College) in 1964. The Indiana University Folklore Archives have nine texts from various midwestern universities, circa 1950-70. One from Kokomo, Indiana, collected by Alan Zirkle in 1967, added this verse:

I love my big cock when it's hard as a rock
In the hairs around her asshole,
And I'd eat her shit
If she'd ask me to.

I love my girl, yes, I do, yes, I do
I love her truly
And I love the hole
That she pisses through.

Air force veteran Wally Fey sang the version here on a tape recording for Bill Getz in the mid-1980s.

Sam, Sam, the Lavatory Man

For such a slight piece of doggerel, this one-stanza poem has certainly traveled the length and breadth of the English-speaking world.

> Sam, Sam, the lavatory man,
> Cleans up the basins in the public can.
> He scrubs up the toilets and puts in the towels,
> And listens to the rumble of the other fellow's bowels.

This scatological essay turns up frequently, another bawdy song apparently inspired by an unrecovered commercial recording. The earliest report, from F. M. Rivinus of Philadelphia, would date it at least to 1950. Rivinus noted, "This song is widely used by all levels of society on both sides of the Atlantic." He recalled an article in the British business press about a department store owner who made unscheduled inspections of restrooms in his emporium. "According to the article, his staff always called him 'Sam, Sam,' behind his back, an obvious reference to this familiar ditty."

Morgan 2 (p. 98); and Hart's *Immortalia*, 3 (pp. 71-73) have the only printed versions noted. This suspected parody of an unidentified popular song is from Rivinus; multiple variants are in the Burson, UCLA, and Western Kentucky collections.

Knock, Knock

This song recycles a group of jokes that have been popular since at least the 1930s, jokes that depend upon outrageous plays upon words. The three stanzas here, set to the melody of that circus perennial "The Billboard March," are but an unfair sample.

She loves a gang - bang, she al - ways will, Because a gang - bang gives her such a thrill. When she was young - er and in her prime, She used to gang - bang all the time. But now she's old - er and turn - ing gray She on - ly gang - bangs twice a day.

[Spoken] Knock, knock!
Who's there?
Sheila.
Sheila who?

[Sung] She loves a gang-bang; she always will
Because a gang-bang gives her such a thrill.
When she was younger, and in her prime,
She used to gang-bang all the time.
But now she's older, and turning gray
She only gang bangs twice a day!

[Shouted]
G-A-N-G-B-A-N-G
Gang bang! Gang bang! Rah!

Knock, knock!
Who's there?
Anita.
Anita who?

I need a blow job. I always do
Because I just can't fuck the likes of you.
Your cunt is rancid and full of scabs.
I bet you'd even give me crabs!

B-L-O-W-J-O-B
Blowjob! Blowjob! Rah!

Knock, knock!
Who's there?
Kenny.
Kenny who?

Can he give cunt licks, or use his hand?
Because I cannot fuck his shriveled gland.
It's always flaccid and way too small
And then I can't feel it at all!
His cock is putrid from fucking sheep.
He can't even come once a week!

C-U-N-T-L-I-C-K
Cunt lick! Cunt lick! Eat me out, rah!

This full text is unique, copied from "Hymenal," the Xeroxed songbook of the University of Southern California Marching Band, in 1988. Christian Gunning, a member of the band, wrote out the music. A portion of the refrain, "She loves a gang bang, she always will, / Because a gang bang gives her such a thrill," circulates as a playground taunt in Southern California junior high schools.

"The Billboard March" was published by John N. Klohr in 1901. It bears at least one other mock, this remembered from the editor's youth:

My name is Jesus,
The son of God.
Hello, hello, hello, hello!
I'm here to save you
And heal your bod.
Hello, hello, hello, hello!

The Rugby Song

Practitioners of the sport insist that "The Rugby Song" is just that, *the* rugby song.

[A]

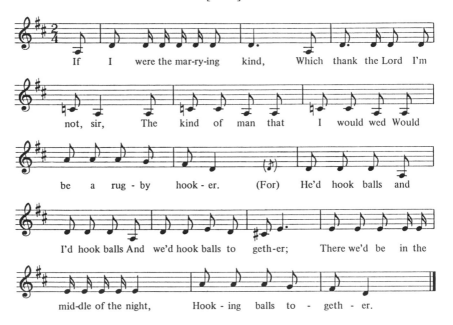

If I were the mar-ry-ing kind, Which thank the Lord I'm not, sir, The kind of man that I would wed Would be a rug-by hook-er. (For) He'd hook balls and I'd hook balls And we'd hook balls to geth-er; There we'd be in the mid-dle of the night, Hook-ing balls to-geth-er.

If I were the marrying kind,
Which, thank the Lord, I'm not, sir,
The kind of man that I would wed
Would be a rugby hooker.
 He'd hook balls and I'd hook balls
 And we'd hook balls together;
 There we'd be in the middle of the night,
 Hooking balls together.

If I were the marrying kind,
Which, thank the Lord, I'm not, sir,
The kind of man that I would wed
Would be a rugby prop.
 For he'd hold it up and I'd hold it up
 And we'd hold it up together.
 There we'd be in the middle of the night
 Holding it up together.

Successive stanzas follow the same pattern:

 Rugby lock . . . screw the scrum
 Break . . . break hard

Scrum half . . . put it in
Standoff . . . feed it out
Wing . . . run hard
Fullback . . . kick hard
Referee . . . blow hard
Spectator . . . come again

[B]

If I were the marrying kind,
And thank the Lord, I'm not, sir,
The kind of girl that I would wed
Would be a hooker's daughter.

Oh, she'd hook balls and I'd hook balls,
And we'd hook balls together,
And we'd be all right in the middle of the night,
Hooking balls together.

Fullback's daughter . . . go to touch
Scrum-half's daughter . . . put it in
Prop's daughter . . . stand erect
Ground-keeper's daughter . . . fill holes
Concessionaire's daughter . . . eat out
Referee's daughter . . . blow hard
Fullback's daughter . . . kick balls
Winger's daughter . . . keep it in
Second row's daughter . . . push hard
Assistant ground-keeper's daughter . . . throw seeds
Ticket-taker's daughter . . . punch holes
Eight-man's daughter . . . she'd be ate
Goalpost's daughter . . . stand erect

This is an adaptation of an older college song clearly related to the cycle of punning songs described under the title "My's Husband's a Mason," above. The college song of old, however, seems to have waned in popularity. In 1967, D. K. Wilgus remembered a bit of that song, learned at Ohio State University about 1940:

If I were a maiden fair,
Fairer than all the others,
I would marry a plumber
As quick as one of the others.
We'd fix a pipe here.
We'd fix a pipe there.

We'd fix a pipe together,
But wouldn't we have a helluva time
Laying pipe together?

A fuller text of this, "Pretty Little Girl"—as it was styled on the
Michigan State College campus in 1956—runs:

I wish I was a pretty little girl and I had lots of money.
I would marry a plumber's son; he'd be as good as any.
He would pump and I would pump and we would pump together.
Oh, what fun we would have, pumping one another.

Carpenter's son . . . pound
Bricklayer's son . . . lay
Driller's son . . . drill
Soldier's son . . . bang

This is one of two versions without melodies in the IU Folklore
Archive, this collected by Virginia Bradway in East Lansing. Another
is in the Western Kentucky collection at UCLA, dated to 1960.

Wilgus's tune is similar to that used by Michael Higer for "The
Rugby Song" "A" text here. Higer recorded it for the editor in Los
Angeles in 1960.

The longer "B" text, without tune, is in a collection of rugby songs
made at Indiana University in 1970 by Drake Francescone and deposited in the IU Folklore Archives.

Apparently the rugby song appeared in print for the first time with
the publication of the first edition of this book. Since then it has
appeared three times: Morgan 1 (pp. 120-23) has a close variant from
Great Britain entitled "If I Were the Marrying Kind"; Laycock (pp.
124-25) offers an Australian text; and Getz 2 (p. MM-3) has a text
from an air force songbook, perhaps traceable to the same collegiate
rugby tradition. Cleveland (p. 95) states "If I Was a Rugby Fullback"
was sung by New Zealanders during the Second World War. Hopkins
prints a text and tune as adapted by Canadian artillerymen in World
War II (pp. 136-37). His tune is a set of Higer's.

Cats on the Rooftops

At one time, this song concerned itself with the idiosyncrasies,
anatomical and amatory, of the animal kingdom. Its attention since
has wandered to higher mammals.

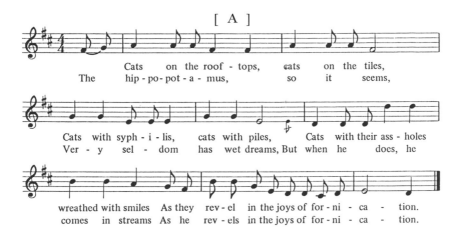

[A]

Cats on the roof - tops, cats on the tiles,
The hip-po-pot-a-mus, so it seems,

Cats with syph-i-lis, cats with piles, Cats with their ass-holes
Ver-y sel-dom has wet dreams, But when he does, he

wreathed with smiles As they rev-el in the joys of for-ni-ca-tion.
comes in streams As he rev-els in the joys of for-ni-ca-tion.

Chorus:
Cats on the rooftops, cats on the tiles,
Cats with syphilis, cats with piles,
Cats with their assholes wreathed with smiles
As they revel in the joys of fornication.

The hippopotamus, so it seems,
Very seldom has wet dreams,
But when he does, he comes in streams
As he revels in the joys of fornication.

The elephant is a funny bloke
And very seldom gets a poke,
So when he does, he lets it soak
As he revels in the joys of fornication.

The ostrich has a funny dick,
And it isn't very often that he dips his wick,
So when he does, he dips it quick
As he revels in the joys of fornication.

Promiscuous girls live under a strain,
Waiting for their monthly pain,
And when it comes, they smile again
As they revel in the joys of fornication.

Oh, you revel in the morning with an upright stand
(It's urinary pressure on the prostate gland),
And you haven't got a woman so you jerk it off by hand
As you revel in the joys of fornication.

The priest of the parish has very little fun.
He doesn't even know how it is done.

369

When it comes to fun, he gets nun
As he revels in the joys of fornication.

The cocksucker blows his friend in haste,
Then he licks it up so it won't go to waste.
Don't think it odd; it's a matter of taste
As he revels in the joys of fornication.

[B]

Chorus:
Cats on the rooftops, cats on the tiles,
Cats with syphilis, cats with piles,
Cats with their assholes wreathed with smiles
As they revel in the joys of fornication.

"Rats!" cried the captain as he thought,
These new ensigns are not so hot
And the admiral takes the best of the lot
As he revels in the joys of fornication.

Do you ken John Peel? Yes, I ken him weel.
He sleeps with his wife but he never gets a feel.
He sleeps by her side, but he never gets a ride
And he wakes up in the morning in frustration.

[C]

Chorus:
Cats on the roof tops, cats on the tiles,
Cats with the clap and cats with the piles,
Cats with their butts all wreathed in smiles,
While they revel in the throes of fornication.

The crocodile is a funny animal;
He rapes his mate only once a year,
But when he does he floods the Nile
As he revels in the throes of fornication.

Now the hippo's rump is broad and round.
One of them weighs a thousand pounds.
Two of them will shake the ground
When they revel in the throes of fornication.

Now the camel has a lot of fun.
His height's ample when he has done.
He always gets two humps for one
When he revels in the throes of fornication.

The queen bees fly out in the breezes,
And consort with who she God damn pleases,
And fills the world with sons of bees
As she revels in the throes of fornication.

The baboon's ass is an eerie sight,
It glows below like a neon light,
It waves like a flag in the jungle night,
As he revels in the throes of fornication.

The monkey's short and rather slow.
Erect he stands a foot or so—
And when he comes, it's time to go
As he revels in the throes of fornication.

Five hundred verses, all in rhyme,
To sing them all seems such a crime,
When we could better spend our time
Reveling in the throes of fornication.

This is one of the more commonly heard bawdy songs, at least within West Coast collegiate circles. The earliest report, dating it to World War II, is in Paul Fussell, *Wartime* (New York: Oxford University Press [1989]: 265). It has been printed, with some scrubbing or judicious selection of verses, by Brand (pp. 32-33), and in an eleven-stanza variant in *New Locker Room Humor* (p. 60-61). An unretouched third version is found in *Songs of Roving and Raking* (p. 101). Getz 2 (pp. CC-3,4) has twelve verses.

Two texts presumably from British currency have been reported. Logue-Vicarion calls his version, No. 48, for no apparent reason, "Nightfuck." Morgan 1 (p. 54) has it with a variant of the Peel verse (p. 84). Hopkins prints a version from Canadian singers (pp. 174-75).

The Peel verse may be a clue to the song's ultimate origin. It is a mock of John Woodcock Graves' "John Peel," an 1820 art song set to a traditional tune, "Bonnie Annie," according to Spaeth (*History*, 63). That melody has been borrowed for "Cats on the Rooftop," and at one time the bawdy song may have had verses, like the last here, closer in parody form to Graves's celebration of the otherwise forgotten huntsman.

There are eight versions of this in the editor's collection, most highly repetitive. The "A" version here, from an anonymous informant, was current in New York college circles circa 1950. The "B" text is from Los Angeles insurance salesman Stuart Grayboyse, who learned it at UCLA in 1950. The "C" text is reprinted from *Songs of Raunch and Ill-Repute* (p. 5), mimeographed and privately circulated

371

at Ricketts House, California Institute of Technology, about the same time. The typographical errors and the orthography have been silently corrected.

Next Thanksgiving

Obscenity is a broad term with no clear meaning, its definition largely subjective. The obscene to one person may mean only the pornographic; to another, it may include the profane. To some, it even includes the impudent, like this satire to the familiar "Frère Jacques."

Next Thanks - giv - ing, next Thanks - giv - ing, Don't eat bread. Don't eat bread. Shove it up the tur - key. Shove it up the tur - key. Eat the bird. Eat the bird.

Next Thanksgiving, next Thanksgiving,
Don't eat bread. Don't eat bread.
Shove it up the turkey. Shove it up the turkey.
Eat the bird. Eat the bird.

Next Christmas, next Christmas,
Don't trim a tree. Don't trim a tree.
Shove it up the chimney. Shove it up the chimney.
Goose Saint Nick. Goose Saint Nick.

Next Easter, next Easter,
Don't color eggs. Don't color eggs.
Shove them up the rabbit. Shove them up the rabbit.
Eat the hare. Eat the hare.

Songs of Raunch and Ill-Repute (p. 15) has a close variant ("Save the bread . . . tree . . . eggs") from Pasadena, circa 1960. It is reprinted in *Songs of Roving and Raking* (p. 65), and from there in Babab (p.

81). Abrahams has forwarded a one-stanza version from Texas. An M.I.T. variant is in "The One, the Only Baker House . . . Songbook" (p. 2).

The text here is from the collection gathered at UCLA in 1960 by Dean Burson.

The Ten Days of Finals

The sacred made profane once more, traditions mocked, piety and sentiment alike ravaged—all to the melody of "The Twelve Days of Christmas."

[A]

On the first day of finals my true love gave to me,
A hand job in a pear tree.

On the second day of finals my true love gave to me,
Two brass balls
And a hand job in a pear tree.

Successive verses are cumulative:

Third day . . . three French ticklers
Four day . . . four cocksuckers
Fifth day . . . five motherfuckers
Sixth day . . . six scrotums swinging
Seventh day . . . seven lezzies licking
Eighth day . . . eight sacks of shit
Ninth day . . . Nine nipples dripping
Tenth day . . . Ten twats a-twitching

[B]

On the first day of Christmas
My true love gave to me
A hand job in a hair tree!

Two brass balls
Three flying fucks
Four flopping whores
Five mother fuckers
Six sacks of shit
Seven semen samples

Eight elegant assholes
Nine gnawed off nipples
Ten dirty douches
Eleven lesbian lickers
Twelve tiny twats.

The gifts vary slightly from day to day, and from campus to campus. The "A" text is one of two versions collected by Linda McAllister in 1969 for the Indiana University Folklore Archive at UCLA.

"B" comes from the USC "Hymenal" songbook, courtesy of Christian Gunning.

Reuss (pp. 144-46), and Edith Fowke ("Sampling," 59) report variants of this song. Ms. Fowke concludes that, on the basis of internal evidence in her version, it was composed in the early 1950s.

Uncle Joe and Aunty Mabel

Much of the humor of parody comes from the use of the incongruous. In this case, the rather basic problems of Uncle Joe and Aunty Mabel are recounted to the festive tune of "Hark, the Herald Angels Sing," a grotesquely inappropriate match.

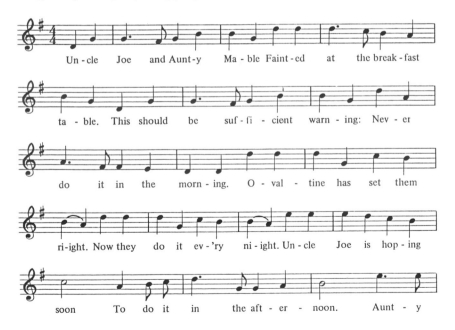

Un - cle Joe and Aunt-y Ma - ble Faint - ed at the break - fast ta - ble. This should be suf - fi - cient warn - ing: Nev - er do it in the morn - ing. O - val - tine has set them ri - ight. Now they do it ev - 'ry ni - ight. Un - cle Joe is hop - ing soon To do it in the aft - er - noon. Aunt - y

Ma - ble will a - gree   It   hits the   spot   at half - past   three.

> Uncle Joe and Aunty Mabel
> Fainted at the breakfast table.
> This should be sufficient warning:
> Never do it in the morning.
> Ovaltine has set them right;
> Now they do it every night.
> Uncle Joe is hoping soon
> To do it in the afternoon.
> Aunty Mabel will agree
> It hits the spot at half-past three.

This is surely the only bawdy song to serve as a national anthem. In 1944, a JEDBURGH team in occupied France, unable to recall the words to "The Star Spangled Banner," instead offered this as a "specially composed anthem of international goodwill." See R. Harris Smith, *OSS: The Secret History of America's First Intelligence Agency* (Berkeley: University of California Press [1972]: 190).

Generally, religious parodies are not malicious or anti-clerical. The songs and prayers are borrowed simply because of the humorous shock effect of unfamiliar words in a familiar setting. Some of the parodies, indeed, are quite moralistic, such as this "Hail Mary" collected in 1960 in Los Angeles by Ms. Jacqueline Brunke from her ten-year-old daughter, Anne:

> Hail Mary, full of grace,
> Bless my boy friend's hands and face.
> Bless his head, full of curls,
> And help him stay away from other girls.
> Bless his arms so big and strong,
> And keep his hands where they belong.
>   Amen.

For a survey of "Parodies of Scripture, Prayer, and Hymn," see George Monteiro's article in the *Journal of American Folklore*, (77 [1964]: 45-52), and the references there. See too Reuss (pp. 276-79).

Religious satire or comic reinterpretation of the Bible is not a uniquely American phenomenon. The Opie's *Lore and Language of Schoolchildren* (pp. 6, 21, 87-89); and Shaw (pp. 94-99) have samplings from England. Robin Hall and Jimmie MacGregor sing a Glasgow children's street song, "Johnny Lad," on *Two Heids Are Better Than One* (Monitor 365) containing these biblical commentaries:

Solomon and David led very wicked lives,
Lunchin' every evenin' with other people's wives.

But sometimes in the evenings when their conscience gave them qualms,
Solomon wrote the proverbs and David wrote the psalms.

In the interest of a complete record, the editor calls attention to one further parody of "Hark, the Herald Angels Sing." Speaking in the House of Representatives on February 27, 1964, New York Representative Emanuel Celler complained, "Some ads are just plain humbug. I am reminded of the doggerel of my boyhood [ca. 1900]:

"Hark the herald angels sing,
Beecham's pills are just the thing.
Peace on earth and mercy mild,
Two for man and one for child."

The editor has handled seven versions of "Uncle Joe," four from college students, as is the one presented here. Three others are from printed sources. The oldest variant, dating to about 1927, is in *Anecdota Americana* 1 (p. 66). Another is in Getz 1 (p. UV-1). Morgan 2 (p. 26) presents a longer version from British singers that does not seem to be common in the United States.

Bless 'Em All

FTER the first flush of patriotic enthusiasm, the foot soldier soon forgets the noble motives that sent him off to war. The militant songs of the home front are replaced with grousing ribaldry, and the stirring sentiments of "The Marines' Hymn" turned to more personal matters:

> From the halls of Montezuma
> To the shores of Tripoli,
> We have fucked the whores and drunk the booze
> Just to prove virility.
> We have used pro kits and rubbers
> To keep our peckers clean,
> Still we have the highest V.D. rate.
> We're United States Marines.

The folks back home may believe all those sons and husbands are caroling such artificial efforts as "The Caissons Go Rolling Along," but then the Pentagon is not going to tell mothers and wives what the men are really thinking and singing about.

In general, combat infantrymen have neither the time nor the inclination to write or sing songs, certainly not while they are on the line. This is a major factor in the content of the songs included here. Troops with more leisure who served in non-combatant or rear area, fliers fresh from colleges in the States who fought their war flying from secure bases far from the areas they bombed, boredom-ridden ensigns on routine watches, these men had a time out of war. (Does the exception prove the rule? Philip Caputo [*A Rumor of War*, reprint, New York: Ballantine, 1978:216] gives the text of a "marching song" written by a marine officer in Vietnam. The last stanza of "A Belly-ful of War" runs: "So you can march upon Hanoi / Just forget this little boy / I don't like it anymore. / For as I lie here with a pout / My intestines hanging out / I've had a belly-ful of war.")

It would be hard to imagine infantrymen singing this marine aviators' adaptation of a World War II ballad. They would have nothing but scorn for the lyric's "gung ho" enthusiasm.

> Up in Korea midst high rocks and snow,
> The poor Chinese Commies [are] feeling quite low.
> For as the Corsairs roar by overhead,
> He knows that his buddies all soon will be dead.
>
> Chorus:
> Hinky di, dinky, dinky di, hinky di, dinky, dinky di,
> He knows that his buddies all soon will be dead.
>
> Li Piao went way up to cold Koto-ri
> His prize Chinese army in action to see.
> He got there a half-hour after the U's,
> And all that he found was their hats and their shoes.
>
> Hinky di, dinky, dinky di, hinky di, dinky, dinky di,
> And all that he found was their hats and their shoes.
>
> Run, little Chinamen, save your ass, run.
> Three-twenty-three is out looking for fun.
> As the big white-nosed Corsairs come down in their dives,
> You'll know the "Death Rattlers" are after your lives.
>
> Hinky di, dinky, dinky di, hinky di, dinky, dinky di,
> You'll know the "Death Rattlers" are after your lives.
>
> Uncle Joe Stalin, your stooges have found
> It just doesn't pay to invade foreign ground.
> For when they disturbed the serene morning calm,
> They brought on the rockets, the bombs and napalm.
>
> Hinky di, dinky, dinky di, hinky di, dinky, dinky di,
> They brought on the rockets, the bombs and napalm.
>
> Here's to the Twenty, the Vought people too,
> And their well-known product, the blue Four F.U.
> To all Gyrene pilots and carriers at sea,
> And the "Death Rattlers" Squadron, ol' Three-twenty-three.
>
> Hinky di, dinky, dinky di, hinky di, dinky, dinky di,
> And the "Death Rattlers" Squadron, ol' Three-twenty-three.
>
> We fought at Pyongyang and at Hagaru,
> At Kumhwa and Kaesong and Uijongbu.
> So here's to our pilots and here's to our crew,
> The target, the shake, and the blue Four F.U.

"Hinky Di," taken from a mimeographed Korean conflict song collection, was written sometime after November, 1950, when the

Fourth Field Army of the Chinese People's Republic overran United
Nations forces around the Choisan Reservoir. ("Shake" in the last
stanza is a rack of bombs or rockets the Vought F4U Corsair carried.
The meaning of "the Twenty" in the fifth verse is unclear.) By that
time, the infantrymen had gained great respect for the ability of the
Chinese as soldiers; no one who retreated from the Yalu River in that
bitter winter scorned them as "little Chinamen." (The bravado of the
marine pilots' "Hinky Di" is explained by Peter Thorpe in his article
"Buying the Farm: Notes on the Folklore of the Modern Military
Aviator," [*Northwest Folklore* 2 (1967): 11-17].)

There are, to be sure, combat soldiers who take pleasure in their
craft and pride in their unit. But the songs they sing would seem to
be shorter ditties, perhaps spur-of-the-moment efforts with a strong
element of angry protest. In January, 1967, *The New Republic* carried
a story by the late Bernard B. Fall, "You Can Tell 'Em, Buddy," with
one such parody (the ellipsis is the magazine's):

> Jingle bells, mortar shells,
> V.C. in the grass,
> You can take your Merry Christmas
> And shove it up your ---.

The combat infantryman would understand this sentiment only too
well.

Snapoo

Folk songs do not respect boundaries or national borders. With
surprising ease they pass from one language into another. "Snapoo,"
for example, started out in life either as a German poem or a French
song; then Prussian officers, according to one authority, parodied the
original song or poem to celebrate the fact that they had arrived in
time to take part in the Battle of Waterloo in 1815. From there it
made its way to sea, and for a hundred years was sung by crews of
deep water sailing ships. During the Civil War, Union soldiers borrowed the tune and poetic form to create "When Johnny Comes
Marching Home." Finally, "Snapoo" the sea song, served as the model
for the original words and music of the song that was to all but drive
it out of oral currency, "Hinkey Dinkey Parlez-Vous." "Snapoo" uses
that same tune.

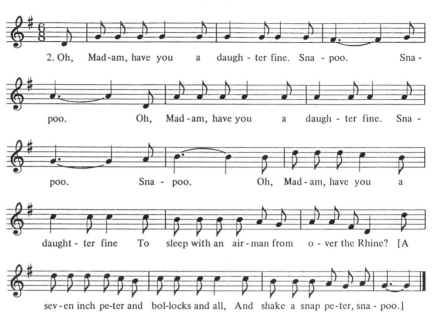

2. Oh, Mad-am, have you a daugh-ter fine. Sna - poo. Sna -

poo. Oh, Mad-am, have you a daugh-ter fine. Sna -

poo. Sna - poo. Oh, Mad-am, have you a

daught - ter fine To sleep with an air-man from o - ver the Rhine? [A

sev-en inch pe-ter and bol-locks and all, And shake a snap pe-ter, sna - poo.]

> Three air force officers flew over the Rhine.
> Snapoo. Snapoo.
> Three air force officers flew over the Rhine.
> Snapoo. Snapoo.
> Three air force officers flew over the Rhine
> * * * * * * * some wine
> * * * * * * * * *
> * * * * * * * * *

Subsequent verses follow the pattern of the first stanza:

> "Oh, madam, have you daughter fine,
> To sleep with an airman from over the Rhine?"

> "Oh, landlady, have you a daughter fair
> With lily-white teats and golden hair?"

> "Oh, sirs, my daughter is much too fine
> To sleep with an airman from over the Rhine."

> "Oh, mother, oh, mother, I'm not too fine
> To sleep with an airman from over the Rhine."

"Oh, mother, oh, mother, he's teasin' me;
He's tickling the hole I use to pee."

"Oh, mother, oh, mother, he's up my bum
And if he don't stop, I will certainly come."

Eight months rolled by and the ninth did pass.
And a little rear gunner marched out of her ass.

The little rear gunner grew and grew,
And now he's chasing the chippies too.

[B]

Three air force officers crossed the Rhine.
Snapoo. Snapoo.
Three air force officers crossed the Rhine.
Snapoo. Snapoo.
Three air force officers crossed the Rhine
Looking for women and searching for wine.
A seven-inch peter and bollocks and all
And shake a snap peter snapoo.

"Oh, landlady, have you a daughter fair?"
Snapoo. Snapoo.
"Oh, landlady, have you a daughter fair?"
Snapoo. Snapoo.
"Oh, landlady, have you a daughter fair?
With lily-white teats and golden hair?"
A seven-inch peter and bollocks and all
And shake a snap peter snapoo.

[C]

Oh mother, oh mother, have you a daughter?
    Snapoo, snapoo.
Oh, mother, oh, mother, have you a daughter
To sleep with a sailor from over the water?
    Snapoo, snapeetah, fie-nanny-go-eat-ah,
    Snapoo.

Oh no, oh no, my daughter's too young
To sleep with that dirty old son of a gun.

Oh mother, oh mother, I'm not too young,
I've done it before with finger and thumb.

So that son of a bitch, he took her to bed,
And crammed it in from its roots to its head.

> Oh, six months came, and six months past,
> The rim of her belly hung down to her ass.
>
> Oh, nine months came, and nine months past,
> And a jolly young sailor rolled out of her ass.

The origin of "Snapoo" and its more widely celebrated relatives seems to be one of the more tangled of folkloristic subjects. The first proposal has it that the song was modeled upon the German Romantic poet Uhland's "Der Wirtin Tochterlein," which Minnie Sears' *Song Index* notes is sung to an eighteenth-century melody. But Robert W. Gordon has suggested instead that "Snapoo" was probably derived from "Drei Reiter am Thor," a German folk song dating from the sixteenth century. Joanna Colcord instead prefers the French folk song, "Le Retour du Marin," as progenitor.

Dolph (p. 82) states that an officer who had soldiered with Kitchener in the Sudan, circa 1884, recalled that British troops sang a song similar in tune and verse structure to "Mademoiselle from Armentieres." He gives one verse:

> Oh, landlord, have you a daughter fair,
> Skiboo, skiboo,
> Oh, landlord have you a daughter fair,
> Skiboo, skiboo,
> Oh, landlord have you a daughter fair
> With lily white arms and golden hair?
> Skiboo, skiboo, skiboodley-boo,
> Skidam, dam, dam.

Nettleingham (*Tommy's Tunes*, 22-23) prints five "well-purged" verses of about forty of a World War I variant, and a tune. De Witt has a twenty-three-stanza version with an introductory headnote (pp. 60-70) linking the song to "Mademoiselle from Armentieres."

The source of the melody is as unsettled as that of the text. Nettl (*Sing a Song of England*, 265) says that the English tune for "Snapoo" is "well known in America, in the minor key" as "When Johnny Comes Marching Home." But how does one reconcile Union Army bandmaster Patrick S. Gilmore's "authorship" of "When Johnny Comes Marching Home" in New Orleans in 1864? Dolph (pp. 357-59) has the Gilmore "original." (Apparently in that same year it was used to carry a satirical pro-Southern song, "For Bales." See Dolph, 297-99.)

In spite of the "Irish" sound of the tune, in spite of the fact that Gilmore was born in Ireland, and in spite of the opinions of most authorities who identify the air as derived from a traditional Irish melody (the usual nominee for honors is "Johnny, I Hardly Knew

Ye"), Gilmore himself said that he learned the *traditional Negro* melody from an unidentified black singer. Gilmore's willingness to credit the tune to someone else—even though his own pseudonym of "Louis Lambert" is on the sheet music—can be accepted at face value. Gilmore's assertion that the melody is a Negro traditional air can be discounted.

The easiest and most logical explanation is that Gilmore did indeed learn the melody from a New Orleans black, but that singer in turn had learned it either at sea or while working on or around the docks.

Hypothetically, the song the black was singing was "Snapoo," a sea chanty before the Civil War. The tune for "Snapoo" was similar to "When Johnny Comes Marching Home," set in the major; that melody, sung by a traditional Negro singer who flatted the third and seventh of the major scale in characteristic blues fashion, would sound *minor* to the formally trained Gilmore.

The original major melody of "Snapoo" having given birth by Gilmore's midwifery to the minor tune that Gilmore called "When Johnny Comes Marching Home," "Snapoo" then went full circle, discarded its own tune and picked up the far more widely known "When Johnny."

The full extent of the tune family has not been explored. The specter of attempting to account for melodies as varied as "Mademoiselle from Armentieres," "Balm of Gilead," and "Son of a Gambolier" is apparently off-putting. Norman Cazden begins the chore in *Folk Songs of the Catskills* (pp. 368-69) and the accompanying *Notes* (pp. 172-73).

Historical notes on "Snapoo" may be found in Nettl (pp. 263 ff.); Dolph (p. 82); Colcord (pp. 110-12); and Hugill (pp. 95-97), which also has other chanties using the same lines. (It may be that "Barnacle Bill" or "Bollochy Bill the Sailor" borrowed its first verses from "Snapoo.") See also Legman (pp. 399-400); and Harlow (pp. 98-99). Silber (pp. 174 ff.); and Heaps (p. 348) offer historical notes on the Civil War marching song. Bronson, 1 (p. 310) has three versions of "The Crow Song" set to "When Johnny Comes Marching Home."

Randolph's "Unprintable Songs" (pp. 288-92) has three versions of "Snapoo," including one said to have been heard near Galena, Missouri, in the 1890s. The first is sung to the music of the verse to the earlier popular song "Life Is a Trial" or "The Housekeeper's Complaint"; the third uses an extended version of "Here We Go Round the Mulberry Bush"/"Three Dukes A- Rovin'."

Other bawdy texts of "Snapoo" are in *Immortalia* ([1927]: 107-8, and 111-12); and the 1968 edition (pp. 120 and 125). In both editions, the second version is sung to "Mademoiselle from Armentieres." Laycock (pp. 130-32) says he learned his variant to the Armentieres tune, in Australian army camps in 1955. Hopkins has a Canadian variant, "Three German Officers Crossed the Rhine" (p. 139) to that melody.

There are four versions of the song in the editor's files. The "A" text and the tune are from the singing of the late Robert W. Kenny, former attorney general of the state of California and Superior Court judge, who said he learned the song in the 1920s while on a visit to New York City. Kenny could not recall the chorus exactly.

The "B" text was collected by a former student of Bess Lomax Hawes from a British veteran of World War II.

Robert G. Gordon got "C" in Berkeley, California, from a group of college men in 1923. It is in the Library of Congress's Archive of American Folk Song, number 400 in the "Inferno" holdings.

In addition to the tune here, "Snapoo" is also sung to "She'll Be Coming 'Round the Mountain When She Comes," a simple-minded offspring of the same "Snapoo" tune family.

I Don't Want to Join the Army

Originally sung during the First World War in the British services, this has since gained wide currency in the colonies.

[A]

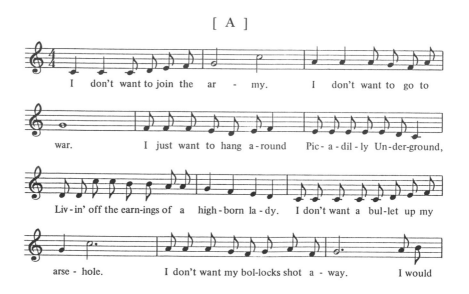

rath - er stay in Eng - land, Jol - ly, jol - ly Eng - land, And

for - ni-cate my fuck-ing life a - way, hey, hey, And way.

I don't want to join the army.
I don't want to go to war.
I just want to hang around Picadilly Underground,
Living off the earnings of a highborn lady [pronounced: "ly-dee"].
I don't want a bullet up my arsehole.
I don't want my bollocks shot away.
I would rather stay in England, jolly, jolly England,
And fornicate my fuckin' life away, hey, hey,
And fornicate my fuckin' life away.

Monday, I touched her on the ankle.
Tuesday, I touched her on the knee.
Wednesday—success! I undid her dress.
And Thursday her chemise, gor blimey!
Friday, I put my hand upon it.
Saturday, she gave me balls a tweak. Woo-woo!
And on Sunday after supper, I shoved the old boy up her.
Now I'm paying seven and six a week. Gor blimey!

[B]

I don't want to join the navy,
I don't want to go to sea.
I just want to mess around
Picadilly underground
Living off the earnings of a high-priced lady.

I don't want a bullet up me asshole.
I don't want me pecker shot away.
I just want to live in England,
In bloody, slimy England,
And fornicate my friggin' life away.

According to Cleveland ("Soldiers' Songs," 81) this song apparently dates from the Napoleonic wars. The tune, however, is of more recent coinage, borrowed from "I'll Make a Man of You" by Herman Finck and Arthur Wimperus, according to popular music scholar Ian Whitcomb. Introduced in the London review *The Passing Show of 1914* (deWitt, 47-48), it is reprinted in *Oh, It's a Lovely War: Songs, Ballads and Parodies of the Great War* (London: EMI [n.d.]: 78), Whitcomb stated.

In addition to the versions in Cleveland and de Witt, other reports from British and/or commonwealth currency are in Vicarion, No. 40; Morgan 1 (pp. 79-80); McGregor (pp. 114-15); Hogbotel and Ffuckes (p. 36); Laycock (pp. 180-81), partially from an American informant; Hopkins (pp. 146-47); and Cleveland, *The Songs We Sang* (p. 21).

American reports include a copy deposited in the Archive of American Folk Song of the Library of Congress by H. L. Goodwin with the note that marine raiders in New Caledonia sang it in 1943; and in Getz 2 (pp. CC-1).

John McVane (*On the Air in World War II*, New York: William Morrow [1979]: 319-20) reports that he, Hal Boyle, and Don Whitehead of Associated Press, and Jack Thompson of the Chicago *Tribune* sang this for a bewildered Russian liaison officer after the link-up at Torgau in 1945.

It is recorded by Oscar Brand on volume four of his bawdy song series (Audio Fidelity 1847); and on *Barely Alive* (Sault Antlers Records) as "The Queen's Marines."

The "A" version here is from the singing of the late Fred Wills of Chicago who said he learned it while serving in the Middle East during the Second World War. The "B" text was collected by Ann Stolz at the University of Texas in 1961. It is to be sung "in a thick cockney accent," she directed.

Fuck 'Em All

It was a poor unit during the Second World War that didn't have at least one version of this classic illustration of what the British army called "The Jack system," that non-Copernican approach to life epitomized by the motto, "I'm all right, Jack; fuck you."

[A]

They say there's a troop-ship just leav-in' Bom-bay,

Bound for Old Blight-y's shore. Heav-i-ly

lad-en with time-ex-pired men Bound for the land they a-

dore. There's man-y a sol-dier has fin-ished his

time; There's man-y a twirp sign-in' on, But they'll

get no pro-mo-tion this side of the o-cean, So cheer up, my

Chorus

lads, fuck 'em all. Fuck 'em all, fuck 'em all,

The long and the short and the tall. Fuck all the

ser-geants and their bleed-in' sons, Fuck all the cor-p'rals and

W. O. ones, 'Cause we're say-in' good-by to them all, As

387

back to the bil-let we crawl. They'll get no pro - mo-tion this

side of the o-cean, So cheer up, my lads, fuck 'em all.

They say there's a troopship just leavin' Bombay,
Bound for Old Blighty's shore,
Heavily laden with time-expired men
Bound for the land they adore.
There's many a soldier has finished his time;
There's many a twirp signin' on,
But they'll get no promotion this side of the ocean.
So cheer up, my lads, fuck 'em all.

Chorus:
Fuck 'em all, fuck 'em all,
The long and the short and the tall.
Fuck all the corporals and W.O. Ones,
'Cause we're sayin' good-by to them all,
As back to the billet we crawl.
They'll get no promotion this side of the ocean,
So cheer up, my lads, fuck 'em all.

[B]

Fuck 'em all, fuck 'em all,
The long and the short and the tall.
Fuck all the blonde cunts and all the brunettes.
Don't be too choosey, just fuck all you gets
'Cause we're saying good-by to them all
As back to the barracks we crawl.
You'll get no erection at short-arm inspection,
So prick up, you men, fuck 'em all.

Fuck 'em all, fuck 'em all,
The long and the short and the tall,
Fuck all the cunts till you break it in two,
You'll get no lovin' where you're going to,
'Cause we're saying good-by to them all
As back to the barracks we crawl,
So get your big prick up and give it a stick up
The cunt or asshole; fuck 'em all.

388

[C]

Fuck 'em all, fuck 'em all,
The Commies, the U.N. and all.
Those slant-eyed Chink soldiers hit Hagaru-ri
And now know the meaning of U.S.M.C.
But we're saying good-by to them all.
We're Harry's police force on call.
So put your pack back on,
The next stop is Saigon,
And cheer up, my lads, fuck 'em all.

As Ewan MacColl has noted, this has been *the* anthem of British fighting men since World War I. According to Hopkins (p. 105), it was written by one F. Godfrey in 1916, and linked with the Royal Naval Air Service. Nonetheless, he gives copyright credit to "Bless 'Em All," a version suited for popular consumption written in 1940 by Jimmie Hughes and Frank Lake, with additional lyrics by Al Stillman the next year. The copyrighted version, published in 1940 by Keith Prowse and Company, Ltd., and Sam Fox Publishing Co., New York, the following year, has only served to teach civilians the proper tune for the many improper verses that circulate.

There are any number of adaptations of "Fuck 'Em All," localized variants and songs of protest. Cleveland, "Soldiers' Songs" (pp. 82-83) has two, Tate (p. 12) another. Getz 2 (p. TT-17) has "Lancaster Leaving the Ruhr," one of the many World War II versions that convey something of the gritty texture of protest in the best versions:

They say there's a Lancaster leaving the Ruhr,
Bound for old Blighty's shores,
Heavily laden with terrified men,
Shit-scared and prone on the floor.
There's many a flak gun shooting them down,
There's many a night fighter, too,
But there'll be no promotions,
This side of the ocean,
So, cheer up my lads, fuck 'em all.

Chorus:
Fuck 'em all, fuck 'em all,
The long and the short and the tall.
Fuck all the sergeants and WO-1s,
Fuck all the corporals and their bastard sons,
For we are saying good-by to them all,
The long and the short and the tall.
There'll be no promotions

This side of the ocean,
So, cheer up my lads, fuck 'em all.

"Fuck 'Em All" was known too in the Pacific theater. A slim collection of jokes, limericks, and songs, "Super Stag Treasury" (rev. ed., Los Angeles: Mada Distributing Co., 1964), contains a Marine Corps version that lampoons the other services. The first and fifth verses of the song are:

Well, we sent for the Army to come to Tulagi,
But General MacArthur said, "No,"
And this is the reason: "This isn't the season.
Besides, you've got no U.S.O."

Then we sent for the nurses to come to Tulagi,
The nurses, they made it with ease,
Their arse on the table, each bearing this label,
"Reserved for the officers, please."

In an open letter from the Marianas, dated September 16, 1945, folksinger Pete Seeger reported that U.S. troops in the Pacific at that time learned the song from the Australians. The text he gives, three verses long, includes the U.S.O. stanza. "Tulagi/U.S.O." is also in Getz 1 (p. B-12). Seeger described the song as "widely known, especially among Marines."

A Korean War air force version grouses about the dangers of breaking the sonic barrier in the first operational jet fighters. As collected by James W. Kellogg in 1963 in Austin, from a Korean War veteran, the song has it:

Bless 'em all; bless 'em all.
Bless tiptanks and tailpipes and all.
Bless old man Lockheed for building this jet,
But I know a guy who is cussing him yet,
'Cause he tried to go over the wall
With tiptanks and tailpipes and all.
The needles did cross and the wings did come off
With tiptanks and tailpipes and all.

Through the wall, through the wall,
That bloody, invisible wall,
That transsonic journey is nothing but rough,
As bad as a ride on the local base bus.
So I'm staying away from the wall,
Subsonic for me and that's all.

> If you're hot, you might make it,
> But you'll probably break it,
> Your butt or your neck, not the wall.

Wallrich (p. 70), and Getz 1 (B-13) both have this "tiptanks" version.

The song continues in oral tradition. Los Angeles attorney Alvin Tenner in 1967 sang a version he had learned in the Marines Corps in 1958-59:

> Bless 'em all; bless 'em all,
> The long and the short and the tall,.
> Bless all the sergeants and W.O. Ones,
> Bless all the corporals and their bastard sons,
> 'Cause we're going back to the front.
> There'll be no more wine, women or cunt.
> We'll lay in our trenches and dream of fine wenches,
> And beat off our meat with a grunt.

Tenner could not recall a second stanza, though it contained a choice threat to gunnery sergeants in general: ". . . And just to be funny, we'll gang-bang the gunny."

Other military versions are in Cleveland (pp. 92-93); Getz 2 (pp. TT-16, 17); and Getz 1 (B-11ff.). Hopkins (pp. 105-8) has four versions, and Wallrich two sanitary air force adaptations (pp. 28, 88). For a recording of a British Army version, see Ewan MacColl, *Bless 'Em All* (Riverside 12-642).

Lynn, *Songs for Singing,* has a sickly parody, "Kiss 'Em All," as well as the copyrighted version (pp. 80-81). Another, more robust civilian version was fashioned by the men of Ricketts Hall at Caltech, about 1960, according to the text in *Songs of Raunch and Ill-Repute* (p. 16).

There are six versions of this in the editor's files. The "A" item here was collected in 1961 by a former student of Bess Lomax Hawes at then San Fernando Valley State College. The student got it from an informant who presumably learned it while serving in His or Her Majesty's armed services.

The second version was given in 1959 to the editor by a former student who said he had learned it while on a Sierra Club outing in Yosemite a few years before. The "W.O." in this chorus (and in several of the other versions) stands for "warrant officer, first class." The third version was learned by the editor in South Korea or in Tokyo from marines. Marines in South Korea sang this in 1953. After that "police action" ended in a truce, the marines sardonically predicted the next.

The Fucking Machine

This song began its career at the beginning of the First World War, probably with one or another of the allied navies. By the end of that conflagration, it was the property of every man in uniform. Unlike "Mademoiselle from Armentieres," which became an unofficial anthem of the doughboys, there is no way to clean up "The Fucking Machine." So "Mademoiselle" went on to fame and glory while "The Fucking Machine" steamed away, underground, to the tune of the honored hymn "Old Hundred."

A sailor told me before he died—
I know not whether the bastard lied—
He had a wife with a twat so wide
That she could never be satisfied.

So he fashioned out a big fucking wheel,
Attached it to a big prick of steel.
Made two balls and filled them with cream,
And the whole fucking thing was run by steam.

'Round and 'round went the big fucking wheel,
In and out went the big prick of steel.
Till at last the maiden cried,
"Enough, enough! I'm satisfied."

But here is a case of the biter bit:
There was no way of stopping it.
The maiden was torn from twat to teat,
And the whole fucking thing went up in shit.

A psychological study of the theme of the great fucking wheel or machine would fill a sizeable volume. For some suggestion of the recurrent popularity of the subject, see Legman's *The Limerick*, number 1325 (pp. 447-48). That limerick, which Legman identified as the most frequently collected in his research, runs:

> There was a young man from Racine
> Who invented a fucking machine.
> Concave or convex,
> It would fit either sex,
> With attachments for those in between.

There are eight versions of the ballad in the editor's collection, the texts remarkable for their similarity. This variant is from New Jersey, circa 1955, and was sung to the author by an engineer living in Los Angeles in 1964.

While the singers frequently mention the solemn quality of the melody, most do not recognize one of the oldest hymn tunes still in use. It is generally credited to Guilliaume Franc, *kapelmeister* in Geneva at the time of the Reformation. The tune dates from sometime before 1554, when it appeared in the *Geneva Psalter* as a setting for the 134th Psalm. Knox's *Anglo-Genevan Psalter* used the melody for the 3d Psalm two years later. In 1562, it first appeared—in Sternhold and Hopkins's *Psalter*—as a setting for the 100th Psalm.

Henry Ainsworth borrowed the song from Sternhold and Hopkins in 1612 for the hymn book that would be taken to the New World by Governor Bradford's Puritan colonists. In 1661, Bishop Ken added new words to the older tune: "Come loud anthems let us sing / Loud thanks to our almighty King." Despite the fact that these are now the most frequently encountered words to the tune, the tune retains the title "Old Hundred," referring to the 100th Psalm once sung to the stately melody.

The tune was a favorite of J. S. Bach. He set it as a chorale three times, including, as legend has it, literally on his death bed with the title "Before Thy Throne I Come Today."

The melody has been borrowed for other secular uses besides "The Fucking Machine." J. Barre Toelken reports it has carried a version of "On Springfield Mountain." A. P. Hudson noted its use in "the South" to carry this:

> I'll eat when I'm hungry.
> I'll drink when I'm dry.
> If the Yankees don't get me,
> I'll live till I die.

A set of "Old Hundred" also appears in Simpson (p. 233) as "Franklin Is Fled Away."

"The Fucking Machine" has been widely printed, with a variety of melodies. The *Songs of Roving and Raking* text (p. 111) uses "Old Hundred" (p. 119), misidentified as "O Master, Let Me Walk with Thee." ("O Master" is presumably Robert Schumann's 1838 composition, which some hymn books name "Canonbury.") Getz 2 (p. BB-16) gives the song under the title of "The Great Bloody Wheel," also stating it is to be sung to the Schumann air. Getz, incidentally, considers it "one of the most popular of the bawdy songs." The Vicarion Anthology also calls for the Schumann tune. Babab (p. 127) prints a version with a repetitive chorus, sung to an unidentified melody. Getz also forwarded a tape recording of "Machine" caroled to "The Strawberry Roan."

British Empire versions without airs are in Morgan 1 (p. 143) and Morgan 2 (p. 136) blaming a blacksmith for the device. Cleveland (p. 95) notes that New Zealand troops during World War II also knew the song, but he gives no melody. Hopkins (p. 160) sets it to "Old Hundred" under the title of "The Great Wheel." Laycock (pp. 226-27) has a doctored text also sung to that melody.

American variants are in *Songs of Raunch and Ill-Repute* (p. 27) and Hart's *Immortalia*, 2 (pp. 34-35). The Reuss thesis (pp. 206-10) lists additional references to the song and gives two versions collected in the Midwest. He provides one tune, again a set of "Old Hundred." The ballad meanwhile persists in oral tradition; Durham's "Bloody Great Wheel" (p. 46) dates from the Vietnam conflict.

Legman discusses this ballad, insisting "it remains only a recitation or chant," in his "Bawdy Monologues" article (pp. 88, 93), and in *The Horn Book* (pp. 327, 422).

Sound Off

This travels under a variety of names. At one or another military installation it is known as "Sound Off," "The Swing Cadence," "The Airborne Chant," or "The Jody Song." There is no one, correct version of the song; it adds and drops verses freely, depending on who is singing it, how long the march is, and, sometimes, how many ladies are within earshot.

At Camp Chaffee, Arkansas, in 1952, the commanding general is said to have issued an order that the song was not to be sung on post. (The orders of general officers are often ill-advised.)

[A]

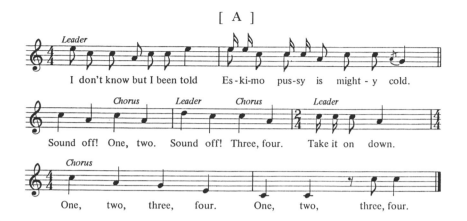

Leader: Sound off.
Chorus: One, two.
Leader: Sound off.
Chorus: Three, four.
Leader: Take it on down. (Or: Cadence, count.)
Chorus: One, two, three, four.
        One, two, three, four.

I don't know but I been told
Eskimo pussy is mighty cold.
        Sound off. (Etc.)

I don't know but I been told
Ass is worth its weight in gold.

I got a gal in Kansas City.
She's got a wart on her left titty.

I got a gal in Baltimore.
She's got a red light on her door.

I know a gal named Frisco Lil,
Touch her tit and get a thrill.

I know a gal from Jacksonville.
She won't do it but her sister will.

I got a gal in Mississippi.
She's got a pimple on her titty.

I got a gal in Monterey.
She makes love the army way.

I got a gal named Sadie Kass.
She's got a face like the sergeant's ass.

I got a gal in San Antone.
She don't like to sleep alone.

If I die on the Russian front,
Box me up with a Russian cunt.

If I die in a combat zone,
Box me up and ship me home.

If I die in Tennessee,
Ship my ass home C.O.D.

I'm out to butcher the butcher's son,
But I'll give you some meat till the butcher comes.

I'm out to plumb the plumber's son,
But I'll fill your hole till the plumber comes.

I got a gal all dressed in blue,
Man, oh man, she likes to screw.

I got a gal all dressed in yellow,
Out every night with a different fellow.

I got a gal all dressed in black,
Makes her living on her back.

I got a gal all dressed in red,
Makes her living in her bed.

Every night before retreat,
Sergeant -------- beats his meat.
If Sergeant -------- didn't beat his meat,
Private -------- wouldn't eat.

[Fill in the appropriate names. This is sung by merely repeating the first two bars of the melody.]

[B]

The "Jody" verses tell the familiar story of the 4-F who steals the soldier's girl friend while the GI is defending flag, country, and mom's apple pie. It is sung to the same tune by repeating the first two bars of the melody.

Ain't no use in writing home,
Jody's got your gal and gone.
Ain't no use in feeling blue,
'Cause he's got your Cadillac too.

Jody's got that gal and gone.
Left me here to sing this song.

Lost your car in a gamblin' game,
Left your gal for another dame.

Ain't no use to mourn and grieve,
Jody's gone, I do believe.
Left your gal in New Orleans
Sellin' pussy to earn her beans.

[C]

I don't know but it's been told
An eskimo's pussy is mighty cold!

Chorus:
Sound off. Eat shit!
Sound off. Douche bag!
Eat shit, douche bag,
Suck off, fuck you!

I don't know but it's been said,
A Stanford squaw is good in bed!

Cal Bear is on the rag.
Stanford Indian is a fag.

The "A" text is a patchwork of stanzas collected between 1955 and 1964 by the editor from Southern California residents Mark Hayworth, Sheldon Horlick, Ed Schweri, Jacques Vidicam, and Gerry Olsen. They had learned these verses while serving at military bases across the country. The editor learned the "B" text during his basic training at Camp Chaffee, Arkansas, in 1952 from his drill instructor, Technical Sergeant Tom Schroeder. The "C" text demonstrates that the song has been fitted to civilian uses. It is taken from "Hymenal," the unofficial songbook of the USC Trojan Marching Band, a copy of which was given to the editor in 1988 by Christian Gunning.

Other versions may be found in Lomax (p. 595); *Hoosier Folklore*, (6 [1947]: 78, 109-10; and 7 [1948]: 54). It is dated in these notes to the First World War. Additional stanzas are in George C. Carey, "A Collection of Airborne Cadence Chants" (*Journal of American Folklore* 78 [1965]: 52-61). Shaw (p. 2) has a two-line fragment, which at least suggests some English currency for this American original.

The "Jody" verses are originally of black, possibly blues currency. Abrahams (p. 170) has "Jody the Grinder," one title of the mosaic of verses and songs celebrating the cocksmith who takes advantage of the husband's absence. See also Bruce Jackson, "What Happened to Jody" (*Journal of American Folklore* 80 [1967]: 387-96). The "Jody" verses do not seem to have been reported prior to the Second World War.

Similarly, the "I got a gal" formula is probably of southern origin. Randolph's "Unprintable" opus has "I Got a Gal in Berryville" (pp. 153-57), with parallel bawdy verses. Randolph says his song is probably derived from a black-face minstrel song to the music of the verse of "Ta-Ra-Ra Boom-Dee-Ay."

Philip Caputo (*Rumor of War*, reprint, New York [1978]: 19-20), offers two stanzas of a related but strikingly different cadence count from Marine Corps tradition, circa 1966:

> I gotta gal that lives on a hill . . .
>> Oh, Little Liza, Little Liza Ja-ane.
> She won't do it but her sister will . . .
>> Little Liza Jane.
>> Whoa-oh-oh-oh Little Liza, Little Liza Jane
>> Oh, Little Liza, Little Liza Jane.
>
> I gotta gal in Lackawanna . . .
>> Oh, Little Liza, Little Liza Jane.
> She knows how but she don't wanna . . .
>> Little Liza Jane.
>> Whoa-oh-oh-oh Little Liza, Little Liza Jane
>> Oh, Little Liza, Little Liza Jane.

Honey Babe

There are any number of tunes used to carry the verses sung or chanted to mark out the cadence of marching men. "Honey Babe," sometimes called "The Swing Cadence," fits many of the verses of "Sound Off" to a different tune.

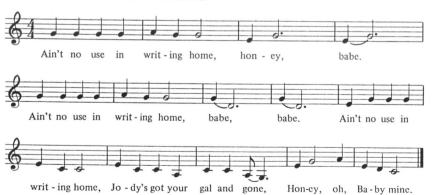

Ain't no use in writ-ing home, hon-ey, babe.

Ain't no use in writ-ing home, babe, babe. Ain't no use in

writ-ing home, Jo-dy's got your gal and gone, Hon-ey, oh, Ba-by mine.

Ain't no use in writing home,
Honey, babe,
Ain't no use in writing home,
Babe, Babe,
Ain't no use in writing home,
Jody's got your gal and gone,
Honey, oh, baby mine.

Similarly:
I've got a gal who lives on the hill,
She won't do it but her sister will.

[B]

I've got a gal in South Sioux Falls.
Honey, honey.
I've got a gal in South Sioux Falls.
Babe, babe.
I've got a gal in South Sioux Falls,
She's got tits like basketballs.
Honey, oh, baby mine.

Similarly:
I've got a gal in New Orleans,
All she does is lay Marines.

I've got a gal in Yucatan,
Sixteen inches she can stand.

I've got a gal in Tijuana,
She knows how, but she don't wanna.

I've got a gal in South Korea,
She's got syph and gonorrhea.

I've got a gal in Kansas City,
She's got a mole on her left titty.

I've got a gal in Iowa City,
Not too clean, and kind of shitty.

I've got a gal, lives on a hill,
If she won't fuck, then her sister will.

I've got a gal from the P.C.C.,
Got the biggest twat that I ever did see.

I've got a gal from Boston, Mass.,
Makes her living with her ass.

I've got a gal from old Coe College,
Only two bits and you're in her cottage.

I've got a gal all dressed in black,
She makes her money on her back.

I've got a gal all dressed in white,
Works all day, and fucks all night.

I've got a gal all dressed in green,
Got the biggest ass you've ever seen.

I've got a gal dressed in green,
She's a walking sex machine.

I've got a gal all dressed in red,
Just two bits, and she'll take you to bed.

If I should die on the Russian front,
Bury me in a Russian cunt.

The "A" version is all the editor can recall of this cadence count, heard first during basic training at Camp Chaffee, Arkansas, in 1952. The "B" text is from the Harry A. Taussig collection made at the University of California, Berkeley, between 1958 and 1963. "P.C.C." refers to Pasadena City College; "Mass." is sung so as to make the obvious rhyme. Though Coe College is in Cedar Rapids, Iowa, that verse and others referring to cities in that state only suggest the provenience of *those* verses, not the entire song.

Getz 2 (pp. II-2, 3) has an air force version. A fifteen-stanza text is in *Songs of Raunch and Ill-Repute* (p. 13). It is reprinted in Babab (p. 109) with a tune from Best, *Song Fest* (New York, 1955).

Too Rally

The new recruit quickly learns the rules of the military game ("Don't volunteer for anything"; "If it moves salute it; if it doesn't, paint it") and the traditions of the service, the most important of which is R.H.I.P. — Rank Has Its Privileges. "Too Rally" is a commentary, probably written by younger junior officers serving in the South Pacific during World War II.

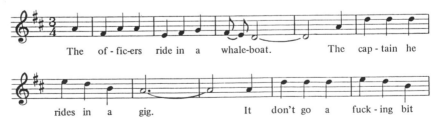

The of-fic-ers ride in a whale-boat. The cap-tain he
rides in a gig. It don't go a fuck-ing bit

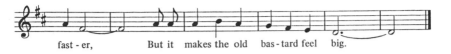

fast - er,   But it makes the old   bas - tard feel   big.

The officers ride in a whaleboat.
The captain, he rides in a gig.
It don't go a fucking bit faster,
But it makes the old bastard feel big.

The officers ride in a whaleboat.
The admiral rides in a barge.
It don't go a fucking bit faster,
But it makes the old bastard feel large.

Chorus:
Sing too rally, oo rally, rally.
Sing too rally, oo rally, ay,
It don't go a fucking bit faster,
But it makes the old bastard feel large.

Oh, the officers eat in the wardroom.
The captain won't eat with the boys.
His chow ain't a fucking bit better,
But the bastard can't stand all the noise.

The officers go to the movies.
The skipper won't sit with the crowd.
He can't see a fucking bit better,
But it makes the old bastard feel proud.

Oh, we're always at general quarters.
The captain, he sits at his desk.
He issues the God damnedest orders
About how all the men should be dressed.

Oh, we may have lost one or two battles,
Or a sub in the midst of a storm,
But there's one thing that you can be sure of:
Our men were in full uniform.

Oh, the officers' head is communal.
The captain, he has his commode,
But his bowels ain't a fucking bit looser,
But his pride swells up like a toad.

At the officers' club in Hollandea,
The captain won't drink with the gang.
He don't get a fucking bit drunker,
But it gives the old bastard a bang.

401

Though he does not have this song, Hopkins has nine others he includes in a chapter devoted to "Songs of Military Hierarchy." He notes (p. 89), "The men at the bottom, prevented from knowing what is really going on at the top, judge the top by what they see. What they see, over and over, is that life at the top carries with it not greater burdens, but greater luxury, less visible work, and considerably less danger. They develop feelings of frustration and resentment against authority." Those sentiments sometimes manifest themselves in song.

"Too Rally" is sung to the tune of the English music hall song "Botany Bay." That fact, plus the whaleboat-gig-barge status ranking in the first stanzas suggests that the song began its career in the Imperial fleet. The last six stanzas here appear to be more recent additions by American sailors.

Songs of Roving and Raking (p. 101), reprinted by Babab (p. 116), has one stanza of "Too Rally" in a quatrain ballad to the melody of "Mush, Mush, Mush Touraliaday":

> The crew they all ride in the dory.
> The captain he rides in the gig.
> It don't go a goddamn bit faster,
> But it makes the old bastard feel big.

Songs of Raunch and Ill-Repute (p. 3) has that verse, the two-stanza "Sexual Life of the Camel" (*supra.*), and these localized quatrains:

> Here's to the girls of P.C.C.
> And here's to the streets that they roam,
> And here's to their dirty-faced bastards,
> God bless them, they may be our own.

> Here's to old Occidental,
> And here's to the old Scripps Trail,
> And here's to those sorority maidens,
> Who gave us our first piece of tail.

According to the Caltech graduate who loaned a copy of the scarce *Songs of Raunch and Ill-Repute*, "P.C.C." is Pasadena City College; "Occidental," spelled as "Oxidental" in the collection, is a nearby liberal arts college. "Few Techmen date there," he added. On the other hand, Scripps College for Women (once just across the street from the Caltech campus) "is one of the most popular date sources for Caltech undergrads. 'Scrippsies' are often bright and intellectual or 'artsy-craftsy.' The girls are not noted for sexual conservatism." The original song from whence the melody was appropriated is in Long and Jenkin (pp. 5-6); and Anderson, *Colonial Ballads* (pp. 18-19).

402

The version of "Too Rally" here was learned by Pete Seeger during World War II, and passed on to Bess Lomax Hawes. It is used with their permission. See, too, the version in Brand (pp. 18-19).

Dinky Die

While serving in the South Pacific during World War II, Pete Seeger learned this classic soldiers' protest song. The melody for the verses is the ubiquitous "Sweet Betsy from Pike." Seeger noted the unusual melody for the chorus.

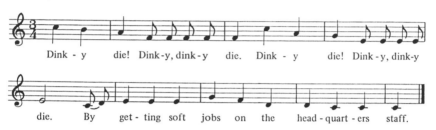

He went up to London and straightaway strode
To army headquarters on Horseferry Road
To see all the blodgers who dodge all the straff
By getting soft jobs on the headquarters staff.

Chorus:
Dinky die! dinky dinky die,
Dinky die! dinky dinky die,
By getting soft jobs on the headquarters staff.

The lousy lance corporal said, "Pardon me, please,
You've mud on your tunic and blood on your sleeve.
You look so disgraceful that people will laugh,"
Said the lousy lance corporal on the headquarters staff.

Dinky die! dinky dinky die,
Dinky die! dinky dinky die,
Said the lousy lance corporal on the headquarters staff.

The digger just shot him a murderous glance.
He said, "We're just back from the shambles in France
Where whizzbangs are flying and comforts are few
[*Slowly*] And brave men are dying [*In tempo*] for bastards like you.

403

Dinky die! dinky dinky die,
Dinky die! dinky dinky die!
[*Slowly*] And brave men are dying [*In tempo*] for bastards like you.

"We're shelled on the left and we're shelled on the right.
We're bombed all the day and we're bombed all the night.
If something don't happen and that mighty soon,
There'll be nobody left in the bloody platoon."

(Chorus as in other verses)

The story soon got to the ears of Lord Gort
Who gave the whole matter a great deal of thought.
He awarded the digger a V.C. and two bars
For giving that corporal a kick in the arse.

(Chorus as before)

Judging from internal evidence, this was written in 1940, not long after the Dunkirk evacuation. The word "blodgers" in the first stanza—apparently a misspelling of "bludgers"—suggests that an Australian had a hand in this. "Bludgers" is Australian slang for someone who lets others do all the work, according to McGregor (p. 87).

Certainly the song has been preserved by antipodalian singers. Cleveland (pp. 26-27) reprints a New Zealand text. Hogbotel and Ffucks (p. 60), Tate (p. 17), and Lahey have it. Wannan (p. 92) asserts that the song dates from World War I, but includes the usual last stanza naming Lord Gort. (As Chief of the Imperial General Staff, Lord Gort led the British Expeditionary Force in France in 1939-40 until the Dunkirk evacuation in June, 1940. Curiously, there were no Australian units included in the 1940 B.E.F., which leaves the dating somewhat a muddle.)

Page (*Kiss Me Goodnight,* 113-14) has a text from British sources with this penultimate stanza:

> You speak to a soldier you meet in the street
> And tell him you suffer with trench-bitten feet,
> While you stopped back in London and missed all the strafe,
> You greasy, big bastard from Horseferry staff.

The Flying Colonel

The men of the air force of World War II produced a number of songs concerned with the problems of flying airplanes longer, harder, faster and higher than they were designed to fly while the Germans and Japanese sought to bring them down. There was little the fliers could do about the occupational hazards; singing about them may have helped. The melody of this parody is appropriately "The Wreck of Old 97," a country ballad about about a fatal train wreck.

We were on our way from Ran-goon-ie to Shan-non, And the flak was burst-in' high, And the P - fif-ty-ones and the P-for - ty-sev-ens were wing-in' their way through the sky.

We were on our way from Rangoonie to Shannon
And the flak was burstin' high,
And the P-51's and the P-47's
Were wingin' their way through the sky.

We were halfway between Rangoonie and Berlin,
Wingin' our way through the blue,
When the Jerries spotted us from five o'clock under,
And came up to see what they could do.

Now the first pass was made on the 497,
Colonel S-----s was up ahead,
And he pissed and he moaned, and he shit and he groaned,
For he thought he would surely be dead.

The colonel called to his brave navigator,
"Give me a headin' home."
But the brave navigator, with his hand on the ripcord,
Said, "Shit, boy, you're goin' home alone."

So the colonel he called to his brave bombardier,
Said, "Give me a headin' home."
But the brave bombadier had already scuttled;
There was silence on the colonel's interphone.

Well, at 24,000 he chewed on his candy,
And his balls drew up in their sack,
And he pissed and moaned, and shit and groaned,
For he thought he would never get back.

> But with four engines feathered he glided into safety
> On the runway of his own home base,
> And it's with great pride that he tells this story
> With a shit-eating grin on his face.

This is one of the few air force songs that seem to have an oral currency apart from frequent reprintings in unofficial unit songbooks. This was collected by Dean Burson in Los Angeles in 1959 from a young man who had earlier learned it at Carnegie Tech.

Getz 2 (p. FF-3) has other versions of "The Flying Colonel." In his first volume (p. R-2) he also has "Recce to Pyongyang," a Korean war adaptation.

Air force songs have been amply anthologized. Wallrich, *passim,* and his "United States Air Force Parodies Based upon 'The Dying Hobo' " (*Western Folklore* 13 [1954]) were the first. Getz's later two volumes of air force songs are virtually encyclopedic in content.

Cohen (pp. 197-226) has a history of the original song, popular with country singers from 1924 on. For other parodies to the same tune, see Wallrich (pp. 23, 54, 75, 104 and 128). (The tunes for the latter two are said to be "Casey Jones," but the stanzas are modeled upon "The Wreck of Old 97.") Getz 1 has other parodies to the tune (pp. O-5, 6, and S-1).

The Sewing Machine

The girl who is sewn-up is pregnant, so it naturally follows that she must have a sewing machine. This song, sung to the tune of "Down in the Valley" by GIs during the occupation of Germany after World War II, is similar to the "Lee's Hoochie" sung by comrades in arms in the Korean War six years years later. The subject, of course, is universal.

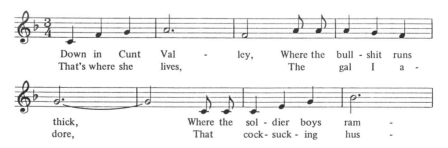

Down in Cunt Val - ley,   Where the bull - shit runs
That's where she lives,   The   gal   I   a -
thick,   Where the sol - dier boys   ram -
dore,   That cock- suck - ing   hus -

ble, And the ba - bies come quick.
sy,   The Hei - del - berg whore.

> Down in Cunt Valley, where the bullshit runs thick,
> Where the soldier boys ramble, and babies come quick,
> That's where she lives, the gal I adore,
> That cock-sucking hussy, the Heidelberg whore.
>
> She took me upstairs and she turned out the light,
> And she said, "Big boy, you're here for the night."
> So I took down my pants and I crawled in between,
> And I started to sew on her sewing machine.
>
> I sewed and I sewed until crack of dawn,
> Then she said, "Big boy, you had better be gone.
> Come back tomorrow night without being seen,
> And you're welcome to sew on my sewing machine."
>
> She gave me the clap and the blue-balls too.
> The clap doesn't hurt, but the blue-balls do.
> For seventeen days, she hasn't been seen.
> I hope she's in Hell with her sewing machine.

This was sung by a student at Carnegie Tech to Dean Burson in Los Angeles in 1959. The singer had learned it during the postwar occupation of Germany at the end of World War II. Apparently it has had only a limited currency, confined to a relative handful of men who served in Europe at that time.

The song seems to have been influenced—in the first stanza, at any rate—by that version of "Charlotte the Harlot" sung to the same tune, "Down in the Valley." The tune may have suggested the borrowing.

Lee's Hoochie

During the Second World War, a new phenomenon entered into the process of oral tradition: the mimeograph machine. Headquarters troops with time on their hands and mimeographs at their disposal took advantage of the situation to turn out reams of copies of bawdy songs. Single songs became anthologies, some running forty pages or more.

By the time of the Korean conflict, the mimeographs had been electrified and the headquarters complements beefed up. The natural result was that songs such as "Lee's Hoochie"—sung to the then-popular song "On Top of Old Smoky"—quickly circulated throughout the Far East Command.

Way down in Seoul cit - y I met a Miss Lee. She said, "For a short time, You can sleep with me."

Way down in Seoul City,
I met a Miss Lee.
She said, "For a short time,
You can sleep with me."

I went to her *hoochie*,
A room with hot floor.
We left our shoes outside,
And slid shut the door.

She took off her longjohns,
And unrolled the pad.
I gave her ten thousand;
'Twas all that I had.

Her breath smelled of *kimchi*.
Her bosom was flat.
No hair on her *poji*,
Now how about that?

I asked "Where's the *benjo*?"
She led me outside.
I reached for Old Smoky.
He crawled back inside.

I rushed to the medics,
Screamed, "What shall I do?"
The doc was dumbfounded;
Old Smoky was blue.

408

If you're ever in Seoul City
On a three-day pass,
Don't go to Lee's *hoochie*.
Sit flat on your ass.

Your ass may get tender,
And she may tempt you,
But better a red ass,
Than Old Smoky blue.

This is just one of a spate of parodies, inoffensive and otherwise, that popped up in the wake of the Weavers' very popular Decca recording in 1951 of the American folk song, "On Top of Old Smoky." One sung by children in Los Angeles that was collected by a number of the editor's former students runs something like:

On top of Old Smoky, all covered with snow,
I saw Georgie Jessel with Marilyn Monroe.
He took of his jacket. He took off his vest.
And when he saw Marilyn, he took off the rest.

Abrahams's thesis, *Negro Folklore from South Philadelphia* (p. 247) has the same with Betty Grable and Gene Autry as stand-ins. He also has forwarded:

On top of old Rachel, all covered with sweat,
I've been fucking two hours, and I haven't come yet.

Other children's parodies of "Smoky" collected by Nancy Leventhal in Hawthorne, California, are printed in *Western Folklore* (22[1963]: 243). Laycock (pp. 165-66) has five stanzas of questionable oral currency from Australia.

The melody used by the Weavers for their recording, which may be found in Lomax (p. 221) was widely borrowed for military parodies. Wallrich has four from the Korean War (pp. 72, 124, 131, and 183). The latter, "On Top of Old Fuji," is a parallel to "Lee's Hoochie," though it contains no censorable lines. Getz 1 (pp. JK-7 and O-12 ff.) has eleven different songs culled from various air force songbooks.

In addition to the sources in Lomax, variants of "Smoky" are to be found in Sulzer (p. 24), and Burton and Manning (pp. 50-51).

"Lee's Hoochie" was second only to "Movin' On" in popularity with troops in the Far East at the time of the Korean conflict. It was current in Japan and Korea in 1951-52 when a mimeographed copy came into the editor's possession. "Hoochie" is, in the GI's trade language, a house; "kimchi" is an odoriferous Korean pickled cabbage; "poji" is the mound; "benjo" is the impolite word for toilet in Japanese, approximately the equal of "shit-house." The "ten thousand" (yen), by the way, would be a bit steep—even in a war-inflated economy—except perhaps for an evening with a true geisha.

Two other texts of "Lee's Hoochie" have been reported. Getz 2 (p. LL-1) has a variant to that here. "Super Stag Treasury," rev. ed. (Maga Distributing Co., Los Angeles, [1964]: n.p.) has it with these introductory lines:

> I'll mention a name, please remember it well,
> The name is Lee's Hoochie, God damn it to hell:
> There's a sign at the door says, "All welcome in here,"
> And each air force man gets a nice souvenir.

The song printed here was learned by the editor while serving in the Far East in 1953.

The Yellow Rose of Taegu

A refurbished soldiers' song from World War II, this was localized to Korea shortly after the outbreak of the police action in that country. The original transplant was probably made by a Regular Army man, but verses of social protest were added by troops less enthused with the military and the war in Frozen Chosen.

She's the yel-low rose of Tae-gu, The girl that I a-
dore. Her cunt it smells like cock juice; She's a
good two-dol-lar whore. You may talk to me of
Se-oul girls Or whores from To-ky-o, But the

yel-low rose of Tae - gu   Beats them all, I'd have you know.

She's the yellow Rose of Taegu, the girl that I adore.
Her cunt it smells like cock juice; she's a good two-dollar whore.
You may talk to me of Seoul girls or whores from Tokyo,
But the yellow Rose of Taegu beats them all, I'd have you know.

Now I was shipped to Taegu; I didn't want to go,
But the Chinks came down from 'Chuko, and I left old Tokyo.
I landed from an LCT; I was left there all alone,
But the yellow Rose of Taegu made me feel right at home.

I didn't want to shoot a gun and that is certain sure.
I didn't want to go on line; I'd rather stayed with her.
They handed me an M-1; it made me nervous more.
The only person I wanted to shoot was my little Taegu whore.

She was a young and charming girl; her age was scarce sixteen.
She took me in and she kicked out a sailor and marine.
She had no titties on her chest; that didn't bother me,
For what she had between her legs was big enough for three.

She liked to play the army way; she damn near broke my back.
My thoughts turn back to her each time I have to tote my pack.
My back she broke; my prick she bent; my balls were hollow too,
But I put calluses on the cunt of my Rose from old Taegu.

I don't care much for GI food, the weather or the work.
I don't care much for the Chinks; up in those hills they lurk.
I don't care much for frozen ears, the colds, the flu, the shits.
I'd trade it all for a dose of clap from the girl without any tits.

I'm going back to see her some bright and sunny day.
I'll go AWOL or on sickcall; I'll get there any way,
I'm sure to get my balls shot off if I stay here on line,
But if my Rose can fuck them off, well, that'll suit me fine.

The editor obtained this from a mimeographed copy while serving
in the U.S. Army in Sendai, Japan, in 1953. "AWOL" is pronounced
"ay-wall."

A version sung by troops in the China-Burma-India theater during
World War II, probably expurgated, is in William R. Peers and Dean
Brelis, *Behind the Burma Road* (New York [c. 1963]: 152). Getz 1 (p.
YZ-1) has a different song from the Vietnam War era sung to the
same tune.

Tinsley (pp. 192-94) states that the original Yellow Rose of Texas was an indentured servant, the "high yellow" Emily Morgan, who kept Santa Anna dallying in lascivious torment so long that his leaderless men lost the battle of San Jacinto on April 21, 1836. The song itself was published only in the late 1850s by Firth, Pond and Co., credited vaguely to "J.K.," according to Spaeth (*History*, 135).

Moving On

This is certainly the most widely known song to come out of the Korean conflict. It was written in 1950-51, after the surprise attack by Chinese Communist troops hurled American and Republic of Korea units into a bloody retreat or "bug out" from the Yalu River. (It's also known as "The Bug-Out Ballad").

Its tone is unflattering and a version of the song sung by marines in at least one case provoked a barroom fight with soldiers who felt themselves slandered. The melody is Hank Snow's phenomenally successful song "Moving On," then popular and now considered a "country classic."

> Hear the patter of running feet,
> It's the old First Cav in full retreat.
> > They're movin' on; they'll soon be gone.
> > They're haulin' ass, not savin' gas.
> > They'll soon be gone.
>
> Over on that hill there's a Russian tank;
> A million Chinks are on my flank.
> > I'm movin' on; I'll soon be gone.
> > With my M-1 broke, it ain't no joke.
> > I'll soon be gone.
>
> Million Chinks comin' through the pass
> Playin' burp-gun boogie all over my ass.
> > I'm movin' on; I'll soon be gone.
> > With my M-1 broke, it ain't no joke.
> > I'll soon be gone.
>
> Twenty thousand Chinks comin' through the pass.
> I'm tellin' you, baby, I'm haulin' ass.
> > I'm moving on; I'll soon be gone.
> > I'm haulin' ass, not savin' gas.
> > I'll soon be gone.
>
> Standin' in a rice paddy up to my belly,
> From then on, they called me "Smelly."

I'm movin' on; I'll soon be gone.
I'm haulin' ass, not savin' gas.
I'll soon be gone.

Here's papa-san comin' down the track,
Old A-frame strapped to his back.
 He's movin' on; he'll soon be gone.
 He's haulin' ass, not savin' gas.
 He'll soon be gone.

Here's mama-san comin' down the track,
Titty hanging out, baby on her back.
 She's movin' on; she'll soon be gone.
 From her tits to her toes, she's damn near froze.
 She'll soon be gone.

I sung this song for the very last time.
Gonna get Korea out of my mind.
 I'm movin' on; I'll soon be gone.
 I done my time in this shit and slime.
 I'm movin' on.

This parody of Hank Snow's recording for RCA Victor was widely known in the Far East, usually under the title of "The Bug-Out Ballad," during the Korean War. It seems to have first appeared in print with a single stanza of "The Bug-Out Boogie" in Harold H. Martin, "How Do Our Negro Troops Measure Up?" (*Saturday Evening Post*, June 16, 1951, 31):

When the Chinese mortars begin to chug,
The ol' Deuce-four [24th Infantry Regiment] begin to bug.

Additional Korean War stanzas, from T. R. Fehrenbach's *This Kind of War* (reprint, New York: Pocket Books, 1963) include:

Lordy, Lordy, listen to me,
While I tell of the battle of Kunu-ri!
We're buggin' out—
We're movin' on! (p. 320)

The Second Division sat on the hill,
Watching Old Joe Chink get set for the kill. (p. 324)

When the mortars started falling 'round the CP tent,
Everybody wondered where the high brass went.
They were buggin' out,
Just movin' on . . . (p. 339)

The version printed here was learned by the editor in Korea in 1953. Jacques Vidicam remembered hearing the song while serving at Fort Sam Houston, San Antonio, Texas, in 1964, where it was sung by Special Service Forces troops, many of whom were Korean veterans. Getz 1 (p. M-9) has a somewhat different version, as does McCarthy (pp. 75-76).

The song has seemingly persevered in oral tradition. In his introduction to a reprint of Bill Mauldin's *Up Front* (New York: W. W. Norton, 1968), David Halberstam recalled an updated variant from the Vietnam War era:

> The McNamara Line is one hundred miles long,
> Completely surrounded by Vietcong,
> I'm movin' on . . .

Bibliography

Aarne, Antti, and Stith Thompson, *The Types of the Folktale,* Folklore Fellows Communications 184 (Helsinki: Academia Scientiarum Fennica, 1961).

Abrahams, Roger D., *Deep Down in the Jungle* (Hatboro, Pa.: Folklore Associates, 1964).

————, *Positively Black* (Englewood Cliffs, N.J.: Prentice-Hall, 1970).

Anderson, Hugh, *Colonial Ballads* (Ferntree Gully, Victoria: n.p., 1955).

Babab, Harry, *Roll Me Over* (New York: Oak Publications, 1972).

Barely Alive at the Antlers (Gettysburg, Pa.: Sault Antlers Recordings, n.d.).

Baring-Gould, Sabine, *Folk Songs of the West Country* (London: Keith Prowse, 1974).

Baring-Gould, William and Ciel, *The Annotated Mother Goose* (New York: Clarkson N. Potter, Inc., 1962).

Barry, Philips, Fannie H. Eckstorm and Mary Winslow Smyth, *British Ballads from Maine* (New Haven: Yale University Press, 1929).

Baskervill, Charles Read, *The Elizabethan Jig* (Chicago: University of Chicago Press, 1929).

Bayard, Samuel, ed., *Dance to the Fiddle, March to the Fife* (University Park: Pennsylvania State University Press, 1982).

————, "Prolegomena to a Study of the Principal Melodic Families of Folk Song," in MacEdward Leach and Tristram P. Coffin, *The Critics and the Ballad* (Carbondale: Southern Illinois University Press, 1961), pp. 103-50.

Belden, H. M., *Ballads and Songs Collected by the Missouri Folk-Lore Society,* 2d ed. (Columbia: University of Missouri, 1955).

Best, Dick and Beth, *Song Fest* (New York: Crown, 1957).

Bold, Alan, *The Bawdy Beautiful* (London: Sphere Books, 1979).

Botkin, B. A., *The American Play Party* (Lincoln: University of Nebraska, 1937).

Brand, Oscar, *Bawdy Songs and Backroom Ballads* (New York: Dorchester Press, 1960).

Broadwood, Lucy E., and J. A. Fuller Maitland, *English Country Songs* (London, n.d. [1893]).

Bronson, Bertrand Harris, *The Ballad as Song* (Berkeley: University of California Press, 1969).

————, *The Traditional Tunes of the Child Ballads,* 4 vols. (Princeton, N.J.; Princeton University Press, 1959-1972).

The Frank C. Brown Collection of North Carolina Folklore, Vols. 2 and 3, edited by H. M. Belden and A. P. Hudson (Durham, N.C., 1952); Vols. 4 and 5, edited by Jan P. Schinhan (Durham: Duke University Press, 1962).

Brunvand, Jan H., *The Study of American Folklore* (New York: W. W. Norton, 1968).

Buchanan, Annabel Morris, *Folk Hymns of America* (New York: J. Fischer, 1938).

Burns, Robert, *The Merry Muses of Caledonia,* edited by James Barke and Sydney Goodsir Smith. Printed for the Auk Society. (Edinburgh: M. MacDonald, 1959).

Burton, Thomas G., and Ambrose N. Manning, eds., *The East Tennessee State University Collection of Folklore: Folksongs,* Monograph 4, Institute of Regional Studies (Johnson City: East Tennessee University, 1967).

Carawan, Guy and Candie, *We Shall Overcome* (New York: Oak Publications, 1963).

Cazden, Norman, *The Abelard Folk Song Book* (New York: Abelard-Schuman, 1958).

————, *A Book of Nonsense Songs* (New York: Crown Publishers, 1961).

Cazden, Norman, Herbert Haufrecht, and Norman Studer, *Folk Songs of the Catskills* (Albany: State University of New York Press, 1982).

————, *Notes and Sources for Folk Songs of the Catskills* (Albany: State University of New York Press, 1982).

Chappell, William, *Old English Popular Music,* reprint edition (New York: Jack Brussel, Publisher, 1961).

————, *Popular Music of the Olden Time,* reprint edition (New York: Dover, 1965).

Child, Francis James, *The English and Scottish Popular Ballads,* 5 vols., reprint edition (New York: Dover Books, 1965).

Cleveland, Les, "Soldiers' Songs: The Folklore of the Powerless," *New York Folklore* 11 (1985): 79-97.

————, *The Songs We Sang* (Wellington: Editorial Services Limited, 1959).

Cohen, John, and Mike Seeger, eds., *New Lost City Ramblers Songbook* (New York: Oak Publications, 1964).

Cohen, Norm, *Long Steel Rail* (Urbana: University of Illinois Press, 1981).

————, "Tin Pan Alley's Contribution to Folk Music," *Western Folklore* 29 (1970): 9-20.

Colcord, Joanna C., *Songs of American Sailormen* (New York: W. W. Norton, 1938).

Collection of Epigrams, A (London: J. Walthoe, 1735).

Combs, Josiah H., *Folk-Songs du Midi des Etats-Unis* (Paris: Les Universitaires de France, 1925).

Cox, John Harrington, *Folk-Songs of the South* (Cambridge, Mass.: Harvard University Press, 1925).

Cray, Ed, *The Anthology of Restoration Erotic Poetry* (North Hollywood, Calif.: Brandon House, 1965).

—————, "Barbara Allen in America: Cheap Print and Reprint," in *Folklore International*, D. K. Wilgus, ed. (Hatboro, Pa.: Folklore Associates, 1967), pp. 41-50.

Creighton, Helen, *Maritime Folk Songs* (Toronto: Ryerson Press, 1962).

Daiken, Leslie, *Out Goes She* (Chester Springs, Pa.: Dufour Editions, 1965).

Davis, Arthur Kyle, Jr., *More Traditional Ballads of Virginia* (Chapel Hill: University of North Carolina Press, 1960).

—————, *Traditional Ballads of Virginia*, reprint ed. (Charlottesville: University of Virginia Press, 1957).

Davison, Peter, *Songs of the British Music Hall* (New York: Oak Publications, 1971).

Dean-Smith, Margaret, *A Guide to English Folk Song Collections* (Liverpool and London: English Folk Dance and Song Society, 1954).

deWitt, Hugh, *Bawdy Barrack-room Ballads* (London: Tandem, 1970).

Dick, James C., *The Songs of Robert Burns*, reprint edition (Hatboro, Pa.: Folklore Associates, 1962).

Doerflinger, William Main, *Shantymen and Shantyboys* (New York: Macmillan, 1951).

Dolph, Edward Arthur, *Sound Off!*, revised edition (New York: Farrar and Rinehart, 1942).

Duffy, Maureen, *The Erotic World of Faery* (London: Hodder and Stoughton, 1972).

D'Urfey, Thomas, *Wit and Mirth: or Pills to Purge Melancholy*, 6 vols. in 3, reprint edition (New York: Folklore Library Publishers, 1959).

Durham, James P., ed., "Bull Durham's Songs of S.E.A.: Over 100 of the Best Songs to Come out of the War in South East Asia" (Copyright SEA [*sic*] 1970, Dur-Don Enterprises), courtesy of Lydia Fish.

Dwyer, Richard A., Richard E. Lingenfelter and David Cohen, *The Songs of the Gold Rush* (Berkeley: University of California Press, 1964).

Eckstorm, Fannie Hardy, and Mary Winslow Smyth, *Minstrelsy of Maine* (Boston: Houghton Mifflin, 1927).

Edwards, Ron, *The Big Book of Australian Folk Song* (Adelaide: Rigby, 1976).

Emmerson, George S., *Rantin' Pipe and Tremblin' String* (London: J. M. Dent and Sons, 1971).

Emrich, Duncan, "Songs of the Western Miners" *California Folklore Quarterly* 1 (1942): 216-32.

Farmer, Henry S., *Merry Songs and Ballads*, 5 vols. (London [?], 1895-97); reprint ed. (New York: Cooper Square Publishers, 1964).

Flanders, Helen Hartness, *Ancient Ballads Traditionally Sung in New England*, 4 vols. (Philadelphia: University of Pennsylvania Press, 1960-1965).

Ford, Ira, *Traditional Music in America* (New York: E. P. Dutton, 1940).

—————, *Traditional Music in America*, introduction by Judith McCulloh, reprint ed. (Hatboro, Pa.: Folklore Associates, 1965).

Fowke, Edith, *Lumbering Songs from the Northern Woods* (Austin: University of Texas Press, 1970).

————, "A Sampling of Bawdy Ballads from Ontario," in Bruce Jackson, ed., *Folklore and Society: Essays in Honor of Benj. A. Botkin* (Hatboro, Pa.: Folklore Associates, 1966).

————, *Traditional Singers and Songs from Ontario* (Hatboro, Pa.: Folklore Associates, 1965).

Fowke, Edith Fulton, and Richard Johnston, *Folk Songs of Canada*, Choral Edition (Waterloo, Ontario: Waterloo Music Company, 1954).

————, *More Folk Songs of Canada* (Waterloo, Ontario: Waterloo Music Company, 1967).

Freud, Sigmund, *Wit and Its Relation to the Unconscious*, as translated by A. A. Brill, and printed in *The Basic Writings of Sigmund Freud*, A. A. Brill, ed. (New York, 1938).

Fuld, James J., *American Popular Music* (Philadelphia: Musical Americana, 1955).

————, *The Book of World-Famous Music*, 3d edition (New York: Dover, 1966).

Furnivall, Frederick J., *Bishop Percy's Folio Manuscript, Supplement: Loose and Humorous Songs* (London: Printed by and for the Author, 1867).

Gainer, Patrick W., *Folk Songs from the West Virginia Hills* (Grantsville, W.Va.: Seneca Books, 1975).

Galvin, Patrick, *Irish Songs of Resistance* (New York: The Folklore Press, 1956).

Gardner, Emelyn E., and Geraldine J. Chickering, *Ballads and Songs from Southern Michigan*, reprint ed. (Philadelphia: Folklore Associates, 1967).

Getz, C. W. "Bill," *The Wild Blue Yonder: Songs of the Air Force*, Stag Bar Edition (Burlingame, Calif.: The Redwood Press, 1986). Cited as Getz 2.

————, *The Wild Blue Yonder: Songs of the Air Force* (San Mateo: The Redwood Press, 1981). Cited as Getz 1.

Goldstein, Kenneth, *A Guide for Field Workers in Folklore* (Hatboro, Pa.: Folklore Associates, 1964).

Greenleaf, Elizabeth B. and Grace Yarrow Mansfield, *Ballads and Sea Songs of Newfoundland* (Cambridge, Mass.: Harvard University Press, 1933).

Greenway, John, *American Folksongs of Protest* (Philadelphia: University of Pennsylvania, 1953).

Grieg, Gavin, *Folk-Song in Buchan and Folk-Song of the North-East*, reprint edition (Hatboro, Pa.: Folklore Associates, 1963).

Grieg, Gavin, and Alexander Keith, *Last Leaves of Traditional Ballads and Ballad Airs* (Aberdeen: The Buchan Club, 1925).

Grotjahn, Martin, *Beyond Laughter*, reprint edition (New York: McGraw Hill, 1966).

Hall, J. Mortimer, *The Unexpurgated Anecdota Americana*, 2 vols., reprint of the 1934 series (North Hollywood, Calif.: Brandon House, 1968).

Hamer, Fred, *Garners Gay* (London: English Folk Dance and Song Society, 1967).

————, *Green Groves* (London: English Folk Dance and Song Society, 1973).

Harlow, Frederick Pease, *Chanteying Aboard American Ships* (Barre, Mass.: Barre Publishing Co., 1962).

Healy, James N., ed., *Ballads from the Pubs of Ireland* (Cork: Mercier, 1965).

————, ed., *The Second Book of Irish Ballads* (Cork: Mercier, 1962).

Heaps, Willard A. and Porter W., *The Singing Sixties* (Norman: University of Oklahoma Press, 1960).

Henry, Mellinger E., *Folk-Songs from the Southern Highlands* (Locust Valley, N.Y.: Augustin, 1938).

Hoffmann, Frank, *Analytical Survey of Anglo-American Traditional Erotica* (Bowling Green, Ohio: Bowling Green Popular Press, 1973).

Hogbotel, Sebastian, and Simon Ffuckes, *Snatches and Lays* (Melbourne: Sun Books, 1973).

Hopkins, Anthony, *Songs from the Front and Rear* (Edmonton, Alberta: Hurtig Publishers, 1979).

Hubbard, Lester, *Ballads and Songs from Utah* (Salt Lake City: University of Utah Press, 1961).

Hudson, Arthur Palmer, *Folk Songs of Mississippi* (Chapel Hill: University of North Carolina Press, 1936).

Hugill, Stan, *Shanties from the Seven Seas* (London: E. P. Dutton, 1966).

"Hymenal," Xeroxed songbook of the University of Southern California Marching Band, dated September 25, 1987.

Immortalia, edited by "A Gentleman About Town" [T. R. Smith?], (n.p., [New York], 1927). Cited as *Immortalia* (1927).

Immortalia, edited by "A Gentleman About Town" [T. R. Smith?] reprint edition (Atlanta: Pendulum Books, 1968). Cited as *Immortalia* (1968).

Immortalia, 3 vols. (New York: Hart Publishing Co., 1971). Cited as Hart's *Immortalia*.

Ives, Edward, *The Man Who Made the Songs* (Bloomington: Indiana University Press, 1964).

Jackson, George Pullen, *Another Sheaf of White Spirituals* (Gainesville: University of Florida Press, 1952).

————, *Down-East Spirituals*, 2d edition (Locust Valley, N.Y.: Augustin, 1953).

————, *Spiritual Folk-Songs of Early America*, 2d edition (Locust Valley, N.Y.: Augustin, 1952).

Jackson, Richard, *Popular Songs of Nineteenth Century America* (New York: Dover Publications, 1976).

Jacobs, Dick, *Who Wrote That Song?* (White Hall, Va.: Betterway Publications, 1988).

Jansen, William Hugh, "The Esoteric-Exoteric Factor in Folklore," *Fabula* 2 (1959): 205-11.

Johnson, David, *Scottish Fiddle Music in the 18th Century* (Edinburgh: John Donald Publishers, Ltd., 1984).

Johnson, James, *The Scots Musical Museum, Containing Illustrations of the Lyric Poetry and Music of Scotland by William Stenhouse*, 2 vols. (Edinburgh, 1853; reprinted Hatboro, Pa.: Folklore Associates, 1962).

Karpeles, Maud, ed., *Cecil Sharp's Collection of English Folk Songs*, 2 vols. (London: Oxford University Press, 1974).

Kennedy, Peter, ed., *Folksongs of Britain and Ireland* (London: Cassell; New York: Schirmer, 1975).

Kidson, Frank, *A Garland of English Folk-Song* (London: Ascherberg, Hopwood and Crew, 1926).

Kronhauser, Eberhard and Phyllis, *Pornography and the Law*, revised edition (New York: Ballantine Books, 1964).

Lahey, John, *Australian Favorite Ballads* (New York: Oak Publications, 1965).

Larson, J. Kenneth, ed., "Barnyard Folklore of Southeastern Idaho," typescript (Salt Lake City, Utah, 1952), a copy of which is in the Archive of American Folk Song, Library of Congress.

————, ed., "Typical Specimens of Vulgar Folklore from the Collection of Gershon Legman," typescript (Salt Lake City, Utah, 1952), a copy of which is in the Archive of American Folk Song, Library of Congress.

Laws, G. Malcolm, Jr., *American Balladry from British Broadsides* (Philadelphia: American Folklore Society, 1957).

————, *Native American Balladry* (Philadelphia: American Folklore Society, 1951).

Laycock, Don, ed., *The Best Bawdry* (London and Sydney: Angus and Robertson, 1982).

Leach, Clifford, ed., *Bottoms Up!* (New York: Paull-Pioneer, 1933).

Leach, MacEdward, *Folk Ballads and Songs of the Lower Labrador Coast* (Ottawa: National Museum of Canada, 1965).

Legman, Gershon, "Bawdy Monologues and Rhymed Recitations," *Southern Folklore Quarterly* 40 (1976): 59-122.

————, *The Horn Book* (New York: University Books, 1964).

————, *The Limerick* (Paris: Les Hautes Etudes, 1953); reprinted (San Diego, 1967).

————, "The Rationale of the Dirty Joke," *Neurotica*, No. 9 (1951): 49 ff.

Levy, Lester S., *Flashes of Merriment: A Century of Humorous Song in America* (Norman: University of Oklahoma Press, 1971).

Limouze, A. S., "The Hump Song," *Journal of American Folklore* 63 (1950): 463-65.

Linscott, Eloise Hubbard, *Folk Songs of Old New England* (New York: Macmillan, 1939).

Linton, E. R. [Ed Cray], ed., *The Dirty Song Book* (Los Angeles: Medco Books, 1965).

Loesser, Arthur, *Humor in American Song* (New York: Howell, Soskin, 1942).

Logsdon, Guy, *The Whorehouse Bells Were Ringing* (Urbana: University of Illinois Press, 1989).

[Logue, Christopher], *Count Palmiro Vicarion's Book of Bawdy Ballads* (Paris: The Olympia Press, 1956).

Lomax, Alan, *Folk Songs of North America* (Garden City, N.Y.: Doubleday and Co., 1960).

Lomax, John A., *Cowboy Songs and Other Frontier Ballads,* revised and enlarged edition (New York: Macmillan, 1938).

Lomax, John A., and Alan Lomax, *American Ballads and Folk Songs* (New York: Macmillan, 1934, 1948).

Long, Lionel, and Graham Jenkin, *Favorite Australian Bush Songs* (Adelaide: Rigby, 1964).

Loth, David, *The Erotic in Literature* (New York: McFadden Books, 1961).

Lowenstein, Wendy, "Shocking! Shocking! Shocking!," Australian Folklore Occasional Paper No. 5 (Prahan, Victoria: The Rams Skull Press, 1974, 1986).

Lynn, Frank, *Songs for Singing* (San Francisco: Leisy and Co., 1961).

————, *Songs for Swingin' Housemothers,* new enlarged edition (San Francisco: Leisy and Co., 1963).

McCarthy, Tony, *Bawdy British Folk Songs* (London: Wolfe Publishing Co., 1972).

MacColl, Ewan, and Peggy Seeger, *Travelers' Songs from England and Scotland* (Knoxville: University of Tennessee Press, 1977).

McCulloh, Judith, "The Problem of Identity in Lyric Folksong," in Porter, James, ed., *The Ballad Image, Essays Presented to Bertrand Harris Bronson* (Los Angeles: Center for the Study of Comparative Folklore & Mythology, UCLA, 1983), pp. 41-58.

————, "Some Child Ballads on Hillbilly Records," in Bruce Jackson, ed., *Folklore & Society: Essays in Honor of Benj. A. Botkin* (Hatboro, Pa.: Folklore Associates, 1966).

McGregor, Craig, ed., *Bawdy Ballads and Sexy Songs* (New York: Belmont-Tower, 1972).

Mackenzie, G. Roy, *Ballads and Sea Songs from Nova Scotia* (Cambridge: Harvard University Press, 1928).

McNeil, W. K., *Southern Folk Ballads,* Vols. 1 and 2 (Little Rock: August House, 1987).

Manny, Louise, and James Reginald Wilson, *Songs of Miramichi* (Frederickton, New Brunswick: Brunswick Press, 1968).

Marcus, Steven, *The Other Victorians* (New York: Basic Books, 1966).

Meredith, John, and Hugh Anderson, *Folk Songs of Australia* (Sidney: Ure Smith, 1967).

Milburn, George, *The Hobo's Hornbook* (New York: Ives Washburn, 1930).

[Morgan, Harry], *More Rugby Songs* (London: Sphere Books, 1968). Cited as Morgan 2.

————, *Why Was He Born So Beautiful* (London: Sphere Books, 1967). Cited as Morgan 1.

Munch, Peter A., "What Became of 'Little Powder-Monkey Jim,' " *Journal of American Folklore* 84 (1971): 311-19.

Nettleingham, F. T., *More Tommy's Tunes* (London: Erskine Macdonald, 1919).

————, *Tommy's Tunes* (London: Erskine Macdonald, 1917).

New Locker Room Humor, revised edition (Chicago: Burd Publishing Co., 1960).

Niles, John J., Douglas S. Moore and A. A. Wallgren, *The Songs My Mother Never Taught Me* (New York: Macaulay, 1929).

O Lochlainn, Colm, *Irish Street Ballads* (Dublin: Printed at the Sign of Three Candles, 1939).

————, *More Irish Street Ballads* (Dublin: Printed at the Sign of Three Candles, 1965).

O'Neill, Francis, *The Dance Music of Ireland* (Chicago: Lyon and Healy, 1907).

————, *The Music of Ireland* (Chicago: Lyon and Healy, 1903).

O'Sullivan, Donal, *Songs of the Irish* (Dublin: Browne and Nolan, 1960).

Odum, Howard W., and Guy B. Johnson, *The Negro and His Songs* (Chapel Hill: University of North Carolina Press, 1925).

"One, the *Only* Baker House Super-Duper Extra Crude Song Book, The" mimeographed (Massachusetts Institute of Technology, ca. 1950).

Opie, Iona and Peter, *The Lore and Language of Schoolchildren* (London: Oxford University Press, 1959).

————, *The Oxford Dictionary of Nursery Rhymes* (Oxford: Clarendon Press, 1951).

Owens, William A., *Tell Me a Story, Sing Me a Song* (Austin: University of Texas Press, 1983).

————, *Texas Folk Songs,* 2d edition (Dallas: Southern Methodist University Press, 1976).

Page, Martin, *Kiss Me Goodnight, Sergeant Major* (London: Hart, Davis McGibbon, n.d.).

Palmer, Roy, *Folk Songs Collected by Ralph Vaughan Williams* (London: J. M. Dent, 1983).

————, *Songs of the Midlands* (East Ardsley, Wakefield: EP Publishing Limited, 1972).

Partridge, Eric, *A Dictionary of Slang and Unconventional English,* 5th edition (New York: Macmillan, 1961).

Peacock, Kenneth, *Songs of the Newfoundland Outports,* 3 vols. (Ottawa: National Museum of Canada, 1965).

Peters, Harry B., *Folk Songs out of Wisconsin* (Madison: State Historical Society of Wisconsin, 1977).

Pinto, Vivian de Sola, and Allan Rodway, *The Common Muse* (London: Chatto & Windus, 1957).

Polwarth, Gwen and Mary, "Folk Songs from the North" (Newcastle Upon Tyne: Frank Graham, 1970).

Purslow, Frank, ed., *Marrow Bones* (London: English Folksong and Dance Society, 1965).

————, ed., *The Foggy Dew* (London: English Folksong and Dance Society, 1974).

————, ed., *The Wanton Seed* (London: English Folksong and Dance Society, n.d. [1968]).

Randolph, Vance, *Ozark Folksongs,* 4 vols. (Columbia: The State Historical Society of Missouri, 1946-1950).

————, " 'Unprintable' Songs from the Ozarks," unpublished typescript with music (Eureka Springs, Arkansas, 1954).

————, *Pissing in the Snow* (Urbana: University of Illinois Press, 1976); reprint edition (New York: Bard, 1977).

Reeves, James, *The Idiom of the People* (New York: W. W. Norton, 1958).

————, *Singing Streets* (Edinburgh, 1964).

Reisner, Robert, *Graffiti* (New York, 1967).

Remick Collection of College Songs, The (New York and Detroit: Jerome W. Remick Co., 1909).

Renwick, Roger deV., *English Folk Poetry: Structure and Meaning* (London: Batsford Academic and Educational Ltd.; Philadelphia: University of Pennsylvania Press, 1980).

Reuss, Richard A., "An Annotated Field Collection of Songs from the American College Student Oral Tradition," unpublished M.A. thesis, Indiana University, 1965.

Roberts, Leonard, and C. Buell Agey, *In the Pine* (Pikeville, Ky.: Pikeville College Press, 1978).

Rosenbaum, Art, *Folk Visions and Voices* (Athens: University of Georgia Press, 1983).

Sandburg, Carl, *The American Songbag* (New York: Harcourt, Brace, & Co., 1927).

Sedley, Stephen, *Seeds of Love* (London: Essex Music Limited, 1967).

Seeger, Charles, "The Folkness of the Non-Folk," in Bruce Jackson, ed., *Folklore & Society: Essays in Honor of Benj. A. Botkin* (Hatboro, Pa.: Folklore Associates, 1966).

————, "On the Moods of a Music-Logic," *Journal of the American Musicological Society* 13 (1960): 224-61.

————, "Preface to the Description of a Music," a report read to the International Society for Musical Research, Fifth Congress, Utrecht, July, 1952.

————, "Prescriptive and Descriptive Music Writing," *The Musical Quarterly* 44 (1958): 184-95.

————, "Systematic Musicology--Viewpoints, Orientations and Methods," *Journal of the American Musicological Society* 4 (1951): 240-48.

Seeger, Peggy and Ewan MacColl, eds., *The Singing Island* (London: Mills Music Ltd., 1960).

Sharp, Cecil, *English Folk Songs from the Southern Appalachians*, edited by Maud Karpeles, 2 vols. (London: Oxford University Press, 1952).

Shaw, Frank, *You Know Me Aunt Nelly?*, 2d edition (London, 1970).

Shay, Frank, *American Sea Songs and Chanteys* (New York, 1948).

————, *More Pious Friends and Drunken Companions* (New York: Macaulay, 1928).

"Shitty Songs of Sigma Chi," mimeographed songbook, n.p., n.d., but apparently from Arizona, ca. 1970, courtesy Guy Logsdon.

Shuldham-Shaw, Patrick, and Emily B. Lyle, *The Grieg-Duncan Folk Song Collection*, Vols. 1-2 (Aberdeen: Aberdeen University Press, 1981, 1983).

Silber, Irwin, *Songs of the Civil War* (New York: Columbia University Press, 1960).

Simpson, Claude M., *The British Broadside Ballad and Its Music* (New Brunswick, N.J.: Rutgers University Press, 1966).

"Songs of Raunch and Ill-Repute," mimeographed (Privately circulated at Ricketts House, California Institute of Technology, Pasadena, Calif., ca. 1960), courtesy of Marc Kaufman.

"Songs of Roving and Raking," dittographed and privately circulated at the University of Illinois, ca. 1962, and credited by Reuss, *supra.*, p. 345, to John Walsh.

Spaeth, Sigmund, *History of Popular Music in America* (New York: Random House, 1948).

————, *Read 'Em and Weep* (New York: Doubleday, Page & Co., 1926).

————, *Weep Some More, My Lady* (New York: Doubleday, Page & Co., 1927).

Stillman, Norton, *Trust Me with Your Heart Again* (New York: Simon & Schuster, 1971).

Stories from the Folk-lore of Russia, edited by Aleksandr Afanasyev (Geneva: Privately Printed, 1872; new translation, Paris: Charles Carrington, 1897); reprinted with a new introduction by Milton Van Sickle as *Ribald Russian Classics* (Los Angeles: Holloway House, 1966).

Stubbs, Ken, *The Life of a Man* (London: English Folk Dance and Song Society, 1970).

Sulzer, Elmer Griffith, "Twenty-Five Kentucky Folk Ballads," Vol. 1, (Lexington, Ky.: Transylvania Printing Co., 1936).

"Supplementary Listing of Recorded Songs in the English Language in the Library of Congress Archive of Folk Song Through Recording No. AFS 4332 (October, 1940)," compiled by Deborah Deems and William Nowlin, Library of Congress, Archive of Folk Song, June 13, 1977.

Tate, Brad, *The Bastard from the Bush* (Kuranda, Queensland: Rams Skull Press, 1982).

Thomson, William, *Orpheus Caledonius* (London, 1733; reprinted, Hatboro, Pa.: Folklore Associates, 1962).

Thorp, N. Howard "Jack," *Songs of the Cowboy* (Estancia, N.M.: New Print Shop, 1908).

Tinsley, Jim Bob, *He Was Singing This Song* (Orlando: University Presses of Florida, 1981).

Toelken, Barre, "The Folklore of Academe," in Jan Harold Brunvand, *The Study of American Folklore: An Introduction*, 2d edition (New York: W. W. Norton, 1978).

Tongue, Ruth L., *The Chime Child* (London: Routledge & Kegan Paul, 1968).

The Unexpurgated Folk Songs of Men, edited by Mack McCormick (International Blues Record Club, Berkeley, Calif., 1964).

Vaughan Williams, Ralph, and A. L. Lloyd, *The Penguin Book of English Folk Songs* (Hammondsworth, 1960).

Wallrich, William, *Air Force Airs* (New York: Duell, Sloan and Pearce, 1957).

Wannan, Bill, *Robust, Ribald and Rude Verse in Australia* (Melbourne: Lands-downe Press Pty., Ltd., 1972).

Warner, Anne, *Traditional American Folk Songs from the Anne & Frank Warner Collection* (Syracuse: Syracuse University Press, 1984).

Warner, Frank M., "Folk Songs and Ballads from the Eastern Seaboard" (Macon, Ga.: Southern Press, 1963).

Wepman, Dennis, Ronald B. Newman and Murray B. Binderman, *The Life: The Lore and Poetry of the Black Hustler* (Los Angeles: Holloway House, c. 1976).

White, John I., *Git Along, Little Dogies* (Urbana: University of Illinois Press, 1975).

Williams, Alfred, *Folk-songs of the Upper Thames* (London: Novello, 1923).

Winslow, David J., "An Annotated Collection of Children's Lore," *Keystone Folklore Quarterly* 11 (1966): 151-202.

Wolfenstein, Martha, *Children's Humor* (Glencoe, Ill.: The Free Press, 1954).

Wolford, Leah Jackson, *The Play Party in Indiana*, revised edition (India-napolis: Indiana Historical Society, 1959).

Index

427

Books in the Series Music in American Life

Resources of American Music History: A Directory of Source Materials
from Colonial Times to World War II
D. W. Krummel, Jean Geil, Doris J. Dyen, and Deane L. Root

Tenement Songs: The Popular Music of the Jewish Immigrants
Mark Slobin

Ozark Folksongs
Vance Randolph; Edited and Abridged by Norm Cohen

Oscar Sonneck and American Music
William Lichtenwanger, Editor

Bluegrass Breakdown: The Making of the Old Southern Sound
Robert Cantwell

Bluegrass: A History
Neil V. Rosenberg

Music at the White House: A History of the American Spirit
Elise K. Kirk

Red River Blues: The Blues Tradition in the Southeast
Bruce Bastin

Good Friends and Bad Enemies: Robert Winslow Gordon and
the Study of American Folksong
Debora Kodish

Fiddlin' Georgia Crazy: Fiddlin' John Carson, His Real World, and
the World of His Songs
Gene Wiggins

America's Music: From the Pilgrims to the Present,
Revised Third Edition
Gilbert Chase

Secular Music in Colonial Annapolis: The Tuesday Club, 1745-56
John Barry Talley

Bibliographical Handbook of American Music
D. W. Krummel

Goin' to Kansas City
Nathan W. Pearson, Jr.

"Susanna," "Jeanie," and "The Old Folks at Home": The Songs
of Stephen C. Foster from His Time to Ours
Second Edition
William W. Austin

Songprints: The Musical Experience of Five Shoshone Women
Judith Vander

"Happy in the Service of the Lord": Afro-American Gospel
Quartets in Memphis
Kip Lornell

Paul Hindemith in the United States
Luther Noss

"My Song Is My Weapon": People's Songs, American Communism,
and the Politics of Culture
Robbie Lieberman

Chosen Voices: The Story of the American Cantorate
Mark Slobin

Theodore Thomas: America's Conductor and Builder
of Orchestras, 1835-1905
Ezra Schabas

"The Whorehouse Bells Were Ringing" and Other Songs
Cowboys Sing
Guy Logsdon

Crazeology: The Autobiography of a Chicago Jazzman
Bud Freeman, as Told to Robert Wolf

Discoursing Sweet Music: Town Bands and Community Life
in Turn-of-the-Century Pennsylvania
Kenneth Kreitner

Mormonism and Music: A History
Michael Hicks

Voices of the Jazz Age: Profiles of Eight Vintage Jazzmen
Chip Deffaa

Pickin' on Peachtree: A History of Country Music in Atlanta, Georgia
Wayne W. Daniel

Bitter Music: Collected Journals, Essays, Introductions, and Librettos
Harry Partch; Edited by Thomas McGeary

Ethnic Music on Records: A Discography of Ethnic Recordings
Produced in the United States, 1893 to 1942
Richard K. Spottswood

Downhome Blues Lyrics: An Anthology from
the Post–World War II Era
Jeff Todd Titon

Ellington: The Early Years
Mark Tucker

Chicago Soul
Robert Pruter

That Half-Barbaric Twang: The Banjo in
American Popular Culture
Karen Linn

Hot Man: The Life of Art Hodes
Art Hodes and Chadwick Hansen

The Erotic Muse: American Bawdy Songs
Second Edition
Ed Cray